Exploring Politics

A Concise Introduction

To our students

Sara Miller McCune founded SAGE Publishing in 1965 to support the dissemination of usable knowledge and educate a global community. SAGE publishes more than 1000 journals and over 600 new books each year, spanning a wide range of subject areas. Our growing selection of library products includes archives, data, case studies and video. SAGE remains majority owned by our founder and after her lifetime will become owned by a charitable trust that secures the company's continued independence.

Los Angeles | London | New Delhi | Singapore | Washington DC | Melbourne

Exploring Politics

A Concise Introduction

Gaspare M. Genna
The University of Texas at El Paso

Taeko Hiroi
The University of Texas at El Paso

Los Angeles | London | New Delhi
Singapore | Washington DC | Melbourne

FOR INFORMATION:

CQ Press
An imprint of SAGE Publications, Inc.
2455 Teller Road
Thousand Oaks, California 91320
E-mail: order@sagepub.com

SAGE Publications Ltd.
1 Oliver's Yard
55 City Road
London, EC1Y 1SP
United Kingdom

SAGE Publications India Pvt. Ltd.
B 1/I 1 Mohan Cooperative Industrial Area
Mathura Road, New Delhi 110 044
India

SAGE Publications Asia-Pacific Pte. Ltd.
18 Cross Street #10-10/11/12
China Square Central
Singapore 048423

Printed in Canada

Library of Congress Control Number: 2022917299

ISBN (pbk) 978-1-0718-0761-3
ISBN (loose) 978-1-0718-9428-6

Acquisitions Editor: Anna Villarruel

Content Development Editor: Tara Slagle

Production Editor: Rebecca Lee

Copy Editor: Colleen Brennan

Typesetter: diacriTech

Cover Designer: Scott Van Atta

Marketing Manager: Jennifer Haldeman

MIX
Paper from responsible sources
FSC® C103567

This book is printed on acid-free paper.

22 23 24 25 26 10 9 8 7 6 5 4 3 2 1

BRIEF CONTENTS

DETAILED CONTENTS

PART II   POLITICAL VALUES AND BEHAVIOR

PREFACE

After more than 30 years of combined experience in teaching introduction to politics in various institutions across the country, we developed a desire to write a book that would engage today's students more effectively. We felt that current approaches to the subject did not fit the needs of the students we taught. No matter our formats (ranging from 50- to 300-student classes, regular semester-long classes as well as short-term classes, and face-to-face and online classes), we noticed that today's students need a different way to engage with the material. We experimented with different techniques that led to our demonstrated student success.

This book fits the needs of students taking an introductory course in political science, which are often titled "Introduction to Politics" or "Introduction to Political Science." Given that many colleges and universities (both public and private) require such a course for graduation, we believe that educating citizens needs to be a critical factor. The average student taking the course will be either first- or second-year students or, in the case of dual college credit programs, high school juniors or seniors. Many students ask themselves why they need to engage with the material. In addition, instructors have become growingly aware that students do not read books with lengthy chapters and without assessments built into the readings. Students quickly calculate that lectures may be a good substitute for reading and thus neglect reading assignments. In addition, the rising costs of education often have led students to forego purchasing the book if they consider it expensive and unnecessary for their academic success.

Our book is written with these challenges in mind. Our task is to be simultaneously accessible and stimulating to both beginning political science majors and non–political science majors. It offers a comprehensive yet concise introduction to the study of politics. It provides major and competing theories in political science with many applications to issues that students find interesting and relevant. As students read each chapter, they will see "Expand Your Thoughts" questions that will arouse students' critical thinking by taking a pensive position on a debated issue. They will also be exposed to "Practical Application" exercises throughout the chapters that ask them to do short research assignments or policy simulations that place their learning into current or recent context.

APPROACH

Our book has ambitious goals: It seeks to overcome the challenges of student engagement, especially for non–political science majors, while simultaneously making sure that it provides a solid political science foundation for political science majors for their success in upper-level courses. Another goal is to keep the price of the book reasonable to ensure that it is also financially accessible to students. To achieve these goals, we wrote this book with the following strategies.

First, it takes on a "no frills" approach. Our book is concise. Students can read and study the material in one sitting. Our approach does not skimp on the introductory material required in such courses. Given that the twenty-first-century university student population often needs to distribute their time for obligations such as employment to pay for school, it is important to balance what we need them to know with the time they have to study.

Second, we organize the book in a manner that is accessible and interesting for the average student taking an introductory course as a graduation requirement. The organization first discusses politics at the individual level, spans to the group level, then the national, and ends with the international level. Chapter 1 introduces politics to students using the game analogy to capture student interest. Chapter 2 emphasizes the importance of objective analysis and presents the use of the scientific method in the study of politics. By examining ideology, culture, and political behavior in the subsequent early part of the book, we get students to understand that politics is relevant to all individuals and groups and not necessarily synonymous with government institutions. The book then provides theoretically informed discussions of states, public policies, political regimes, domestic governmental institutions, elections, and political parties illustrated by contemporary and relevant issues, such as state failures, today's prominent dictators, and executive-legislative conflict in presidential systems. The last four chapters of the book deal with topics to which both political science majors and nonmajors can relate: economic development and policy, democratization, international peace and conflict, and globalization. Thus, our book is simultaneously accessible and stimulating to both political science majors and nonmajors.

Along the way, we wish to give students portable ideas that they can carry with them as lifelong learners. One such idea is the understanding that democracy is not a one-size-fits-all arrangement. By exposing students to how others practice democracy around the world, they will have greater insights into how to improve the way to practice democracy at home. Another is the role identity plays in political decision-making. Identity can often answer the question of why people vote against their economic self-interest. In addition, the various theories and investigative methods introduced in this book with ample examples will enable students to conduct their own analysis of politics outside the classroom. With this in mind, we have wide geographic cover in illustrative examples and pay particular attention to the growing need to address issues related to gender, race, and ethnic politics.

Lastly, we embed the book with discussion questions that students can address either individually or in a team. The pedagogical advantage is in the active engagement students have with the materials. In addition to introducing concepts and theories and multiple real-world examples, throughout the book, it asks students to answer questions that require them to exercise their analytic skills and their ready use of the internet to fill in the gaps. In one sense, we are "flipping" the process of individual study. Traditionally, students are asked to read and memorize in introductory courses. With this book, we ask them to know the basics and then quickly turn their attention to application and discovery. Instead of doing the thinking for them, which will be boring for most students, we ask them to think for themselves. In addition, instead of having students wait until the end of each chapter to see what discussion questions and other learning materials are available for each chapter (most students do not explore these materials if they are made to wait until the end), we embed questions and exercises throughout each chapter. We believe that our approach is unique among the books currently on the market, many of which do not address these critical challenges.

ORGANIZATION OF THE BOOK

The book is divided into four parts. The first three parts give students the basic tools and concepts that will be used deeply in the last part. **Part I** covers the fundamentals of contemporary political analysis. **Chapter 1**, **Analyzing Politics**, begins by understanding the importance of analytic thinking and removing emotions from political analysis. Students discover the meaning of politics and its importance in daily life: in government, society, economics, and individual behaviors. We emphasize that politics and games have common elements and that focusing on these elements helps us understand political events and political behaviors. We illustrate strategic interactions common in political events and their implications with interesting and relevant real-world examples.

Chapter 2, **Studying Politics**, provides a basic knowledge of how the scientific method can be used in political analysis. We start by recognizing the value of evidence-based reasoning and move to an understanding of the scientific method. We then explain how theories and hypotheses are developed in political research. This section also discusses some of the limits of applying the scientific method in the social sciences as well as its strengths. We guide students in recognizing intended and unintended biases in research and their consequences for our understanding of politics. The chapter ends by describing the role of normative theory in political science.

Part II continues with a look at individual and group dynamics. **Chapter 3**, **Political Ideologies and Political Thoughts**, discusses some of the more salient classical and contemporary political ideologies and political thoughts. It begins by defining political ideology and examines the three functions of political ideologies. We then outline the major tenets of political realism, describe liberal ideology and compare classical liberalism with modern U.S. liberalism, look at conservatism and how it manifests in modern U.S. politics, and explain the differences in the various types of socialism. The chapter then introduces ideologies developed in the twentieth century: fascism, religious fundamentalism, environmentalism, and feminism.

Chapter 4, **The Cultural Dimension of Politics**, continues the examination of individual political behavior by looking at the cultural dimension of politics. We define political culture and its role in explaining political behavior and describe the process of political socialization, including the transfer of values and norms between generations. Students also learn how political culture can dramatically change between generations through the exploration of the logic and evidence of postmaterialist theory. The chapter ends by showing how values manifest themselves in various political attitudes regarding authority, society, and individualism.

The book then explores concepts and theory associated with rational choice theory and political psychology in **Chapter 5, Trust, Identity, and Political Behavior**. We introduce a simple definition of political behavior and explain how it is influenced by information. The role of the media is explained through the importance of one- and two-way communication and how changes in technology produce new types of mass media communication. We then look at how the average individual processes information and come to understand the limits to rational decision-making. The chapter then explains why trust is important in a well-functioning society and for effective government, and why people place themselves into social identity groups. We demonstrate how identity affects politics in different parts of the world. Finally, the chapter examines the differences between traditional and new social movements and the roles they play in producing political and social change.

We move from individual and group behavior to government institutions and political processes, which are introduced and detailed in **Part III**. **Chapter 6**, **States, Nations, and Varieties of Political Regimes,** identifies the characteristics of modern states. First, we explore how the concept of state sovereignty developed, and we describe its limits. We then recognize the fundamental functions of states, the features of state capacity, and the challenges posed by weak and failed states. Students then move toward understanding the differences between democratic and nondemocratic regimes, characteristics of liberal democracy, and subtypes of autocratic regimes.

Chapter 7, **Interests, Policy, and Public Goods**, examines the interplay of actors' interests, policy development, and the production of collective goods. Students explore the roles and types of interest groups as well as the various ways in which they influence the policymaking process. We then discuss the differences between national, public, and private interests and models to explain policymakers' motivations for national and public policies. Next, we identify examples and characteristics of public goods and common pool resources. The chapter shows how ecological health and environmental issues can be understood and analyzed as public good and common pool resource questions. Finally, the chapter discusses two collective action problems: the free rider's problem and the tragedy of the commons.

Chapter 8, Institutions of Government, starts the discussion on government institutions. It reviews the debate about the role of political institutions and "new institutionalism" in the study of politics. Students then examine the characteristics of presidential, parliamentary, and semi-presidential systems, the fundamental differences among them, and their implications for policymaking and political behavior. We then break down the institutions and help students understand the differences between the types of democratic executives and their primary functions, identify the principal functions of legislatures and understand how legislative institutions differ across democracies, and examine the key functions and characteristics of various types of judicial systems. The chapter examines the differences between federalism and unitary systems and analyzes the reasons for and against the centralization of state power. Finally, students explore institutions of nondemocratic regimes (with attention to China and Iran) and learn that their functions and goals differ from those in democratic regimes.

Next, we examine electoral systems and political parties in **Chapter 9, Elections and Political Parties**. The evolution of democracy and the important role of elections begin our discussion. The importance of elections requires us to investigate voter participation. The chapter introduces the paradox of voting and the varied patterns of voter turnout in democracies. It also discusses the characteristics of a typical voter. We then identify the various electoral systems used around the world and understand the pros and cons of each with respect to political representation, governing efficiency, and voter-representative relationship. We review the patterns of recent electoral system reforms around the world. Understanding political parties' functions, types of political party systems, and the relationships between electoral systems and political party systems connects the two halves of the chapter. We finish the chapter by exposing students to the roles that elections and political parties play in nondemocratic regimes. A case study on "democratic" decisions made by the Communist Party of China illustrates how important decisions are made in the country.

The last set of chapters (**Part IV**) brings the lessons learned by examining the most salient political issues researched in political science. **Chapter 10, Economic Development and Policy**, covers the different ways states craft economic development around the world. After defining economic development and exploring the classifications of countries based on levels of economic development, we examine three major economic strategies: market-led development, centrally planned (command) economies, and state-led development models. Each strategy's outcomes are critically analyzed. Students then look at the roles that education and infrastructure policies play in economic development. The final topic of the chapter is fiscal and monetary policies and how they impact the demand for goods and services and thus economic performance.

Chapter 11, Democratization, begins by identifying historical waves of democratization, tracing the evolution of the meaning of democracy, and exploring the current state of democracy around the world. Next, students examine the characteristics of consolidated democracies and the challenges to democratic consolidation. Those foundational concepts are followed by the three major approaches to explain democratization: economic development, culture, and international factors. Last, students explore various explanations for the breakdown of democratic regimes.

Chapter 12, International Peace and Conflict, compares different types of state relations and identifies the major actors involved in international relations, their interests, and how they make decisions. The chapter explains how international actors' power impacts their behavior and reviews current major international issues. The main theories of international relations introduced in the chapter include power transition, balance of power, democratic peace, commercial liberal peace, and constructivism.

Chapter 13, Our Globalizing World, examines globalization and regionalization. It identifies the characteristics of globalization and regionalization and the types and functions of international institutions, including the United Nations, the major global economic institutions, and the European Union and other regional integration institutions. We finish the chapter by recognizing the principal critiques of globalization.

ACKNOWLEDGMENTS

Many people contributed to making this book a reality. We owe a great many thanks to each for their important roles. First, we owe gratitude to Scott Greenan for his belief in our approach. As a senior acquisitions editor for political science books at SAGE, he was invaluable in helping us draft our proposal and guiding us through the first stages of the book's development. We thank our content development editors, Alissa Nance, Tara Slagle, and Anna Villarruel, whose patience and dedication to improving our manuscript led to its finalization. Anna Villarruel's new role as acquisitions editor is also much appreciated. Of course, the wonderful students we have had the privilege to teach over the years at The University of Texas at El Paso, the University of South Florida, and Winona State University motivated this work. It was their feedback and willingness to try out pedagogical innovations that helped us develop our book. Finally, we would like to thank the following reviewers who provided invaluable feedback, which improved the content and the coverage of this book greatly:

Jesse Cragwall, Pellissippi State Community College

Deborah D. Ferrell-Lynn, University of Central Oklahoma

Julie L. Hershenberg, Collin College

Brian D. Jones, Northern Virginia Community College

Lisa Langenbach, Middle Tennessee State University

Sharon Manna, North Lake College

Ronald McGauvran, Tennessee Tech University

John Patrick Afamefuna Ifedi, Howard University

Constance Pruitt, Howard University

Kerry R. Stewart, University of North Georgia–Gainesville

Gwyn Sutherland, Elizabethtown Community and Technical College

Charles M. Swinford, Southern New Hampshire University

Anca Turcu, University of Central Florida

ABOUT THE AUTHORS

Gaspare M. Genna is Professor and Chair of Political Science and Public Administration, as well as the Director of the North American Studies Program at The University of Texas at El Paso (UTEP). He is a Pastor Scholar, Robert A. Pastor North America Research Initiative, with the Center for Latin American and Latino Studies at American University, an Associate Research Fellow for the Institute on Comparative Regional Integration Studies at the United Nations University, and Senior Research Fellow for the TRC Institute at Portland State University. His research interests include the application of political economy and political psychology approaches to the understanding of issues related to regional integration (structural conditions for regionalization, political decision-making, public opinion on integration, and policy implications). His geographical area of specialization is in Europe and the Americas. He is a coauthor or coeditor of six academic books and has publications in such journals as *Geopolitics, International Interactions, Review of International Political Economy, European Union Politics, Journal of European Integration*, and *The Journal of College Student Retention*. In 2013, he won a University of Texas System Regents' Outstanding Teaching Award and is now a UTEP Distinguished Teaching Professor.

Taeko Hiroi is Professor of Political Science at The University of Texas at El Paso and a contributing faculty to the Center for Inter-American and Border Studies, Asian Studies, and Brazilian Studies Programs. Her research areas include political institutions, legislative politics, presidential and legislative coalitions, electoral systems, governance and accountability, democratization, political instability, comparative and international political economy, and health politics and policy. Her recent publications appear in *Comparative Political Studies, Democratization, International Political Science Review, Journal of Legislative Studies, Legislative Studies Quarterly, Publius: The Journal of Federalism*, and *Studies in Comparative International Development*. She is a coauthor of the book *Regional Integration and Democratic Conditionality*.

BRENDAN SMIALOWSKI/Contributor/Getty Images

1 ANALYZING POLITICS

What kind of world or local events have drawn your interest lately? Are you puzzled why SARS-CoV-2 (also known as COVID-19), first identified in Wuhan, China, in December 2019, spread worldwide, infecting hundreds of millions of people and claiming millions of lives? Have you wondered why government responses to the COVID-19 pandemic and the infection and death rates have varied significantly across countries? Do you wonder what caused the tragic death of George Floyd, a 46-year-old Black man, in the hands of police officers in Minneapolis, Minnesota? Why did this event, and not similar previous tragedies, trigger a resurgence of the Black Lives Matter movement in the United States and other countries? Or are you concerned about the vulnerability of the electoral system to foreign influence and attacks?

Politics is present in all of these and other issues that impact our lives. Discussing and examining politics can be exciting, but its analysis requires a cool head. If done with logic and unbiased evidence, we can learn why political phenomena occur. Such knowledge is also useful for taking actions to solve problems we confront.

Take, for example, a topic that is critical for everyone: health care. A country's health care policies can literally be a life-or-death outcome for some. How should health care be provided? Some believe that health care should be an individual responsibility. Others believe that the government should guarantee it. Yet others believe in a mixed system where people could choose between government-provided and private health care systems. This example also leads us to wonder how societies come to terms with different opinions. Analyzing politics can help us explain why countries make different choices.

We study and attempt to understand politics because of its importance in our lives. This chapter will guide you in understanding that human political interactions have detectable patterns. We will also see how analytic frameworks using game analogies can help us identify those patterns and predict likely outcomes.

THINKING ANALYTICALLY

LEARNING OBJECTIVE

1.1   Understand the importance of analytic thinking and removing emotions from political analysis.

Prior to this course, your exposure to political discussion may have been largely at the emotional level. This happens when individuals exchange strongly held opinions with selected facts that may support their claims. Most political discussions center on topics about which individuals deeply care. Therefore, it is natural, and could be useful, that people use strong emotions when discussing politics. Doing so demonstrates passionate concern about what is "right" or "wrong" regarding how specific issues are dealt with. In many cases, seeing people care enough about an issue to discuss it is more appealing than people acting in an apathetic manner.

When you turn on the television, this is what you tend to see nowadays. Programs conveying news objectively without emotions have become rare. From CNN to MSNBC and Fox News, America's major TV networks are broadcasting news talk shows in which the hosts passionately and emotionally discuss political, economic, and social issues using selective evidence. Many of these shows do not allow viewers to be neutral; the division of the good from the bad is clear and polarization is ubiquitous. Their mission is not an objective analysis but to convince people that their side is correct.

When emotions are the main factors involved, things can get tense if we disagree, or relaxed if we agree. Tension resulting from a heated disagreement can prevent people from resolving issues, which is the reason why people generally want to discuss politics in the first place. The analysis of politics attempts to emphasize, as much as possible, a logical discussion. In having such discussions, people can move toward some possible solutions that would promote the well-being of as many people as possible. Even if solutions obtained may not satisfy a majority of the people, open discussion and analysis of politics with cool heads are likely to help yield a solution with which everyone affected can, at minimum, live.

Analytic thinking is a process of solving problems by breaking down complexity into components and seeing how the parts fit together. The aim of analysts is to put the puzzle pieces together so that we can solve the problem at hand. As we will discuss further in Chapter 2, the process requires analysts to step outside of the problem and let the gathered information tell the story. Analysts ask questions like: What are the sources of the problem? What is the scope of the problem? Can we change the sources and scope of the problem to solve it? If so, how can we do this? Notice that each of these questions lacks emotional considerations. When analysts release emotional ties, answers that could be uncomfortable become acceptable.

Gathering of information also needs to be systematic. A common mistake is that individuals tend to jump to a conclusion based on a specific experience that happened to them or people close to them. Another common mistake is that people tend to only search for and accept "facts" that corroborate their beliefs and look away when they see contrary evidence. Systematic analysis of evidence—one where analysts collect and analyze all evidence in an objective manner—is necessary. A more objective and systematic inquiry increases the likelihood that the answers and solutions to problems will be effective.

Psychological experiments demonstrate that focusing on emotions—both positive and negative emotions—reduces the use of logic in making decisions. Removing emotions from analysis is important to accurately understand the problem at hand and come up with a helpful solution. Likewise, analyzing politics objectively does not make the study of politics boring. In fact, as we will see later in this chapter, many political scientists consider that politics and games have similar structures, and that analysis of politics is a fun and serious endeavor at the same time!

WHAT IS POLITICS?

LEARNING OBJECTIVE

1.2 Define politics and its importance in daily life.

Until now, we've discussed politics without defining what politics is. Some people think politics is about government and governance. Others consider politics as it pertains to power. Yet others view politics as being about the distribution of resources and how people relate to one another. American political scientist Harold Lasswell developed one of the most commonly used definitions of politics. According to Lasswell, **politics** is about "who gets what, when, and how" (Lasswell, 1936). In other words, politics is about how people distribute and obtain resources and power within a society and across countries.

If all people always attained whatever they wanted, whenever they wanted, and however they sought it, then we would not have politics. In reality, that is not the case. Therefore, questions related to politics are everywhere and important. Should the state provide health care services to its citizens, or should individuals be responsible for their own health care? How high should taxes be, and who should pay them? Who should own guns, and under what conditions can people justifiably use them? Should capital punishment be legal, and when is it allowable? Are resources available to some and not others based on race, ethnicity, gender, kinship, or religion? If this is the case, how does one end this practice? When should we go to war with another country? Moreover, if a war breaks out, who is going to fight? Should we erect tariffs on certain imports, and how high should the tariffs be? Or should we even trade internationally? Overall, who should make all these important decisions?

The study of politics involves understanding the mechanisms for making decisions about "who gets what, when, and how." The rest of this chapter will start you down the path of analyzing politics by examining certain cases from recent history and some current affairs. You will see that the examples are very complex if you look at all the parts at once. However, after we break them down using an analytic game-like framework, you will see noteworthy patterns and they become easier to understand.

POLITICS AS A GAME

LEARNING OBJECTIVE

1.3   Describe politics using the common elements and structures of a game.

Politics is structurally a lot like games. Games have a certain common structure. A game involves two or more players that interact to achieve one or more goals within a framework of rules. Players may have different preferences and have stakes in the outcomes. They try to win or obtain the best possible outcomes. Their ability to obtain preferred outcomes depends on many factors like knowledge, resources, and experience. Outcomes also depend on the choices made by other players. Everyone, therefore, cares about the choices that everyone else makes, and this encourages **strategic interaction** among actors. Strategic interaction refers to a calculative interaction between players in which (a) a player's ability to obtain the desired outcome is dependent on the move of at least one other player and (b) all players know this condition and make calculated moves in order to attain the best possible outcome.

Consider an election in which incumbent politicians are facing a threat to their reelection due to the possibility that well-qualified rivals may enter the race. Money is very important in modern-day elections. Candidates and political parties seek to raise campaign donations so that they can run effective campaigns. Many election analysts analyze the size of the war chest—the campaign fund available to a candidate—as a crucial factor in predicting the likelihood of a candidate's election victory. Candidates monitor the amount of the funds that they and their rivals garner to assess the viability of their candidacy. If other candidates are raising significantly more money than they are, perhaps they have little chance of winning the election. Knowing this, an incumbent politician facing the possibility of a competition with a high-quality candidate may expend much effort in raising campaign contributions in order to deter the potential challenger from entering the race. If the incumbent can demonstrate their ability to raise a considerable amount of funds, the potential challenger may think that their chance of defeating the incumbent is slim and may give up challenging the incumbent. This illustrates a strategic interaction that frequently occurs in politics. Janet Box-Steffensmeier (1996) and others have discovered that the size of war chests influences the entry decisions of high-quality candidates.

Players' choices are also constrained by the existing rules. In the example of the war chest and election entry, we can think about campaign finance laws and other rules and constraints that candidates and political parties face. Those laws and rules vary from one country to another. However, all democracies have laws, rules, and conventions that govern electoral competition.

Let us summarize the key elements common in games and politics:

- Players: Who are the key players?

- Goals: What goals or stakes do they have?

- Strategies: What actions (or strategies) are available to them?

- Rules: What rules constrain or influence actors' choices and behavior?

The game-like nature of politics is obvious in many situations—when the U.S. president negotiates denuclearization with North Korean leader Kim Jong-un, when members of Congress consider alternative tax bills, when candidates raise money for elections, and when abortion supporters and opponents try to influence laws.

You may associate games with having fun and think that we should not use this word since the stakes of politics are often very serious. By no means do we imply that using the "game" analogy to analyze politics reduces politics to a frivolous activity. You are correct in thinking that politics is a serious business—it involves interactions that affect the lives of real people. The examples we use in this book attest to the importance of politics.

EXPAND YOUR THOUGHTS
BENEFITS AND DRAWBACKS OF THE GAME ANALOGY

We discussed how we could use the metaphor of a "game" to analyze politics. Some would argue that politics is too complex to describe it as a game. Others, instead, believe that by structuring politics as a game, we can put the different parts together to see the overall picture. What is your position? Do you think it is useful to use the game analogy to understand politics? What benefits and drawbacks are there in using the game analogy? Illustrate your answer with examples from politics and political situations that this chapter does not use.

STRATEGIC INTERACTIONS IN REAL-WORLD EVENTS

LEARNING OBJECTIVE

1.4 Recognize strategic interactions when analyzing real-world events.

In the remainder of this chapter, let's take a look at a few examples of politics to understand its game-like nature.

Strategic Voting

Political scientists have long studied strategic voting by individuals. In an election, a naive observer may think that people vote, in each election, for their most preferred candidate or party. That would be great if your preferred candidate has a real chance of winning the election. Yet sometimes that is not the case. What if the candidate, which some voters like, has little to no chance of winning? In such cases, voters may abandon the candidate and vote for another candidate in order to prevent a candidate that they really dislike from winning. When voters do this, we say they are voting strategically. **Strategic voting** occurs when voters, instead of voting for their most preferred candidate, vote for another candidate in order to prevent a candidate that they really dislike from winning.

Strategic voting is a common occurrence, and everyone has the potential to be a strategic voter. Knowing this, politicians and parties have also tried to convince voters to vote strategically (of course in their favor) to block the election of a candidate they dislike. Have you ever heard people say that a candidate has no chance of winning, so why not vote for someone else who has a more realistic chance of winning? In asking this question, people are starting to convince others that strategic voting may be in their best interests.

Consider the 2000 and 2004 U.S. presidential elections. The 2000 presidential election was a very close, contested race between Republican candidate George W. Bush and Democratic candidate Al Gore. Usually, elections experts can predict the winner reasonably well because of a combination of exit polling and expected early returns. The 2000 presidential contest was so close that we did not know who the winner would be until the vote's final tally. Initial election returns showed that Gore had won the popular vote, but neither candidate had gained the 270 electoral votes required to win the presidency. It turned out that the results from the state of Florida would determine the winner. In Florida the tally showed Bush was leading Gore by only 537 votes. That difference was very small, causing a dispute over the count, which mandated a recounting of the Florida votes. The U.S. Supreme Court ultimately decided the outcome of the election, which ruled in favor of Bush in a 5-to-4 vote, thus giving Florida's 25 electoral votes to Bush. With 271 electoral votes, Bush became the 43rd president of the United States.

This presidential election drew a lot of attention and outcry questioning the legitimacy of the United States' unique institution, the Electoral College. Was there widespread electoral fraud? Was the vote count accurate? Shouldn't the popular vote winner become the president just like any other presidential democracy outside the United States? While interesting, our focus here is not on who really won the 2000 election, whether we should abolish the Electoral College, or whether it was correct for the Supreme Court to decide the election outcome. We want to point out another factor. Although candidates from the two major parties usually draw the most attention in U.S. presidential elections, there are usually more than two candidates. In 2000, there was a third candidate, Ralph Nader of the Green Party.

Ralph Nader was considered more progressive than the Democratic candidate, Al Gore. Nader's campaign addressed the pervasiveness of corporate power, environmental justice, universal health care, affordable housing, free college education, and workers' rights and living wages. In the 2000 election, Nader received 2.7 percent of the popular vote nationwide. In Florida, where Bush defeated Al Gore by only 537 votes, Nader received 97,421 votes. If about 600 of the Nader voters had voted for Gore instead, the Democratic Party candidate would have won Florida and would have had enough electoral votes to become president. This led many to claim that Nader acted as a third-party spoiler and was responsible for Gore's defeat.

Four years later, in 2004, Nader competed in the presidential election once again, this time running as an independent candidate. The election was a close race again, between Republican and incumbent president George W. Bush seeking reelection and Democrat John Kerry. This time, however, Nader faced an uphill battle. His campaign had a hard time getting people to sign on the petitions to put him on the ballot. The 2004 election results indicated that Nader received only 0.38 percent of the popular vote, compared to 2.7 percent in 2000. This is a significant decline in the popular support for Nader. What happened? What changed so much in just four years? Do you think many former Nader supporters voted strategically? Some analysts think so. To prevent the repeat of the 2000 presidential election, it is possible that many former Nader voters abandoned the candidate and chose to vote for the Democratic candidate in order to block the reelection of President Bush, who was the least favored among many Nader voters.

Strategic voting is indeed more common than you might think. During the 2016 Democratic Party presidential primaries and caucuses, there were many that claimed that Bernie Sanders was too left wing to win nationally and that Hillary Clinton was the better choice to beat a Republican candidate. Four years later, in 2020, seeking the Democratic Party's nomination, many moderate presidential candidates within the party once again emphasized their electability as one of their main appeals that would help defeat the incumbent, President Trump of the Republican Party.

EXPAND YOUR THOUGHTS
IS STRATEGIC VOTING REALLY A GOOD IDEA?

Strategic voting is a way for voters to attempt to get their next best candidate, or at least one that is most acceptable among the viable candidates, in office. Many democracy advocates do not view strategic voting favorably. If too many people vote strategically, the politicians and political parties do not really reflect or represent the true interests of the people. In considering strategic voting, what is your opinion of people's decision not to vote for their clear favorite candidate when such an option is present? Do you consider that strategic voting is a wise decision? Do you think strategic voting lowers the quality of democracy? Why or why not? Under what conditions would voters not engage in strategic voting?

The Cuban Missile Crisis

In October 1962, U.S. President John F. Kennedy learned that the Soviet Union (officially the Union of Soviet Socialist Republics or USSR) was constructing nuclear missile sites in Cuba, which is located only 90 miles from the Florida coast. Being so close to the U.S. mainland and given the technology of the time, missiles could be launched and hit their targets before the United States could react. For months, there had been charges of the Soviets building nuclear missile sites in this Caribbean country, which both the Kennedy administration and the Soviets had denied.

However, a U.S. U-2 spy plane produced clear photographic evidence of medium-range and intermediate-range ballistic missile facilities under construction on the island. Upon this confirmation, President Kennedy, on October 22, notified Americans in his televised speech about the presence of the nuclear missile site construction on the island and explained his decision to implement a naval blockade around Cuba. The blockade would prevent the Soviet Union from sending more materials to Cuba and thereby prevent the completion of construction, which many believed at that time not to be operational. Kennedy made it clear that the United States

On October 29, 1962, President John F. Kennedy met with the Executive Committee of the National Security Council in response to the Cuban Missile Crisis, White House, Cabinet Room.

Image courtesy of the John F. Kennedy Presidential Library and Museum, Boston. Image in the public domain. https://commons.wikimedia.org/wiki/File:EXCOMM_meeting,_Cuban_Missile_Crisis,_29_October_1962.jpg

was prepared to use military force if necessary to defuse this threat to national security. Many people feared the possibility of this confrontation escalating into an all-out nuclear war between the superpowers. Kennedy himself estimated the probability of this happening as "between one out of three and even."

You can readily see the game-like nature of the Cuban Missile Crisis. In the overall picture, President Kennedy determined that the presence of Soviet missiles in Cuba was unacceptable. The challenge was to arrange their removal without escalating into a nuclear war that seemed imminent in the view of many people. Kennedy and his team of advisors and officials in the Executive Committee of the National Security Council, or ExComm for short, discussed a wide range of options, from using diplomacy to launching air strikes and a full-scale invasion of Cuba. How would the Soviets respond to each of these options? Would diplomacy put enough pressure on Soviet leader Nikita Khrushchev to remove the missiles from the Caribbean Island country? If the United States launched massive air raids to destroy the missiles, would it provoke a nuclear retaliation by the Soviet Union? President Kennedy and his advisors needed to weigh each option carefully by considering the Soviets' likely response.

To consider the Soviets' likely response, we need to assess Soviet leader Khrushchev's preferences and constraints. As the head of an undemocratic country, he could quickly lose his leadership position if he made the Soviet Union look weak in the eyes of the world. Why? Nazi Germany invaded the Soviet Union only 20 years prior. The invasion and consequent struggle to win World War II resulted in an estimated 20 to 27 million Soviet deaths. That was approximately 11 to 14 percent of the country's population. There was also a very large cost in physical damage and painful memories during the Nazi occupation. Khrushchev himself was at the Battle of Stalingrad, one of the worst battles of World War II. The Soviet leadership vowed that it would not suffer like that again and suspected the United States of trying to bring down the Soviet government through force.

It is also important to note that Khrushchev became the Communist Party leader in the aftermath of a fierce struggle with his rivals after the death of Joseph Stalin. Getting to the position of Soviet leader involved many sacrifices and maneuvering. There were many backroom deals and conspiracies. Sometimes those who attempted to obtain or secure the Soviet leadership would imprison or kill their opponents. Therefore, the stakes were high for him in many ways. Giving up the missile sites in Cuba without something of substance in return would lead to his downfall.

PRACTICAL APPLICATION
ADVISING PRESIDENT KENNEDY ON THE CUBAN MISSILE CRISIS

During the Cuban missile crisis, U.S. President John F. Kennedy needed to make some of the most difficult decisions in human history. His mistakes could lead to the annihilation of living species through an all-out nuclear war. What options did President Kennedy have in response to the news that the Soviets were constructing nuclear missile sites in Cuba? President Kennedy sought to rid Cuba of Soviet nuclear missiles at the same time avoiding an escalation of this crisis into a nuclear war between the two superpowers. Given President Kennedy's goals, which of the options you listed were more likely for him to use? Consider probable Soviet responses to each of these options. Given your assessments of the Soviets' likely responses, how would you advise President Kennedy about how to respond to this crisis?

You can also see the game-like nature of the crisis in many tense sub-episodes where the framework of a game is useful to analyze the event. Let's go back to the U.S. choice. After several agonizing days, President Kennedy made his decision: The United States imposed a naval blockade of the island to prevent the Soviets from delivering additional missiles and military equipment while giving an ultimatum that the USSR must remove the existing missiles. On the other hand, Soviet ships prepared to run the blockade. A decisive moment arrived on October 24, when Soviet ships bound for Cuba came close to the line of U.S. vessels enforcing the blockade. Both sides recognized the prospect of an escalation into a nuclear war, but both wanted the other to be the one to back down. Political analysts understand this type of brinkmanship using the **game of chicken,** where players benefit if the other side yields, and the worst outcome for both sides is when neither side swerves, resulting in an outright collision (or a nuclear war in this case). Therefore, the players' optimal choice depends on what their opponent will do: if the opponent yields, the player should not, but if the opponent does not yield, then the player should yield. In this particular sub-episode, the Soviet ships stopped, and thus the world avoided a nuclear war.

Climate Change Negotiations

Scientists who study the relationship between global climate change and the amount of carbon in the atmosphere have demonstrated that significant, long-term changes in the global climate have been happening. Some of the notable changes in the global climate include more intense heat waves, melting glaciers, increasing sea levels, increased frequencies of more violent hurricanes, and extended periods of droughts. These scientists state that the main culprits of climate change are human activities that increase carbon in the atmosphere, such as burning fossil fuels and destroying forests. Carbon dioxide, methane, nitrous oxide, and other substances we release into the atmosphere (called **greenhouse gases**) function like a blanket, trapping the sun's heat, causing the planet to warm. Scientists warn us that unless we do something about it, there will be dire consequences. Since climate change affects everyone on this planet, you would think that it would not be difficult for governments of all countries to come together to work out solutions to curb greenhouse gas emissions. However, global climate change negotiations have faced significant challenges. One of the most recent challenges came from the U.S. government.

On June 1, 2017, President Donald Trump's announcement that the United States would withdraw from the 2015 Paris climate change agreement unsettled the world. The Paris agreement established a global target to hold the increase in the global average temperature to well below 2°C above preindustrial levels, primarily by reducing greenhouse gas emissions. One hundred ninety-five countries ratified the treaty and agreed to strengthen their efforts to monitor and cut greenhouse gases. Why would President Trump withdraw the United States from the agreement, and what effect might it have on other countries and climate change?

President Trump cited the "unfairness" and "economic burdens" of the Paris agreement on the United States. He estimated that if implemented, it would cost the United States $3 trillion in lost GDP and 6.5 million industrial jobs. The United States would have possible short-term benefits by withdrawing from the agreement so that it could maintain flexibility in how to promote economic growth while free riding on other countries' efforts to combat climate change, that is, taking advantage of the benefits produced by other countries' efforts to curtail climate change without contributing to the efforts. However, the United States is the second-largest emitter of greenhouse gases after China (and cumulatively the largest producer), and without U.S. cooperation, it would be difficult to achieve the agreement's goals. This puts other countries in a difficult position. Why should they sacrifice their economic growth and budgets trying to help achieve the agreement's goals, especially since without the United States, they would be unlikely to achieve them? The political leaders of other countries also face domestic pressures for jobs and energy resources, so they may also leave the agreement, putting the system at risk of breaking down.

The climate change example illustrates a situation known as the **prisoner's dilemma**. It explains why perfectly rational individuals do not want to or cannot work together even when it is beneficial to do so, resulting in a socially worst outcome. The prisoner's dilemma story goes like this. Two criminals are confined in separate prison cells and are barred from communication. A prosecutor offers to drop all charges if one confesses to their crimes, but the other does not. The one who does not confess would get 10 years in prison. The prosecutor does not have enough evidence to convict them on the principal crime without a confession, so if neither confesses, they both get one year in prison for minor charges. Finally, if both confess, they each get six years in prison. So the prisoners face the dilemma: Whatever the other chooses, each is better off confessing than remaining silent. The prediction of the game is that individually rational prisoners will confess, resulting in combined 12 years in prison. The problem is that they collectively would obtain a better outcome if they both remained silent. The "dilemma" faced by the prisoners here is that, whatever the other does, each is better off confessing than remaining silent. But the outcome obtained when both confess (combined 12 years in prison) is worse for each than the outcome obtained if both remain silent (combined two years in prison). The prisoner's dilemma is used to illustrate how players acting in their own individual self-interest can lead to socially suboptimal outcomes.

Applying the prisoner's dilemma to understanding our example of climate change negotiations, each country has an incentive to not cooperate regardless of what other countries would do. The result is the continued threats of climate change that are in everyone's interest to avert. Although the prisoner's dilemma predicts lack of cooperation and collectively undesirable outcomes, it is possible to change people's behavior. Under what conditions do you think people or governments are more likely to cooperate?

PRACTICAL APPLICATION
U.S. CARBON POLICY

Think about the reasons why the United States would be reluctant to limit carbon emissions as part of an international effort. What would convince the U.S. leaders to cooperate internationally in limiting carbon emissions? Is "It's in everyone's best interest" enough? What reasonable incentives would convince people like former President Trump to change their minds?

The Syrian Civil War

In spring 2011, a wave of protests swept North Africa and the Middle East. What would later be referred to as the **Arab Spring** saw citizens of various countries rise up against long-time dictatorships and demand democratic reforms. Some of the protests ended in democratic reform. However, many efforts developed into new dictatorships. In a small set of cases, the protests turned into violent revolts, which then spiraled into civil war. The Syrian Civil War, which is still ongoing, is such a case. Why would the sides of this conflict continue to fight after approximately 10 years? You can answer this question by examining the actors and their conflicting goals. Although the following is a simplified accounting of the war, its description will help us understand why it has lasted so long and why there is no end in sight.

A **game of attrition** involves interactions where actors attempt to "wait out" each other. Actors believe that the other side will give up eventually. They reason that it is better to keep incurring costs until the other side gives up since the benefit of winning is worth the costs. As you can imagine, if both sides follow this approach, then the conflict would go on, almost indefinitely, so long as all sides have the resources to carry on. However, if one side decides that the conflict is no longer worth the cost, then they will back out. A central question is: How will we know when one side believes it is no longer in its interest to keep going?

To answer this question, we need to know what is at stake for the competing sides. In the case of the Syrian Civil War, the stakes are very high. It is very possible that Syrian President Bashar al-Assad believes that in the event of his defeat, not only will he lose his position as ruler, he will also lose his life. An armed revolt removed a similar dictator, Libyan leader Muammar Gaddafi, during the Arab Spring and then captured and executed him. The video of his brutal execution went viral on social media. Similarly, the Syrian rebel forces must be concerned that they would face execution by al-Assad if they surrendered given the ruthless reputation of his government. Therefore, it is not surprising that both sides would want to continue until the other gives in. They literally believe their lives are at stake.

The limiting factor for either side is, of course, the resources to continue fighting. Without arms and personnel, it would be difficult to carry on. The limitation of resources has not been a large problem, however, since both sides are receiving aid from foreign allies. On the government side, al-Assad has received material support from Iran and Russia. The rebel side has multiple factions with one group getting support from Turkey and another from the United States. Some international terrorist organizations are supporting other rebel factions. The foreign actors have vital interests in making sure that the side they support will eventually win. For them, the costs of maintaining support are fairly low compared to what would happen if their side lost. So long as all sides of the war have ample supplies and they fear death should they surrender, we will likely see a continuation of this civil war.

PRACTICAL APPLICATION
IS THERE AN END GAME FOR THE SYRIAN CIVIL WAR?

The Syrian Civil War is one of the Arab Spring events and is still ongoing more than 10 years since the war broke out. Review the barriers to ending the Syrian Civil War as discussed in this chapter. Imagine that you are a foreign policy analyst and your task is to make recommendations about how to end the civil war in Syria. How would you end this game of attrition? What incentives would you give the conflicting parties to stop the war? What confidence would they have in you that you could deliver your promised incentives? How would you deal with the foreign interventions?

ZERO SUM OR NON–ZERO SUM?

LEARNING OBJECTIVE

1.5 Explain how perceptions of outcomes in zero-sum terms influence interaction among political actors and the degrees of conflict among them.

The perception of "winning" and "losing" greatly affects how political actors behave and make choices. In using the framework of a game as a way of analyzing politics, you may think that a game's outcome must produce a clear winner and a clear loser; that is, someone wins a prize and the other loses the prize. After all, when you play a game, you expect this sort of outcome. This can surely be the case in certain situations. However, it does not always have to be the case. Let's take a look at games that may lack a clear winner-and-loser outcome.

Zero-Sum Games

First, let's define a **zero-sum game**. A zero-sum game is a situation in which one player's win is another player's loss. If we add up the total gains and losses of the players, the sum equals zero. If we think about gains and losses in terms of wealth, in a zero-sum game situation, no new wealth is created, and therefore someone's gain must necessarily come from another person's loss. The term comes from the quantifiable payoffs of the outcome. If two people bet on a contest, say who can eat the most pizza, the winner will get some amount of money from the loser. If both parties bet $20, the person who wins gains $20 and the person who lost, loses the same amount. When we add the two amounts together, we have zero: $20 + (-$20) = $0. Someone's gain is another person's loss. Consequently, in a zero-sum game there is a clear winner and loser outcome.

A government's redistributive policy is an example of a zero-sum policy. Consider a situation in which the government decides to equalize wealth in the society by taxing the rich heavily and giving that money to the poor. Since the government did not produce any new wealth but simply reallocated the existing wealth from the rich to the poor, it is a zero-sum policy. As you can easily imagine, a zero-sum policy is prone to generate conflict because it necessarily creates losers and the stakes of the losers may be high.

Non-Zero-Sum Games

A **non-zero-sum game** produces an outcome that is either more or less than zero. This means that one's gain does not necessarily come from another's loss. It is possible that all players win; it is also possible that all players lose. If the total of gains and losses is greater than zero, we call this a **positive-sum game**. If the total of gains and losses is smaller than zero, then we call it a **negative-sum game**.

Positive-Sum Games

Consider a scenario where a government policy increases employment in a society. This is a positive-sum situation because the policy's net effect on employment is more jobs available to workers. Since workers' employment results from additional jobs created by a government policy, you would expect little to no conflict among workers because someone's employment does not mean another's unemployment. There will simply be more employment. It is also a win-win situation because jobs are desirable and politicians gain support due to the policy's success in creating employment.

It is important to keep in mind that positive-sum outcomes do not mean that everyone "wins" equally. Employment increases may mean that some are getting better paying jobs than others are. A positive-sum game also does not mean that everyone gains. It is possible that some players lose. It is still a positive sum if the net outcome is positive, that is, the total of the gains is greater than the total of the losses. What is important is that it is possible for players to gain without taking things away from other players. Therefore, in a positive-sum situation, political interaction is not necessarily competitive or conflictual. It is possible for all parties to gain.

At the same time, it is imperative to remember that people do care about how much they gain relative to others. Therefore, competition and conflict are possible even in positive-sum games. For example, consider international trade where mutual gains from trade occur. For instance, the trade relationship between the United States and China can be considered a positive-sum outcome in the sense that China exports products to the United States at prices that the average U.S. consumer can afford to buy. China gains by selling its products to the United States and the United States benefits by making affordable Chinese products widely available. Therefore, this is a win-win situation. However, we also know that there have been long-standing trade disputes between the United States and China. One of the causes of the trade disputes is the perception on the part of some businesses and individuals in the United States that the trade relationship disproportionately favors China, that even though the United States is gaining, China has gained much more.

Negative-Sum Games

An example of a negative sum is environmental damage. Some businesses have aggressively sought profits by neglecting their impact on the environment. Many factories have polluted air and water. The total cost to the society from environmental degradation—the cost to clean up water, the additional health care costs that people have to pay to care for compromised health due to pollution, and so on—often significantly outweigh the profits that the firms responsible for the pollution make. However, because the benefit is concentrated (the firms make money) and the cost is diffuse (many people share the cost of environmental issues), environmental issues, despite their importance, generally do not receive the kind of attention they deserve. In the meantime, the environment continues to deteriorate.

Perceptions of Zero-Sum and Non-Zero-Sum Games

Sometimes people may perceive an outcome as zero sum or non–zero sum with no basis in reality. People may believe that if someone or some group is "winning," then they must be losing. We see this frequently in many aspects of politics. As we saw earlier, some may argue that if China's economy is growing due to trade with the United States, then they are "winning" and the average American is "losing." They may point to certain types of job losses as an example. However, they do not consider the lower prices trade has made possible as a net benefit.

Another set of cases where we can find perceptions of zero-sum outcomes is in multiethnic societies. In societies where there are many different identities, a fear often arises that one group's success is another group's loss. Let's look again at policies that promote job growth. Perhaps the government policy strongly effects job growth in a particular region of a country and not in other regions. In a country with multiple ethnicities, there could be a good chance that ethnic groups are concentrated in specific regions. In such cases, the regional job growth could also mean job growth for a specific ethnic group. This result could lead other ethnic groups to believe that jobs are growing for the other ethnic group at their expense. They may believe that if one group is getting jobs, then other groups must be losing the opportunities for those jobs. This may or may not be the case. However, the perception that the outcome is zero sum can generate conflict among ethnic groups.

We see this in many countries that have multiethnic societies. For example, the West African country of Nigeria is home to over 250 different ethnic groups. The three major groups are the Hausa-Fulani, Yoruba, and Igbo. These groups also split along religious and regional lines. For example, the Hausa-Fulani people are predominately Muslim and are located in the Northeast of the country. The Yoruba people are located in the Southwest, with roughly half being Christian and the other half being Muslims. Tensions among Nigerian ethnic groups tend to develop due to the uneven economic development within Nigeria and perceptions that one group gains by another group's loss of opportunities to economic resources. Even if the government policies may not have intended such an outcome, people will likely perceive that the outcome was intentionally zero-sum. To keep conflict at a minimum, policies in Nigeria need to keep in mind the possible regional disparities of outcomes.

Another example involves the advancement of racial equality in the United States. Norton and Sommers (2011) found that white people see racism as zero-sum. White people in their study believe that the decline in biases against African Americans since the Civil Rights movement has resulted in increases in perceived bias against white people. African Americans in the study did not share this notion. In other words, they did not believe that lower levels of discrimination against them meant higher levels of discrimination against white people. Perceiving that one group gains (or loses) due to losses (or gains) in another group can make mending race relations in the United States a great challenge.

You may notice that how people perceive the possible outcomes, whether it be zero sum or non–zero sum, can strongly influence their behavior in the political game in question. If one believes that job growth is a zero-sum outcome, then voters in a multiethnic society may wish to vote for political parties that best represent their ethnicity's interests. This behavior furthers competition among the ethnic groups. However, if a non-zero-sum perception is prevalent, then voters may choose a political party that is more nationally oriented instead of ethnically oriented. If we take the concept further, we can see how consistent perceptions of zero-sum outcomes over time can possibly trigger violent actions such as a civil war.

EXPAND YOUR THOUGHTS
ZERO SUM OR NON–ZERO SUM, THAT IS THE QUESTION

We learned that whether political actors see outcomes as zero sum or not influences the intensity of political conflict and the interaction among the actors. A zero-sum game is a situation in which one player's win is another player's loss. A non-zero-sum game produces an outcome that is either more or less than zero. This means that one's gain does not necessarily come from another's loss. It is possible that all players win; it is also possible that all players lose.

Go back through the examples found in the "Politics as a Game" section and select one case. How would the actors perceive the potential outcome in your selected example? Did they see them as zero sum or non–zero sum? Why do you believe this to be the case? Do you think it makes a difference if the actors view the outcomes as one way or the other? Why do you think so?

SUMMARY

Harold Lasswell defined politics as "who gets what, when, and how." Understanding politics requires analytic thinking with systematic use of evidence to come to a valid conclusion. Analyzing politics requires a cool head and distancing ourselves from our emotions. However, it does not mean that the study of politics must be boring. On the contrary, it is quite interesting!

As the chapter shows, politics and games have common elements. We can therefore analyze politics using game frameworks because political actors often need to make decisions considering other actors' actions and reactions within the constraints of rules and resources. We also need to understand how they perceive possible outcomes. Hence, to understand politics we need to identify key actors, their goals and values, the range of alternative options available to them, and existing rules of the game. That means that it is important for us to understand what their political values are and where they come from, as well as the formal institutions and informal rules that may constrain actors' choices and behavior. Subsequent chapters address values and ideologies, how actors make decisions, and political institutions within which actors make those decisions. However, before delving into those substantive areas, we will examine in Chapter 2 how political scientists today conduct empirical analysis of politics.

KEY TERMS

Analytic thinking (p. 2)

Arab Spring (p. 11)

Game of attrition (p. 11)

Game of chicken (p. 9)

Greenhouse gases (p. 10)

Negative-sum game (p. 13)

Non-zero-sum game (p. 13)

Politics (p. 3)

Positive-sum game (p. 13)

Prisoner's dilemma (p. 10)

Strategic interaction (p. 4)

Strategic voting (p. 5)

Zero-sum game (p. 13)

FURTHER READING

Jung, N., Wranke, C., Hamburger, K., & Knauff, M. (2014). How emotions affect logical reasoning: Evidence from experiments with mood-manipulated participants, spider phobics, and people with exam anxiety. *Frontiers in Psychology*, *5*, 570.

Marcus, G. E. (2000). Emotions in politics. *Annual Review of Political Science*, *3*(1), 221–250.

McGhee, H. (2021). *The sum of us: What racism costs everyone and how we can prosper together*. One World.

2 STUDYING POLITICS

LEARNING OBJECTIVES

2.1 Recognize the value of evidence-based reasoning.

2.2 Understand the process of scientific inquiry.

2.3 Understand how theories and hypotheses are developed in political research.

2.4 Understand the roles that intuition and evidence perform in political science inquiry.

2.5 Recognize intended and unintended biases in research and their consequences for our understanding of politics.

2.6 Describe the role of normative theory in political science.

What explains the breakdown of democracy in various countries? Why is voter turnout low in legislative elections? What explains voter apathy? What accounts for the inability of government to enact a sweeping health care reform? Why do countries go to war? How can we explain significant variations in economic wealth within and across countries? These are some of the common questions political scientists seek to answer. How do political scientists answer the questions they have?

Most, if not everyone, reading this chapter have had some exposure to science, or to be more precise, the scientific method. This exposure likely came in the form of understanding and explaining the natural world in subjects like biology, chemistry, and physics. We envision people in lab coats conducting experiments in a laboratory or others out in the field taking geological samples or studying animal behavior.

Humans are also members of the animal kingdom. Therefore, it should not be a surprise that a researcher can study human behavior, human-created institutions, and societies using the same methods. In other words, the methods scientists employ to explain why planets form orbits, water dissolves most substances, and some bacteria are helpful for our digestion can also help us explain, and perhaps predict, political phenomena.

The study of human interactions and societies falls under the label of social science. When we study the political dimension of humanity, we are now in the realm of political science. Simply put, **political science** is the examination of politics using the scientific method.

EVIDENCE-BASED CLAIMS

2.1 Recognize the value of evidence-based reasoning.

You may be surprised to know that contemporary political science predominantly uses the scientific method to research and test claims. Is the scientific method the only way to examine politics? The answer is no. Over the many millennia of human existence, people have used many different methods to explain why people do the things they do. Ideologies are one example, which we will discuss in Chapter 3. It is common for people to make arguments based on what they believe rather than what the data dictate. People in authority sometimes propose ideas as if they are facts when there is often little or no evidence to support them. Evidence-based claims, however, helps us to demystify our world. Answering questions in this way helps us become better equipped to solve problems facing humanity.

The study of the natural world also had a nonscientific phase. There was a time when many people believed that bad air caused diseases like the plague, which periodically killed off large numbers of people. People believed that they could protect themselves from evil odors by wearing masks with long chambers filled with nice smelling herbs and flowers. For centuries, authority figures told people that this was true when in fact it was a nice story that had no evidence supporting it.

Using the scientific method, however, researchers discovered that the plague results from the bacterium *Yersinia pestis*, which attacks our immune system, producing symptoms that our bodies cannot tolerate and leading to death if not treated. Researchers also discovered that the disease was not airborne. Instead, it gets into our bodies through fleabites. Fleas, which rats carry, pass the bacteria from animals to people and from people to people by drawing in blood from one and then passing the bacteria to another with the next bite. The medieval doctors usually did not contract the disease because they covered themselves from head to toe and therefore did not leave skin open for fleabites. The masks

Plague masks were worn by medieval doctors, such as the one seen here, due to the belief that the illness was caused by bad air. It was not until scientific studies conducted hundreds of years later revealed that these assumptions were false and it became known that the plague was in fact spread by flea bites.

"Historiae anatomicae" by Thomas Bartholin. In the public domain. https://commons.wikimedia.org/wiki/File:Paul_F%C3%BCrst,_Der_Doctor_Schnabel_von_Rom_(Holl%C3%A4nder_version).png

did not prevent the disease, but because they usually did not get sick, authorities kept the "bad air" idea alive. Instead, the scientific method showed that if you get rid of the fleas by removing rats that passed them around, then you could solve the problem.

The COVID-19 pandemic also helps us understand the use of the scientific method. At first, we puzzled as to how the virus spread. Researchers have shown that the virus spreads through tiny droplets in the air and that wearing a mask, distancing in social gatherings, and limiting large gatherings will slow down the spread of the disease. Along with vaccinations, the knowledge of the airborne transmission helps us develop public policies that guide people to the behavior needed to control the spread of COVID-19. Questions of interest to political scientists is why some locations have mandates to limit its spread and why some people do not wish to follow such mandates if they exist.

Today, many political scientists study politics scientifically. In examining data and drawing conclusions, we may sometimes find evidence that go against conventional wisdom on a topic or issue. We may discover something similar to whatplague researchers found—what we think is causing a problem may be untrue even if we strongly believe it to be the case. The point is to solve problems based not on what we assume to be true but where the evidence takes us.

STUDYING POLITICS SCIENTIFICALLY

LEARNING OBJECTIVE

2.2 Understand the process of scientific inquiry.

How many of your political beliefs have a basis in a sound scientific study? Or, like the average medieval subject, do you hold beliefs that sound reasonable and yet have no basis in reality? We first introduce the basic steps in explaining political phenomena scientifically. We then move to a deeper understanding of scientific inquiry in the study of politics in the next section.

Karl R. Popper (1902–1994), one of the most influential philosophers of science of the twentieth century, emphasized the quest for truth rather than the possession of absolute knowledge in defining science. According to Popper, all human knowledge is tentative and thus needs continuous testing. The **scientific method** is a systematic way to test hypotheses and answer questions using observable data. We say the scientific method is systematic because it has specific steps accepted by the community of scholars that they can repeat to see if the findings are valid. Replication is critical because a finding may be a coincidence. If others can repeat the steps and get the same or similar results, then we have more confidence in the findings.

The Steps of the Scientific Method
1. Come up with a research question.
2. Develop a theory-based hypothesis that will answer the research question.
3. Test the hypothesis by observing the values of your variables while considering other factors.
4. Compare your results with your expectations.
5. Draw conclusions.

The first step is to be curious about why certain things happen in the political world. Researchers look around the local, regional, national, or international landscape and notice differences and similarities. In the political world, important questions abound. Why are some countries rich while others are poor? Why are some countries democracies while others are not? Why do some countries fight many wars, but others do not? Why do some cities have cleaner air than other cities? Why is government corruption rampant in certain countries? Why do countries sometimes go to war with each other but resolve disputes peacefully using diplomatic means in other times? What institutional arrangements strengthen voters' ability to hold elected politicians accountable? Why do racial and gender discriminations persist? These are just a small sample of questions we will answer in this book.

To figure out why things are the way they are, political scientists do some preliminary research. First, they may notice patterns and come up with some starting ideas. They make observations and examine previous studies to see what other people have discovered. Perhaps someone already saw the same pattern. Perhaps others discovered that the pattern exists, yet more questions came up. Researchers can then use this knowledge to refine their ideas and formulate an explanation that is new and interesting.

Suppose we are interested in figuring out why some countries sign free trade agreements and others do not. A **free trade agreement** is a treaty between two or more countries that reduces barriers to imports and exports among them. Such agreements allow goods and services to move more freely among countries. Let's say that we notice the following pattern: Countries that sign free trade agreements have large businesses organized into powerful associations. These associations try to convince political leaders that greater international trade would help the domestic economy because more exports mean more jobs. After doing some reading, the researcher discovers that no one examined the connection between signing a free trade agreement and large business associations.

The researcher, then, develops or uses an existing explanation, a **theory**, as to why this connection would be so important. Briefly, a theory is a possible explanatory answer to a question. We can also define a theory as an estimation of how the world works. Formally, a theory is a set of interrelated concepts and propositions that explain or predict events and behaviors. A theory provides a systematic way of understanding events, behaviors, and other types of phenomena.

A **scientific theory** is a theory that is well tested using the scientific method and offers a broad explanation of a natural or social phenomenon. As discussed in the introduction of this chapter, not all ideas or explanations become scientific theories. Some ideas are simply held as true (which is often the case with religious beliefs), and others have no ground in empirical reality. In contrast, theories in political science should be testable, and should be falsifiable if evidence indicates the contrary. However, theories typically comprise multiple concepts and propositions and may be too complex to test them in one setting.

To create an estimation of the world, we explain how actions and concepts connect with each other. Theories are important because they can generate hypotheses that explain political phenomena as small as a local election result or as large as the initiation of a global war. The logic of a theory will produce a hypothesis or several hypotheses. A **hypothesis** is a simple and clear statement that describes a presumed relationship between (usually) two variables that can be tested with empirical data. A **variable** is a measurable property or trait of people or things that can take on different values. The values of a variable may change across space and time. By space, we mean across individuals, groups, and geographic regions—regions within a country, across countries, or across world regions. Perhaps we wish to compare different counties or regions within a country or compare a set of countries with respect to the strengths of their democratic institutions. If a researcher is interested in voting decisions of individuals, they may compare voting behavior of a sample of voters. Variables also change values across time. Researchers use many different time measurements: years, quarter years, months, or days. If you observe an item that does not change across space and time, then it is not a variable; it is a constant.

A good example of a variable would be wealth. We can measure the wealth of people or countries. If we measure the wealth of people, then we can observe the annual income of citizens within a country or across different countries. If we make observations of wealth within a country, then we can see how wealth changes across parts of a country (changing values across space) and how this wealth changes from year to year (changing values across time). We can also measure the wealth of countries. The variable will change from country to country (changing values across space) and from year to year (changing values across time).

In order to meet the requirements of the scientific method, we need to word the hypothesis in a way that makes it testable. This means that the concepts need to be observable. It may take the form of a cause-effect statement, "if x, then y." The cause, x, is called the **independent variable**. It is a factor that causes the phenomenon. The effect, y, is called the **dependent variable**. It is a phenomenon that is being caused. If a theory is too complex to test in one setting, a researcher can test a part of the theory using a hypothesis derived from it. As researchers test more parts of the theory, they contribute to the accumulation of knowledge.

Getting back to our free trade research example, we can summarize an answer to the question (why do some countries sign free trade agreements while others do not?) in a simple and clear hypothesis: Having large business associations in a country increases the chance that politicians will sign free trade agreements. Our independent variable is the existence of large business associations in a country. The dependent variable is likelihood of signing a free trade agreement.

Next, we need to gather evidence to test the hypothesis. This step can be tricky because we can introduce bias if we are not careful. Biased data are information that favors supporting our hypothesis. It is tempting to seek out evidence that will support our hypothesis and ignore any evidence that may contradict it. We often see examples of biased analysis on TV, the internet, and other media outlets. Such analysts have a conclusion that they badly want to "prove" and therefore leave out evidence that could harm their arguments. However, the scientific method requires an objective analysis. We need to gather evidence without considering whether or not the evidence will support our claims. For example, we could search only for cases that uphold our claim that countries with large business associations tend to sign free trade agreements than countries without such associations. In other words, we could choose only those cases that fit our claim. However, this would be a bias in favor of our claim and thus is not a real test. Instead, we would need to examine a representative sample of all countries regardless of whether they signed free trade agreements or whether they have large business associations, and then see what proportion of them fit our claim.

Now that the evidence is in front of us, we can compare the results with the expectations. Perhaps we will discover that 30 percent of the agreements demonstrate that the political leaders were convinced to sign the agreement by large business associations. Or maybe 50 percent follow our expected pattern, or maybe 80 percent do.

So how can we conclude whether we have evidence to support our claim? A researcher can come up with one of three possible conclusions. First, the researcher may discover that the evidence is contrary to the expectation. If we find that only 30 percent of the free trade agreements fit our claim, we can conclude that the percentage is too low and therefore we lack strong enough evidence. We say that the data falsified the claim, meaning that the researcher will reject the hypothesis.

Second, the researcher may discover that there is not enough evidence to support or falsify the claim. For example, if the researcher discovers that 50 percent of the cases followed the expected pattern, then the evidence is not sufficiently strong to conclude that the hypothesis is correct. In this case, the researcher may say that that evidence is inconclusive. In other words, the researcher does not know if the claim is accurate or not. In such circumstances, scientists usually side with caution and reject the hypothesis as well. However, this time it is because we simply do not know if we are correct or not.

The last possible conclusion would be that the evidence supports the claim. Let's say the researcher determines that if they find that 80 percent of the cases fit the expected pattern, the evidence is strong enough to support the claim. How can we conclude if we have support with 80 percent of the cases? Do we not need 100 percent? Not necessarily, and here is why. Humans are very complex beings, and as a result, no one claim is likely to explain 100 percent of human-related activity. Think about all the reasons you are reading this chapter. Is there one and only one reason you are reading this chapter? Therefore, any claim a researcher makes will only be part of the story. Perhaps the claim is a large part of the story, but it will not likely be the entire story. However, if the researcher can make a claim that explains a large portion of the story, then we have something important to say. In such circumstances, the researcher can accept the hypothesis because there is enough evidence. We can have a good degree of confidence that the claim is correct.

The last step involves writing up the analysis and getting it evaluated. The write-up needs to communicate all the previous steps so that there is transparency in how the research was conducted and tests were performed. It must communicate all the steps that the researcher followed. The researcher must tell the readers why the research question is important and how it fits with what we already know. The reasoning behind the claim must be logical and understandable. The researcher must discuss the evidence and be able to demonstrate that no bias is present. Finally, the researcher needs to defend the appropriate conclusions using the evidence. If other researchers agree that the study is valid, then it is published in a peer-reviewed journal or book, where it becomes part of the larger literature on the topic and the findings will make their way into someone else's future study.

MORE ON THEORIES AND HYPOTHESES IN POLITICAL SCIENCE

LEARNING OBJECTIVE

2.3 Understand how theories and hypotheses are developed in political research.

Theories and hypotheses of scientific research require a little more detail so that we can keep certain factors in mind when using them in political research. First, we look at why theories rely on assumptions. We will see that assumptions are important if they are reasonable. We then examine how much any one theory can explain and why political science has so many theories. While having a single grand theory to explain all political phenomena sounds like a great idea, formulating one has proven to be very difficult. Next, we try to understand the differences between causal hypotheses and ones that describe an association between our independent and dependent variables. We conclude that without true experimental conditions, it is difficult to demonstrate a causal relationship. We end this section by providing some thoughts on political science's ability to predict outcomes.

The Role of Assumptions in Theory Building

First, theories are built on assumptions. Theoretical assumptions are our starting points—they are items that we hold as true when we begin our explanation. Some researchers state theoretical assumptions clearly, while others do not. Some stated assumptions require more explanation so that the reader will accept them. For example, perhaps a theory assumes that a person's upbringing plays no role in making a political decision. Only current factors, like the person's material wealth, are important. By assuming that a person's upbringing plays no role, we do not imply that the way people are raised does not matter at all in their political choices. Rather, it means that there are other factors (in this example, current conditions) that are much more important in explaining political decision-making.

Why make theoretical assumptions? As mentioned earlier, humans are complex beings, as are their behaviors. Many factors can contribute to our behavior. As a result, we need to simplify our complex world with certain assumptions. Simplification does not necessarily harm our ability to explain political phenomena. Simplification allows us to narrow down the list of factors that are most important in explaining a particular political phenomenon. Many political scientists strive to develop a **parsimonious theory**—a theory that can explain a phenomenon with a few factors. In general, if the two theories can explain the same set of phenomena, then the more parsimonious theory is preferred.

What if theoretical assumptions are wrong? First, if assumptions are completely incorrect, theoretical predictions about human behavior and society are likely to be wrong as well. Therefore, when you follow the scientific method and test a hypothesis derived from the theory with data, you will probably find disconfirming evidence. This gives you an opportunity to reevaluate the theory, including its assumptions. If the assumptions are inaccurate and they lead to incorrect predictions, you need to revise the assumptions. What if the assumptions are not accurate but they still help the theory to generate predictions that approximate reality?

The "utility maximizer" assumption of the rational choice theory is one such example. Many political science theories begin by assuming that people are rational and make decisions by examining how they can maximize benefits and minimize costs. People will therefore gather information they need to make decisions, compare all the different options, and choose a strategy that leads to an outcome that most benefits them. Some scholars have challenged the assumption when stating that humans lack cognitive capabilities to be utility maximizers.

They disagree with this utility maximization assumption of rational choice theory because they observe that people may not seek, or may not be able to seek, all the information needed to make a decision that will maximize their benefits. In addition, some nonmaterial benefits are hard to compare with material ones. For example, how can we compare the utility of a "good feeling" one has when making a decision with a monetary payoff of a different decision? Which has more value? It is therefore difficult to observe what exactly a benefit entails. Does this mean we should dismiss the rationality assumption?

Nobel Laureate in Economic Sciences Milton Friedman argued in his 1953 essay, "The Methodology of Positive Economics," that theories should be judged not by their psychological realism but by their ability to predict behavior. Even though we know that humans do not behave in a perfectly rational manner, we still try to be rational, and the utility maximization model is a close approximation of human behavior. Friedman's view was that, as long as a theory is useful, its assumptions need not be perfect.

Is a Grand Theory of Political Science Possible?

Another item to keep in mind is the range of questions political science theories can answer. It would be great if we have a grand theory of politics. We could use such a theory to explain all political phenomena. A single grand theory could explain, for example, both the results of a local mayor's election and why countries fight wars. However, as you will see in this book, no such grand theory exists. Efforts to create such a paradigm in political science were not successful. Instead, political science has middle-range theories. These theories only attempt to explain a set of similar political phenomena. We have theories, for example, that attempt to explain the occurrence of war. Notice that we used the plural word *theories*, and not *a theory*, of why wars among countries exist. Even within a subset of research questions, no one theory dominates. Instead, we have multiple theories that rely on differing assumptions and logical mechanisms to explain war across time and around the world. The same applies to other political events such as why some countries are democratic, why some societies continue to have low levels of economic development, or why some citizens trust their governments more than other citizens do.

EXPAND YOUR THOUGHTS
POLITICAL SCIENCE LAWS?

Some political scientists argue that we should strive to build law-like theories that are more common in natural sciences. Some do not consider finding laws of political science likely and instead advocate that we should develop theories that are more probabilistic—those that do not predict or explain with 100 percent or near 100 percent accuracy but do so with good probabilities, say 80 percent. Yet others are skeptical of political science ever being able to develop predictive theories. What is your position?

Let's examine one theory a bit more closely. Modernization theory explains why stable democracy develops in certain countries and not in others. Modernization theory emphasizes the role of economic development in accounting for democratic development. Factors such as higher per capita income, industrialization, and urbanization will lead to the growth of the middle class. The middle-class people are educated and capable. They would thus demand political power. Once this group becomes large enough in the society, according to modernization theory, the country becomes and stays democratic. You can see that modernization theory contains parts—propositions and concepts—that are interrelated and that together explain democratization and stability of democracy. The theory also assumes that people prefer to control political power than to be controlled by others. Education and economic wealth give them the tools to achieve this power. Another attribute of a theory is that it is general; that is, it is not an explanation for just one or a few cases but is an explanation that accounts for a large number of cases. Indeed, many political scientists regard a theory that can explain more cases as a more preferred theory.

Causation Versus Association

Another point that requires more detail is the difference between causation and association. In political science, is it possible to verify that x (the independent variable) causes y (the dependent variable)? Or do we just happen to observe x and y to occur together? These questions are at the heart of the "causation versus association" problem. Often times, theories are worded so that they are explaining a causal relationship. This would require us to test to see if a causal relationship is really happening. However, many studies do not employ this level of testing. Instead, they often demonstrate that x and y are observed in the way the theory predicts. Since the theory gives a reasonable explanation, we conclude that x caused y. This poses a challenge in empirical testing because it is possible that x did not cause y. X and y could appear together by coincidence, or perhaps something else produces x and y. We call this type of false association that appears to be causal but in fact is not a spurious relationship. As you can see, simply observing x and y happening together may lead to some false conclusions.

How do we resolve this problem? Ideally, we would run controlled experiments like researchers do in laboratories. You may have done some simple experiments in your school life. For example, consider a plant experiment. You have three plants. Each plant is the same, with the same soil and amount of water. The hypothesis we want to test is if sunlight causes the plant to grow. Since the plants, soil, and water are the same (they are all constants), we can vary the amount of sunlight to see if, in fact, it helps the plants to grow. We keep one in dark, another with little sunlight, and third with a good amount of sunlight. After measuring the plants over time, we discover that the plant with the most sunlight grew more than the other two. We have demonstrated causation by controlling the plants' exposure to the sunlight while holding other factors constant: The sunlight caused the plant to grow.

The plant experiment will not win us a Nobel Prize, but it does show that controlled experiments can demonstrate causality. Do we have such experiments in political science? The brief answer is, generally speaking, no. While there has been some experimentation in certain areas of political science, such as studies that involve psychologically based theories, most of the findings rely on statistical operations that mimic experimentation conditions but are not exactly experiments.

Why is experimentation not common in political science research? Well, in many cases we are ethically and practically limited. Take any hypothesis regarding the causes of war. Would it be ethical, or even possible, to manipulate a set of countries to see if they will wage wars against each other? In another example, is it ethical to lie intentionally to voters to see if we can change their decisions on a candidate and find the causes behind voter choice? Would it even be possible for researchers to manipulate levels of countries' economic development so that they can test if democracy does not break down beyond a certain level of economic development? Instead of experiments, many political scientists examine the natural laboratory as events occur in the mostly uncontrolled world. They seek to approximate controlled experiment through quasi-experimental research design using statistical techniques or by case matching. They gather data as events unfold or look at the historical record for sound case comparisons. From these studies, we approximate a causal finding.

Political science is not alone in dealing with the "causation versus association" problem. A few natural sciences also face the same dilemma. Seismologists (people who study earthquakes) cannot create an earthquake to see if their hypotheses can predict when they will occur. It would be great if we knew when an earthquake would hit a heavily populated area. However, the ability to create a real one in the earth is impossible for many reasons. Semiologists instead rely on data gathered when earthquakes do occur to see if their hypotheses are correct. After gathering enough data in the natural world, these researchers can piece together a highly predictive theory. Political scientists work in a similar manner.

PRACTICAL APPLICATION
A HYPOTHESIS THAT IS IMPORTANT TO YOU

Political science research often begins with important questions in our lives. A hypothesis is a simple statement that describes a relationship between variables. Think about something related to real-world politics about which you care. State your hypothesis in a clear and concise manner regarding why you believe such a phenomenon happens. Which one is the independent variable (or the factor that causes the phenomenon), and which one is the dependent variable (or the phenomenon to be explained)? What is your explanation as to why the dependent variable occurs as a result of the independent variable?

Predictions in Political Science

If theories are useful in answering important questions, then they may also help us predict how events will unfold. With the ability to predict outcomes, political scientists can suggest policies that will promote benefits for a society or prevent undesirable outcomes from happening.

In the previous section, we learned that modernization theory consists of various concepts and propositions, which makes it difficult for us to test the entire theory at once. One frequently tested hypothesis derived from modernization theory is that per capita income and the likelihood that a country is democratic is positively correlated. In other words, the higher per capita income, the more likely that the country is a democracy. Per capita income is the independent variable and the likelihood that a country is democratic is the dependent variable. Many researchers have found that per capita income and the likelihood that a country is democratic are indeed positively correlated. If modernization theory is a good scientific theory, that is, if the theory has withstood repeated tests with consistent evidence supporting the theoretical claims, we should be able to use modernization theory to predict if and at what level of wealth a country will become a democracy.

Recall that most political science theories are probabilistic. They do not explain political phenomena 100 percent of the time. Instead, good political science theories should explain political phenomena reasonably well. That means that while researching, you may encounter observations that are not consistent with theoretical predictions. For example, the People's Republic of China is not a democracy, yet its economy is growing (in other words, people are becoming wealthier). Does this imply that China's chances of becoming a democracy are increasing? According to past findings of modernization theory, we could expect this to be the case. However, no single theory, especially one regarding human activity, will explain all events. The complexity of human behavior requires us to have multiple theories and hypotheses to approximate events found in our world. If China does become a democracy because of economic development, then we have one more data point supporting modernization theory. If China stays autocratic despite its economic development, that does not necessarily negate the explanatory power of modernization theory. Yet we need to suspect that perhaps another factor or other factors are at work that prevents China from democratizing.

DISCOVERY IN POLITICAL SCIENCE

LEARNING OBJECTIVE

2.4 Understand the roles that intuition and evidence perform in political science inquiry.

This book contains many findings that may sound intuitive to you. This means that you "feel" or have a "hunch" that the findings are true because they make logical sense. Therefore, you may think that seeking evidence to support claims is not necessary. You may believe that people are wasting their time since the claim is "obviously" true. The problem is: How do we know if a claim is true unless we find evidence to support it?

We need to recognize that intuition is an important part of the scientific process because it offers us a good starting point. Our minds come up with ideas that seem reasonable given what we already know. After all, scientists generally do not go out to see if there is evidence for relationships that they believe are incorrect. They seek observations based on what they believe to be true. It is intriguing, however, when we discover evidence that contradicts our intuitive starting point.

Take, for example, the start of a **social movement** or revolution. A social movement occurs when citizens of a country organize in a sustained manner to seek some sort of change in the politics of a society. Members of a social movement use protest, public meetings, and rallies (often peaceful, but not always) as well as various forms of civil disobedience to get the message for change in the ears of governmental leaders. Social movements are prevalent in democracies, but sometimes occur in nondemocracies. The Civil Rights movement in the United States is an example of citizens demanding the improvement of political rights for Black Americans as part of the overall fight to end racism.

In contrast, a **revolution** aims to produce a complete change. A revolution is a complete overhaul of a political system often through a violent overthrow of the previous political regime. Citizens are so unhappy with their political, social, and economic conditions that they demand an entire change in the political system. Revolutions are mostly violent affairs with citizens taking up arms against their current government. They demand the removal of the incumbent political leaders to install a new social, economic, or political system. The French Revolution is an example of people wanting to remove a monarchy and establish a democratic form of government.

We may think that social movements or revolutions are spontaneous protests of people gathered to change undesirable circumstances. We picture people participating in civil disobedience or marching with others to show dissatisfaction. In the case of revolutions, we may picture people organizing themselves into military units to fight the current regime. The reality, however, is far from this. People generally do not spontaneously organize themselves for change. Instead, certain individuals acting as leaders organize and inspire people into action against the political system. These leaders communicate the legitimacy behind people's dissatisfaction and explain why it is in their best interest to organize, protest, and, sometimes, conduct armed rebellion.

The claim that people will act against an unsatisfactory political condition sounds intuitive. Nonetheless, the evidence shows us that this will not be the case unless a robust leadership is present. In fact, current and past events show that it is common to have many dissatisfied people, but most of the time they do nothing to change their political systems. The finding that most dissatisfied people do nothing to change their systems opens up another avenue of questions: Why do people fail to act if they are unhappy? Who becomes leaders of contentious politics, such as protests and revolutions? Why are some political leaders unable to communicate the legitimacy behind people's dissatisfaction? Why do people sometimes choose democratic means (such as elections) to make changes while in other times they resort to violence?

In our brief example, we described a discovery that may challenge our intuition. We may believe, intuitively, that dramatic changes brought about by social movements or revolutions are due to people being very dissatisfied by their circumstances. Instead of people spontaneously getting together because they are "fed up" by the current political system, evidence points to people doing the opposite. The discovery that dramatic change requires more than simply being dissatisfied requires us to ask and answer even more questions on this topic, which will lead to us to other avenues of discovery.

GETTING RESEARCH RIGHT: BIAS AND PREDICTION IN THE STUDY OF POLITICS

LEARNING OBJECTIVE
2.5 Recognize intended and unintended biases in research and their consequences for our understanding of politics.

We may perform a scientific study of politics inappropriately if we are not careful. If we scientifically study other creatures or organisms, we can easily distance ourselves from the subject. In studying politics, we are studying ourselves, which may cause us not to be as objective as we should. In addition, political scientists often cannot conduct laboratory experiments. Since we are unable to control for many factors like in a laboratory, we may believe that one variable is related to another when in fact it is not. Poor research design and the lack of objectivity can lead to biased conclusions. To be sure that we are on the correct track, we need to consider all the biases that may present in a study.

Bias is an inclination or prejudice in favor of or against a particular thing, view, person, or group compared with another in an unfair way. Bias is not uncommon in political claims. In this chapter, we have emphasized the important role that the scientific method plays in testing hypotheses. Although the scientific method provides a way for us to test the empirical validity of various ideas and claims, researchers need to take necessary care if their research is to serve as a valid test. One of the sources of bias is one's values. While there is a debate about whether value-neutral research is even possible in political science, the scientific study of politics requires one not to allow one's values and desires to interfere in the research process. Such interference may lead to biased collection of information just to validate one's claim—that is, only gather data that fit the story and ignore other data that contradict, or otherwise may cause distortion in, the interpretation of the data.

Bias in research can also arise even without researchers' intent due to poor procedures for collecting data or data unavailability. For example, many studies have shown that democracies tend to do a better job than dictatorships in promoting citizens' well-being, especially in prolonging life expectancy and reducing child deaths. However, Michael Ross (2006) points out that one of the reasons why democracies *appear* to perform better than dictatorships in earlier studies is that data on many nondemocratic countries that tended to perform well were not available. Therefore, many studies predominantly included dictatorships that did poorly while omitting many that did well. Although to what extent democracies are better at promoting citizens' well-being compared to dictatorships remains a subject of intense debate, Ross made an important and valid criticism in this literature. If investigators do not follow proper procedure in making sure that the sample of individuals that they decided to study closely mirrors the population they are trying to understand, they can make costly mistakes.

Case Study: Biases in Predicting the 1936 U.S. Presidential Election

One such mistake from the use of a biased sample occurred in the United States in the 1930s. In 1936, U.S. President Franklin Roosevelt, a Democrat, was seeking reelection against Republican candidate Alf Landon. The *Literary Digest* was one of the most respected magazines of the time and had correctly predicted the winner of the presidential election since 1916. In 1936, the *Digest* conducted perhaps the largest poll ever taken in the history of electoral politics. The *Digest* mailed over 10 million questionnaires to its subscribers and names drawn from lists of automobile and telephone owners, and over 2.4 million people responded. Based on the responses obtained from this sample, the *Digest* predicted a landslide victory by Landon, by 57 to 43 percent. The election indeed produced a landslide: Roosevelt won with 62 percent of the vote. And the *Digest* went out of business.

What went wrong? The *Digest*'s polling techniques were the main culprit. By its polling method, it polled people who were much wealthier than most, and wealthy people tended to support the Republican candidate. Just think about who would be able to afford to subscribe a magazine like the *Digest* during the Great Depression or own telephones and cars at that time? Although unintended, the magazine polled a biased sample of voters, which ended up causing the embarrassing failure in prediction.

This example shows you the importance of obtaining data appropriately if you are to make a general conclusion from them. It also cautions us against making generalizations based solely on our experience or the experiences of a few people with whom we associate. When we do that, there is a significant chance that our sample will be biased, that is, not representative of the larger population. When you draw conclusions based on a study using a biased sample, the likelihood that your conclusions are wrong significantly increases.

Science Gone Wrong: The Case of the Eugenics Movement

It is important to spotlight the times in recent history when researchers and political leaders incorrectly used the scientific method and thereby produced tragic consequences. The following discussion of the eugenics movement demonstrates how biased studies produced invalid findings that influenced U.S. laws and court rulings.

Eugenics is a belief that people biologically inherit socially desirable human traits, such as intelligence and proper behavior. Eugenicists believe that they can improve the human condition by limiting the reproductive ability of, or otherwise excluding, people and groups judged to be inferior, while promoting the procreation of those who they judge to be superior. Advocates referred to the practice as "race hygiene."

The ideas of eugenics have a long history. Plato, an ancient Greek philosopher, in his book *The Republic*, suggested that the ideal society should apply principles of selective human breeding. In modern times, the eugenics movement began in the late nineteenth century and had popular appeal until the 1940s in the United States and Europe. Even after its decline in popularity, we still see its lingering effects. Charles Darwin's half-cousin Francis Galton introduced eugenics and its related concepts in 1883. You may know Darwin as the founder of the theory of evolution. Galton and others took the ideas from this theory and extended them into the pseudoscience of eugenics.

What is wrong with the science behind eugenics? First, the traits that eugenicists declared to be socially desirable are subjective. What does it mean to be intelligent? How does one objectively measure such a trait? Numerous studies have pointed to the biases associated with defining and measuring intelligence. In addition, it is very difficult to remove the social conditions that contribute to someone's intellectual development. For example, we know that wealth is a major contributor to a person's ability to get a good education. Other social conditions, such as racism and sexism also produce barriers. Finally, members of the eugenics movement believed that one's physical appearance was an indicator for undesirable human traits. For example, they believed that an individual's skull shape or nose size was a good indicator for intelligence or even the likelihood that the person was capable of criminal activity. By using physical appearance as an indicator, proponents could target members of specific ethnic groups as being undesirable.

In the United States, the popularity of eugenics was behind several political decisions in the early twentieth century. Numerous states passed laws permitting the sterilization of individuals who specialists deemed unfit to have children. Doctors would carry out the procedures without a person's consent or knowledge. State and lower federal courts subsequently struck down some of these laws. However, in their ruling in *Buck v. Bell* (1927), the Supreme Court declared, by an 8-to-1 decision, that laws permitting forced sterilization were constitutional. Also during the same period, the U.S. government passed the Immigration Act of 1924. The act's immigration laws introduced quotas on individuals that could immigrate to the United States based on the 1890 census data. Using the 1890 data was intentional. During this time, most immigrants came from northwest Europe (Britain, Germany, Scandinavia, etc.). Advocates of the new immigration laws viewed people from these countries as having socially desirable traits. The laws attempted to exclude the rising number of individuals from East Asia (mainly China and Japan) and southern and eastern Europe (Italy, Spain, Portugal, Poland, Russia, etc.) because they believed these people held socially undesirable traits. One of the major religious considerations was limiting the number of Jews coming from eastern Europe.

The eugenics movement hit its highpoint in 1932 when the Nazis seized power in Germany. Their fascist ideology (Nazism, which we will discuss in greater depth in the next chapter) led them to enact a series of "racial purity" laws. Such laws removed the citizenship of Jews and other "undesirable" Germans, robbing them of their property. The Nazi's thinking eventually led to the murder of millions of people in numerous death camps in Germany and eastern Europe. After the Nazis conquered eastern Europe, their murderous policies extended to Poles and Russians because they deemed the Slavic peoples as inferior. The defeat of Germany in World War II ended the Nazi atrocities and the open use of eugenic beliefs in the creation of laws and other policies. Interestingly, Nazis leaders that were on trial for crimes against humanity cited the U.S. Supreme Court case *Buck v. Bell* as a partial justification for their actions.

In sum, sound scientific reasoning was not the basis of the so-called biology-based political decisions that led to numerous tragedies. Instead, they were actually propagating the socially constructed discrimination already in place. Eugenicists had already viewed certain people as inferior and simply used "science" to justify their beliefs. It is therefore not a surprise that today the term *eugenics* is closely associated with the concepts of scientific racism and white supremacy.

PRACTICAL APPLICATION
THE BIASES OF "I JUST KNOW IT'S TRUE"

We discussed that bias is an inclination or prejudice in favor of or against a particular thing, view, person, or group compared with another in an unfair way. One of the sources of bias is one's values. You may have been involved in a discussion when someone's facts are questioned, only to hear the challenged person say, "I just know it's true!"

Although the scientific method provides a way for us to test the empirical validity of various ideas and claims, researchers need to take necessary care if their research is to serve as a valid test. Firmly believing that something is true when it is not may cause problems in the analysis of politics. How would you deal with the "I just know it's true" attitude when faced with it?

NORMATIVE STUDY OF POLITICS

LEARNING OBJECTIVE

2.6 Describe the role of normative theory in political science.

Although the use of the scientific method is common in today's political science research, not all scholars in the discipline apply the scientific method. This branch of the discipline is referred to as political theory. Many such scholars employ **normative theory**, which concerns the evaluative judgments about what is right or wrong, just or unjust, or desirable or undesirable in a society. It is not a part of the scientific branch of political science, and it makes no claims to follow the scientific method. Instead, its primary role is to evaluate phenomena and offer alternatives on how the world "ought to" or "should" be. The focus is on prescribing changes that would form an ideal world. It does not seek to explain politics in the scientific sense but attempts to explain why things are undesirable based on specific value judgments.

The values espoused in normative theory are subjective since they are based on a scholar's moral views. Perhaps the scholar will argue that society should be set up to benefit the greater good by focusing on society as a collective unit. Other scholars will conversely argue that only through individual self-reliance will we achieve the greater good for society. Yet others will argue that the greater good for society is unachievable and/or perhaps unworthy of pursuit.

There is debate among political scientists regarding the role of normative theory. Some argue that it plays a critical role in our understanding of the human condition. Others are skeptical about the role of political normative theory in contemporary political science due to how the discipline has developed. We, the authors of this book, consider normative theory as an important part of the study of politics. As you will see in the next chapter, normative political theory is frequently the basis of ideology that motivates political action. In the end, the relationship between the government and the governed is a perpetual question for many of us who study politics. We conjecture how the world ought to be and seek improvement in the way we live and relate to one another.

The role of ideology is also interesting and can be studied scientifically as well as normatively. Why do some ideologies evolve and have lasting appeal while others do not? What explains the attractiveness of an ideology? Why do some people adopt a specific ideology while most people do not? The next chapter will start us down the road of discovery by examining some of the more popular ideologies of our times as well as major classical ideologies that have had significant impact on the way we interpret the world.

SUMMARY

Political science is the scientific study of politics. This chapter introduced you to a specific way of analyzing political phenomena using the scientific method of discovery. The scientific method allows us to make reliable evidence-based claims by requiring our evidence to be objectively collected and therefore free of biases. The first steps of analysis involve asking important questions and using theories to provide preliminary answers. Theories help us develop hypotheses that need testing using real-world observations. Conclusions drawn from the evidence promote reaffirmation or discovery, which may sometimes be counterintuitive. In fact, many of the more exciting discoveries are not what we expect.

Biases in research could be intentional or unintentional. Researchers need to remove their own values as much as possible from the research process if they are to understand how the world works. It is also imperative for researchers to pay adequate attention to how the observations they use in research are collected and analyzed so as not to introduce unintended biases to their research.

Although much of political science today relies on empirical testing, some scholars do explore problems facing society using normative theories. Normative theories are an important part of the study of politics because of the fundamental questions they address and the insights they offer in guiding human behavior. In the next chapter on ideologies, we will examine normative ideas and examine how people use them in political life.

KEY TERMS

Dependent variable (p. 23)

Free trade agreement (p. 22)

Hypothesis (p. 22)

Independent variable (p. 23)

Normative theory (p. 34)

Parsimonious theory (p. 25)

Political science (p. 19)

Revolution (p. 30)

Scientific method (p. 21)

Scientific theory (p. 22)

Social movement (p. 30)

Social science (p. 19)

Theory (p. 22)

Variable (p. 22)

PHILOSOPHI QVAM MODICE HABITAT

W. Faithorne sculp.

THOMAS HOOBS Malmesburiensis.
Aet: suæ. 76.

POLITICAL IDEOLOGIES AND POLITICAL THOUGHTS

LEARNING OBJECTIVES

3.1 Define ideology and understand the three functions of political ideologies.

3.2 Describe the tenets of political realism.

3.3 Compare classical liberalism and modern U.S. liberalism.

3.4 Discuss conservatism and how it manifests in modern U.S. politics.

3.5 Identify the various views of social contract.

3.6 Explain the different types of socialism.

3.7 Identify the key features of fascism.

3.8 Explore how religious doctrine can be used as a political ideology.

3.9 Describe environmentalism and its relation to sustainable development and social equity.

3.10 Identify the three major forms of feminism.

Who has the right to rule? What are the ideal political, economic, and social systems? What should be the relationship between the government and the governed? Should the state distribute resources to its citizens, or should individuals be responsible for their own welfare? If there is a conflict between individual rights and collective welfare, should societies sacrifice individual freedom to achieve a greater good? From ancient Greek philosophers such as Plato and Aristotle to contemporary politicians, scholars, and citizens, people have debated these questions for thousands of years. As you might imagine, the answers vary greatly. Some believe that the state's power should be limited for fear that it will use its power against citizens. Some believe that the state should be powerful enough to solve most, if not all, of society's problems. Yet others glorify the state and its leaders, viewing as legitimate the state's quest for total control over all major parts of society and a citizenry's self-sacrifice and complete obedience.

Many people answer fundamental political questions through their worldviews. Scholars commonly refer to such worldviews as ideologies. Although there could be as many different ideologies as there are the number of people, certain ideologies have been more influential in explaining political events and political behavior than most others. Indeed, many ideas and beliefs that people hold are variants of major ideologies. In this chapter, we will discuss some of the major ideologies and political thoughts that have exerted significant influence in politics over many centuries around the globe, including realism, liberalism, conservatism, and socialism. We will also examine in this chapter more contemporary ideologies, such as fascism, religious fundamentalism, environmentalism, and feminism. The two chapters that follow will address the complexity of societal and individual political beliefs and behavior in more detail.

WHAT IS AN IDEOLOGY?

LEARNING OBJECTIVE
3.1   Define ideology and understand the three functions of political ideologies.

What is an ideology? Formally, we define **ideology** as a comprehensive system of beliefs about political, social, and economic institutions, processes, and goals. Such systems of beliefs also offer to explain, evaluate, and provide remedies for social problems. Succinctly, an ideology is a worldview that motivates action. A political ideology often starts by offering a critique of a country's politics and then proposes a vision of the way in which the world ought to be. Ideologues are people whose personal belief systems capture a specific ideology. Understanding ideology is important to understanding politics and human behavior because the values and beliefs that ideologues hold influence their behaviors and choices.

A political ideology has three interrelated functions. First, a political ideology furnishes answers to questions. It explains why things are the way they are. For example, you may observe a significant inequality in the distribution of wealth in the country. Consider the United States. Undoubtedly, there is tremendous wealth in the United States. The United States is one of the wealthiest countries in the world with an advanced and complex economy. Despite the significant amount of wealth, poverty is a serious issue in the country. The U.S. Census Bureau reported that the official poverty rate in 2019 was 10.5 percent, down from 14.8 percent in 2014. This is the lowest rate observed since 1959, which is when the Census Bureau first began publishing poverty rate estimates. Still, approximately 34 million people were in poverty in 2019 (U.S. Census Bureau, 2020). On the other hand, the 10 richest American billionaires hold combined assets of around $1.05 trillion. This is about the size of the Mexican or Indonesian economy. Despite the COVID-19 pandemic, the 10 richest Americans substantially increased their wealth, thereby widening economic inequality. Why are there so many poor people in a society with a tremendous amount of wealth? Why is wealth concentrated in a small group of people? How do we explain this? Different political ideologies provide different answers in explaining why the distribution of wealth is skewed.

Second, a political ideology provides a normative evaluation of the situation; that is, it states if the situation is good or bad. Is it right for so many people to live in poverty when sufficient wealth exists in the society? Alternatively, is economic inequality justified and not a problem in need of a solution? Is it just for political leaders to repress the people's political rights for the sake of national security and social stability? Political ideologies provide answers to these and other questions. They inform followers if actions and current conditions are right or wrong. For example, classical liberalism, one of the most influential political ideologies that we will examine later in this chapter, holds individual liberty as its highest value and would be opposed to suppression of the people's political rights even if it seems necessary for national security.

Given the diagnosis and evaluation, the third function of a political ideology is programmatic: It provides a guide for specific action to solve the problem (assuming that the ideology suggests that a problem exists). It tells the ideology's followers what they need to do to solve the problem and how to do it. For example, the Marxist or communist ideology (we will also review this ideology in this chapter) considers unequal distribution of wealth in a society as an unjust condition. Furthermore, it identifies that the operation of the capitalist economy underlies the inequality between the property-owning class (who exploits the workers) and the working class (the exploited). Further, it calls for the overthrow of the capitalist system, the abolition of private property, and the establishment of a classless society. During much of the twentieth century, the Marxist ideology motivated many revolutionary movements in various parts of the world, including Russia, China, and Cuba.

It is important to emphasize that different ideologies explain and evaluate the same situation differently and thus recommend different programs of action. For example, the concentration of wealth may be a problem for the ideologies of the left. However, classical liberal and conservative ideologies do not necessarily see it as a problem.

POLITICAL REALISM

LEARNING OBJECTIVE
3.2 Describe the tenets of political realism.

Political realism is a political philosophy that attempts to explain and prescribe political activities and relations. It views politics as the struggle for power. Political realists thus believe that only the powerful can rule. Followers of political realism believe that ethical and moral questions need to be subjugated in favor of focusing on attaining and maintaining power. For them, power is right.

One of the most famous and earlier political realists is Niccolò Machiavelli (1469–1527). Machiavelli lived during the difficult time of war-torn Renaissance Florence in the fifteenth and the sixteenth centuries. He served as a senior official in the city-state responsible for diplomatic and military affairs. Before Machiavelli, the predominant stance among political philosophers was that rulers must be virtuous and morally upright, which would legitimize their exercise of authority. Machiavelli was very critical of this moralistic view of authority. His experience as a senior political advisor taught him that deception, treachery, and crime prevailed in politics. In his famed treatise, *The Prince*, he argued that there is no moral basis on which to judge what is right and what is wrong, and whoever has power has the right to command. He further stated that being virtuous does not ensure power and authority. Consequently, Machiavelli teaches

that the only real concern of the political ruler is, and should be, the acquisition and maintenance of power necessary to care for the state. Machiavelli writes in *The Prince*:

> Many have imagined republics and principalities which have never been seen or known
> to exist in reality; for how we live is so far removed from how we ought to live, that he
> who abandons what is done for what ought to be done, will rather bring about his own
> ruin than his preservation. (Machiavelli, 1532/1908)

Political realism has had a long history in the perspective of authority and human
interactions. It portrays appalling images of human nature and human behavior as true.
Seventeenth-century philosopher Thomas Hobbes (1588–1679/1968) assumed that humans
are by nature selfish and their behavior is competitive and nasty, driven by greed and fear of
death. Hobbes characterized human interaction in the absence of a powerful ruler as "war of
all against all" and life in the **state of nature**—a hypothetical condition of human life before
government or society—as "solitary, poor, nasty, brutish, and short."

In his renowned book, *Leviathan*, Hobbes describes how humans would live without political authority:

> In such condition, there is no place for industry; because the fruit thereof is uncertain:
> and consequently no culture of the earth; no navigation, nor use of the commodities
> that may be imported by sea; no commodious building; no instruments of moving, and
> removing, such things as require much force; no knowledge of the face of the earth; no
> account of time; no arts; no letters; no society; and which is worst of all, continual fear,
> and danger of violent death; and the life of man, solitary, poor, nasty, brutish, and short.
> (Hobbes, 1588–1679/1968)

You can find contemporary examples of Hobbes's state of nature in countries wracked by
civil war and violent political strife, such as in Syria and Afghanistan. In Syria, unrest grew in
2011 out of discontent with the Syrian government. The unrest spiraled into an armed conflict after the government violently suppressed protests calling for President Bashar al-Assad's
removal. Since then, a civil war has been fought between the Ba'athist Syrian Arab Republic led
by Assad, who is trying to hold onto power, and multiple domestic and foreign groups fighting
with Assad's group and with one another, all vying for power. With over 400,000 deaths and
the displacement of millions of Syrians, the war is still ongoing with no ending in sight. Hobbes
would say that such miseries and instabilities occur because there is no powerful authority who
can "keep them all in awe." Political realists' likely solution would be the creation of a very powerful government that could enforce stability, with force if needed.

Today, political realism is one of the popular schools of thought in international relations,
which has influenced many foreign policymakers. Henry Kissinger, former U.S. Secretary of
State and National Security Advisor, who served under the presidential administrations of
Richard Nixon and Gerald Ford, is one such figure. As a practitioner of **Realpolitik** (politics
or diplomacy based on practical rather than ideological or moral considerations), Kissinger
believed that moral impulses and crusading ideals should not guide foreign policies. He engaged
in a number of controversial U.S. policies, such as U.S. involvement in the 1973 Chilean military coup that ousted the democratically elected socialist president, Salvador Allende.

EXPAND YOUR THOUGHTS

DOES POLITICAL REALISM PROVIDE AN ACCURATE UNDERSTANDING OF HOW WE BEHAVE?

Political realism refutes idealistic and moralistic approaches to politics and advocates instead that one needs to see the "reality" of politics. For realists, politics is the struggle for power, and the winners are the ones that use both force and cunning wisely. Those who insist on morality as the basis of their action tend to ruin themselves. Does political realism provide an accurate understanding of political relations and human behavior? What examples can you give?

LIBERALISM

LEARNING OBJECTIVE

3.3 Compare classical liberalism and modern U.S. liberalism.

Traditionally, individual liberty is the hallmark of liberal ideology. It may be a surprise to you that the way Americans understand **liberalism** today is different from how people around the world understand it. The rest of the world's understanding of liberalism goes back to its original ideas. We will first review the original ideas and then discuss how these ideas differ from the contemporary American usage of the term.

Classical Liberalism

Classical liberalism, or simply liberalism, holds individual liberty in high regard and advocates for civil liberties under the rule of law. It began with a focus on individual freedoms at a time when monarchs were absolute rulers or shared power with a small elite. Under a monarchy, social mobility was nearly impossible. If you were born a peasant, you died as one, no matter how hard you tried to move up socially and economically. Politically, you had no rights except the ones dictated by the monarch, which could change depending on the circumstances.

John Locke (1632–1704) was one of the most influential classical liberals. He argued that all individuals were rational and born with inalienable natural rights that include perfect equality and liberty. Locke wrote in his *Second Treatise of Government* in 1689—at the time of England's Glorious Revolution—"Being all equal and independent, no one ought to harm another in his life, health, liberty, or possessions." A state should not take these rights away, and society should be as free as possible from government interference.

John Locke's view of the government and the people provided one of the most influential social contract theories. A **social contract theory** explains why and whether members of society need to comply with the fundamental social rules, laws, and institutions of the society (more on this later in this chapter). John Locke is also widely considered the father of liberal democracy. Since individuals could live reasonably well with their rationality and inherent rights even in the absence of authority, Locke defended the creation of limited constitutional government based on popular consent. His contributions to classical republicanism and liberal theory influenced the U.S. Declaration of Independence.

Another contributor to classical liberalism was the economist Adam Smith (1723–1790). Smith maintained that the free market is the path to prosperity and that government interference hinders economic growth. Smith and others argued that the market could self-regulate and self-correct when a problem arises, and thus no intervention by the government is necessary. On the contrary, governmental attempts to solve economic problems would only make things worse.

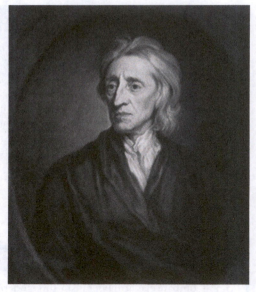

John Locke

Image by Godfrey Kneller, courtesy of the Hermitage Museum, in the public domain. https://commons.wikimedia.org/wiki/File:Godfrey_Kneller_-_Portrait_of_John_Locke_(Hermitage).jpg

John Stuart Mill (1806–1873) continued the evolution of liberalism when he argued in his book, *On Liberty* (1859), that governments can only exercise power to prevent harm to others. In addition, the economic and political rules of the society should allow individuals to make full use of their talents and not limit their ability to enrich themselves. If states allow individuals full expression, then the society as a whole could progress.

In sum, classical liberalism emphasizes individual liberty, individual rights, and private property, and calls for minimal intervention by the government in the affairs of private agents.

Modern U.S. liberalism

By the beginning of the twentieth century, it was clear that the free market was not as self-regulating as classical liberals once believed. Economic depressions were hurting the working class and poor people disproportionately. The Great Depression of 1929 marked the worst economic decline in the history of the industrialized world. It was during this time in the United States that the liberal ideology began to change. American liberals started to consider that the government should protect poor and working-class people and play an active role in removing social barriers that limited opportunities.

Classical liberalism assumed that if you remove a monarchy, you would achieve a free society where all individuals have the same opportunities. However, many modern liberals saw that this was not truly the case. For example, in the United States, African Americans did not have the same opportunities as white people even after the abolition of slavery. Women and men did not share the same rights. Individuals born in poverty did not have access to the same educational opportunities as the wealthy. Poverty also limited individuals' health conditions, which would harm their chances to succeed. Therefore, it seemed that governments needed to do more to realize the liberal ideals.

The Great Depression dragged on during the 1930s. U.S. President Franklin D. Roosevelt took office in 1933, amid the darkest moment of the historic depression. Banks were failing across the country and a quarter of Americans were unemployed. The Roosevelt administration implemented a set of economic programs called the New Deal, intended to mitigate economic hardships and unemployment, provide greater opportunities, such as jobs and training, and restore economic growth. Some call the ideas and policies of Roosevelt's economic and social programs New Deal liberalism.

More generally, **modern U.S. liberalism** combines ideas of civil liberty and equality with support for social justice and equalization of opportunity through government intervention. To address social barriers, modern U.S. liberals contend that more government involvement in citizens' lives is necessary. They advocate laws that remove and punish discriminatory norms and behaviors, thereby heavily regulating human interaction. They also promote programs to improve material well-being of all citizens. Such programs include unemployment benefits, public compensation for work-related injuries, retirement benefits, and many others. Ironically, classical liberals rejected government involvement in the economic lives of citizens while modern U.S. liberals brought it back in.

CONSERVATISM

LEARNING OBJECTIVE
3.4 Discuss conservatism and how it manifests in modern U.S. politics.

Conservatism seeks preservation of the current political and socioeconomic system or a return to a political and social system more in line with traditional values. Conservatives believe that humans are morally and intellectually imperfect, and human nature, if not controlled, can lead to social breakdown. As a result, one of the central tenets of conservatism is to control moral behavior and individual liberty. High moral standards would produce a more stable society by reducing self-indulgence and other behaviors, which they consider would lead toward instability. To achieve this, leaders should use state power to preserve traditions and control society with laws that would limit behavior deemed immoral. Ideal rulers should have wisdom and a strong moral background. They should use the wisdom carried by past generations, those who demonstrated the highest regards to societal traditions.

Edmund Burke's (1729–1797) work exemplifies classical conservatism. Burke was an Irish statesman and philosopher, who, after moving to England, served for many years in the House of Commons of Great Britain. In his book, *Reflections on the Revolution in France* (1790), Burke fiercely attacked the French Revolution for its level of violence, brutality, and destruction, warning the British against the dangers of revolutions. Burke instead defended the hereditary monarchy. He stated, "But what is liberty without wisdom, and without virtue? It is the greatest of all possible evils; for it is folly, vice, and madness, without tuition or restraint."

Burke accepted that monarchs make mistakes but argued that making mistakes still would not be justifiable grounds to remove the monarchy. Ultimately, Burke defended a **prescriptive constitutional government**, which is a government based on a constitution that is the "historical choice of successive generations, the successful inheritance of those who have gone before, and the embodiment of the wisdom of the species over time." Such government needs to be embraced and preserved since its continuation is the evidence that it has passed the "solid test of long experience." Drastic political changes are prone to grave and irreparable mistakes, according to Burke. Consequently, no radical change in the political system should occur.

Edmund Burke.

Image by James Barry, courtesy of the National Gallery of Ireland, in the public domain.https://commons.wikimedia.org/wiki/File:Portrait_of_Edmund_Burke_128.jpg

Consider contemporary examples of Communist revolutions that occurred around the world in the twentieth century. Communist revolutionary leaders vowed the creation of a society where people would be equal and treated with dignity. They promised that the state would guide the people in economic development, without exploitation, to achieve affluent societies. However, those countries ended up with tyrannical governments that often turned against their own people, and citizens suffered from repression, poverty, and shortages of even basic products. In the Soviet Union, Communist Party leader Joseph Stalin launched a massive campaign of political repression known as the Great Purge of 1937, which resulted in the removal of the members from the Communist Party. The Great Purge also saw the removal and imprisonment of government officials and members of the Red Army, repression of the peasantry, ethnic cleansing, widespread police surveillance, and arbitrary imprisonment and executions. Stalin had as many as 950,000 to 1.2 million people killed during this campaign from 1937 to 1938.

Modern U.S. Conservatism

Since what is traditional varies depending on the country and time, what conservatives believe in and promote will also vary. Classical liberal ideas had strong influence in the establishment of the United States and its earlier period. Thus, our previous discussion of classical liberalism forms a big part of what we call conservatism in the United States today. In the United States, conservatives believe that individuals should retain ample self-determination to achieve what they can, given their talents and ambitions. Not everyone will be successful, nor do conservatives believe that the political system should produce equal outcomes among individuals. U.S. conservatives believe that should the government attempt to produce equal outcomes, individuals will not be industrious and will attempt to rely on the work of others. If society bases rewards on individual work, it can grow and prosper.

Modern U.S. conservatives also believe that citizens should have a strong sense of national pride. They favor strong loyalty to national institutions and the ideals of the nation, which often translates into encouraging military might. Indeed, one of the primary roles of government is in protecting the country from outside threats. However, many conservatives differ on how to protect the country. The isolationist view seeks to reduce involvement in international affairs. This includes limiting national exposure to the international economy by favoring high tariffs on imports and other policies that reduce trade. They also do not favor labor migration into the country. The internationalist conservative view seeks out involvement in the international arena by engaging in trade and projecting military force. Internationalists believe that projecting the country's strength will allow it to spread its values and create norms that will favor its positions. Modern U.S. conservatives also emphasize traditional values in social aspects, especially religion. They support prayer in public schools and are opposed to same-sex marriage and abortion.

PRACTICAL APPLICATION
DOES TRUMPISM REPRESENT THE NEW CONSERVATISM IN THE UNITED STATES?

Like the label of liberalism, the meaning of conservatism has also changed over time. In the United States, we would not necessarily consider conservatives today individuals that we would have considered conservative in the 1950s. Trumpism incorporates the ideas, style of governance, and movements associated with former U.S. President Donald Trump and his political base. How closely do Trump's ideas represent modern U.S. conservatism?

SOCIAL CONTRACT AND THE STATE

LEARNING OBJECTIVE

3.5 Identify the various views of social contract.

Have you ever wondered how governments emerged and why we need to obey them? If you have, you are not the only one. In fact, the relationship between the government and the governed is an enduring question about which many pundits have pondered and sought an answer. Scholars developed some of these ideas into what we know as social contract theories.

A social contract theory purports to show why and whether members of society need to comply with the fundamental social rules, laws, and institutions of the society. The idea of the social contract is old—it goes back to ancient Greece. However, Thomas Hobbes popularized the modern form of the idea. John Locke, Jean-Jacques Rousseau, Edmund Burke, and others then developed it further in different ways. They each provided a unique view of the relationship between the government and the people.

As we mentioned earlier in this chapter, Thomas Hobbes was a political realist who viewed human nature as something horrible. Without constraints by a powerful authority, according to Hobbes, we would kill and steal from each other, thus barring ourselves from leading a productive and fulfilling life. We would instead live short, poor, and nasty lives. However, we would also cherish a long and commodious life if it were obtainable. Therefore, in order to escape the miserable and fearful life in the state of nature, we would sign up for a social contract to establish a powerful government. This government, which Hobbes called *Leviathan*, would enforce order and stability, with force if necessary. According to Hobbes, society comprises a population underneath a sovereign authority, and all individuals in that society cede some rights to the authority in exchange for protection.

The government that Hobbes envisioned was very powerful. You may be concerned that a very powerful government may abuse its power. We have seen so many dictators using their power against the people that they govern. In the Hobbesian view, people must accept abuse of power by the sovereign authority as the price of peace.

John Locke did not agree with Hobbes. Like other classical liberals, Locke believed in human rationality and individual rights. He believed that people in the state of nature live reasonably well, with their "inalienable rights to life, liberty and property." But without rules and without government, these rights are not secure. According to Locke, people accede to a social contract to create a government by conditionally transferring some of their rights to it so that they can safeguard the stable, comfortable enjoyment of their lives, liberty, and property. Since governments exist only with the consent of the people for the purpose of protecting the rights of the people and promoting the public good, citizens can resist and replace governments that fail to do so with new governments. John Locke's work had an enormous influence on the founding of the United States.

Conservative Edmund Burke had a different idea about social contract. For both realists and liberals, social contract is contemporaneous; that is, it is between the government and the people living at the same time. In contrast, Burke, who, as a conservative, cherished tradition and continuity, maintained that social contract is an intergenerational partnership. Burke wrote in his *Reflections on the Revolution in France*: "As the ends of such a partnership cannot be obtained in many generations, it becomes a partnership not only between those who are living but between those who are living, those who are dead, and those who are to be born."

SOCIALISM

LEARNING OBJECTIVE

3.6 Explain the different types of socialism.

Socialism is an ideology that seeks to change political systems that support a market-based economy to ones where opportunities and resources are more evenly distributed. At the heart of socialism is the desire to end perceived suffering of people due to human exploitation by other humans and to establish an egalitarian society where all people are equal and have access to commodities necessary to live a decent and fulfilling life. Socialism assumes that humans are caring by nature, but they do not always act in such a way because of the environment in which they live. If human exploitation happens, it is because of the systems that encourage such behavior. Hence, to end exploitative relationships and to create a more egalitarian society, the political structure would need to change in dramatic ways and the state would need to be more involved in economic matters.

In a socialist economic system, the state owns or controls either the entire economy or large sectors of it and manages the economic sectors in the name of the people. In doing so, the state seeks to remove profit from the price consumers pay, distribute wages more equally among workers, and guarantee the provision of social needs such as housing, health care, and education. Achieving such an outcome will require shifting property from private hands to public ownership. Socialists on the extreme end of the spectrum advocate the elimination of all private property. The state would control all property, services, and institutions, including manufacturing industries, service sectors, agriculture and farmlands, housing, education systems, and more. If the state does not own property, then groups of workers would own it collectively and manage it cooperatively. Another socialist view advocates for the state's control of major economic sectors while allowing small private holdings.

Given its desire to produce fundamental change, socialism is an ideology that can ignite strong reactions. The years of the Cold War produced a negative feeling among many Americans about socialism because they tended to equate it with the terrors and failures of the centrally planned economic system of the Soviet Union (see Chapter 10 for details). However, in various other parts of the world, socialism is an ideology that legitimately stands alongside liberalism and conservatism.

We have already hinted that there are many variations of socialism. There are socialists who accept only an extreme version, which advocates the violent overthrow of the current capitalist system and then ushers in a socialist system. On the other side of the spectrum, we have people that seek out change using peaceful democratic methods to achieve a socialist ideal. Therefore, it may be difficult to know what type of socialism they are referring to when people label themselves as socialists. We review the different variations of the socialist ideology in the following sections.

Communism

The extreme version of socialism comes under the label of communism, the principles of which Karl Marx and Friedrich Engels authored in the *Communist Manifesto* (1848). In fact, the label Marxism is synonymous with communism. Marx summarized all human development into five stages (see Figure 3.1). The progress through the stages occurs due to **historical materialism**. Historical materialism is a theory of human development that emphasizes the internal contradictions in the system of material production and economic relations as the engine for societal

FIGURE 3.1   ■   Marxist Stages of Development

Historical Development

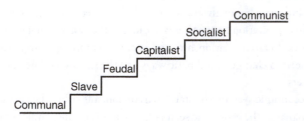

development. At each stage, there are two opposing classes: one that owns the means to produce things and the other that does not. Those that own the means of production are wealthy because they use their ownership of land, factories, or other resources to make profits, or what Marx referred to as **surplus value**. Those in the non-owning class can only meet their needs with the sale of their labor, which the owners of production exploit when they sell products and collect the surplus value. Each stage includes a struggle between the owners and non-owners. The end of their struggles leads to a new stage and the formation of a new struggle.

The cycles of class struggle began at a point in time when the level of technology was very low and the concept of property was at its infancy. This early stage of **communal society** is one where people participated in hunting and gathering activities. Generally, such activities consumed a great deal of time with little to show for some days. Even on the more successful days, people consumed all the products of their labor with little to no surplus. In addition, almost all group members needed to contribute in some form if they wished to consume.

With the introduction of horticulture and then agriculture, a class of people began forming in the **slave society** stage. Agriculture advanced human production of the vital needs of life. With the development of irrigation, seed planting, and animal domestication, individuals could now produce more than they needed for personal consumption. The producers could sell the additional production to others. This new mode of production, however, required a labor force that would tend the fields and animals. To maximize the wealth gained from production, landowners created institutionalized forced labor in the form of slavery and therefore ushered in slave societies. In these societies, slave holders supplied enslaved peoples with their minimal needs and therefore maximized their own wealth. In other words, surplus value was for the first time created and owned by the owner of the means of production—the landowners. At this stage, the means of production were the lands, equipment, and the enslaved people themselves.

The struggle between slave holders and the enslaved resulted in the creation of the next stage of economic development in the Marxist ideology: **feudalism**. This stage saw the rise of the nobility as the dominant class and serfs and peasants as the exploited class. The nobility owned the lands while peasants were required to work the lands and send their surplus output to the nobility. The system tied the peasants to the land by birth, meaning that they could not leave the property and were subject to the rules, laws, and traditions created and enforced by the local nobility. Within the feudal system, peasants obeyed the nobility because the nobility protected them from external threats, primarily members of the nearby nobility. Finally, the local religion gave the nobility the right to rule.

From this peasant class, a merchant class began forming. This merchant class would later become, in Marxist terminology, the bourgeoisie. This class was able to move from the land to the cities by buying out their position in the feudal system. Since the nobility was always in need of money, they sometimes welcomed peasants buying themselves off the land. In the cities, the new merchants bought and sold products they produced as well as lent out money. As time went on, the merchant class greatly improved their economic status. This new wealth allowed them to live like the nobility: They wore the same fashions, ate the same types of foods, and had their children educated by the same tutors. Because the bourgeoisie were now the major lenders, many of the nobility were dependent on them to finance their wars and noble lifestyles. The bourgeoisie saw that their economic power could be used for political advantage. They eventually removed the nobility's authority to rule, which they did either by revolution or other forms of rebellion. The triumph of the bourgeoisie over the nobility produced the next stage: capitalism.

In Marxism, **capitalism** is a stage in the historical progression of economic systems that follows feudalism. The capitalist stage has an industrialized economic system in which the owners of the means of production, called the **bourgeoisie** or capitalists, exploit the industrial workers to generate economic surplus value. Marx developed his ideas during the mid-1800s, in the era of industrialized capitalism in western Europe. He surmised that the cycles of class struggle that produced the slave societies, feudalism, and capitalism were continuing. The current owners of the means of production, the bourgeoisie, were simply carrying on the exploitative conditions that the slave holders and nobility had created before them. They just did it in a different way. Under capitalism, Marx referred to the exploited class of workers as the **proletariat**. These people were the economic class who could sell only their labor since they owned no property. They worked in severe conditions of the mines and factories in the market economy for a small wage with all the resulting surplus value going to the capitalists.

The Marxist ideology predicted that the time was right for another revolution and the introduction of a new stage of human development. Living in the nineteenth century, Marx saw around him the results of economic inequality. He lived, researched, and wrote in the major cities of Germany, France, and Britain. He also visited the major industrial centers where he saw people (including children) working under harsh conditions and living in poverty. For example, at the time there were no aid programs if a worker became unemployed or disabled as the result of a work injury. Being injured on the job meant economic destitution. In addition, workers could not demand better work conditions because doing so would lead to quick unemployment. Marx believed that workers would become conscious of their exploitation. They would see that they created the wealth for capitalists, without improvement in sight for their lives. Eventually, Marx predicted, the exploited workers would overthrow the capitalist system through a revolution and take over the means of production.

The next stage, socialism, would reduce the level of exploitation by eliminating private property and establishing the collective ownership of production. Since workers would be in sole control of economic output, all the surplus value would go to them alone. With the self-management of the means of protection, Marx saw that the lack of an exploited class would lead to the final stage of human development, **communism**. At this stage, workers' ownership and management of production would cause the state—considered the instrument of the ruling class—to become obsolete and disappear. This final stage of a classless and stateless society would end the exploitation of people, which was the goal that followers of communism hoped to achieve.

Democratic Socialism

Another version of socialism is **democratic socialism**. Democratic socialists abandon the idea that only a violent revolution can produce socialism. Instead, they advocate for change through elections and other democratic means. Through elections, democratic socialists seek to create laws and policies that will gradually reform their economies with the aim to create a more equitable society. Over the years, democratic socialists in power have effected the government takeover of major resources such as oil and coal. They have established inexpensive or free delivery of a wide range of social services, such as health care, elementary and higher education, and housing, to name a few. They have also sought to reduce income inequality by redistributing wealth through greater taxes on the wealthy, empowering workers to form labor unions that are able to negotiate higher wages, and the establishing minimum wages that produce a dignified standard of living. Recently, U.S. Senator Bernie Sanders ran presidential campaigns promising democratic socialist reforms.

FASCISM

LEARNING OBJECTIVE
3.7 Identify the key features of fascism.

The Italian dictator Benito Mussolini (1883–1945) developed the fascist ideology during the early twentieth century. However, most people are more familiar with how Adolf Hitler's Nazi Party of Germany used the fascist ideology. **Fascism** is a radical right-wing ideology that promotes extreme nationalism, seeks to blame outsiders for a country's problems, and emphasizes the supremacy of the state.

Extreme nationalism is the first recognizable principle of fascism. **Nationalism** is an elevated sense of national consciousness that emphasizes the unity of a nation and promotes its interests and culture to the detriment of other nations. This is different from **patriotism**, which is the devotion to one's country. Extreme nationalism characterizes one's nation as being so superior that its interests outweigh all other nations' interests. This belief leads fascists to think that there would be no reason to compromise with others given others' inferiority. For example, fascism legitimizes forceful foreign actions such as the taking of territory.

The Nazi concept of *Lebensraum* captures the principle of extreme nationalism. The ideology's followers believed in the superiority of the German nation above all others, especially relative to the nations of eastern Europe. *Lebensraum*, which means "living space" in German, meant that land to the east of Germany, as far as Russia, and to the north (Norway and Sweden) were lands into which the German people needed to expand. The Nazis believed that their superiority gave them the right to conquer the land and remove the existing populations. During World War II, the expansion into these lands were followed by the establishment of concentration camps for the "extermination" of people who were deemed inferior. The long-term plan was to move Germanic peoples into the land newly vacated through genocide.

Scapegoating, or blaming "outsiders" for one's problems, is another key feature of fascist belief. Scapegoating is a way for fascists to explain and solve situations that are not going well. After all, if extreme nationalism states that they are so superior, why would they have problems? According to fascists, it was due to foreign elements that were occupying the country and attempting to put down the nation with the help of traitors. As you can tell, the idea of scapegoating is very connected to extreme nationalism. Fascists believe that if they removed foreigners and their influence, they could achieve the benefits of their superiority. Their perceived superiority gives them the right to deal with the scapegoats as targets for their violence.

You likely know that the main scapegoating target for the Nazis was the Jews. They believed that Jews were foreigners and not true Germans. Nazis argued that Jews practiced a non-Christian religion, with the more orthodox practitioners of Judaism dressing differently and speaking in a different language. Nazis viewed Jews as the cause of all of Germany's problems, even though Jews were patriotic Germans who lived in the country for many generations and fought bravely in wars as German military officers and enlisted personnel. The solution, using the Nazi elites' words, was the final solution. The final solution was the specific plan to remove all Jews from their homes, steal their property, and then systematically murder them in gas chambers or through forced labor. The Nazis believed that once the Jews were gone, the German people would not have any further problems.

While Jews were the main target of Nazi scapegoating, they were not the only victims. Nazis believed that anyone who did not follow their norms and beliefs or did not pass their racial purity tests were subject to arrest, detention in concentration camps, and eventual death. This included men, women, and children whom Nazis considered dangerous because of their political or religious beliefs, sexual orientations, or national origin. The massive death camps, therefore, also housed such groups like the Jehovah's Witnesses, Romani, gay people, and eastern Europeans such as Poles and Russians. The Nazi deaths during the Holocaust—the systematic murder of the European Jews by the Nazis—numbered approximately six million. The other groups combined amounted to about another 10 million murders.

Last, fascists believe that citizens need to hold the nation in sacred regard. They often promote a mythic past detailing historic sacrifices by heroes in producing the greatness of the nation. For them, there was a glorious past when the nation was great and respected by all. However, they argue that certain events reduced this greatness. Since the nation is pure and just and only "outsiders" can cause problems, the people need a strong state to return to the nation's original greatness. In sum, they believe the only protector of the nation is the state. For the state to achieve its goals, each citizen has a duty to pledge absolute obedience to the country's leaders and accept total rule by completely surrendering daily life to the needs of the state. In addition, government leaders do not tolerate group conflict within the society. All groups and organizations are agents of the state and must be loyal to the fascist ideology. The state does not permit dissenting thoughts.

The Nazis instituted their ideology during their reign between 1932 and 1945. Their supreme leader, Adolf Hitler, embodied the state. Every member of the Nazi Party had to pledge absolute loyalty to him. The Nazis also expected the same loyalty from all citizens. All social organizations, no matter how small or harmless, needed to include a pledge of loyalty to the Nazi cause and serve the interests of the state. Labor unions, for example, were agents of the state and needed to assist the state in its economic policies. To keep critics of the state under control, the Nazis created secret security agencies that had the power to quickly arrest and deport accused dissenters to concentration camps, where they met the same fate as Jews, eastern Europeans, and other "undesirables."

PRACTICAL APPLICATION
REVISITING FASCISM

Fascism is a radical right-wing ideology that promotes extreme nationalism, seeks to blame outsiders for a country's problems, and emphasizes the supremacy of the state. Conduct research to learn about the resurgence of fascism in Europe, also known as neofascism and neonazism. What actions or slogans do these new fascist groups have in common with the first fascists? Do they follow the same fascist principles?

RELIGIOUS FUNDAMENTALISM

LEARNING OBJECTIVE

3.8 Explore how religious doctrine can be used as a political ideology.

We can consider religion an ideology when people exercise its tenets for political gain. **Religious fundamentalism** refers to the unwavering belief that an individual or a group of individuals has in the infallible and absolute authority of a sacred religious text or teachings of a particular religious leader or deity. Religious fundamentalists believe that only one view of the world can be true, and their view is the only correct one. Because of this belief, religious fundamentalists seek to force their view on others and attempt to eliminate competing religious beliefs and ideas. Religious leaders use the fundamental doctrines of a religion to exercise theocratic power by emphasizing their exclusive interpretation of sacred texts. As the holders of orthodoxy of the faith, their view of how society should be organized and how individual behavior should be regulated cannot be questioned. Therefore, the average person cannot enter into most debates regarding matters that will influence their lives because they lack the legitimate authority to interpret religious principles.

Religion's role in politics is not a new phenomenon. Earlier in this chapter, we discussed how liberalism ran counter to the idea of an established monarchy. Monarchs, in their various forms, based their legitimacy to rule on the concept of **divine right**. This means that they ruled on behalf of a deity or multiple deities. They, and their heirs, received the right to rule thanks to a victory in some sort of violent struggle that religious leaders claim was a sign from their deity (or deities) that bestowed legitimacy. The concept of divine right was so central to the legitimacy of monarchs that they would fight individuals that tried to produce an alternative interpretation of the religion. Examples include the splits in Christianity (Catholics, Protestants, and Eastern Orthodox) and Islam (Sunni and Shia). In each case, monarchs persecuted those who proposed alternative views because they put the monarch's right to rule in question.

The advent of liberal democracy attempted to put religious affairs outside government since freedom of worship and prohibiting official state religions are central liberal tenets. However, this did not end the influence of religion both in and out of such democracies. It is therefore not surprising that many religious fundamentalists still wish to either rid their country of other religious doctrines or make them insignificant. Today, people often equate religious fundamentalism with Islam. When people think about religious fundamentalism and theocratic states, the Islamic Republic of Iran comes to mind. Iran is a theocratic state with the ultimate authority vested in the religious "Supreme Leader," a position held by Ali Khamenei since the death of the first supreme leader, Ruhollah Khomeini, in 1989. The terrorist attacks on the United States on September 11, 2001, by al-Qaeda, a militant Islamist terrorist organization, imprinted a lasting and incorrect impression in some people's minds that all Islamic groups are religious fundamentalists and religious fundamentalists are Islamic. However, many countries throughout the world have experienced or are currently experiencing the use of religion as an ideology. This includes, but is not limited to, Christianity, Hinduism, and Buddhism.

As an example, consider Buddhism. Buddhism, at least among some westerners, is often associated with nonviolent doctrines. Yet, even in the twenty-first century, we see examples of organized violence towards non-Buddhists by members of this religion. Multiple acts of anti-Muslim violence by Buddhists in Myanmar (also known as Burma) broke out in 2013. Much of the violence resulted from individual-level conflicts that broadened to community violence. Mobs attacked the Mingalar Zayone Islamic Boarding School, killing 32 teenage students and four teachers. Outside the largest city, Rangoon, hundreds of militant Buddhists destroyed mosques, homes, and shops. The religious conflicts seen in Myanmar are similar to those in Sri Lanka and Thailand.

EXPAND YOUR THOUGHTS
WHEN IS A RELIGION A POLITICAL IDEOLOGY?

Religion, by itself, is not necessarily a political ideology, although many believe it to be one. What behaviors do we need to observe from religious leaders and spokespeople before we can treat religions as a political ideology? Why would these observations tie directly into politics?

ENVIRONMENTALISM

LEARNING OBJECTIVE

3.9 Describe environmentalism and its relation to sustainable development and social equity.

Environmentalism centers on concerns of ecological well-being, specifically the improvement and preservation of the natural environment by advocating for cleaner air, water, and soil. The ideology traces its origins to the back-to-nature and conservation movements of the late nineteenth and early twentieth centuries in the United States and Europe. In the United States, President Theodore Roosevelt (1858–1919) was a big advocate of the conservation movement. He established the U.S. Forest Service and created five National Parks. These days, the reach of the environmentalist ideology has expanded globally to include less developed countries.

The increases in pollution due to heavy industrialization have produced poor quality-of-life conditions in all the major cities around the world. The early ecology movement of the 1960s and 1970s brought to popular attention the effects of various types of pollution on human health. Rachel Carson (1907–1964), in her book, *Silent Spring*, was among the early pioneers. She brought to the world's attention the harmful effect that pesticides had on human health. Other adverse outcomes included severe air pollution, which produced acid rain that was responsible for killing off forests and damaging property. The polluted air also contributed to the rise in respiratory diseases. Polluted water in various rivers and streams produced undrinkable water and killed fish and other aquatic life. In the United States, the pollution levels of the Cuyahoga River in Ohio reached such a frightening level that it would literally catch on fire!

The clearly visible dangers of pollution were not the only concerns of environmentalists. They also expressed their apprehension that nuclear energy accidents could produce devastating outcomes. More recently, many have drawn attention to the effect of greenhouse gases on the global climate. International cooperation is required to reduce the levels of these gases.

The problems just listed, as well as many others, influence the local, national, and global arenas and have been a call to action by environmentalists. The arguments aimed at promoting regulations that would limit, if not eliminate, declining environmental conditions are often opposed by those who believe that new rules will have a negative impact on economic productivity. For every new regulation, opponents argue that the cost of doing business will increase. The added regulatory costs will raise prices and could force some businesses that cannot adapt to close down, leading to job losses. Environmental advocates counter that an absolute focus on the economic concerns in the short term means that people would eventually pay higher costs in the long term, such as health-related costs and quality-of-life issues due to environmental degradation.

The struggle between improving the environment and economic concerns introduced important ideological principles. One such principle is **sustainable development**. Policies that advance sustainable development encourage economic development without compromising the environmental conditions for future generations. Sustainable development, therefore, requires a balance between economic and environmental progress. For example, one major way governments around the world help promote economic gains is to offer tax breaks and other subsidies. Environmentalists argue that it would be more sustainable to subsidize renewable energy sources (e.g., solar and wind) instead of subsidizing polluting activities, like mining and burning fossil fuels (e.g., coal, petroleum, and natural gas). By doing so, economic policy would still encourage economic activities while not harming future generations' quality-of-life standards.

Sustainable development also introduces other dimensions of environmentalism. One is the development of environmentalist political parties, commonly referred to as "green" parties. Leaders of various green political parties began the development of the environmentalist ideology in the 1960s and 1970s. Green parties are single-issue parties because their objective is not to change all laws and policies but only those that influence a single issue, namely, the environment. Their sole aim has been to introduce and promote standards that would clean up the environment.

In addition to its effects in the economic and political realms, the principle of sustainable development has influenced the social realm by advancing the idea of **social equity**. Social equity refers to developing conditions of equal opportunity and fairness to all members of a society. Environmentalists point out that the economically disadvantaged often live in more polluted areas of a country due to the community's political inability to fight against businesses that produce environmental problems. Producing change would require knowledge, time, and money that economically poor communities do not have. Moreover, since these communities need more economic activity, many residents resist environmental changes because they fear that they will lead to fewer jobs. In addressing the problems of the environment, environmentalists argue that societies should also address problems surrounding poverty.

Another aspect of environmentalism is the international component. Environmentalists claim that creating change at the national level is not enough; rather, there is a need for international cooperation. Therefore, environmentalism includes principles associated with foreign policy, or the types of relationships states have with each other. If environmentalists were successful at the national level, would this mean that the global environment would no longer be a problem? Unfortunately, uneven economic development around the world poses a significant barrier to efforts at solving global environmental problems. Like poor areas of a country, poor areas of the world have economic incentives to exploit their natural resources and participate in other economic activities that generate income but also could harm their environments. Their desire to "catch up" economically puts them in a similar situation that wealthier countries faced one hundred or so years ago.

In addition, the level of environmental degradation in poorer countries has worsened due to social dumping. Social dumping occurs when a business transfers economic activity that is no longer allowed in the home country, because of advanced environmental regulations, to another country that lacks those regulations. For example, if one country forbids a type of manufacturing that produces high levels of greenhouse gases, that business could take its manufacturing operations to another country that does not regulate the emission of greenhouse gases. Overall, the amount of greenhouse gas produced stays the same, or it could even be worse. Therefore, even if one country puts a limit on greenhouse gas emissions, as long as businesses can move their operations to places with lax environmental regulations, the problem will continue.

The result is that environmentalists not only demand international cooperation in the area of environmental policy; they also seek to influence international economic cooperation. International cooperation on environmental policy would include negotiating and enforcing treaties on topics like reducing carbon emissions and deforestation. The **Paris Agreement on Climate Change**, adopted by 196 countries in December 2015, is an example of an international environmental treaty. This agreement established the intentions of the signatory states to reduce their greenhouse gas emissions.

The environmental issues are also part of international economic cooperation, such as free trade agreements, which attempt to limit or prevent social dumping. In the early 1990s, Canada, Mexico, and the United States negotiated the North American Free Trade Agreement (NAFTA). During U.S. ratification of NAFTA, environmentalists raised the concern of social dumping by Canadian and U.S. firms. They protested the ability of firms to move manufacturing from Canada and the United States to Mexico to take advantage of Mexico's lower environmental standards. They pressured the U.S. Congress not to ratify the treaty unless there were provisions to mitigate the environmental harm produced by Canadian and U.S. companies participating in such practice. Environmentalists were successful in getting the three NAFTA partners to negotiate and ratify a side agreement that sought to address their concerns.

EXPAND YOUR THOUGHTS
SHOULD LONG-TERM INTERESTS OUTWEIGH SHORT-TERM INTERESTS?

Much of the environmentalist ideology focuses on the long-term consequences of the activities that people do in the short term. However, for many, short-term activities and outcomes are very important as well. Consider, for example, the arguments by political and economic leaders of poor countries. Current rich countries have engaged in economic production that has generated environmental degradation. Many people in developing and impoverished countries think it is unfair that current wealthy countries are asking poor countries to sacrifice their economic growth for the sake of environmental protection. They contend that they also want to grow, and grow as fast as they can. How would an environmentalist justify sacrificing short-term economic gains for long-term environmental protection? Is there a way to obtain short-term economic gains without harming the environment in the long term?

FEMINISM

LEARNING OBJECTIVE

3.10 Identify the three major forms of feminism.

Feminism, like many of the ideologies we have discussed, has many branches that have developed over time to include many different meanings, approaches, and focal points. We will first identify the feminist foundations and then discuss the three major forms of feminist thought: the liberal, Marxist, and radical branches.

The feminist ideology is a **critical theory**. A critical theory begins by discussing the problems in society and the need for change. All branches of **feminism** recognize that society discriminates against women based on their gender by denying or limiting opportunities for their well-being in the social, political, and economic arenas. Discrimination against women relegates them to a subservient role to men, making women's ideas and actions invalid or less valid than men's ideas and actions.

The manifestation of the subservient role traditionally placed women in the private sphere (the home) and not the public sphere (the workplace). Not being in the public sphere relegated women to tasks associated with reproduction: childbearing, childcare, and household duties. Even when women ventured out into the public sphere, their roles were very limited. It is significant to point out that the limited roles did not come out of women's choices but due to societal norms and traditions codified in laws determined by men. The outcome was that the contributions of approximately half the population (women) were dictated by the wishes of the other half (men). The lack of choice and inability to take advantage of their talents and capabilities held back women's progress and societal development.

Although discrimination against women and gender inequality were more acute in the past, the problems persist today in varying degrees around the world. Feminists argue that solving the problem of gender inequality requires a massive change in thinking about the role of women. The first actions toward gender equality began in the United States with the Seneca Falls Convention of 1848 and the *English Woman's Journal* established by members of the Langham Place Group in Britain during the 1850s. The Seneca Falls Convention gathered women to draft a declaration outlining a list of grievances that required resolution. The most controversial item was to give women the right to vote. The Langham Place Group was an organization of women in London that launched the *English Woman's Journal*, dedicated to address equality for women, especially in the workplace.

The different branches of feminism vary in how they address the issues of discrimination and inequality. They often take on one or more intersectional identities of women. This means that while women share the same gender identity, they differ in many other ways, including economic class, race, ethnicity, religion, national identity, and sexual orientation. Therefore, to address the problems of inequality faced by women, various branches of feminism advocate the need to examine other identities as well. One branch is **liberal feminism**, also known as mainstream feminism, which is the oldest of the three we will examine. Liberal feminism traces its roots to Mary Wollstonecraft (1759–1797). In her book, *Vindication of the Rights of Woman* (1792/2014), she argued that women possessed the same intellectual abilities as men but were unable to express their talents because they lacked access to education. She stated that the classical liberal ideals of individual freedoms needed to include women as well as men. She proclaimed that women are humans and thus should possess all the social, political, and economic rights that Locke and others stated are "inalienable." Put simply, all the rights associated with life, liberty, and property apply to women as well as men. Liberal feminism, therefore, advocates for a guarantee of these rights using the democratic processes to reform the legal structure that was stripping women of their rights as persons.

Another important branch of feminism examines the oppression of women through a Marxist approach. **Marxist feminism** argues that gender inequality is part of the larger set of inequalities found in the capitalist system. The exploitation of workers, which we discussed earlier in the chapter, extends to the exploitation of women in the workforce and in the home. Recall that under feudalism, peasants worked the land for members of the nobility. The family unit at this stage worked together with each member's role in production determined by their gender. Although women and men worked the land together, women would sometimes need to shift their role to rearing children and other associated household duties.

Capitalism further segmented labor by gender. Under capitalism, the role of income and the rise of private property devalued, in monetary terms, the labor of women. Labor shifted from earning a living from the land under feudalism, to working in the factory under capitalism. The value of labor, as a result, shifted from compensation based on agricultural outputs to a wage based on hours worked. However, women were remaining at home because the factory work would not allow women to carry out family duties as they did while working the land. The result was that women's labor was now uncompensated. In the final analysis, the surplus value (profits) produced by capitalists depended directly on the exploitation of workers, who were mainly men, and indirectly on the exploitation of women as uncompensated homemakers.

According to Marxist feminists, the only way to remove inequality between women and men is to remove the exploitative structure of capitalism, either through revolution or through radical reform. The next stage of socialism would see women liberated from gendered economic roles and participating as equals in production. Their new economic roles would give them true equality in the political and social arenas.

Feminism took another turn in the 1960s with the advent of **radical feminism**. As the name indicates, radical feminists take a more critical look at the role of women in society. This branch argues that the **patriarchy**—a social system in which men hold power and privilege and predominate in government, moral authority, economic roles, and social functions—is the fundamental organization of society. The social system is characterized by the intentional domination and oppression of women by men through societal norms and traditions. The deeper criticism involves not only the lack of full rights that prevents equality but also the structural and physical violence that keeps women in a state of oppression.

To end the patriarchy, radical feminism argues that societal norms regarding differences between women and men would need to change. Changing laws (as advocated by liberal feminists) or economic structures (as advocated by Marxist feminists) will not be enough if societies maintain the same practices that uphold the patriarchal system. Such changes include the elimination of the different gender roles when assessing the person's value and capabilities. To this end, women need to have full control of their reproductive choices and a voice in workplace matters.

SUMMARY

Ideologies are systematic beliefs that people use to make sense of their political environments. They answer basic questions regarding legitimacy of governance. These beliefs explain current situations and offer remedies to solve problems. Ideologies perform these functions because they envision the way the political world ought to look like. Liberalism (both classical and modern U.S. liberalism), conservatism, socialism, fascism, religious fundamentalism, environmentalism, and feminism all envision the creation of an ideal world although what the ideal world should be varies significantly depending on a particular ideology. This idealism contrasts with the realist views that all politics is a simple quest for personal or group power.

Ideologies vary greatly in their worldviews. We see a wide scope of differences not only among different ideologies but also within them. We also see that ideologies change over time. We should note that ideologues usually do not need empirical evidence to support their beliefs. What evidence they do present is usually selective. Therefore, an ideology is more about what one believes is true rather than facts guiding us to the truth. The next set of chapters explores the origins and impact of societal and individual beliefs in more detail.

KEY TERMS

Bourgeoisie (p. 49)

Capitalism (p. 49)

Classical liberalism (p. 41)

Communal society (p. 48)

Communism (p. 50)

Conservatism (p. 43)

Critical theory (p. 57)

Democratic socialism (p. 50)

Divine right (p. 53)

Environmentalism (p. 54)

Fascism (p. 50)

Feminism (p. 57)

Feudalism (p. 48)

Final solution (p. 51)

Historical materialism (p. 47)

Holocaust (p. 51)

Ideology (p. 38)

Liberal feminism (p. 58)

Liberalism (p. 41)

Marxist feminism (p. 58)

Modern U.S. liberalism (p. 43)

Nationalism (p. 50)

Paris Agreement on Climate Change (p. 56)

Patriarchy (p. 58)

Patriotism (p. 50)

Political realism (p. 39)

Prescriptive constitutional government (p. 44)

Proletariat (p. 49)

Radical feminism (p. 58)

Realpolitik (p. 40)

Religious fundamentalism (p. 52)

Scapegoating (p. 51)

Slave society (p. 48)

Social contract theory (p. 41)

Social equity (p. 55)

Socialism (p. 47)

State of nature (p. 40)

Surplus value (p. 48)

Sustainable development (p. 55)

FURTHER READING

Delmar, R. (2018). What is feminism? In A. C. Herrmann & A. J. Stewart (Eds.), *Theorizing feminism: Parallel trends in the humanities and social sciences*. Routledge.

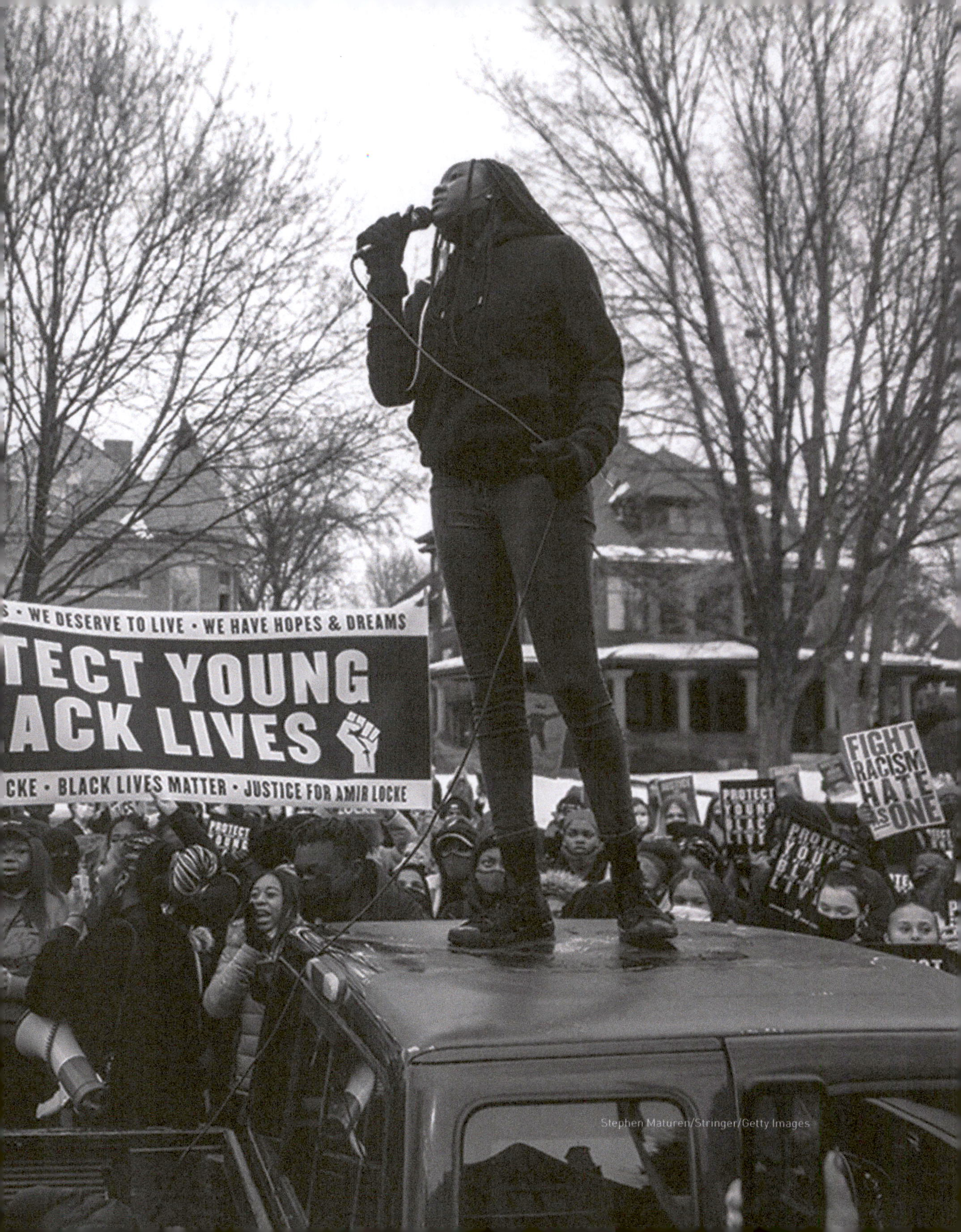

Stephen Maturen/Stringer/Getty Images

4 THE CULTURAL DIMENSION OF POLITICS

Researchers find it interesting to explain how a society's culture influences political opinions. Since the foundation of a democracy is the will of the people, understanding how voters reach their decisions is important. Even in dictatorships, it is important to know why some people legitimize a regime that gives them little to no freedoms. The study of a country's culture also provides important insights like tolerance for violent protests, attitudes toward immigrants, and opinions regarding the environment. This chapter will introduce some societal norms and values that current research indicates have an influence on politics. We will also examine one interesting finding, namely, that political culture is not constant. Although it may not change rapidly (in other words, within a single generation), political culture can change from one generation to another due to various factors. Such factors produce a new generation of values that influence where people stand on political issues.

POLITICAL CULTURE

Political culture can be an important tool in analyzing public opinion because we dig into people's belief systems. A **belief system** is the collection of views people hold regarding what they believe the political world to be and what it should be like. Some individuals' belief systems are very close to ideologies, many of which we presented in the previous chapter. However, many have personalized their beliefs, and therefore their belief systems may not clearly fit into any particular ideology. In fact, many people hold beliefs that are a mixture of a few ideological principles. Sometimes individual beliefs may seem inconsistent in that different parts of their beliefs contradict other parts. Investigating the impact of a political culture on politics requires an analysis of individuals while acknowledging that the interaction of individuals collectively makes up a country's culture.

Political culture comprises a society's shared norms and values that are relevant to the analysis of politics. **Norms** are what a society views as acceptable behavior. In societies with many different ethnicities, races, and religions, there can be more than one accepted way to behave. A quick example of a norm is how people greet one another. In some cultures, it is the norm to shake hands. In another, people bow to each other. In yet other societies, kissing each other on the cheek is the norm. As you may imagine, not getting the correct greeting is a violation of the culture's norms and would make people uncomfortable or even angry. Although this example may not reflect a political issue (unless of course you are a foreign diplomat), we can intuitively see that norm violations that affect politics can be a very large problem.

An example of a norm that can influence a country's politics is a mode of protest. A mode of protest refers to how people conduct themselves during an act of protest and the type of action. You may be familiar with people standing in front of an important political building with signs and shouting slogans related to the injustice they feel needs correcting. Other forms of protest can be a large march across a city or town. In the 1960s, during the Civil Rights movement in the United States, African Americans would sit at lunch counters reserved for whites to protest segregation in the American South. In some cases, protestors intentionally wanted police to arrest them so that they could continue the protest in the judicial system with the goal of getting the change they sought.

In some societies, protests that disrupt people's lives are not welcome because they violate cultural norms. Disruptive protest can actually reduce the chances that the government will address protesters' grievances because public opinion will turn against the protesters. Disruptions could include adding difficulty to a person's daily routine and/or the destruction of public or private property. In other countries, such disruptive protests invoke sympathy among the public because citizens believe protestors' actions are justified. This can cause public opinion to swing in favor of the protesters' grievances, depending on the level of disruption.

France, for example, has had a long history of disruptive protests. In 2018, it experienced a widespread protest against proposed increases in fuel taxes. The *Gilets Jaunes* (Yellow Vests) movement staged acts of civil disobedience, many of them violent and destructive. Although this generated severe problems for the French, many citizens became sympathetic, causing the French government to end the new taxes. In the eyes of French citizens, conducting protests that disrupt daily life is acceptable behavior. They see people voicing complaints that make life uncomfortable as a norm for demanding change. This is perhaps not surprising given France's history of revolutionary movements.

In Britain, the opposite is true. Long-distance transport drivers staged a protest in 2000 over increases in fuel taxes. Their protests involved blocking oil refinery deliveries and blocking traffic on two of the main British freeways. Public opinion quickly turned against the protesters when gasoline shortages began to have a ripple effect across the country. In this example, the average British citizen did not feel that these protests, which disrupted daily life, were acceptable

Gilets Jaunes protestors block a French motorway.
NICOLAS TUCAT/AFP via Getty Images

behavior. The low level of public support gave the British government the ability to take a hard stance against the transportation drivers. The government did not give into the protestors' demands and arrested those who impeded normal daily activities. The show of the government's resolve ended the protests without a decrease in the fuel taxes. Again, this may not be surprising given Britain's long history of government success in battling protests and rebellions. The only revolution they experienced occurred in 1688, the Glorious Revolution, which restored the protestant monarchy. This is an illustration of the conservatism found in British politics.

Values are items that people hold in high regard. If you think about all the goals an individual hopes to achieve, certain goals have higher priorities than others do. For example, you may value being with friends. Your friendships can improve your quality of life and are important to your mental health. However, you may value doing well in your college courses more than socializing with friends. Doing well in college, for many, is a means of social mobility and achieving career-centered aspirations. Therefore, doing well in your courses has significant value. Doing well, however, requires studying for exams and performing well on assignments. You may therefore prioritize doing well in your college courses over participating in a social gathering with friends given your time limitations. On the other hand, you would do the opposite if you value friendship more than doing well in your courses.

Political values are the values that exert an impact on political behavior. Just like studying for an exam and spending time with friends, political decisions have their trade-offs. If you value a very strong military, then you are likely in favor of greater governmental spending on the military and consequently may accept less funding for other social needs, such as health care. This comes from an understanding that budgetary trade-offs are necessary due to the limit on the amount of money that a government can spend. The differences in the priorities in the government's spending can cause tension between voters who believe that their society should place a higher value on the military and others who believe that health care should have the higher priority. If a sufficient number of people in a society value a very strong military over health care, the country may have the latest fighter jets, naval vessels, and other armaments, but not an accessible health care system.

Another example would be the debates on capital punishment, also known as the death penalty. Although most people value human life, societies sometimes divide themselves over the authority of the judicial system to punish some criminals by executing them. Even those who value human life see the need for the death penalty. Those who favor the death penalty may hold other values, such as a particular view of justice and the value of deterring crimes by having strong punishment. Others argue that the death penalty arguments are not strong enough to justify executing a person and may instead value life in prison as a suitable punishment. As the two examples show, political values, particularly when governments put them into action, can have a very real impact.

SOCIALIZATION: HOW PEOPLE LEARN THEIR VALUES AND NORMS

LEARNING OBJECTIVE

4.2 Describe the process of political socialization, including the transfer of values and norms between generations.

How do people acquire their values and learn social norms? Since people are not born with them, one generation has to transmit its political culture to the next through a process called **political socialization**. Simply put, political socialization is the process of teaching and learning the society's norms and values. Socialization agents are the people who teach the society's values and norms. Agents come in two forms: primary agents and secondary agents. **Primary agents of political socialization** are those who have the most influence. They include family members and members of someone's educational system, such as school teachers. Friends, fellow members of a religion or other social group, and people associated with the media would all be considered **secondary agents of political socialization**. They are less important than the primary agents but nonetheless make a significant impact.

Political socialization is the first step in understanding the impact political culture has in explaining personal choices (see Figure 4.1). After acquiring political norms and values through socialization, individuals will acquire attitudes toward political actors and institutions. People then make choices based on these attitudes. We will first detail the process of political socialization by explaining the role of agents and then discuss various types of attitudes.

FIGURE 4.1 ■ From Cultural Transmission to Individual Choices

Political Socialization → Norms and Values → Attitudes → Choices

Agents of Socialization

Political socialization is a complex process that requires us to consider two important components. First, we classify some agents as primary or secondary based on average experiences. It is possible that agents who we just classified as secondary are actually more important for some people than the ones commonly considered the primary agents. For example, for some, friends may have a more important role in teaching political values and norms than family members. Recall in Chapter 2 we discussed that no political science theory or approach will explain 100 percent of the cases examined. When we identify the primary agents, we are including those who have the most influence on the average person.

Second, agents can teach culture in direct or indirect ways. The direct transfer of values and norms occurs when both the agent and recipient are aware that a lesson is underway. That is, everyone involved knows that a political lesson is being taught, like when students study in school how their government works. Students might learn about the value of democracy, for example, or the norms associated with a secret ballot. An indirect transfer occurs when a person witnesses an agent's actions and learns a conscious or unconscious lesson from that experience. In such cases, people see the political actions around them and believe that such actions are normal and valued.

Primary Agents of Socialization

Members of our family and educational systems make the largest impact on our belief systems because of the vast amount of time we interact with them when we are young. Childhood is a period of great learning and mental development. As previously stated, we are not born with specific values and norms and therefore are susceptible to acquiring new knowledge. Those whom we spend the most time with during our youth will make the largest impact on our personal political development. For the average person, family and members of the educational system fit this category. School teachers are usually the ones that directly teach us about our society's political values and norms through history, government, and civics courses. They also influence our behavior through day-to-day lessons regarding civility.

In a democracy, for example, educators teach students the value of political participation. They emphasize not only the value of voting in a practical sense but also the sacrifices prior generations made to secure the vote. The idea is if everyone before you fought for the vote, then the vote must be valuable. In addition, teachers may place an emphasis on how some classes of people (such as people of color and women) could not vote, but they fought for this right because they valued the right to vote.

In a nondemocracy, educators may teach the value of obeying the governmental authorities. The emphasis here is not to criticize the government or the political system. They may point out that before the current political system was in place, there was instability, which produced violence and poor living conditions. They teach that historical leaders established the current government to make life better for the people. Teachers will include lessons on how life is better for the country's citizens today. They may then conclude that criticizing the government will lead to a return to instability and the "bad old days."

Political socialization by family members is more complex because we often learn indirectly from them. It is possible for parents and guardians to provide direct lessons to children. This tends to happen when children ask questions or if family members are politically active and feel the need to teach lessons regarding politics. A young person may also learn indirectly when older family members do or say something political that affects them. For example, if we see family members vote on a regular basis, then we learn that voting is an important duty. This is especially the case if young people see family members take precious time out of their days to vote. If family members bring children to peaceful protests, then the children learn the value of voicing dissatisfaction and the actions needed to obtain change.

In addition, families sometimes discuss political issues with children because they want children to know their views. For example, a family member who is very loyal to government leaders may mention the value of obedience. Children in this family will likely learn to value being loyal and obedient to government leaders. What happens when families never discuss politics, vote, or attend protests? Young people in these situations learn the norm of being apolitical, which refers to not being interested in their political environment. Therefore, young people learn a great many lessons from primary agents, even if the lesson is about not being interested in politics.

Secondary Agents of Socialization

Secondary agents are the second most important actors in the process of political socialization. Secondary agents—typically friends, religious or civic organization members, and members of the media—are those with whom young individuals generally interact less than they do with primary agents. Friends are influential if they discuss politics. They may talk about the choices in upcoming presidential and legislative elections. They may discuss the merits of the health care system or how the government should respond to a pandemic. They may share their opinions about immigrants and immigration policy. It is important to note that small children are unlikely to discuss politics, so most of a young person's life may not have the influence of friends. However, as people get into their teens, they become more aware of the world around them. They begin to understand the stakes, in varying degrees, about the decisions that society makes. Friends, therefore, play a more intensive role later in a person's life.

The media can also influence the formation of people's values. An important factor here is the type of media since events are filtered and portrayed in different ways. In prior generations, only television, radio, and printed press (newspapers and magazines) comprised the media. People's choices of these traditional media outlets were also limited. For example, television viewers in the United States used to get all their news and other information from only four channels until cable-TV came into people's lives. In some countries, governments control the information that traditional media outlets report. Media censorship and control by the government is particularly prevalent in autocratic countries. In such cases, the media limits information that is not convenient to the government or the political leader. In some instances, they produce or transmit false information. In countries where political leaders have developed the cult of personality, the government and the media present an ideal world to the people, one that emphasizes the greatness of their political system and leaders.

Today, the growth of social media platforms has dramatically increased the volume of information and misinformation. This change significantly influences a young person's political socialization. The development of various platforms, and the ability to access them free of charge if you have a "smart" device, can give virtually anyone the ability to influence people. Such an ability has had some positive and negative impact on socialization. On the positive side, people have more access to local, national, and world events than ever before. People post their own videos of critical events, which can become viral in a manner of minutes. Everyone who sees the video is then a witness to the event, in a sense. What makes this especially important is how it can influence people's values. In traditional media, people saw or read someone else's interpretations of events; now people can see events unfold for themselves.

Viral social media videos of police violence against Black people in the United States, many of which result in death, can challenge people's values. People who are taught that the United States is not a racist society, or that the society has made many significant changes to reduce racism, may have second thoughts after seeing such videos. In addition, such videos may challenge the view that the police are enforcing the democratic value of equality under the law. In the past, people often discounted accusations against police made by members of minority groups because it was their word against law enforcement's. If a person values the important role of the police, then that person is likely to believe a law enforcement officer who denies accusations of abuse. A video, however, may lead that person to rethink the motivations of some members of law enforcement.

Social media's negative impact on socialization is due to the level of misinformation available. Quality information is important to form opinions, such as those needed before casting a vote. Misinformation, especially the kind that people intentionally release on social media, not only leads individuals to draw incorrect conclusions but can also reduce people's confidence in the information they see. When people start distrusting traditional reporting, everything may seem suspect, and they may value traditional media less and less. This can be a problem in a democracy since reliable information is essential for citizens to make good choices. In many cases, only the media can provide that information.

Social media misinformation spread during the 2016 U.S. presidential election alarmed many and put in question the wisdom of allowing people to post anything about candidates. In addition, people voiced concern about foreign influence on the election, as many experts suspected that outside state agencies operated social media accounts to post about the candidates. Suspicion was that Russian agencies specifically posted misinformation to influence people's opinion of the candidates and potentially steer the public toward their desired outcome. Recent research indicates that concerns about social media on political socialization have merit. Edgerly et al. (2018) show that social media volume has significant importance in providing young adults with opportunities to learn about politics. Specifically, they were able to demonstrate that the more a political event is circulating in social media, the higher the young citizens' knowledge will be about the event. Therefore, higher circulation of misinformation will produce a negative impact on knowledge.

It is important to note that secondary agents often (but not always) hold values and norms that overlap with those of primary agents. In such cases, they reinforce the values and norms that primary agents transmit to individuals. Take a person's religious membership. For many, a family's values mirror the values of their religion. Therefore, we see the religious group members (secondary agents) as reinforcing values and norms taught at home (primary agents). Parents also attempt to influence their children's friendship circles. They encourage friendships with those who share similar values while discouraging friendships with those who do not share their values. We similarly observe parents' influence over a young child's education. The home-schooling movement in the United States is in many ways a response to parents' attempts to better influence their children's values and norms by removing them from the social interactions introduced by public education.

Contradictory Values: The Case of Apartheid South Africa

Primary and secondary agents of political socialization can sometimes transmit contradictory norms and values. This can happen between primary and secondary agents or among similarly classified agents. For example, values and norms taught at home may differ from those taught at school. In addition, friends may demonstrate values and norms that are different from those taught at home or school. In such cases, agents deliver a puzzling set of messages to the person learning about their country's political culture. So, what if the knowledge a person learns does not fit reality or if one set of values are at odds with another set of values? As you would imagine, the politics of a country may need to undergo some important changes to reconcile the contradictions.

To illustrate how contradictory norms and values can be reconciled, we will look at the Republic of South Africa during the apartheid period. South Africa implemented a system of institutionalized racial segregation called apartheid between 1948 and 1994. We can trace the origins of the apartheid system to South Africa's Dutch and British colonial days. It was a system of institutionalized racism based on the concept of white supremacy. South African law during this time required the extreme segregation of all social, economic, and political activities between officially designated racial groups: Whites, Asians (mainly Indians), Black Africans, and people of mixed heritage.

Apartheid was an extreme version of the Jim Crow laws of the American South. Whole cities and towns in South Africa were determined to be "White only" or "Black African only." Political power was also in the hands of the Whites. Whites were the only group that had the full right to vote. Other groups were given a limited right to vote, and voting was prohibited for Black Africans. The laws also prohibited Black Africans from taking part in the educational system, enjoying property rights, and access to other resources for economic advancement. Marriage between members of the racial groups was against the law as well as any sexual relations. Another important difference between the segregation in the American South and apartheid is the demographic numbers. Whereas Black people comprise an overall minority in the United States, they were a large majority in South Africa, approximately 80 percent of the country's entire population.

The values of the apartheid system were at odds with the democratic values that the South African government professed. The cultural foundation of apartheid was the belief in the superiority of the Europeans, specifically those of British and Dutch descent. The White minority government believed that given their low numbers, the perceived inferior African culture would overcome them, which would lead to the decline of South African economic and political development. The logic of apartheid stated that keeping the racial groups separate would cause each group to develop in their own way. This would keep resources in the hands of the Whites, who acquired their wealth through past colonial conquest.

Democracy, on the other hand, values equality among all individuals and that the governed will hold political leaders accountable. Without the right to vote, access to education, property rights, or other economic advantages, the Black Africans could only obey decisions made by the White government. Therefore, for the apartheid regime to profess democratic principles ran counter to the definition of being a democracy. Democracy for the few is not a true democracy.

The system socialized children of all racial groups under these conditions. The majority Black African population clearly understood the injustice and contradictions of the system. Educated Whites who grew up in the 1970s and 1980s also saw the hypocrisy of the system. In addition, the outside world became more democratic and intolerant of discrimination among racial groups. The United States abandoned its own segregation laws in the name of fulfilling its democratic credentials. The desire for Black South Africans to enjoy democratic values resulted in the armed insurrection against the apartheid regime. Many White South Africans also could not justify the contradictory values within the system. The international community condemned apartheid and imposed economic and other sanctions on South Africa.

The inability to sustain the system led the White minority government to negotiate the end of the apartheid regime in relative peace. The government released Nelson Mandela, the imprisoned leader of the major anti-apartheid political party, the African National Congress (ANC). Soon after, Mandela and the White leaders negotiated a transition from White minority rule to true democratic government. Universal adult suffrage was installed, and the election was held on April 27, 1994. Twenty million South Africans cast their votes in the election that was deemed free and fair by the international community. The ANC won 62.65 percent of the vote, and in May 1994, Nelson Mandela became the first Black president of the new South Africa.

PRACTICAL APPLICATION
HOW DID YOU GET YOUR POLITICAL VALUES AND NORMS?

We learned that people acquire their political values and norms through socialization with primary and secondary agents. Think about the political norms and values you hold. Choose a political value or norm that is very important to you and explain how agents (primary and/or secondary) in your life transmitted it to you. Keep in mind the direct and indirect methods in the transmission of political values and norms.

GENERATIONAL POLITICAL CULTURE CHANGE: THE CASE OF POSTMATERIALISM

The complex transferring of culture would lead one to believe that culture can change, if only gradually. However, political scientists have detected interesting patterns that help explain how political culture can dramatically change from one generation to the next. In the 1970s, American political scientist Ronald Inglehart observed that the younger generation of people held values and adopted norms that were very different from those of their elders. He theorized and demonstrated that people from the more economically developed parts of the world are shifting from **materialist values** to **postmaterialist values**. A review of postmaterialist theory will help in further understanding how culture influences public opinion and how opinion can dramatically change from one generation to the next.

The Logic of Postmaterialist Theory

Inglehart (1977) began developing his theory by restating findings by psychologist Abraham Maslow (1908–1970). Maslow (1943) theorized that people have a hierarchy of needs. Some items needed in life are more important than other needs. Once people have their most important needs met, they move on to fulfill their higher needs. At the low end of the needs hierarchy are basic ones needed for survival: food, water, shelter, and security. Without meeting these needs, a person can no longer exist. Once the basic needs for survival are satisfied, people then have the time and energy to get their higher needs met. Higher needs include social belonging, self-esteem, and self-actualization. Fulfilling these needs is important since they help improve the quality of a person's life.

Thought experiments are an easy way to understand new concepts, such as the hierarchy of needs. Picture yourself worrying about when you will have your next meal. Your efforts in solving the food acquisition problem will very likely crowd out any thoughts about other needs. Alternatively, picture yourself lacking physical security. Each time you venture outside your home, there may be threats to your life due to crime or social unrest. Your thoughts will likely focus on how to keep safe. Perhaps you do not have a good place to shelter from the elements. You therefore are more likely to spend your time looking for a secure place to sleep. After you are food-secure and physically secure, then your mind has the room to think about higher order needs, such as achieving your full human potential or understanding your role in society.

With the hierarchy of needs in mind, Inglehart theorized that growing up in prosperous economic environments produces adults with different values than those socialized in poorer ones. If individuals grow up in an environment where they are not having their basic needs regularly met, their socialization teaches them not to take those needs for granted. As a result, they continually focus on their basic needs throughout their adult lives. Alternatively, if socialization occurs under prosperity, then individuals may take for granted things like economic and physical security.

Let's go back to our thought experiment. If you had to worry about getting a proper meal— or any meal—during most days of your youth, then it is likely that you and your family will have given most of your time and thoughts to the efforts needed to feed yourselves. You are likely not going to learn about higher order needs from parents or guardians, or at least they will not place much emphasis on learning about higher order needs under these conditions. Even at school, you may question the value of learning about higher order human needs because you are continuously worried about the basic survival needs. As a result, you will likely hold on to the values that focus on meeting basic needs into your adulthood and pay little (or no) attention to the higher order needs found in Maslow's hierarchy.

On the other hand, if you grow up in an environment where your basic needs are regularly met, you will likely take those needs for granted. In other words, basic needs for survival are so available that you will likely not give them much thought because you assume that they will be present. It is not that those needs are unimportant to you, it is more that you won't need to focus on them. Thus you will have time and energy to learn and think about other issues as you grow up. Family conversations will likely focus on other matters, resulting in learning values associated with higher order needs. At school, you might have more willingness to learn about higher order needs or at least understand their value. As a result, you will likely focus on your higher needs as an adult. You will spend more time thinking and learning about self-esteem and how you can reach your full human potential. You will have the mental space to think about what you want out of life instead of how to survive.

Inglehart's theory refers to individuals who hold materialist values as those who prioritize economic and physical security (materialists). People who hold postmaterialist values prioritize self-expression and quality of life (postmaterialists). His theory tells us that primary and secondary agents are not alone in influencing political socialization. Economic conditions matter as well. If the economic environment dramatically improves, then the average person's political values between generations will change as the focus shifts from basic needs to higher order needs. We should then ask ourselves: If economic conditions worsened between generations, would we see a shift once again to values associated with basic needs?

Inglehart argued that a generation's average values can transform if there is a period of economic prosperity. If large portions of society grow up having their basic needs met, then we should see a society having more postmaterialists than materialists. It will take time for this change to occur. Postmaterialists will need to develop, and the natural mortality rate would remove the older materialists from society. In the following section, we will see how Inglehart collected survey data from around world and repeatedly saw this pattern over many decades.

Why does a shift in values from one generation to another matter? The answer involves how this shift would affect people's opinions on specific policies. Materialists prefer policies that focus on economic prosperity and physical security. They set their priorities on such items as job growth, the ability to purchase products such as cars and houses, and decreasing crime through stronger law enforcement. Postmaterialists may also want these things, but they place a higher priority on other types of policies. Postmaterialists favor policies that focus on such factors as environmental protection, a kinder society, and giving people more say in political decision-making. Materialists may also think postmaterialists' priorities are also important, but not at the expense of their priorities. Therefore, people will need to decide what the best policy trade-off is using their political values. Should the country adopt stricter environmental standards with the understanding that it may reduce economic performance, or should it focus on economic performance with the understanding that environmental conditions may worsen?

PRACTICAL APPLICATION
PRESERVING OR HARVESTING OLD-GROWTH TIMBER

We learned that materialist values are political values that place an emphasis on physical and economic security as opposed to self-expression and quality-of-life issues. Postmaterialist values are the ones that place an emphasis on self-expression and quality of life as opposed to economic and physical security. Materialist values are on one end of a spectrum of values associated with postmaterialist theory. Postmaterialist values are on the other end of the spectrum. Now, let us put this knowledge to practical use through a simulation.

Imagine a town located close to a very large old-growth forest. Old-growth forests refer to forests that have had little impact by people, have complex ecological systems, and usually take thousands of years to develop. Suppose that a logging firm wants to harvest the trees from this forest and has approached the owner of the land to start cutting. The town's governing council will need to approve permits so the logging firm can cut down the trees. Some people want the council to approve the permits since the logging firm will produce jobs that will significantly improve the town's economy. Others want to deny the permits so that the town can preserve the forest in order to maintain a healthy environment for the townspeople. Each side of the debate is seeking advice from political consultants so they can successfully argue their position to the town council. The group that wants to preserve the forest has hired you. How would you advise them?

The first step could be to figure out why the townspeople would, or would not, want to cut down the trees. How would knowing the ratio of materialists to postmaterialists help you explain the decision the town will ultimately make? Suppose that you discovered that there are more materialists than postmaterialists in the town. What sort of decision do you believe the townspeople would want the council to make? Even if there were more materialists than postmaterialists in the town, how would you convince the townspeople to preserve the forest?

The Evidence of Postmaterialist Theory

The scientific method requires us to collect data so that we can test whether or not our hypotheses have real-world support. How would a political scientist know if someone is a materialist or postmaterialist? Surveying a sample of people is one of the methods to determine to which category people belong. Researchers have asked individuals in various countries the same two-part question on the World Values Survey (WVS) over time. The WVS question asks:

"There is a lot of talk these days about what the aims of this country should be for the next ten years. On this card are listed some of the goals which different people would give top priority. Would you please say which of these you, yourself, consider the most important? And which would be the next most important?"

First Most Important Priority

1. Maintaining order in the nation

2. Giving the people more say in important government decisions

3. Fighting rising prices

4. Protecting freedom of speech

Second Most Important Priority

1. Maintaining order in the nation

2. Giving the people more say in important government decisions

3. Fighting rising prices

4. Protecting freedom of speech

Can you figure out which of the four priorities are materialist and which are postmaterialist? If you selected choice 1 and 3 as materialist, and 2 and 4 as postmaterialist, then you would be correct. Priorities 1 and 3 talk to values associated with physical and economic security. Priorities 2 and 4 pertain to values associated with higher order needs. When a person answering the question selects the materialist choices in both parts, then the researcher codes that person as a materialist. Similarly, if a person selects the postmaterialist choices in both parts, then the researcher codes that person as a postmaterialist. If a person selects a materialist choice first, and then a postmaterialist second, the researcher codes that person as holding mixed values. The researcher will do the same if a person selects a postmaterialist priority first and a materialist one second. Analysis over time demonstrates that it does not matter if a person selects the materialist (or postmaterialist) choice first or second. Therefore, we can place either type in the "mixed" value category.

The World Values Survey researchers have asked these questions since 1981 in about one hundred countries that represent approximately 90 percent of the world's population. They, of course, ask many other questions. The wealth of data accumulated from these surveys over time allows social scientists to track important cultural changes that may explain significant political phenomena.

Knowing the ratio of materialists to postmaterialists among voting citizens can help explain why countries make certain choices. Figure 4.2 plots the data collected in four waves of surveys from 1994 to 2014 among the world's wealthiest countries by the consortium of researchers using surveys around the world under the World Values Survey project. The data tell us that there was a small increase in postmaterialist values between 1994–1998 and 1999–2004. However, the data show a reversal of the trend when we compare the last three waves. While the percentages of individuals in the "mixed" values category (those who have both materialist and postmaterialist values) have stayed consistent, the percentages of materialists have increased and postmaterialists have decreased.

We can also examine the U.S. trends using the World Values Survey data. Surveys going as far back as the late 1970s have shown a steady increase of postmaterialist values in the United States. However, current trends seem to have changed direction. Figure 4.3 plots the percentage

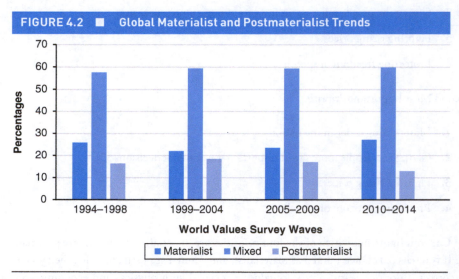

FIGURE 4.2 ■ Global Materialist and Postmaterialist Trends

Source: Based on data from World Values Survey https://www.worldvaluessurvey.org/WVSContents.jsp

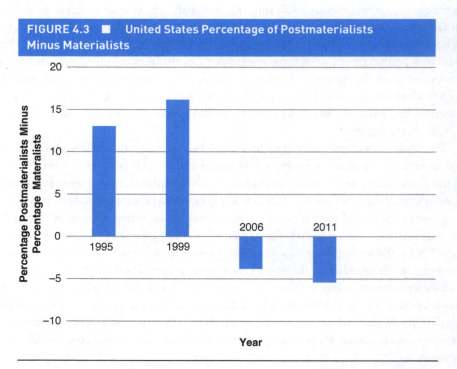

FIGURE 4.3 ■ United States Percentage of Postmaterialists Minus Materialists

Source: Based on data from World Values Survey https://www.worldvaluessurvey.org/WVSContents.jsp

of postmaterialists minus the percentage of materialists. Values greater than zero indicate more postmaterialists than materialists; values smaller than zero suggest more materialists than post-materialists. From 1995 to 1999, there was an increase in the percentage of individuals surveyed as postmaterialists. In 1995, there was an approximate 13 percentage point difference between the two categories (more postmaterialists than materialists). This number increased to an approximate 16 percentage point difference in 1999. This continues a trend that researchers are used to seeing.

However, the numbers decrease dramatically from 2006 to 2011. In 2006, the survey data indicate that there is an approximately negative 4 percentage point difference, which means the number of materialists surpassed the number of postmaterialists. In 2011, we see a further decline to an approximately negative 6.7 percentage point difference. If the trend of declining postmaterialists continues, we should expect to see voters demanding policies that favor economic prosperity and physical security over stronger environmental protection, a kinder society, and giving people more say in political decision-making.

POLITICAL ATTITUDES

LEARNING OBJECTIVE
4.4 Explain the connection between political values and attitudes.

The roles of **political attitudes** are the last subject in our exploration of how culture affects political choices. A political attitude is an established way of thinking or feeling about something or someone that a person expresses in their political behavior. A person's political values help explain the types of attitudes expressed. Examples can include attitudes toward authority, society, and individualism. Individuals often make decisions with limited information. As a result, attitudes toward particular political issues and actors serve as shortcuts for making a decision. Attitudes result from values and norms that people hold; they are an established way someone thinks or feels about something or someone. Among the multitude of all possible attitudes, we will examine attitudes toward authority, society, and individualism. In each type, we map out attitudes with extreme cases at opposite endpoints. Although we can find individuals at either endpoint, there are many more who fit somewhere between both extremes.

Authority

Attitudes toward authority involve how much importance one gives to a hierarchically organized society. Political institutions and leaders represent **authority**, which is the power or right to give orders, make decisions, and enforce compliance. Hierarchies are a traditional method of allocating authority so that members of an organization know who can give the orders and who must obey. The resulting power relationship among organizational members prompts us to ask how much individuals respect and obey authority. The answer can help us explain why some people in societies, on average, have negative attitudes toward those who do not obey their political structure's authorities. On the flipside, we can also ask why others have positive attitudes toward members of society who rebel. These two differing outcomes depend on the underlying attitude toward authority.

Attitudes toward authority develop from the importance someone places on conventional values. By valuing the prevailing status quo, people believe in the legitimacy of those who are in authority to make and enforce rules. They will have favorable attitudes toward authority figures even if they may not understand the complexities of a particular issue or have the relevant information.

There is a spectrum of attitudes toward authority. At one end of the spectrum, there is the complete disregard for authority. Individuals at this end do not respect, trust, or obey authority figures or institutions. They question conventional values because they lack the legitimacy required for absolute obedience. As a result, those who have a disregard for authority wish to limit the hold that political institutions and leaders have on their lives. They tend to react unfavorably to policy regulations and reject conventional norms. They manifest their attitudes in choices like not obeying law enforcement, not adhering to conventional norms, or participating in protests.

On the other end are individuals who have a great deal of respect and trust for authority figures and institutions. They will likely obey laws without question because they believe political leaders have the legitimate right to rule. Laws, in their view, are for the good of society and need to be strictly enforced.

A recent example in the sporting world shows how a seemingly small act of protest can generate a large impact due to differing attitudes toward authority. In 2016, National Football League (NFL) quarterback Colin Kaepernick started a protest movement that brought greater awareness of institutional racism in the United States to the national stage. He began by sitting during the singing of the national anthem at the opening of NFL games and later moved to kneeling during the anthem. The goal of the protest was to spotlight racial injustice in the United States and police brutality against people of color. His protest was highly controversial because many viewed not standing during the national anthem as a sign of disrespect to the country. The protest created renewed dialogue in the media regarding when it is proper to protest. His actions also brought new attention to the issues of institutional racism in the public discourse. Other athletes joined in the kneeling protest, thereby widening the discussion.

The United States has had a long history in coming to terms with **institutional racism**, a condition where societal institutions have embedded racist norms. So deeply seeded are such norms that some people question if racism is actually present. Although individuals acting in these institutions may not believe themselves to be racists, the rules and policies produce uneven advantages and disadvantages based on the person's race. An example would be harsher prison sentences for crimes committed by Black Americans than white Americans.

The protest against institutional racism started by Colin Kaepernick and the backlash against it involve attitudes toward authority. People who have a strongly positive view of authority believe that not standing for the national anthem disrespects the foundational principles that govern the country and those in authority. Since the primary targets of the protest were the actions of police around the country, people who value authority did not like the protest because it specifically targeted those who are essential to enforcing the law. The protesters believed that questioning and highlighting the wrongs of people in authority are important. They held a very different attitude toward authority, one that called out injustices in a very dramatic and public manner.

In this example, we see a clash between differing value sets when expressed in their attitudes. On one side, we have people who highly value law and order, with the other side valuing peaceful protest. Both sides likely value both "law and order" and "peaceful protest"; however, each side values one much more than the other. They expressed their values through their attitudes toward authority. One side saw the protest as a perfectly acceptable method to draw attention to a wrong. The other side considered the protest an unacceptable attack against authority.

Attitudes toward authority have significant political implications because they affect government resources. The more citizens who disobey a government's authority, the more resources the government would need to expend in order to maintain power. On the other hand, if there is voluntary compliance for authority, then citizens are self-regulating and fewer resources are needed. People would obey the authorities because they believe it is the correct thing to do, meaning that fewer law enforcement and security agencies are needed, which would lead to less government expense, and perhaps, fewer taxes. When authorities need to rely on force to enforce rules, they must expend more resources and will likely need to collect more money in taxes. Collecting more taxes from a society that does not have a positive attitude toward authority is difficult. The alternative would be to move expenses from other government spending, such as education, infrastructure, and health care, to public security agencies. The result would lead to a society with growing negative attitudes toward authority. As one can imagine, this sequence of actions (negative attitudes toward authority → less law compliance → more resources for law enforcement and security → more negative attitudes toward authority) is unsustainable. The cycle will likely lead to political instability. To break the cycle, the laws and policies of the country would need to match the values and norms found in society.

EXPAND YOUR THOUGHTS
IS DISSENT HEALTHY FOR DEMOCRACY?

Some argue that dissent is an important part of any healthy democracy. They argue that the people's right to protest is vital when they feel their rights are under attack. Others argue that dissent actually undermines democracy. Since societal, economic, and political conditions come out of democratic practices and decisions, dissent means that the democracy is not working. How would members of a democratic political system tolerate dissent when the average person has a very positive attitude toward authority? How would the dissenters need to act if they wanted to be heard in such a society? How would this society evaluate dissent if the average person had a negative attitude toward authority? Would dissenters choose a different way to act in such a case?

Society

Attitudes toward society pertain to how likely a person will interact with others in a constructive manner. People interact with others in a constructive manner if they trust others in their society. Trust gives individuals the confidence that others will act according to expectations without the need for oversight. In other words, individuals believe that others will follow through on what they say without some sort of enforcement. We will discuss trust and its role in politics in more detail in the next chapter. For now, we will focus on the level of social interactions among individuals.

In highly trusting societies, people tend to interact more in associational groups. Such groups can focus on activities like a particular amateur sport, hobby, or an organization that fosters community involvement and improvement. Since people wish to interact, there is more community spirit and institutions tend to be more effective. We refer to such societies as consensual. **Consensual societies** are societies with high levels of interpersonal trust and individuals willing to associate with community groups. Cooperation is easier in these societies as is reaching mutually acceptable decisions. Their strong attitude for a collaborative society is an outcome of valuing tolerance and compromise. To be clear, disputes do occur in those societies. The point is in how societal members resolve disputes. Consensual societies use trust, tolerance, and compromise to reach resolutions.

In societies where trust is low, individuals prefer not to associate with others. In these societies, people keep social interactions to a minimum because they suspect others will take advantage of them. The lack of community engagement or person-to-person interactions prevents people from gathering to discuss matters that are important to them. We refer to such societies as contentious. **Contentious societies** are societies with low levels of interpersonal trust and deep divisions among individuals and groups. Individuals in contentious societies also value tolerance and compromise less than those in consensual societies do. Having a negative attitude toward others in society likely results in heated debates on how to solve problems. People would demand that their specific way of solving problems is best and would therefore be less likely to consider other views. Members of contentious societies have difficulty cooperating with others and reaching mutually acceptable decisions. At the very extreme, such attitudes can lead to armed conflict within the society or even **genocide**, which is the systematic mass murdering of a specific group of people, usually those of a particular ethnic group or nation. Examples of genocide include the Holocaust, the Ottoman Empire's genocide of Armenians, Rwanda, and Bosnia-Herzegovina.

The issue of social interactions is especially important for heterogeneous societies. A heterogeneous society is a society composed of many different identity groups. It could be a society where there is one large majority group and various smaller minority groups. Or there could be multiple groups of various sizes without a dominant group. Homogeneous societies, on the other hand, comprise people with mostly identical identities. When we see multiple identity groups, they tend to split themselves along various dimensions. Examples include ethnicity, religion, and language, among others.

Having different identities can result in deep differences on how to approach issues. In a consensual society, the various groups will likely come to some sort of resolution with which almost everyone agrees. Contentious societies, in contrast, will have trouble developing a mutually acceptable resolution. In cases where a large majority group exists, disagreements often continue even after a decision has been reached. In countries where a dominant majority group exists, there may be long battles that are verbal or physical.

We can examine two European countries to illustrate the effects of consensus and contentious attitudes in societies with many different identity groups. Switzerland's society comprises four language groups (French, German, Italian, and Romansh). Although approximately 70 percent of the population speaks German, their constitution recognizes the other three languages. As a result, all four languages are given equal status and rights in official government deliberations. In addition, the country's main religions are Catholicism and Protestantism (Swiss Reformed Church). Although Switzerland is very heterogeneous, it has not seen significant internal (or external) conflict since its modern founding in the mid-nineteenth century. Scholars argue that the Swiss' attitude toward resolving problems through consensus, which is enshrined in their constitution, has prevented major internal conflicts.

This was not the case of the former Federal Republic of Yugoslavia, another heterogeneous society made up of different linguistic and religious groups. At the end of the Cold War in 1990, the single-party dictatorship ended, after having been in power since 1945. This prompted the regions that made up Yugoslavia to seek independence. The demographics of the regions were mostly internally homogeneous but were markedly different from one another. For example, Croatia includes people (Croats) who speak a language using the Latin alphabet and who are mainly Catholic. On the other hand, people from Serbia (Serbs) use a language based on the Cyrillic alphabet and are mainly Orthodox Christians. Yugoslavia splintered into the countries of Croatia, Serbia, Kosovo, Montenegro, North Macedonia, Slovenia, and Bosnia-Herzegovina.

The independence movements that split Yugoslavia into many countries turned violent, leading to a lengthy set of civil wars and wars of independence. The movements justified their regions' independence by invoking the right to rule by reason of their differing ethnic identities. They maintained that it would be easier to rule without the involvement of other ethnic groups. There was one region, however, that included three different groups. Bosnia–Herzegovina has individuals that identify themselves as Bosniaks, Croats, and Serbs. The differences are stark. Bosniaks are mostly Muslim, which are very different from the Croat Catholics and the Serbian Orthodox Christians. The Bosnian Civil War (1992–1995) witnessed massive genocidal campaigns that aimed to "purify" the land by ridding it of opposing ethnicities. The lengthy conflict demonstrated a clear conflictual attitude that encompassed the values of intolerance and mistrust.

EXPAND YOUR THOUGHTS
ARE SOCIAL INTERACTIONS IMPORTANT FOR A FUNCTIONING DEMOCRACY?

Some scholars argue that democracies need to have societies where people typically interact with one another in both political and nonpolitical situations. Others argue that interactions in nonpolitical situations are not very important. Why would these scholars believe that nonpolitical social interactions are important? What effect might infrequent social interactions have on the functioning of a democracy?

Individualism

Individualism favors autonomy between people and between individuals and the state. As a result, this attitude affects the amount of cooperation people have with one another and through governmental institutions. People with **individualistic attitudes** value the importance of individual efforts in making their own futures and taking exclusive responsibility for outcomes. Individualists do not view the role of others or the state as a method to make their lives better. In fact, they believe that the more others and the state are involved in their lives, the worse off they will be. This would also include government financial assistance since they believe individuals are at their best when they can resolve their own problems without such assistance. Assistance, according to this attitude, promotes dependence on others and the government, which could lead to limiting individual efforts in the future.

At the other end of the spectrum, people with **collectivist attitudes** value the importance of cooperation and group efforts in producing successful outcomes. They hold that society is more successful when people come together and participate in collective efforts. They believe that no one can succeed on their own. Instead, people rely, to some degree, on the efforts of others. When individuals are not successful, the society and government should step in to help solve the underlying problem. The assistance from government or others in society improves society as a whole because individual success leads to overall societal success. In general, people that hold collectivist attitudes do not place a significant value on self-made success stories.

We can see how these attitudes play out by examining different opinions about policies that aim to address poverty. Every country has a part of its population that is economically poor. Almost all countries view poverty as a problem that needs a solution. The question is what policies a government should adopt to solve the problem of poverty. More specifically, what methods should be in place to improve the lives of the poor so that they can have at least a minimally acceptable standard of living? Should the state adopt a policy solution focusing on a collective approach or an individualistic one?

People that hold strong individualistic attitudes would not favor government involvement in any way. They would argue that policies that assist in subsidizing housing, health care, income, or food purchases would not solve the underlying problem of why people are poor. Individualists would argue that people are poor because of badly formed choices that led them to their present condition. Such attitudes favor an approach that requires people to look at their life choices and see which ones they can change. They also favor the idea that individuals should examine their future goals and see which choices will get them to their aims. If they make wise choices, they will not be poor. Government assistance, in an individualist's opinion, could actually keep them in poverty because they lack the individual incentive to help themselves. They would enter a cycle of dependency and poverty that would be difficult to break.

People with collectivist attitudes would disagree. They do not believe that individuals are poor solely because of their own choices. They point out that many are born into poverty and may not have the skills or resources to get themselves out of their situation. In addition, they argue that there are structural or institutional conditions that keep particular groups of people in poverty. They believe that biases, such as racism and sexism, prevent some from taking advantage of opportunities. In such cases of institutionalized discrimination, members of a minority group or women do not have the same access to resources that will get them out of poverty. Given that society, as a whole, has failed people in poverty, it is up to society to correct the problems. Collective solutions through government action are the best way to solve the problem of poverty. This may involve establishing programs that support those in poverty while advancing opportunities by building a level economic playing field.

Note that in this example, neither individualists nor collectivists approve of poverty. Their attitudes, however, influence their views about the appropriate role of the government in solving the problem. One side calls for government intervention; the other does not. Their differing values lead to differing attitudes toward the role of the individual in society. One side sees individuals needing to help each other; the other side views the need for individuals to help themselves.

PRACTICAL APPLICATION
PANDEMIC MASK WEARING AND INDIVIDUALISM

During the COVID-19 pandemic, health experts argued that one simple and effective way to prevent the transmission of the virus was for people to wear facemasks. However, some national and local governments did not make this practice mandatory and instead only gave strong encouragement for people to wear masks. Even when governments made masks mandatory, they had little power to enforce the regulation. Could you predict how well people would follow mask regulations if you knew the degree to which a country's population had either individualistic or collectivist attitudes? In general, how well would a society comply with a mandatory mask ordnance if everyone adopted an individualistic attitude?

How Dictatorships Depend on Certain Attitudes to Survive

Dictatorships may have a right-wing or a left-wing ideological focus. They also may have a close affinity with differing attitudes of authority, society, and individualism. Dictatorships place importance on strong control over citizens' political behavior. As a result, they suppress individual freedoms.

The major difference between the right-wing and left-wing dictatorships involves the policies that their ideologies promote. We learned in Chapter 3 that leftist ideologies tend to support policies that require state control of economic activities. The extreme versions of leftist ideologies require complete state ownership of all the "means of production." We also learned that right-wing ideologies tend to support policies that promote the superiority of one's country and people over other countries and people. The more extreme versions of right-wing ideologies require people to declare other countries and people to be so inferior to one's own that they often do not recognize those individuals as full human beings.

The political attitudes discussed in this section can help explain why some societies tolerate dictatorships. If the average citizen strongly believes in the power and legitimacy of the state's authority, the unimportance of societal interactions outside state-sanctioned groups, and the power of the collective over the individual, then we may have a population that is willing to accept dictatorial rule. Dictators have a population willing to accept their rules and policies because citizens' attitudes align with strong support of the state's right to limit individual interactions and freedoms.

PRACTICAL APPLICATION
EXTERNAL SECURITY THREATS AND PUBLIC OPINION ON LEADERS

Researchers have demonstrated that external threats, such as possible terrorist attacks, can change people's views regarding their leaders. They explain that a perceived increase in terrorist threats makes current leaders seem more capable. How and why do you think external threats would influence attitudes toward authority, society, and individualism?

SUMMARY

The norms and values of a society help us explain why people hold particular political views and opinions. One way to study political culture is to examine how people prioritize their needs and how they vary in what they believe is acceptable or unacceptable behavior. People learn their norms and values from various agents. In general, primary agents of political social-ization—commonly family and school teachers—exert the most influence on people's value and norm formation. Secondary agents, such as peers, friends, media, and social organizations, also contribute to the development of one's values and norms.

Culture can change from one generation to another if the environment of political socialization changes. We saw that young people's socialization under very good economic conditions has led to the rise of postmaterialist values in many countries with advanced economies. As values change, we should see changes in attitudes that affect opinions of specific policies. Individuals also vary in their attitudes toward authority, society, and individualism. The differences in peo-ple's attitudes explain their opinions about public policies and the degrees of submissiveness that individuals have to government authorities. In the next chapter, we will examine another aspect of individual political behavior by examining mental and emotional factors.

KEY TERMS

Authority (p. 77)

Belief system (p. 63)

Collectivist attitudes (p. 82)

Consensual societies (p. 80)

Contentious societies (p. 80)

Genocide (p. 80)

Individualistic attitudes (p. 82)

Institutional racism (p. 78)

Materialist values (p. 72)

Norms (p. 64)

political attitudes (p. 77)

Political culture (p. 64)

Political socialization (p. 66)

Political values (p. 65)

postmaterialist values (p. 72)

Primary agents of political socialization (p. 66)

Secondary agents of political socialization (p. 66)

FURTHER READING

Inglehart, R. (1997). *Modernization and postmodernization: Cultural, economic, and political change in 43 societies*. Princeton University Press.

Sapiro, V. (2004). Not your parents' political socialization: Introduction for a new generation. *Annual Review of Political Science*, *7*, 1–23.

Sevi, B., Altman, N., Ford, C. G., & Shook, N. J. (2019). To kneel or not to kneel: Right-wing authoritarianism predicts attitudes toward NFL kneeling protests. *Current Psychology*, *40*(6), 1–8.

Triandis, H. C. (2018). *Individualism and collectivism*. Routledge.

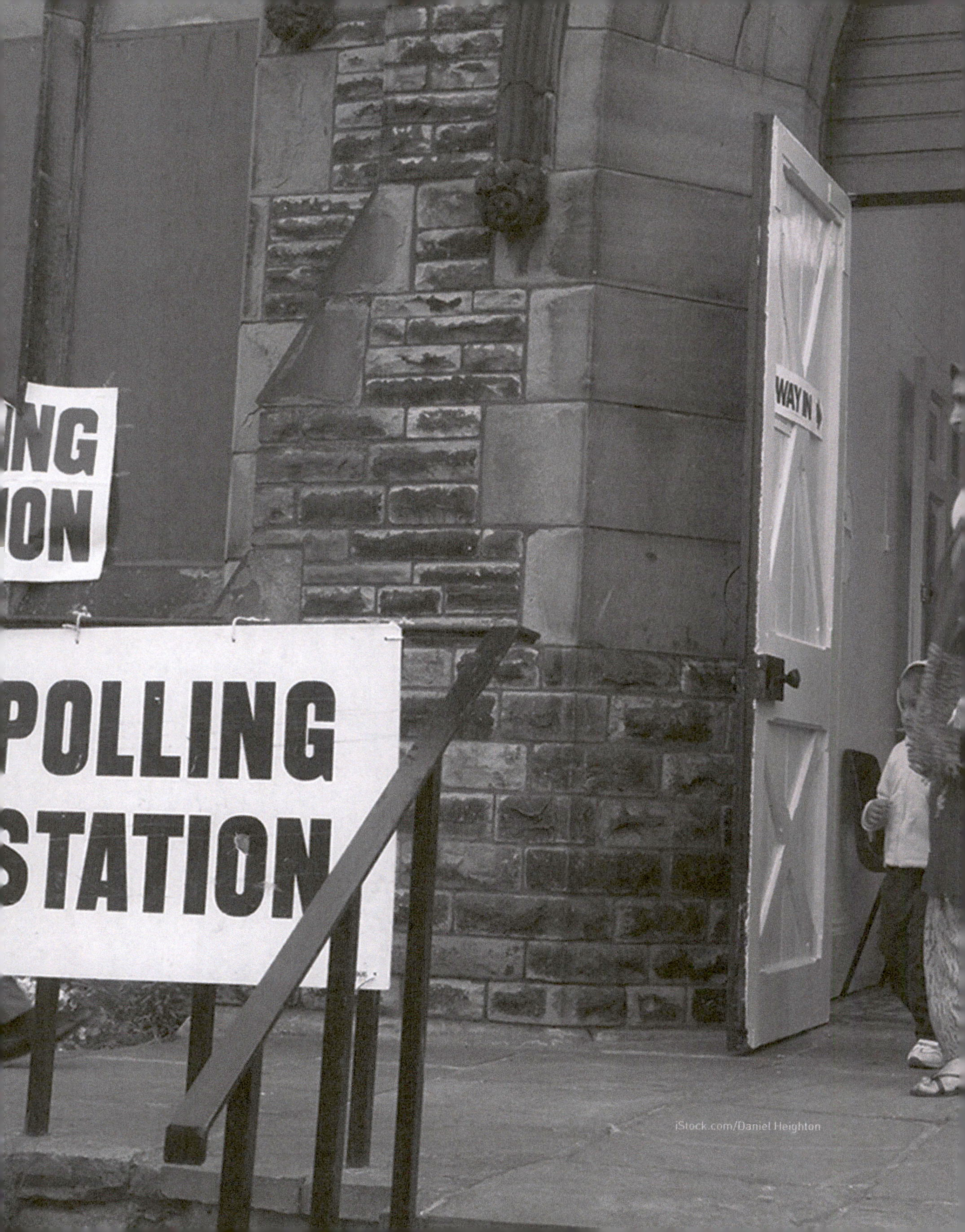

iStock.com/Daniel Heighton

5 TRUST, IDENTITY, AND POLITICAL BEHAVIOR

LEARNING OBJECTIVES

5.1 Define political behavior and explain how it is influenced by information.

5.2 Explain the importance of one- and two-way communication and how changes in technology produce new types of mass media communication.

5.3 Describe the limits to rational decision-making and alternative ways for decision-making.

5.4 Explain why trust is important in a well-functioning society and for effective government.

5.5 Explain why people place themselves into social identity groups and demonstrate how identity affects politics in different parts of the world.

5.6 Describe the differences between traditional and new social movements and what roles they play in producing political and social change.

Humans are complex beings and it is impossible for researchers to explain their behavior by one simple set of ideas. In the previous chapter, we looked at how culture can help to explain the manner in which individuals' beliefs influence their political choices. An analysis of political values can offer us some understanding of human choices and behavior given that people emphasize things that they hold in the highest regard. However, how do people know if a given choice will actually lead them to their preferred outcome? What are the ways people gather and process information before making choices? Can the answers to these questions also help explain decisions that seem to go against their values or even economic self-interest?

In this chapter, we examine the ways in which people gather and use information to make decisions. Although people try to make rational decisions, it is not always feasible for the average person to make precisely calculated decisions based on the information available to them. To understand how people reach their choices, we will investigate the rational actor model as well as psychological approaches that examine political behavior using emotional responses. We will also examine the ways by which individuals work together to produce social and political change.

POLITICAL BEHAVIOR AND THE ROLE OF INFORMATION

LEARNING OBJECTIVE
5.1 Define political behavior and explain how it is influenced by information.

Much of political science is an examination of political behavior. **Political behavior** pertains to any form of engagement in the political process or any activity that has political or policy consequences. Political behavior can be individual or group based. It includes both democratic forms of political participation (such as voting in elections, lobbying by interest groups, and actions of social movements) and nondemocratic political activities (such as coups, terrorism, and revolutions). Scholars who study political behavior examine not only behavior or action itself but also opinions, beliefs, values, norms, and institutions that influence decisions and behaviors. When we examined political culture in Chapter 4, we learned that a society's norms and values can influence people's decisions and behaviors. In Chapters 8 and 9, we will see how the rules of different institutions influence decisions and outcomes.

We will examine political behavior in this chapter by first examining the rational actor model and then psychological models. Rational choice theory forms the basis of the **rational actor model**, which is heavily influenced by the economic sciences. The rational actor model seeks to explain human behavior in terms of expected utility maximization—the quest for maximizing anticipated benefits and minimizing anticipated costs—by individuals or groups (see Chapter 2). **Political psychology** examines how people process information employed in political decision-making with attention to conscious and unconscious processes involving emotions. By including the examination of information processing, we can better understand how people use their values to form attitudes and how information can help people adapt attitudes before making choices.

Before going further, we will take a moment to partake in a detailed discussion about information. The information people use in making political decisions can take many forms. We often think of information as a set of facts. This can be the case, but information can also include opinions as well. Consider information regarding a city's water quality. There are many facts a person can consider when assessing their water quality. This may include the levels of bacteria, minerals, carcinogens, chlorine, or other possible pollutants. Another piece of information is the valued opinion of a person. This person might be an expert, politician, friend, or other trusted person. Accepting the opinion of others as true in making decisions is all the information many people need. Therefore, facts and the opinion of others can form the set of information a person uses.

Two characteristics of information are important for us to consider. The first is the amount of information. Does the person hold a sufficient amount of information? That is, is it enough information to make a decision that reflects what they really want or need? As you can imagine, having too little information can lead to making the wrong decision. Sometimes we only know that we have too little information after we make our decision. The second characteristic is the quality of information. Does the person hold information that truly reflects reality? Is it accurate? Just like too little information, incorrect facts or opinions of others might lead to a decision that goes against what the person wants or needs.

Last, we need to understand the mechanics of processing information. If we focus on facts, and assume that we have a sufficient amount of information and the information is of good quality, then how do we use facts in our calculations? Does the person have the technical training needed to process the information? Going back to the city's water quality, if a person knows the amount of bacteria or other substances in the water, will the person know if the levels are too high and therefore the water is harmful for human consumption? After all, we may never see water coming out of our taps that is 100 percent pure. Unless people have technical training in water quality and are aware of the latest research, they may not be able to process the information effectively and decide whether the water is sufficiently clean. In these circumstances, people may do some research or rely on the opinion of others. However, how do people know whether the opinions they receive are accurate? Should they examine the opinion leaders' expertise credentials? Some people tend to accept the opinion of others when they believe they share the same ideology. Would this also apply to the evaluation of water quality? As you can see, the understanding of how people process information is complex, with different people coming up with their decisions in different ways.

Figure 5.1 offers a quick look at how people can use their values to process information into an attitude and how information can affect choices. Let's take as a starting point an individual who holds a set of specific values. If the person is a postmaterialist (discussed in Chapter 4), then we know they value the environment as well as having citizen input in policymaking. We would then ask what type of information our postmaterialist possesses that could influence their attitude on how their government formulates environmental policies. Suppose that the person receives information that the government did not include citizen input in creating a specific policy. Whether this information is true or not is of little relevance. What is more important is that the person believes that the information is true. If the person values citizen input, there is a strong likelihood that this person will start forming a negative attitude toward the way the government created the policy. The information will therefore cause the postmaterialist to oppose the policy, even though the policy's goal may align with the person's values. Perhaps this person believes that the policy will not be effective because there isnot enough citizen input. In other words, the information that the postmaterialist possesses canproduce an effect that runs counter to what we would expect the person to choose. This example shows how people process information to form political attitudes and choices. Ultimately, these attitudes inform and drive a person's political behavior.

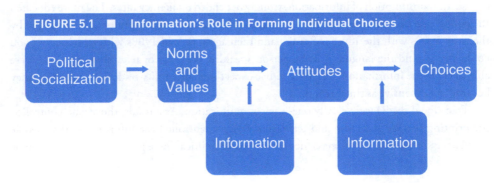

FIGURE 5.1 ■ Information's Role in Forming Individual Choices

Political Socialization → Norms and Values → Attitudes → Choices

Information → (Norms and Values)

Information → (Attitudes)

SOURCES OF INFORMATION: MEDIA AND POLITICS

LEARNING OBJECTIVE

5.2 Explain the importance of one- and two-way communication and how changes in technology produce new types of mass media communication.

Before discussing how individuals process information, we begin by examining the sources of information and how technological innovations have impacted the ways by which people distribute and receive information. Much information comes to people through **mass media**, which are methods of communication that attempt to reach a wide audience. Other sources may include communication from friends, relatives, coworkers, and other individuals in a person's network.

Many mass media sources distribute political information through one-way communication. This means that a person can receive the information, but they cannot respond to the source. In other words, one-way communication lacks a dialogue between those who deliver information and those who receive it. If a dialogue is possible, then we refer to it as two-way communication. We make this distinction because of the power of one-way communication. If you read or hear something that you believe is inaccurate, you can personally dismiss the information. However, in one-way communication you lack the ability to voice criticism of the information and for others to hear your views. As a result, most people believe that the information is accurate because no one is criticizing it. The inability of people to interact with the standard model of one-way communication—which has been around for hundreds of years—incentivizes other forms of communication.

Traditional Media Sources

Traditional media sources include print media, such as newspapers and magazines, and electronic media like television and radio. Print media have been around since the invention of the printing press by Johannes Gutenberg in the mid-1400s. By the 1500s, print media spread in Europe to everyone who could read. This revolutionary technology dramatically increased the volume of information compared to the slow speed of the older method of hand copying. Of course, the consumption of information strongly depended on literacy rates. The more educated the population became, the more mass media could influence public opinion. This changed by the early 1900s with the advent of radio, and then again in mid-1900s with television. If you could understand the language of the person speaking on radio or television, then you were able to consume information. The only setback was the affordability of devices, although they became less expensive as time went on.

Traditional media were clearly one-way communication. As a result, those who controlled the printing presses and radio and television stations controlled the information that people could access. In democracies, mass media are a major political force given their ability to shape opinion on various matters. If a newspaper had a strong view on a political event, then it had the ability to let its readers know. In addition, traditional media served a gatekeeping role: It determined what was worthy of being reported and what was not. The magnification of such power occurred if a local area had few newspapers and radio and television stations. Therefore, very few groups or individuals had such power during these times. The consequential influence of mass media led to calls for ethical journalism. Ethical practices meant that media would factually report news at the front end of the print media or at the start of a broadcast, with opinion on matters regulated toward the end. However, this has not always been the case. For example, the rise of tabloid journalism focuses on sensationalist or scandal reporting and is not necessarily true.

In a democracy, regulating the media is difficult since it can lead to violating the principles of freedom of speech and expression. For example, a government that tells a traditional media outlet not to print something, even if the story has falsehoods, would typically be considered a form of censorship. While it would be harmful if the public receives false or biased information that could dramatically influence political decisions and events, no one has developed clear criteria on how to regulate information while protecting these basic democratic rights. The closest some societies have come have been on moral grounds, which are very culturally specific. Many people believe that in a free society, it is up to the consumer of mass media to decide what is worth reading, listening, viewing, and believing.

The combination of one-way communication and freedom to provide information in the form of opinions launched an innovative and powerful U.S. radio-formatting technique in the 1980s: talk radio. Talk shows were not a new phenomenon on radio or television. The format began in the early days with a host mediating a conversation between individuals who supported different sides of an issue. Another example is a radio host interviewing someone, with a dialogue between the interviewer and the guest. Sometimes the listeners could ask questions or make comments by calling into the radio station. However, radio station employees screened the calls and decided who could and could not ask questions, which limited opportunities for listeners to call in with opposing views. Also, the amount of time allowed to call-ins was very limited.

The innovation in talk radio came when one person, the host, controlled all the information delivered during the program. The host simply gave a monologue expressing a large array of opinions. The shows completely lacked guests, which meant that no one could challenge the views of the host. The host had the power of the airwaves to disseminate any view the audience was willing to accept and businesses would support through advertising. One of the earlier pioneers of this format in the United States was Rush Limbaugh (1951–2021), who hosted the most listened-to show with an estimated 15.5 million weekly listeners. Listeners included members of the U.S. military through its government broadcasting service, Armed Forces Network. Research demonstrates that his conservative views were influential in many elections and provided important talking points for others in his field, not only in the United States, but also abroad.

This new format accelerated the formation of **media echo chambers**. This term refers to programing where the audience tunes in because they are likely to agree with the host's views. The result is that no diversity of ideas exists to challenge either the host or the audience's positions on critical matters. In a sense, the host and the audience echo each other's views. The phenomenon reinforces what the listeners believe and gives them a safe place to enjoy their ideas.

Media echo chambers are popular because of a psychological condition referred to as **cognitive dissonance**. Imagine being in a situation that challenges your worldviews. You believe in something, but someone gives you some strong evidence that the way you think about things is incorrect. Such a condition makes people uncomfortable or even causes stress because they would need to rethink or defend their positions, which they may not be able to do. To reduce the possibility of stress, and enjoy the company of like-minded individuals, people tend to avoid media outlets that challenge them and instead gravitate to those that support their views.

Importantly, media echo chambers have an effect of polarizing politics. First, people are galvanized into entrenching their thoughts. They often reason that if there are millions of people listening, then the views must be true. If it is true, then why should they change their minds? Second, echo chambers have an effect on beliefs that people have yet to form. If someone agrees with most of what a media personality says about other topics, then it will be easier to convince someone when a new topic comes up.

Let's say you do not have a view regarding the motivations of a foreign government. In fact, you know nothing about the country in question. Your favorite program host or author, one whom you often agree with, labels the foreign government as evil (or good). You are likely to use your favorite host's opinion as your own. You would reason that since you have agreed with this person in past, you must have common values. Therefore using the host or author as a "shortcut" to get to an opinion is a good use of your time. The net effect in the galvanization of thoughts and assisting in the formation of new opinions is the production of political camps that are likely to keep their beliefs regardless of any contradictory evidence.

Nondemocracies also have traditional mass media. Although information in democracies is free of government censorship, dictatorships strongly control information. One way that many dictators control information is by directly owning print and broadcast outlets. The media's sole purpose is to distribute information that favors the government's political leaders and policies. It is often the case that government-controlled media is the only source of information available to most citizens. The news reported is generally favorable to the government so that citizens can view the current political leadership in a positive light. When they report bad news, it is often blamed on foreign actors or domestic opponents. News from outside the country is also limited or not allowed to come into the country. Thus, the dictatorship guarantees that no message from the outside world will contradict the official news of the government. The most extreme example of information control is found in North Korean reporting, where the government, especially its paramount leader Kim Jong-un, is seen as flawless and the conditions of the average North Korean citizen are seen as the best in the world. This is far from true.

New Media Sources

The number of media information sources dramatically increased with the creation and development of the internet. Even in democracies, there was a limit to the number of traditional outlets for information. Their one-way communication and gatekeeping often meant that information was narrowly distributed. This changed with the development of social media in critical ways.

First, new media allowed people to obtain information on an on-demand basis. Traditional media had a specific schedule to distribute information, especially anything involving politics. Newspapers delivered information in the morning, with some having an evening edition. News and political magazines came out weekly or monthly. Television and radio hosted morning and evening news programs. With broadcasts, if you missed a scheduled program, you could not get a recap. After video recording became accessible, people could theoretically record news programs, but very few did. With the internet, outlets could store their programs and wait for the consumer to be ready to view or listen to them.

On-demand information, however, requires outlets to broadcast the news as soon as possible. In the traditional schedule, outlets all waited until five or six in the evening to get their stories ready. Newspapers had a longer lag time since the fresh news would appear in the morning editions. Therefore, if an outlet did not have a piece of information early, they had sufficient time to get all the basic information by the time of airing or printing. With on-demand, outlets need to have the information ready as soon as possible so that consumers see them as the best place to get their news. This can lead to stories with errors and stories with incomplete reporting.

Another change is the increase in the number of outlets due to lower production costs. Running traditional media is expensive. Hiring technically trained employees and purchasing expensive equipment is out of the reach for most. Technological innovations have lowered the cost barriers, thereby allowing greater access. Consider, for example, operating a radio station. Aside from hiring people that know how to produce the programing, run the technology, market your station, and manage its affairs, you would also need to buy a facility and equipment such as multifaceted recording studios and transmission towers. Another needed item is a license from the government to transmit at a specific frequency. As you can imagine, these things do not come cheap.

The advent of the internet, and associated computing technology, dramatically reduced these costs. You can create a page on a social media platform and start distributing whatever information you like. You can also produce a podcast, which only requires you, your ideas, a microphone, and a computer with the appropriate recording application. If you add a video component and some creativity, you can produce a news program of decent quality. People can deploy such programs onto the internet at a fraction of the cost it would take to do the same on radio or television. To repeat, you can do this on your own. In traditional media, a station would need to hire you to do some of the tasks and then you would be limited to what the station manager says you can or cannot broadcast. Since these barriers are not present, you have more freedom to broadcast your ideas to an audience that would find you appealing.

With little or no gatekeeping or regulations, the new media methods can lower quality while increasing the volume of information. People hired in traditional media received an education from journalism schools that professionalized them into applying ethical standards. While some in social media also apply such standards, many do not. This makes it difficult for the average person to figure out what is true and what is not. The lack of quality control was a major problem during the 2016 U.S. presidential election when many suspected that actors, especially foreign ones, were distributing false information that favored one candidate. The COVID-19 pandemic also saw the spread of false information, first regarding the existence of the virus and then the effectiveness of the vaccines.

The concern about "fake news" has been growing in many corners of the world. At the same time, many politicians today dismiss inconvenient reporting as fake news on their social media platforms to communicate directly with their supporters who are ready to accept such claims. The development of social media has enabled people to stay within their own circle and not hear alternative views. This has contributed to the growth in political polarization as people have increasingly become intolerant of different perspectives and refuse to have a dialogue with whom they disagree. The ease of obtaining low quality information that people can quickly agree with lowers the chances of making prudent choices given the effect that cognitive dissidence has on producing media echo chambers.

PROCESSING INFORMATION: RATIONALITY OR BOUNDED RATIONALITY?

LEARNING OBJECTIVE

5.3 Describe the limits to rational decision-making and alternative ways for decision-making.

As we discussed, there are many different ways in which people process information in order to come to a conclusion, such as which politician to vote for or which side of a political issue to support. Some political scientists argue that people make decisions by considering how a political outcome can benefit them. According to the **rational actor model**, individuals choose options that maximize their self-interest. Doing so requires knowing the range of options available to them, obtaining accurate information about these options, and being able to process the information in a way that leads the rational actor to choose the option that generates the optimal outcome.

The rational actor model has explained politicians' behavior reasonably well, especially when the stakes are high. It is common for politicians to gather information about different options and try to choose a strategy that maximizes their payoffs. Recall the case of the Cuban Missile Crisis we examined in Chapter 1. With the discovery that the Soviet Union was constructing nuclear missile sites in Cuba, U.S. President John F. Kennedy analyzed all the possible options with his advisors when searching for a solution. The goal was to develop the best strategy that would remove the missiles while avoiding the crisis escalating into a nuclear war. President Kennedy was acting rationally.

You may question whether anyone can be perfectly rational in the way assumed by the rational actor model. Political actors may examine a *nearly* entire set of options instead of a truly entire set of options. They may not have perfect information all the time but seek to acquire as much and as accurate information as possible. Political actors may not be flawless computational machines but will still try to be as calculating and as strategic as possible. Rational choice scholars maintain that the theory is still useful because people try to be or behave *as if* they were rational.

Now imagine your situation: If you had to make a very important decision, do you have a ready team of experts to help you gather all the relevant information and rank the benefits of possible decision outcomes? We may see less evidence of rational behavior, particularly with an average person. Even well-resourced politicians' behaviors sometimes defy the expectations generated by the rational actor model. It is a daunting task to think about all the possible options, acquire information on all of them, and analyze each one of them carefully. For one, it takes time to investigate political issues. The average person often lacks time to obtain important information because of other competing commitments such as work, family, and leisure. Knowing where to get accurate information can also be a substantial obstacle in itself. In addition, people will need to understand the information and be able to calculate potential benefits and costs. They may lack the technical background or resources to do so.

One political decision that citizens in a democracy make is choosing which election candidate will help make their lives better. Politicians usually make broad promises, which makes choosing a candidate difficult. One common promise is looking out for the economic interests of people that support them. They may be a little specific by saying that they will cut taxes and/or increase spending in certain areas, like welfare benefits and infrastructure. To get accurate information, voters need to find out what exactly candidates plan on doing. Of course, this assumes that the candidates will provide a specific plan. Voters could investigate past decisions made by the candidates or look into who contributes to their campaign fund to figure out how they will likely decide important issues. Doing so will require spending time and having the ability to access information that may not be easily available.

There is also another factor to consider: If the voter can get the information, will they be able to process it? For example, let us say that the candidate wants to make it more difficult for foreign imports to come into the country. They can campaign that free trade has harmed the country's economy and cost jobs. They therefore promise to limit products coming in from abroad. How will this influence the voter? If the voter works in an industry benefiting from closing off trade, then you may think that the voter will likely support the candidate. However, even this choice, which seems easy, is actually not so straightforward. For example, restricting foreign imports reduces consumer choices and may lead to higher prices. All voters are consumers. Then, to what extent would the promised trade restriction on balance affect the overall economic welfare of the voter? Would voters facing similar situations consider all the possible costs and benefits of all possibilities before making a decision as assumed by the rational actor model?

Herbert Simon proposed **bounded rationality** as an alternative model of decision-making. Bounded rationality is the idea that we make decisions that are rational, but they are within the limits of the information available to us and our cognitive capabilities. Decision-makers, in this view, act as **satisficers**. Rather than optimize, they choose the option that will satisfy their needs and desires without putting too much effort into making sure they consider every single possibility. In elections, for example, boundedly rational voters may compare only the candidates from major political parties when deciding whom to vote for, instead of seeking information about all of the candidates in the race and deeply scrutinizing their proposals, as assumed by the rational actor model.

In sum, bounded rationality assumes that people's information processing capability is limited. Even if people try to be rational, they often do not consider all options or do not seek out all the available information about those options. They do research and consider options that are sufficient in their view. They may use shortcuts to decision-making, like using the opinions of technical experts, ideological leaders, or political party affiliations to make a candidate choice in an election. Indeed, people use some sort of shortcut to make decisions in everyday life. To understand how this can happen, we next examine the roles of social and political trust.

PRACTICAL APPLICATION

What information would voters need to determine whether a candidate's promise to cut taxes would benefit them? Where would they get this information? How would they know if the information is reliable?

EXPAND YOUR THOUGHTS

Considering the differences between maximizers and satisficers, which model do you think better describes how people make decisions? Would your answer depend on the occupations or positions of the individuals? Would it depend on the nature or the importance of the decision issues?

SOCIAL AND POLITICAL TRUST

LEARNING OBJECTIVE

5.4 Explain why trust is important in a well-functioning society and for effective government.

Given the complexity of gathering and processing information, many political psychologists believe that it is more likely that citizens will use their feelings when making political decisions, such as choosing candidates or holding positions on particular issues. Trust is a powerful emotion because it can facilitate cooperative behavior among people when it is present or cause institutions to operate poorly in its absence. When we **trust** others, we believe that they will act in a way that may benefit us, or at least not harm us, without the need for oversight. Overseeing everyone who we depend on will dramatically increase our burden in many ways.

Take buying a car or medicine. We assume that the car is safe to drive or medicine is safe to take and effective because of government regulations ensuring safety. If you trust the government and the policies and regulations it creates, you do not have to worry if companies performed the proper testing to make sure the car brakes work or your medicine will not have an unknown harmful side effect. Imagine needing to investigate these situations, and many more, on your own. Doing so would require you to forgo the time you could spend on other things, like family obligations, studying, reading, working, sleeping, and exercising, so it is costly to you. Most people also do not have the expertise or resources to test and ensure the safety of automobiles, drugs, and other items. If you can trust your government regulators to do their jobs, then you do not have to conduct all this oversight. Trust is something people feel frequently and helps reduce what researchers refer to as **transaction costs**. Transaction costs are the time, effort, and other resources required to make and enforce individual and collective decisions.

COVID-19 vaccines are another example of how trust in government institutions and regulations reduces transaction costs. Several vaccines were developed to fight against the COVID-19 pandemic. Many people hoped the vaccines would work so that they could return to normal life. Some questioned if the vaccines would be effective and, more importantly, if harmful side effects would be present. Without some way of verifying the answers to these questions, some people thought they were taking a chance on their health. If one wanted to personally verify the consequences of the vaccine, one needed to examine all the data that showed that people had a very good chance of being protected by the vaccine and would not be harmed. Again, we face the same dilemma: Do we have the ability to gather sufficient information and analyze it? Trusting institutions, like the global and national health agencies, and leaders, such as those in public office and health care, removes the transaction costs associated with the decision to get a vaccination or not. If people trust leaders and institutions, and these trusted institutions and leaders assure you that vaccines are safe and effective, then people do not need to personally conduct the oversight investigation.

PRACTICAL APPLICATION

Do you trust most people? Think about an interaction that requires you to trust someone you do not know well. Now think about how you would execute the interaction without trust. Does trust dramatically reduce transaction costs in your example?

Trust is important because it allows us to do more with our time. It lowers transaction costs so that people can use their time more productively instead of making sure that others are not taking advantage of them. We will explore two types of trust that scholars demonstrate are important in explaining political behavior. The first is **social trust**, which is the trust that people have for one another and for social institutions. Countries with strong levels of social trust have people that interact more with each other outside of family life. They are more likely to enjoy memberships in leisure clubs like bowling teams or volunteer to help others through civic organizations. With greater interactions, people form solid bonds that improve the likelihood of collaboration and aids in solving common problems. Because solutions are jointly developed, there is higher likelihood that they improve the overall quality of life. In sum, highly trustful societies tend to be friendlier ones, encourage collaboration, and produce societies that are more cohesive.

A high level of civic engagement is an outcome of a society with a large amount of social trust. **Civic engagement** is the set of voluntary actions by individuals, often times in groups, to identify and try to solve problems in their local community, country, or even around the world. In other words, civic engagement occurs when people get involved in their communities. The forms of civic engagement vary widely. It could be volunteering for a community project, such as covering up graffiti at a playground. It could also include getting involved in changing rules or regulations, such as revising city ordinances so that the community has more green spaces. Social trust is critical in creating an environment where civic engagement will thrive. Trust brings people together when there is a common cause because they believe that others will work for the benefit of all. If people lack trust, then they may feel that volunteering for community activities is not worth the effort. They may feel that people in their neighborhoods are only looking out for themselves and any effort to improve their community will have little or no impact.

There is a common link between a well-functioning democracy and civic engagement. Since democracy is "government by the people," citizen action should be the foundation of any decisions that affect local, national, and perhaps international environments. If people keep to themselves, they will not solve community problems from the grassroots of society. A lack of trust, which causes suspicion of others, prevents mobilization and leaves problems unanswered. The exception is when elites promote change. Such cases may help communities, or harm them, depending on the motivations or interests of elites. We do see community involvement in dictatorships, for example, but such actions are usually set up to promote and legitimize the ruling elite and the regime. The rulers give approval for such actions, which are always top-down. Rulers do not allow grassroots, or bottom-up, actions because such activities may pose a threat to their hold on power.

Social trust not only improves the development of civic mindedness, but it helps facilitate economic transactions. Businesses and financial institutions give credit to people that they trust will pay back their debts. They gather information on people to improve the likelihood that they can trust them. When someone writes a check for a purchase, the person receiving the check needs to trust that the person writing the check has cash in the bank to cover it. Without trust, people would need to pay for all goods and services in cash. In addition, without some degree of trust, businesses would not accept credit card payments. After all, how do they really know you are good for the credit? Without trust, we would need to carry all the cash needed to spend in a given day, week, or month. Even keeping money in the bank relies on trust that the bank will give you back your money when you ask!

Ultimately, even cash transactions rely on trust. Currencies are valuable only so far as people can trust the values of the currencies and the institutions that issue them. In many countries that have experienced hyperinflation (i.e., extremely high inflation) and where the government has no credibility, many people and businesses prefer to save and conduct economic transactions using trusted currencies like the U.S. dollar because they do not trust their countries' currencies. In many of these countries, governments have adopted economic policies to "borrow" the credibility of the U.S. dollar to boost confidence in their national currencies by guaranteeing a fixed rate conversion between their own currency and the U.S. dollar. Some countries have even adopted the U.S. dollar as their countries' official currency. This measure is known as dollarization.

Political trust is the trust citizens give to political institutions and politicians. Imagine a society where no one trusts the government at any level. Police cannot rely on citizens to help solve crimes because citizens lack the trust that the police are actually helping the neighborhood. Citizens may try to figure out creative ways to avoid paying taxes because they lack the trust that the money they pay to the government will go toward worthwhile projects. They may not volunteer to join the armed forces because they don't trust that politicians are looking out for the citizens' best interests. In democracies and autocracies with elections, citizens may lack the desire to vote because they have low or no trust that ballot counting will reflect the will of the people, or they do not believe that the results will change the political situation. Such a society will require more coercive force to obtain citizen cooperation and make sure people follow the laws and regulations. The need for greater governmental law enforcement will require more resources and may harm the civil rights of citizens. When political trust is high, people are more likely to volunteer their efforts in scenarios like those just mentioned, which makes the operation of government activities easier to carry out.

One detailed study on the relationship between trust and government performance, by American political scientist Robert Putnam (1993), demonstrated that institutions work well when trust is present. Putnam examined Italy, which displays an interesting feature. Due to a divided history, Italy's northern and southern regions have different levels of social and political trust. In the north, people are more trusting and therefore engage in community associations. The opposite is true in the southern regions. Using a detailed measurement of government performance, Putnam discovered that the more trusting northern regions also have higher levels of effective government. This should not be a surprise given our understanding of trust. If people voluntarily obey laws and contribute to civic needs because they trust fellow citizens and their government, governments can be more effective in carrying out policies and accomplishing societal goals.

SOCIAL IDENTITY THEORY

LEARNING OBJECTIVE

5.5 Explain why people place themselves into social identity groups and demonstrate how identity affects politics in different parts of the world.

Since trust aids us in explaining political behavior, it is helpful to know how trust develops. One widely cited theory that can help us understand trust within and among groups is **social identity theory**, which was developed by Henri Tajfel and John C. Turner in the 1970s and 1980s. Social identity theory explains how improved self-esteem develops through group formation and helps to explain intergroup behavior (i.e., behavior between groups).

Everyone holds more than one identity. We are born in, socialized to accept, or choose to belong to many identities. Some identities are transitional, like being a child, whereas others are more permanent, like being an adult. According to social identity theory, which identity we choose to emphasize depends on our most important social group affiliation. A **social identity group** is one with membership restricted to people who hold the same identity. An ethnic group is a good example. While people interact with members of their ethnic group daily, there are people that belong to the group that they do not know personally. Even if they do not know them personally, they are still willing to accept them into their group because of identity.

Why do people form groups based on identity? People identify as a group member (referred to as the in-group) because the affiliation enhances their self-esteem, which is how much they value their own worth. People view their in-group as having a special status within the society, which gives a member a degree of importance that would not be available if the member were not in the group. Members reinforce each other's self-esteem when interacting in, or associating with, the group. The importance given to the group helps build trust and therefore creates a bond among members.

PRACTICAL APPLICATION

Do you consider yourself a member of an important social identity group? Explain why this group is or is not important to you. Be as specific as possible.

One important implication of social identity theory is a phenomenon known as **in-group favoritism**. In-group favoritism is the desire to distribute resources to members of the in-group and keep resources away from members of the out-group (people who are members of other groups). The phenomenon develops from the self-esteem bonding that promotes in-group trust and the associated lack of trust in out-group members. People skew resources to members of their in-group because they view the in-group members as legitimately more important than out-group members and therefore more deserving of favoritism. By doing so, in-group members who engage in in-group favoritism improve or reinforce their self-esteem. In-group members recognize their special value to each other by channeling resources toward their group.

In-group favoritism has important implications for explaining political behavior. Since societies have group divisions, we can predict with a good likelihood that there will be favoritism in distributing resources to a decision-maker's in-group. Even countries with seemingly homogeneous societies will have group divisions and are therefore susceptible to in-group favoritism.

The detection of in-group favoritism came through lab experiments that test social identity theory's claims with people who just met each other. Researchers placed complete strangers into groups using arbitrary reasons. However, the researchers told the participants that they placed them into groups because of a specific trait their in-group possessed. By telling the group members that they had a unique identifying trait, individual group members were more likely to skew resources to members of their group, even when resources would not come to the individual making decisions about resources. According to social identity theory, this is the power of social group identification. Although people do not personally know everyone in their group, they will favor them nonetheless. With this approach in mind, we can predict that people are more likely to keep or wish to redistribute resources to members of their in-group not because people believe that resources are likely to benefit themselves but because more resources to members of their in-group are likely to benefit people *like* them.

PRACTICAL APPLICATION

How could you use in-group favoritism to explain how people would behave if they believed the out-group is a threat?

Take, for example, the issue we raised earlier in this chapter regarding trade. Voters may not know if closing off trade will benefit them or not. However, if they are told that it would benefit people like them, then social identity theory predicts that they will be in favor of closing off trade. Emotion associated with group membership drives the decision, not a logical calculation based on maximizing narrowly defined individual self-interest.

We see this in current debates in the United States and Britain. During Donald Trump's 2016 and 2020 campaigns for U.S. president and during his administration, he linked trade policy with working class identity. The focus on trade harming manufacturing jobs persuaded working-class voters (especially white working-class voters) to support trade reform even though there was little evidence that current trade agreements harm them personally. According to social identity theory, it was the perceived threat to people like them that triggered their choices.

This Brexit campaign ad states that the money Great Britain spends on the European Union could be used for national health care.

Image by Abi Begum under CC BY 2.0 via Flickr. https://www.flickr.com/photos/141776778@N02/26969015773

The same occurred in Britain during the referendum campaign to remove the country from the European Union economic bloc, known as Brexit. The message to voters was that the out-group (Europe) was harming the in-group (British working class). The advocates for Brexit continued by stating that the resources that the in-group shared with the out-group should stay with the in-group. The message was successful. The majority of British voters decided to leave the European Union.

EXPAND YOUR THOUGHTS

Consider two social identity groups that are different and yet have many similar characteristics. Do you think their intergroup relationship would be more cooperative or conflictual? Please explain.

Case Studies: Ethnic Conflicts of the 1990s

The following two cases offer examples of how societies, which on the surface seem to include people with similar identities, separate themselves into various social groups with deadly consequences. In each case, we see social identity groups unable to collaborate because of their in-group favoritism of resources. The first case we will examine occurred in Northern Ireland. The people of the area refer the years of intergroup violence (1966–1998) as "The Troubles."

The conflict involved Protestants on one side and Roman Catholics on the other. The divide also included an ethnic characteristic with Protestants identifying themselves as Ulster and Catholics as Irish. The origins of intergroup conflict, like many others, have a long history. What is now the Republic of Ireland was at one time part of the United Kingdom (UK). It gained independence through violent struggle in 1922. However, the UK did not grant the entire island independence. The northeastern corner fought to stay in the union with the UK. Unlike the southern majority of the island, the people of this corner (Ulster) claimed a different heritage due to their migration to the island from Britain over many years. They feared domination by the overwhelming majority Catholic society of the south. By continuing their membership in the UK, the Protestants believed that they could maintain their identity.

The intergroup conflict continued to be a problem since there was a minority Catholic population in Northern Ireland. Although the two religions are similar (they are both Christian), they saw their identities tied to two different destinies. Protestants wanted to maintain power, and to do so, had to remain in union with the UK. Catholics wished for Northern Ireland to unite with the Republic of Ireland. In doing so, Catholics in Northern Ireland saw Irish unification as a way to gain power over resources.

As time went on, political decisions regarding resources in Northern Ireland favored the Protestants over the Catholics, given the former's majority status. Relations became more contentious in the 1960s when Catholics began their own civil rights movement. The aims of the movement were to end job and housing discrimination, expand the vote in local elections to all adults (not just to property owners who were mainly Protestants), terminate electoral boundaries that favored Protestants, implement police reform, and revoke laws that limited the political rights of Catholics.

Violence developed after not being able to achieve political aims quickly, with armed civilian groups pitted against each other. They engaged in street violence, but the main method was a terror campaign using targeted bombings. The introduction of British troops into the conflict only escalated the violence with soldiers killing unarmed civilians. Approximately 3,000 people lost their lives during the years of The Troubles.

Most of the violence ended with a complex power sharing arrangement specified in the multiparty Good Friday Agreement in 1998. Under power sharing, the two social identity groups worked together so that both sides had fair treatment. However, the violence has not come to a complete end due to retaliatory acts that seek to punish those involved in the years of violence.

The second illustrative example is the Rwandan Civil War (1990–1994) fought between the Hutu and Tutsi identity groups. There is some debate regarding the origins and divisions of the two groups. Both are part of the greater Bantu ethnic group that populates much of Africa. Political scientist Mahmood Mamdani claims that the division was a creation of the Belgian colonial occupiers who designated Tutsi as those who owned cattle and Hutus as people that did not. After independence, the two identities persisted with predicted skewed allocation of resources to whichever group was in power.

During the colonial days, the Belgians placed a Tutsi monarchy in power. A Hutu majority government replaced the monarchy after independence. Tutsis left Rwanda in large numbers to escape Hutu-led violence shortly after independence. The Tutsi refugees, who mainly settled into neighboring Uganda, lost property to the Hutu elite. While in Uganda, Tutsi leaders (mostly children of refugees) organized an armed invasion in 1990 in order to reinstate Tutsi political power. The violence was supposed to end when both sides agreed to a power sharing arrangement (the Arusha Accords) in 1993. However, the death of President Juvénal Habyarimana (a Hutu) in a plane crash sparked the genocide of Tutsis living in Rwanda by Hutus. The genocide was perpetrated by government officials and civilians incited to violence by government-owned radio programing that laid the blame of the plane crash on the Tutsi political leaders. In the one hundred days of the genocide, an estimated one million Tutsis were murdered. The violence ended when leaders of both identity groups decided to resume the power-sharing arrangement started in 1993.

SOCIAL MOVEMENTS

LEARNING OBJECTIVE

5.6 Describe the differences between traditional and new social movements and what roles they play in producing political and social change.

Trust and identity are also important ingredients in the development of another form of political behavior: the formation of and individual participation in social movements. When communities and countries face problems to solve, it is difficult to get people organized to create solutions. Why is it difficult to bring people together to start social movements? To put it another way, what are the factors that lead to the formation of social movements?

Traditional Social Movements

Social movements are a complex grouping of people acting for the goal of producing change. Traditional social movements attempt to change the politics of a country by influencing the creation of new laws, modification of existing laws, or the repeal of laws with which they disagree. Social movements are complex because there may not be a central organization attempting to produce change. There may be multiple organizations, which have similar goals and only sometimes act in a coordinated manner. There are many instances when a movement's actors and organizations advocate for using different methods to achieve the same aims.

To understand the factors that lead to the formation of social movement activity, we need to revisit a concept we covered in Chapter 1. Recall that the prisoner's dilemma game describes a situation where people do not or cannot work together even when it is beneficial to do so, resulting in a socially worst outcome. Rational individuals' acting in their self-interest prevents participation in activities that would produce collectively desirable outcomes. Participation in a social movement will incur costs such as an individual's time, among other resources. Since individuals incur a cost, they may ask themselves if contributing time and money to a cause is worth it. Will the actions that movement leaders propose really produce the change demanded? Will enough people take action to produce the change?

Another rational calculation considers if the actions of one person will really matter. If the social movement produces the needed change, but one person does not participate in getting the change, will the nonparticipating individual still benefit from the change? If the answer is yes, then a person can calculate that incurring no cost by not participating in a social movement, while getting all the benefit from the change, seems like a good deal. Scholars refer to this as the free rider problem. Individuals see an advantage in deciding not to participate in obtaining the collective good because they expect other people to participate, while still being able to take advantage of the benefits that others made possible. The free rider problem is a part of collective action problems, which we will discuss further in Chapter 7. For now, we can see that there are multiple disincentives for someone to participate.

Trust and identity are variables that may help people overcome collective action problems, such as participating in a social movement. As discussed earlier, people are more likely to work together if they share a common identity and trust each other. The common identity works as a way to recognize the members of the in-group. The identity could be racial, ethnic, religious, or sharing the same political idea that unite people under a common cause. While identity brings people together, trust will be the "glue" that keeps them together. Believing that members of the movement are true in their word and deed will offset the transaction costs of getting involved in the cause.

The abolitionist movement in the United States and western Europe from the late 1700s to the 1800s is a prime example. The movement attempted to abolish slavery around the world. The focus was generally at the national level through attempts to outlaw the practice in the movement followers' home country and its colonial possessions. Its origins began in Britain when followers of the Quaker faith and others sought to ban slavery there and in its colonies. They argued that slavery was an immoral institution that went against the ideals of the Enlightenment, which was the foundational thinking behind classical liberalism (see Chapter 3). The Enlightenment's principle that people have basic rights at birth because they are human ran against the idea that a person could hold another person against the latter's will and force the person into labor.

The abolitionist movement considered all people, regardless of their race, skin color, or place of origin, as humans and therefore endowed with these rights. The leaders, especially in the early days of the movement, were white people, whereas the enslaved peoples were mainly Black Africans (or their descendants) and native peoples. Even though the members of the movement had different skin colors, they saw their common human identity as the reason to end slavery.

The abolitionist movement achieved some success with the British ruling in *Somerset v. Stewart* (1772) in which the court ruled that since no law allowing slavery existed in Britain, it was unlawful for the institution of slavery to continue. While this ruling outlawed slavery in Britain, it did not apply to its colonies. During this time, the abolitionist movement spread to other countries that used slavery in their colonies: France, the Netherlands, Portugal, and Spain. Each practiced the enslavement of Africans or people of African descent in their colonies.

The movement attempted to outlaw slavery in the American colonies and then in the United States after independence from Britain. The U.S. branch of the movement included varied opinions on how to best abolish slavery throughout the country. Leaders of the movement included Harriet Tubman, Harriet Beecher Stowe, William Lloyd Garrison, Frederick Douglass, Henry David Thoreau, Oren Burbank Cheney, David Walker, Nat Turner, and Sojourner Truth. Some of the abolitionist movement leaders were born into slavery, whereas others were not. Some were Black and others were white. They all, however, opposed slavery on humanitarian grounds, believing that each person was a human being and therefore born free.

Again, their common human identity united them in attempting to end slavery. The major difference was that in the United States, slavery was a legally recognized institution. If you were in the U.S. South, then your abolitionist actions could be considered a criminal offense if it meant attempting to free the enslaved. As you can imagine, trusting others in the movement was critical for achieving common goals. While united in ending slavery, the people involved relied on differing methods. Some saw that the U.S. South would not change unless someone forced the Southerners through armed struggle. The idea of an armed struggle led to the creation of a more militant faction. Others advocated for changing laws at the national level. They believed armed struggle was unnecessary, and perhaps counterproductive. They preferred a legal change, using courts and changes in legislation. The social movement, therefore, carried a diversity of methods in seeking the same goal.

An example of the movement's violent methods took place before the outbreak of the American Civil War. As the geography of the United States expanded westward, the national debate centered on the expansion of slavery into the new territories and states. Armed conflict between pro- and anti-slavery groups erupted in Kansas over the debate of admitting the state into the Union as free or slave. Veterans of this fight, such as John Brown (1800–1859) and his followers, also attempted to free enslaved people in the American South by force. Brown tried to convince other leaders, such as Frederick Douglass, to join his crusade, but others did not trust in Brown's ability to achieve success. They argued that such plans were more likely to harm the movement than help it. Brown's rebellion ended quickly when he tried to capture guns and ammunition from the federal armory in Harpers Ferry, Virginia, which he wanted to use in a campaign that would spread a revolt among the enslaved throughout the South. His attempt failed and state authorities captured Brown and his followers. They tried and executed Brown for the charge of treason in 1859.

New Social Movements

Researchers note that since the end of World War II, and particularly since the late 1950s, a new set of movements have appeared. The scholars labeled them **new social movements**. New social movements differ from past social movements in that the former attempt to influence the changing of societal norms and values, as well as a country's laws and policies. Scholars note that the change in focus is due to the rise of postmaterialist values (see Chapter 4). Members of new social movements believed that unless people's attitudes changed, it would be difficult to change laws in a democracy. Furthermore, without a change in attitudes, any changes in laws would have little effect because they may not be enforceable.

For example, extending rights to those who had not enjoyed them would be meaningless in a society where individuals would not respect these new rights. This was at the core of the American civil rights movement. Although African Americans had the same constitutional rights as white Americans, they did not enjoy the same rights in real terms. Especially, but not exclusively in the U.S. South, they had unequal access to public and private resources, such as education and housing. In addition, electoral rules and overall racist attitudes limited their ability to vote.

Many see Martin Luther King Jr. as the leader of the Civil Rights movement. While he was certainly a major leader, like most other movements, there were many leaders and organizations: Congress of Racial Equality, Leadership Conference on Civil Rights, National Association for the Advancement of Colored People, Southern Christian Leadership Conference (which King led), Student Nonviolent Coordinating Committee, and Southern Student Organizing Committee, just to name a few. The movement also used a large array of tactics to achieve aims, although most of them were peaceful given their commitment to the philosophy of civil disobedience.

True to its nature as a new social movement, the Civil Rights movement achieved victories in many legal challenges and produced new laws while also focusing on changing how white people viewed Black Americans. The movement argued that until white people saw Black Americans as equal citizens, the latter would not enjoy all the political rights and economic opportunities afforded in American society due to racial discrimination. As evidenced by the formation of the Black Lives Matter movement, the early twenty-first century in the United States demonstrated that more societal change is necessary.

Black Lives Matter: From Hashtag to New Social Movement

Scholars date the end of the American Civil Rights movement with the assassination of Martin Luther King Jr. and the Civil Rights Act of 1968. It would be incorrect to assume, however, that with these events, U.S. law and practices fully guaranteed civil rights for African Americans and other people of color. In fact, events would open up new chapters in this struggle. In the early twenty-first century, advancements in technology and social media assisted in exposing and addressing institutional racism. U.S. society now could see systemic racism in action. Recall that this form of racism is a condition where societal, economic, and political institutions have embedded racist norms. Although individuals acting in these institutions may not believe themselves to be racists, the rules and policies produce uneven advantages and disadvantages based on the person's race. The focal point was the treatment of Black Americans in the judicial system, primarily in contact with law enforcement and their use of force.

The story of the Black Lives Matter (BLM) movement begins in 2013 following the murder of an Black teen, Trayvon Martin, by George Zimmerman. Zimmerman stated that he was acting in the capacity of a neighborhood watch coordinator and shot Martin in an act of self-defense under Florida's "stand-your-ground" law. The local police decided not to charge Zimmerman even though Martin did not possess a weapon, lethal or otherwise. The national news coverage of the case prompted the state of Florida to charge Zimmerman with murder through a governor-appointed special prosecutor. The jury acquitted Zimmerman in July 2013.

The acquittal sparked outrage throughout the Black community and the country as a whole. There has been a long history of violence against the African American community, with many perpetrators of this violence, specifically those who have murdered Black people, walking away without meeting justice. From the time of slavery to the lynching during the segregationist period, and to modern times, African American deaths seem to have had little value for American society and its justice system. Social media were the principal avenue of communication for voicing this anger using the hashtag #BlackLivesMatter. By including the hashtag on any statement of protest, movement members could quickly identify allies and promote their message effectively. It leapt from social media platform to street protest by the originators of the hashtag, Alicia Garza, Patrisse Cullors, and Opal Tometi. They developed a decentralized national network of local chapters of activists with no formal leadership hierarchy.

The deaths of two other Black men, Michael Brown and Eric Garner, amplified the cause further. Local law enforcement shot the unarmed 18-year-old Brown while investigating an incident of stealing candy. Garner, also unarmed, had his life ended when law enforcement placed him in a chokehold that compressed his neck, causing asphyxiation. His crime was selling loose cigarettes. Garner's death added a new item, a witness video recording of the incident on a smartphone.

The recordings of Garner's death and those of other Black Americans in the hands of law enforcement cast a large spotlight on how police routinely treated members of this community. Past incidents often pitted two stories, one voiced by the victims (if they could) and the other by the officers, with the latter often believed over the former. Video recordings provide evidence independent of personal accounts. These recordings are especially powerful on social media and often go "viral," meaning that millions of views can occur in seconds.

The latest round of national protests resulted from the death of George Floyd in 2020. A Minneapolis police officer murdered Floyd by kneeling on his neck for nine and half minutes during his arrest for the alleged charge of using a counterfeit $20 bill. Like others, Floyd did not possess a weapon. The video of the murder went viral. The media put the number of participants in nationwide protests over the Floyd murder in the tens of millions. One major protest occurred in Lafayette Square, Washington, D.C., which sits across from the White House.

BLM is a good example of a new social movement. As stated, it did not have a centralized leadership and members associated themselves with the cause instead of being part of a formal organization. One major aim of the movement is to change people's views on the role of racism in law enforcement and their use of force. It attempts to show that police officers conduct themselves in racist ways as a result of the institutionalization of racism in law enforcement. BLM activists want the mass public to also accept a potential victim's side of the story and not jump to the conclusion that a police officer's story is true. The preliminary evidence shows that there may be a societal change in this direction as indicated by the dramatic increase in the favorable public opinion given to the movement. On the policy side, the BLM movement advocates diverse changes, such as shifting funding from law enforcement to community services (also known as police defunding) and criminal justice system reforms.

Also notable is the international spread of the movement. Various European countries, Canada, Brazil, Australia, and New Zealand have active chapters. The commonality of these countries is the presence of minority groups that have had a history of abuse in the hands of law enforcement. The international movement, just like its U.S. counterpart, makes wide use of social media and witness video recordings of incidents.

SUMMARY

In this chapter, we explored modes of decision-making and human behavior in politics. One of the principal approaches to human decision-making that is commonly used is the rational actor model. The rational actor model has been an influential approach in the study of political behavior. It assumes that political actors make decisions and choose actions based on a cost-benefit analysis to maximize self-interest. The rational actor model has explained politicians' behavior reasonably well.

The chapter also elaborated on why information is an important factor. Information will guide people in the use of their values and help form attitudes before making final choices. Information comes to the average person through mass media outlets. Traditional mass media provide a one-way communication of information using print and electronic sources. We sometimes see the one-way communication method of mass media outlets present multiple views of an issue. However, some outlets have developed biased reporting and facilitated echo chambers in a country's politics. New methods of disseminating information use the technological advances through use of the internet. The innovations reduce the barriers to being a mass media outlet and make it easier for anyone to enter the industry. Their downside has been the proliferation of misinformation and further polarization of politics.

We also understand that the average person works with imperfect information on many occasions and has limited capabilities to process information. Therefore, it is unlikely that people will always use a calculated method assumed by the rational actor model. Instead, political psychology theories expect people to use limited information to satisfice through bounded rationality or by employing emotional responses. Trust is one such emotion that can help explain why people make their choices. Trust in others and their political leaders and intuitions helps promotelevels of citizen collaboration and obedience to laws without government coercion.

Another important psychological factor is an individual's most important social identity. Belonging to an in-group has the psychological benefit of enhancing a person's self-esteem. The desire to belong to and develop strong bonds within a group produces behavioral consequences such as in-group favoritism. Social identity can facilitate trust in some ways and lowers trust in others. In this way, we can see why both collaboration and conflict occur.

We also saw how trust and identity are important variables in the formation of traditional and new social movements. Identity brings people together while trust keeps them together to achieve common goals through group collaboration. We also learned that social movements are complex phenomena that include multiple organizations and leaders. Scholars distinguish new social movements from traditional ones by the former's desire to change societal attitudes as well as laws and policies.

Our exploration of political behavior is not complete. In the next set of chapters, we will examine how political regimes, governments, and institutions also play their parts.

KEY TERMS

Bounded rationality (p. 95)

Civic engagement (p. 98)

Cognitive dissonance (p. 92)

In-group favoritism (p. 100)

Mass media (p. 90)

Media echo chambers (p. 91)

New social movements (p. 106)

Political behavior (p. 88)

Political psychology (p. 88)

Political trust (p. 99)

Rational actor model (p. 94)

Satisficers (p. 95)

Social identity group (p. 100)

Social identity theory (p. 99)

Social movements (p. 104)

Social trust (p. 97)

Transaction costs (p. 97)

Trust (p. 96)

FURTHER READING

Dixit, A. K., Skeath, S., & McAdams, D. (2020). *Games of strategy* (5th ed.). Norton.

Jamieson, K. H., & Cappella, J. N. (2008). *Echo chamber: Rush Limbaugh and the conservative media establishment.* Oxford University Press.

Shepsle, K. A. (2010). *Analyzing politics: Rationality, behavior and institutions* (2nd ed.). Norton.

6 STATES, NATIONS, AND VARIETIES OF POLITICAL REGIMES

LEARNING OBJECTIVES

6.1 Describe the differences between states, nations, governments, and regimes and the relationships among them.

6.2 Identify the characteristics of modern states.

6.3 Explain how the concept of state sovereignty developed and its limits.

6.4 Identify the fundamental functions of states, the features of state capacity, and the challenges posed by weak and failed states.

6.5 Describe the differences between democratic and nondemocratic regimes, characteristics of liberal democracy, and subtypes of autocratic regimes.

Is Canada a state, a nation, or a political regime? Is democracy a state, a political regime, or a government? So far, we have loosely talked about states, nations, governments, and regimes. Indeed, many people frequently use these concepts interchangeably in casual conversations. Are they different from one another? In political science, while interrelated, they are unique and distinctive concepts. We will distinguish between these concepts in this chapter. Doing so will help us begin to address many important questions in politics, such as: What is nationalism? How do states emerge, and why do they fail? Which countries are more vulnerable to civil wars and secessionist movements? What is democracy, and how can we ensure the stability and quality of democracy? Why do certain autocracies persist, while others are vulnerable to collapse? How do governments form and endure?

WHAT IS THE STATE? STATES, NATIONS, GOVERNMENTS, AND REGIMES

LEARNING OBJECTIVE

6.1 Describe the differences between states, nations, governments, and regimes and the relationships among them.

Understanding states, nations, governments, and regimes requires us to define these concepts and identify their characteristics. We will start with the definition of the state. We will then define the nation, political regime, and government.

Defining the State

The state is a core analytic concept and one of the key areas of study in political science. The origin and development of the modern state—and its failures—have fascinated many political scientists and represents one of the main areas of concern for policymakers today. According to Republican U.S. President George W. Bush in his letter introducing the National Security Strategy in 2002, the events of September 11, 2001, "taught us that weak states, like Afghanistan, can pose as great a danger to our national interests as strong states. Poverty does not make poor people into terrorists and murderers. Yet, poverty, weak institutions, and corruption can make weak states vulnerable to terrorist networks and drug cartels within their borders" (Bush, 2002). Before becoming a U.S. president, Democrat Senator Barack Obama agreed when he said, "We know where extremists thrive: in conflict zones that are incubators of resentment and anarchy; in weak states that cannot control their borders or territories, or meet the basic needs of their people. From Africa to Central Asia to the Pacific Rim—nearly 60 countries stand on the brink of conflict or collapse" (Paddock, 2009). As these quotes demonstrate, concern for weak and failed states transcends political party identification and ideology. Failed and weak states pose serious challenges to the global community in terms of refugee flows, trafficking in illicit commodities, and peacekeeping and humanitarian assistance. Terrorists have taken advantage of weak and failed states to use as safe havens where they train, indoctrinate, recruit, gather, prepare, and support their operations.

Before we can talk about strong states, weak states, and failed states, we need to understand what a state is. One of the most cited definitions of the state is Max Weber's. According to Max Weber, a state "is a human community that (successfully) claims the monopoly of the legitimate use of physical force within a given territory" (Weber, 1918/1946, p. 78). Another often cited definition of the state is proposed by Douglas North (1981, p. 21). North defines a state in terms of taxation power: A state is "an organization with a comparative advantage in violence, extending over a geographic area whose boundaries are determined by its power to tax constituents." Charles Tilly (1985) argues that "war makes states." Successful war-making not only secures the country from external enemies but also helps the rulers disarm domestic rivals and consolidate the monopoly of coercive power in their hands. War-making also spurs the development of state institutions (such as a court system) and apparatus (such as one for tax collection). Tilly conceptualizes states as "relatively centralized, differentiated organizations, the officials of which, more or less, successfully claim control over the chief concentrated means of violence within a population inhabiting a large, contiguous territory" (Tilly, 1985, p. 170).

Although the precise definitions of states by different scholars vary, two common factors stand out. One is territory, and the other is coercive power. We define a **state** as an administrative apparatus that makes and implements public policies and uses coercive power to rule within a given territory. The idea that the state uses coercive power to rule may be alarming to people living in a democracy. Wouldn't only autocrats use coercion to rule? Aren't people free in democracies? In fact, both democratic and authoritarian states use force and other coercive power to govern. Think about why you stop at a red light when there is no car or person around you. Most likely, you stop when the traffic signal light is red because the law says the red light means stop. The law may also state that if you violate the red-light law, you will get a ticket. Making you stop at a red light, which you may not do otherwise, is a power of coercion. Assessing a fine for rule violation, sending someone to jail, sentencing a capital punishment for unlawful behavior, collecting taxes, and using the threat of punishment to force people to behave in a certain manner all involve the use or threat of coercive power.

Different states use coercion for different purposes, in different ways, to different extents, and with different effects. In the example of the law regarding traffic signals, a state uses coercive power to ensure the safety of the people. Some states collect taxes widely and heavily from the society to provide for fundamental services to ensure social rights, including education, health care, housing, and protection against unemployment. In other countries, states levy taxes from the society to enrich the ruling elite. In an autocratic country, political leaders may use violent repression to silence their opposition. All these examples involve different types of coercive power, used for different purposes and with varying degrees, producing wide-varying effects on the society. The point is that all states, democratic or autocratic, use coercive power to rule.

Although the term *state* is also often used interchangeably with the term *country,* strictly speaking, a state is an administrative entity that governs a country. For example, Brazil is a country, but you can also talk about the Brazilian state when you are referring to the administrative apparatus of the Federative Republic of Brazil.

What Is a Nation?

Although colloquially the term *nation* is often used synonymously with *state,* they are two different concepts. A **nation** refers to a group of people who perceive themselves as sharing a sense of belonging and who often have a common language, religion, culture, and/or historical experience. In short, a nation is an expression of identity. Sometimes the people of a nation may identify as belonging to a particular state, which enhances the legitimacy of the state. Some nations, such as Japan, significantly intersect with states. A country where a significant majority of its population shares the same national identity is called a **homogenous state**.

However, states may contain more than one nation. Catalonia in northeastern Spain is a nation within a state. It has a distinct history dating back almost a thousand years, and the Catalans consider themselves as distinctive and different from the rest of Spain. Another example of multiple nations within a single state comes from the United States. In the United States, there are 573 federally recognized tribes of American Indians and Alaska Natives. American Indians and Alaska Natives are members of the original Indigenous peoples of North America. Native American tribes in the United States are often referred to as nations because members of a particular tribe share a common language, history, and culture, and a sense of belonging that differs from those of other Native American tribes. Tribal nations in the United States self-govern in order to protect their culture and identity.

Some nations exist across several state borders or may occupy only part of a state. The Kurds are mostly Sunni Muslim people who share a unique language and culture and a long history of oppression. The Kurds form a nation but live across the borders of at least five states—Armenia,

Iran, Iraq, Turkey, and Syria—and have suffered oppression and discrimination and engaged in armed struggle in those countries. The Syrian government stripped 120,000 Kurds of their Syrian citizenship in the 1960s, making them stateless people who were unable to travel. The Saddam Hussein government in Iraq launched the al-Anfal ("the spoils") Kurdish genocide campaign in 1988, and killed tens of thousands of Iraqi Kurds, destroyed thousands of villages, and used chemical weapons against civilians. In Turkey, successive Turkish governments have persistently assailed Kurds on their ethnic, cultural, and religious identity and their economic and political status. The struggle between the Kurdish separatist fighters and the Turkish government's attempts to eradicate the Kurdish language and culture have led to countless arrests, imprisonments, and torture, claiming numerous lives. Kurds in Iran, viewed with suspicion and hatred as Sunni Muslims in a Shiite state, have also experienced extensive oppression.

With the dissolution of the Ottoman Empire following World War I, the Allies created the modern Middle East. Although the Treaty of Sèvres in 1920, which was not ratified, envisaged an independent state of Kurdistan, the 1923 Treaty of Lausanne created the states of Turkey, Iraq, and Syria, but ignored Kurdistan. The Kurdish territory was split among Turkey, the French mandate of Syria, the British mandate of Iraq, and Persia.

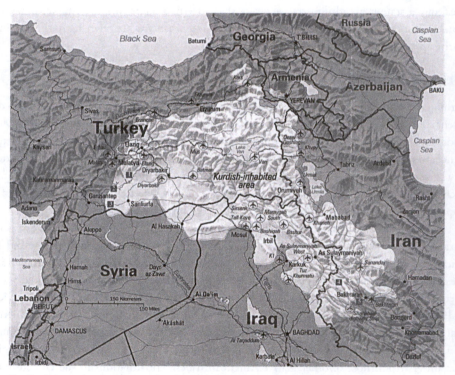

The Kurdish people, who form a nation, live across the borders of at least five states: Armenia, Iran, Iraq, Turkey, and Syria.

Image courtesy of the U.S. Central Intelligence Agency, in the public domain. https://commons.wikimedia.org/wiki/File:Kurdish-inhabited_area_by_CIA_(1992)_box_inset_removed.jpg

The Kurds are today one of the world's largest peoples without a state, making up sizable minorities in Iran, Iraq, Syria, and Turkey. For over a century, their quest for independence has met with marginalization, oppression, and repression, with no sight for the establishment of the state of Kurdistan in the near future.

Political Regimes and Governments

A state is also different from a political regime or government. A **political regime** is a set of formal and informal rules, norms, and institutions that determine how the government is organized and how governmental decisions are made. Political scientists commonly identify two broad categories of political regimes: democracies and nondemocracies. A nondemocratic regime is also called authoritarianism, autocracy, dictatorship, and the like, to refer to a general category of various types of nondemocratic regimes. Each of these broad categories is further subdivided into various groups depending on its features. For example, democracies can be classified into presidential, semi-presidential, and parliamentary regimes. Alternatively, if you wish to classify democracies based on the characteristics of political party systems, you can distinguish among dominant party, two-party, and multiparty democracies.

Arend Lijphart (2012), noticing that modern democracies are based on two competing visions of democratic ideals, developed a new typology of democracies. A **majoritarian democracy** emphasizes majority rule and is based on a concentration of power. In an ideal-type majoritarian democracy, an elected (single-party) majority has an unfettered mandate to govern within its term to implement its policies decisively. Voters evaluate government performance and use elections to hold the government accountable. If voters are dissatisfied with government performance, they elect a new majority with an unblocked mandate to govern until the next election. As you can see, a majoritarian democracy promotes government decisiveness, clarity of responsibility for policy and government performance (because policy and performance responsibility is clear since who is the majority is clear), and accountability. A majoritarian democracy seeks to advance these democratic ideals by a combination of institutions that concentrate power in the hands of a majority—plurality electoral rule, two-party system, unitary system, unicameral legislature, and so forth.

A **consensus democracy**, on the other hand, prioritizes representation and inclusiveness. It promotes the idea that democracy should represent as many citizens as possible, that a simple majority should not govern unfettered, and that power should be shared by different groups. The institutions that foster a consensus democracy include proportional representation electoral rule, multiparty system, federalism, a bicameral legislature, and other institutions that divide power among different groups. The majoritarian and consensus models of democracy are ideal types; democracies in most countries fall somewhere between these two "pure" types.

Government is also distinguishable from a political regime or state. A **government** is a set of people who have the authority to act on behalf of the state. In other words, a government is the means through which a state exercises its power and establishes and enforces policies. All but failed states and developing societies have had governments. In parliamentary systems, the head of government (often referred to as prime minister) and their cabinet comprise a government.

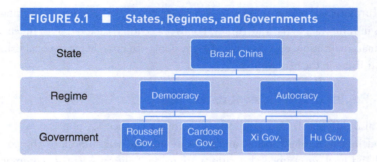

FIGURE 6.1 ■ States, Regimes, and Governments

In presidential systems, a government consists of a president and their cabinet. In the United States, government is more commonly called administration.

Generally, states are more enduring than regimes or governments. In Figure 6.1, Brazil and China are identified as states. Brazil has had both democratic and authoritarian regimes while maintaining itself as Brazil. China has been a nondemocratic country, which has gone through various types of autocratic regimes. Since 1949, China has been a dominant party dictatorship ruled by the Communist Party.

States can cease, as had happened to the Soviet Union when it broke up in 1991 and created Russia and 14 other states. However, states usually last longer than regimes. Since achieving independence in 1822, Brazil has gone through a monarchy, an oligarchy, fascism (called the *Estado Novo* or New Republic in Brazil), democracy, military rule, and the current democratic regime. Regimes are, in turn, usually (but not necessarily) more persistent than governments. It is common, and in fact expected, that in democratic countries different governments can form and depart within the same regime. For example, since democratization in 1985, Brazil has had 11 governments under the most recent democratic regime as of this writing.

EXPAND YOUR THOUGHTS

Many people believe that heterogeneous states are prone to violent internal conflict such as civil wars and coups. However, some recent research indicates that ethno-religious fractionalization of a society is not associated with a country's tendency toward violent internal conflict. Which hypothesis is more plausible? Why?

THE ELEMENTS OF THE MODERN STATE

LEARNING OBJECTIVE

6.2 Identify the characteristics of modern states.

We now understand that states are conceptually different from nations, regimes, and governments. Next, we examine the essential characteristics of modern states. Argentina, China, France, Italy, India, Iran, Nigeria, and Zimbabwe are all states. What do they have in common? Modern states have the following elements: territory, population, government, diplomatic recognition, and sovereignty. These five elements are necessary conditions; absence of any of these elements disqualifies an entity as a state. Let's take a close look at each of the essential state characteristics.

A state must have a **territory**—a geographic area with clearly defined borders separating itself from other states. States' territorial requirement may sound obvious, but it is not necessarily so in the reality of many states and non-state communities. Territory can change through independence, secession, acquisition, and other means. Many disputed borders also exist in the world. For example, India, Pakistan, and China currently dispute the ownership of Kashmir, which is in the northernmost geographic region of the Indian subcontinent. Border disputes do not automatically disqualify a political community as a state so long as most of the land it claims is accepted by the international community of states as comprising its national territory. India, Pakistan, and China are all recognized as states. However, some cases do not have recognized national territories.

The case of the Kurdish nation and Kurdistan discussed earlier is an example of a nation without a state with internationally accepted national boundaries. Another example of a nation without a state is the Palestinian Arabs. When Jews established the state of Israel in 1948 and fought wars with their Arab neighbors, Palestinians were displaced. Palestinians now have a strong commitment to establishing their own state. Due to ongoing disputes with Israel, they do not command a geographic area that they can call their territory with clear borders.

Every state also has people within its borders. A state may be relatively homogeneous in its population composition with an overlapping national and state identity among its inhabitants. A state can also be a multinational state where many ethnic, religious, or other identity groups exist within its borders. Such states are called **heterogeneous states**. Today, news of insurgencies, terrorism, secessionist struggles, and other civil strife come from countries where multiple identity groups reside. You may wonder if having multiple identity groups inevitably undermines state stability. In fact, the rise in civil wars and other types of internal conflict since the end of the World War II has often been attributed to ethnic fractionalization in societies (i.e., the degree to which a society is divided into different ethnic groups). However, the presence of multiple identity groups within a single state does not necessarily weaken the state or cause its breakup. For example, the United States is sometimes referred to as a melting pot due to its multicultural society consisting of different nationalities, ethnicities, and other forms of identities. Despite having those identities, people in the United States have also developed a strong sense of shared identity: being American. Thus, the existence of multiple identity groups does not automatically threaten or challenge the state. On the other hand, strong national consciousness and loyalty to a group that differs from the state in which people live have led to demands of greater autonomy or even secession from the state.

The third element of statehood is government. As discussed previously, government, which usually comprises a head of government and a cabinet, is the means through which state power is exercised and state policy is determined and carried out. Government may be democratic or autocratic, or elected or unelected, but all states have a single national government that makes, implements, and enforces state policies. Heads of state and government also represent their states in international affairs. The degree of legitimacy that a government has in the society and the amount of resources at its disposal vary considerably, which in turn impacts the effectiveness of the government in producing desired outcomes. As we will see in the next section of this chapter, those factors at least partially determine whether a state is strong or weak. An utter dearth of government legitimacy and/or resources can lead to a state failure.

For a political community to be considered a state, it also must be sovereign. **Sovereignty** refers to states' authority to govern autonomously over a given territory. Colonies, such as India under Britain and Brazil under Portugal, became states only after they achieved formal independence. States' subnational units, such as California in the United States, Buenos Aires in Argentina, and Catalonia in Spain, are not states in the international community because they lack sovereignty. Historically, the international community viewed the concept of national sovereignty as absolute in the sense that one state could not interfere in the affairs of another state. However, we have seen increased debate and transformation of this view since the mid-twentieth century.

Finally, whether a political community can achieve a state status is really a political decision by other countries in the international community. It must obtain, and retain, **diplomatic recognition** by the international community of states, especially by the more powerful ones, that it is a sovereign state. This happens when the community of states legally recognizes it as the sole legitimate governing authority within its territory and as legally equal to other states. With diplomatic recognition come the exchanging of ambassadors and opening of embassies. Most major international governmental organizations, such as the United Nations, also require as a condition of membership that countries be recognized by the international community as sovereign states.

The Palestine Liberation Organization (PLO) has aimed to gain the international recognition of statehood since the Palestinian Declaration of Independence proclaimed the establishment of the State of Palestine in November 1988. Within a year, more than 80 countries recognized the proclaimed state. As of 2021, 137 of the 193 United Nations member states and two nonmember states have recognized the State of Palestine. However, Israel, the United States, Canada, Japan, Republic of Korea, Mexico, Australia, New Zealand, most of the European Union member states, and other countries have not recognized Palestine as a state.

In contrast, the international community of states quickly recognized the independence of East Timor. East Timor, located in Southeast Asia, was a Portuguese colony and gained independence in November 1975. However, Indonesia invaded East Timor shortly after its independence and annexed the territory as its 27th province. Despite heavy investments by the Indonesians in East Timor and robust economic growth over the next 20 years, resistance to the Indonesian occupation continued by the Timorese, who were determined to preserve their culture and national identity. A United Nations (UN)-sponsored referendum took place in August 1999, in which an overwhelming majority of East Timorese voted for independence from Indonesia. Immediately following the referendum, anti-independence Timorese militias, organized and supported by the Indonesian military, commenced a widespread campaign that resulted in the death of approximately 1,400 Timorese, forced dislocation of approximately 300,000 people into West Timor as refugees, and the destruction of most of the country's infrastructure. In September 1999, the multinational, non-UN-sponsored International Force for East Timor led by Australia was deployed to end the violence. Following an UN-administered transition period, the Democratic Republic of Timor-Leste was internationally recognized as an independent state on May 20, 2002.

PRACTICAL APPLICATION

Conduct research on the Republic of China (also known as Taiwan). Is it a state? Why or why not?

PRACTICAL APPLICATION

Consider Somaliland. Is it a state? Why or why not?

THE DEVELOPMENT AND LIMITS OF STATE SOVEREIGNTY

LEARNING OBJECTIVE

6.3 Explain how the concept of state sovereignty developed and its limits.

Have states always been sovereign? One of the required elements of a modern state is sovereignty. However, the idea of the state having the exclusive power to govern within their territory free from external interference is somewhat of a new concept, considering the length of human history. Moreover, since the end of World War II, the international community has challenged and questioned the ability of states to be truly sovereign.

Traditionally, the ability of a state to maintain its sovereignty depended in large part on the level of its military power. Throughout history, strong military powers were on the quest to build empires. As a result, a state that was weaker would either be fully conquered or incorporated into the empire, with the imperial state having strict control over it. This was the practice on almost every continent. Therefore, in highly competitive parts of the world, states were only as sovereign as they were powerful. Some would argue that this is still the case. Weaker states often need to bend to the will of stronger ones.

After the fall of the Roman Empire and the rise of Christianity in Europe, a new phenomenon developed. The empire's collapse produced a large number of new monarchies with one practice in common: Each monarch obeyed the commands of the Roman Catholic Church through its leader, the Pope. This obedience was required since their ability to rule depended on the Pope's approval. Upsetting the Pope could mean excommunication from the Church, which would end their right to rule. Obedience, therefore, limited their ability to be absolute state rulers. In fact, they could often not marry unless the Pope approved. The Church could also tax the nobility and operate as an independent law enforcement agency within the monarch's borders. In sum, during these times, there were two ruling powers operating in a European country, a secular power and a spiritual power.

The two powers' level of authority started to shift when Martin Luther, a German Catholic cleric, began the Protestant Reformation in 1517. The Reformation challenged the foundational ideas behind the Catholic Church's teachings, such as the absolute authority of the clergy, including the Pope. In very brief terms, Luther stated that one could be a good Christian even if one did not obey the Pope. His ideas started a wave of Protestantism throughout Europe, one that some monarchs took advantage of. Once kingdoms converted to Protestantism by establishing their own churches, monarchs governed spiritually as the head of their own churches. In other words, they now had sovereignty over all lawmaking and law enforcement, both secular and spiritual, within their territory.

As one would imagine, the Catholic Church's leadership was not happy about this. The Pope excommunicated all clergy that adopted Protestant beliefs (especially Martin Luther) and all monarchs that established their own churches. With this, the Pope gave his blessing to all Catholic monarchs to wage wars against the Protestant kingdoms because their monarchs no longer had the right to rule. Victory meant expanding the kingdoms that were still loyal to the Pope.

The Thirty Years' War (1618–1648) between the Catholic and Protestant monarchs ended with two peace treaties that are collectively known as the Treaty of Westphalia. The treaty established the modern concept of state sovereignty because each kingdom was allowed the right to establish its own religion (so long as it was based in Christianity) and kingdoms agreed not to interfere in each other's domestic affairs. The treaty therefore outlawed states from starting wars because they did not like how another state conducted their governance. Monarchs were sovereign in their territory. The idea that states would not interfere in the internal affairs of other states lasted for about three hundred years.

The twentieth century witnessed new challenges to state sovereignty and created limitations to states' powers. At the end of World War II, the Allied countries put on trial the former leaders of Japan and Nazi Germany for war crimes and crimes against humanity. Each of the top leaders claimed that their trials were not valid since the accused leaders operated as a sovereign state. They argued that all the laws, including ones that killed millions of innocent people, were created using legitimate government processes. The claim of sovereignty meant that the Allied powers could not interfere in their domestic affairs and could not convict them.

The tribunal judges of the Nuremburg and Tokyo Trials disagreed. They ruled that sovereign states could not create laws that violated universal basic human rights and that the international community was empowered to bring in humanitarian intervention as necessary to stop and punish such violations. This doctrine was applied again at the International Criminal Tribunal for Rwanda (1994–2015) and the International Criminal Tribunal for the former Yugoslavia (1993–2017). It formed the basis for establishing the International Criminal Court in 1998. Therefore, today national leaders are accountable for violations of international law governing human rights and cannot defend such violations under the cover of state sovereignty.

STRONG, WEAK, AND FAILED STATES

LEARNING OBJECTIVE

6.4 Identify the fundamental functions of states, the features of state capacity, and the challenges posed by weak and failed states.

Not all countries have functioning states. You may have heard policymakers talking about countries like Somalia and Syria as "failed states." Some countries are considered "strong" states and others as "weak" states. Earlier in the chapter, we saw U.S. President George W. Bush and Senator Barack Obama expressing concern about "weak states." What do they mean? What are the characteristics of strong, weak, and failed states, and what makes states strong or weak, or even fail? Why should the international community care about state failures?

States use their institutions and resources to provide political goods to their population. According to Robert Rotberg (2004), **political goods** include security, the rule of law, a functioning legal system, and infrastructure, such as roads, public education, and health care. Citizens also expect modern states to provide and promote economic prosperity and help enhance the population's well-being in general. From these expected roles of a modern state, we can define a strong and a weak state as follows. A **strong state** is a state that is generally capable of providing adequate political goods and economic well-being to its citizens. Most developed countries, such as Australia, France, Japan, the United Kingdom, and the United States, meet the criteria of strong states. A **weak state** is a state that insufficiently provides political goods or economic well-being to its citizens. Many developing or poor countries belong to this category because they cannot provide adequate economic well-being to their populations. Additionally, many of those countries do not provide sufficient political goods. In practice, however, strong and weak states are more appropriately considered on a continuum where most countries fall somewhere between the strong and weak state marks.

At the lowest end of the continuum is the failed state. **Failed states** effectively have no recognized or accepted national government that can enforce policy. The state is so weak that it virtually loses control over part or all of its territory and is unable to make its inhabitants obey. For example, countries in civil war are failed states because states cannot coerce and are unable to control the inhabitants successfully in their territories. Recent examples of failed states include Afghanistan, Somalia, Congo, and Syria, among others. In essence, failed states are quasi-state entities because they do not meet the characteristics of modern states in major ways.

There is a growing international concern about weak states and state failures, as epitomized by the 2002 U.S. National Security Strategy issued by U.S. President George W. Bush discussed at the beginning of this chapter. Failed states often serve as breeding grounds for international terrorism and destabilize world peace. Somalia's lack of a state has led to an increase in terrorist activity by al-Shabab and piracy by various actors in the northwestern Indian Ocean. Significant human miseries due to the lack of security, food, and shelter have also been documented in weak and failed states. Such miseries produce large migrations of refugees that overwhelm neighboring states. This has been the case of European states being unable to accept people from the Middle East and North Africa. Some scholars associate weak states with a type of colonial rule and the way states achieved independence.

Many political scientists have also identified what is known as a **resource curse** as a potential cause of weak and failed states. Contrary to the common belief, according to this perspective, having significant amounts of natural resources, such as oil and diamonds, is not a blessing but rather a curse for economic development, democracy, and political stability. States with significant revenue from mineral extraction do not need to tax the population, producing government that is unaccountable to the people. Those resources are also lootable resources. Revenues from such resources not only create an incentive and opportunities for corruption, but rebels also have an incentive to try to control minerals, which occasionally leads to civil war.

EXPAND YOUR THOUGHTS

What do you think are potential determinants of state strengths and state failures? Many factors may influence state strengths and failures. What would be the most important cause of state strengths?

VARIETIES OF POLITICAL REGIMES

LEARNING OBJECTIVE

6.5 Describe the differences between democratic and nondemocratic regimes, characteristics of liberal democracy, and subtypes of autocratic regimes.

Are democracies more adept at economic growth than dictatorships? What factors increase the probability that a dictatorship will become a democracy? What types of political regimes are more likely to end up in failed states? There are many interesting and pressing questions related to political regimes. To be able to answer these and other questions, we need to conceptualize and measure political regimes and their varieties. Regime classification represents an important first step in this endeavor.

The most fundamental contemporary categorization of political regimes distinguishes democracies from nondemocracies (see Figure 6.2). In this approach, scholars typically begin by enumerating the basic defining elements of democratic regimes and classifying states that meet all those elements as democracies. Others that do not meet all or some of the necessary elements are classified as nondemocracies. The nondemocratic category may be called dictatorship, autocracy, or authoritarian regimes. Classifying political regimes requires clear conceptualization of each regime type.

EXPAND YOUR THOUGHTS

For you, what is democracy? How do you define it? What characteristics are fundamental in democratic regimes? Compare your answer to the subsequent discussion of democracy in this chapter.

Conceptualizing Democracy

Conceptualization of democracy starts with how we understand what democracy is. There are two different views of democracy: substantive and procedural. The **substantive view** classifies political regimes in terms of the outcomes that they engender, whereas the **procedural view** emphasizes institutions, rules, and procedures that govern political competition and citizens' rights. To understand the differences between the two, it is helpful to consider what rights citizens may have. Broadly speaking, citizens may have three types of rights. **Civil rights** refer to individual freedom and fair treatment. This includes the rule of law, freedom of expression, freedom of association, and other freedoms. **Political rights** are the rights of citizens to political participation and include such fundamental rights as the right to vote and the right to

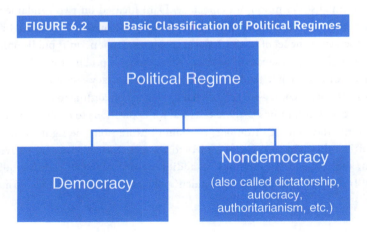

FIGURE 6.2 ■ Basic Classification of Political Regimes

Political Regime

Democracy

Nondemocracy
(also called dictatorship, autocracy, authoritarianism, etc.)

compete for elective office. **Social rights** are the rights of citizens to socioeconomic well-being. These rights may include, for example, public education, pensions, employment, decent wages, national health care, and so forth. Societies, groups, and individuals differ in their views about what should constitute social rights and to what extent the state should assume the role of providing or guaranteeing those goods to its citizens. The substantive view essentially argues that democracy should secure social rights of the people and that countries should be judged based on the extent to which they guarantee and deliver those outcomes.

However, people tend to differ in their views about what should constitute social rights and to what extent the state should assume the role of providing or guaranteeing those goods to its citizens. For example, in the United States some argue that health care is people's essential social right, and the government must ensure that everyone has access to decent health care services. Others vigorously oppose that view. Another example is the right to bear arms: What right do people really have with respect to weapons? There is a sharp divide in the U.S. public's opinions on this and other issues. The controversies and highly tense and polarized nature of discussion concerning these and many other social issues make the point: There are significant disagreements over what constitutes social rights and the role of government in the society. If people cannot agree on what social rights are and the role of government in their society, how are we to judge countries based on the **substantive view of democracy**?

The procedural view, on the other hand, classifies political regimes more objectively, in terms of their institutions and procedures to safeguard citizens' political and civil rights. The procedural view does not consider the provision of social rights as an essential characteristic of democracy but instead focuses on the rules, institutions, and procedures that govern competition for public office and ensure citizens' participation in the political process. This is the approach commonly adopted today by political scientists, many governments, and international organizations. Researchers developed many different classification schemes of democracy based on the procedural definitions of democracy. They are often referred to as minimalist because they strip down political regime characteristics to the most basic institutional features that define democracy.

However, how minimal the required components are varies substantially among different classification schemes. Robert Dahl (1971), half a century ago, proposed one of the most influential minimalist definition of democracy. Dahl focused on two fundamental dimensions of democracy—contestation for office and broad participation of citizens—and defined political democracy as the set of institutional arrangements that permits public opposition and establishes the right to participate in politics. Since his conceptualization of democracy does not encompass all that people tend to associate with democracy—it emphasizes institutions and rules rather than outcomes—Dahl called it **polyarchy**. According to Dahl, polyarchy must have seven necessary conditions that are essential for oppositions to compete and take office: freedom to form and join organizations, freedom of expression, the right to vote, eligibility for public office, the right of political leaders to compete for support, alternative sources of information, and free and fair elections. In addition, Dahl added an eighth requirement for polyarchies: Institutions that make government policies depend on various forms of citizen preferences.

More recently, Przeworski and his colleagues (Alvarez et al., 1996) developed a new classification of political regimes based on only one of the two underlying theoretical constructs of polyarchy: contestation for public office. According to these authors, a country is a democracy if it meets all of the following conditions: (a) The chief executive is elected, (b) the legislature is elected, (c) there is more than one party competing in elections, and (d) there has been an alternation in power under identical electoral rules. Otherwise, a country is a dictatorship. This definition of democracy is truly minimal; it does not consider the other theoretical constructs of Dahl's polyarchy, that is, broad participation of citizens. One of the key institutions of modern democracies that enable citizens' broad participation in political processes is universal adult suffrage. Przeworski and his colleagues' minimalist definition does not even consider this fundamental political right as a necessary requirement for democracy. This may be surprising to you—how can a country be considered a democracy without guaranteeing all adults the right to vote?

As we will see in Chapter 11, the meaning of democracy and its institutional attributes have evolved over time. Universal adult suffrage—or the right of practically all adult populations to vote—is a relatively recent phenomenon in the history of democratic regimes. Not including participation in the conceptualization of political democracy has at least two advantages. First, it allows researchers to ask questions related to how variables of political contestation, such as the competitiveness of elections, may lead to the expansion of suffrage. Second, focusing on contestation enables researchers to compare democratic regimes across long periods. There are various ways to conceptualize and define democracy. What is important is that researchers use the definition of democracy that is appropriate given the kind of questions they investigate.

In Chapter 8 we will discuss finer classifications of subcategories of democratic regimes based on political institutions (e.g., parliamentary vs. presidential democracies). In the following section, we focus on a standard definition and criteria of democracy in today's world—liberal democracy.

Liberal Democracy

When scholars, politicians, and governmental and nongovernmental organizations talk about democracy, they usually mean **liberal democracy**. This notion of democracy combines the idea of popular rule (literally so, as *demo* means people and *cracy* means rule in Greek) and liberalism, which is concerned with the protection of individual rights and liberty. Liberal democracy is based on a **procedural view of democracy** and thus emphasizes institutions, rules, and procedures that govern political competition and participation as well as the protection of civil liberties.

Political Rights

The two pillars of liberal democracy are political rights and civil liberties. Political rights include universal adult suffrage; the right to run for elected office; free, fair, and competitive elections; periodic elections; and equality in voting.

Universal adult suffrage gives the right to vote to all adults in a society. Denial of the right to vote based on race, ethnicity, sex, socioeconomic status, or educational attainment violates the fundamental principle of democracy—rule by the people. How universal the universality of adult suffrage is can be nuanced. For example, in most U.S. states, convicted felons do not have the right to vote after being released from prison. In most countries, the right to vote is generally limited to citizens of the country. Nonetheless, many countries extend voting rights to noncitizen residents in some limited capacity, such as the right to vote only in certain local elections. A few countries, such as New Zealand and Uruguay, grant noncitizen permanent or long-term residents the right to vote in national elections. These examples show that universal adult suffrage is not literally universal. However, the fundamental principle still stands: All liberal democracies must achieve nearly universal adult enfranchisement, subject only to minor exceptions.

In addition, liberal democracies must also guarantee near universality of the **right to compete for elective office**. What use would it be if all adult citizens have the right to vote but only individuals from a particular socioeconomic status, a particular racial group, a particular sex, or a particular region could run for public office in elections? In a liberal democracy, the right to compete for elective office needs to be guaranteed for practically all adult citizens without discrimination.

Free, fair, and competitive elections are also requirements of a liberal democracy. A **free election** refers to the right of voters to cast their votes for the candidates or the parties of their choice, free of constraints or coercion. For example, if incumbent politicians threaten voters that they would lose their jobs if they do not vote for them, it would be a violation of the free election principle.

A **fair election** guarantees all candidates and parties the right to compete on a level-playing field. It does not mean that all candidates or parties have equal chances of winning—naturally, candidates' qualifications and ideas differ so their appeals to the voters should also vary. Rather, it is to ensure that no candidates or parties are systematically advantaged or disadvantaged in a way to skew the outcomes of elections. This includes equal application of electoral rules and procedures for all, but also those rules and procedures themselves must be fair. For example, if candidates of the governing party are allowed to have television advertisements, then this right cannot be denied to opposition candidates.

A **competitive election** ensures that voters have meaningful choices. At minimum, there must be two candidates from at least two different political parties. If there is only one candidate in an election, then the election is not competitive. In dictatorships where the ruler runs uncontested, the election is not considered competitive and thus is not democratic. However, the existence of meaningful choices is also important. Therefore, elections are not considered competitive if they happen in countries where the ruling party has a monopoly or near-monopoly of political representation.

Consider the Democratic People's Republic of Korea (North Korea) where elections occur every four to five years for the Supreme People's Assembly (SPA), the country's national legislature. Although multiple parties exist in the country, they participate in the ruling Democratic Front for the Reunification of Korea led by the Workers' Party of Korea. According to official reports, voter turnout in national legislative elections in North Korea is nearly 100 percent, with 100 percent or nearly 100 percent of the voters approving the Democratic Front's candidates, and the Democratic Front wins 100 percent of the legislative seats. North Korea's elections do not meet the competitive election requirements because voters do not enjoy meaningful choices (all parties are in the ruling Democratic Front alliance), and the outcomes of elections are clearly foreseeable.

PRACTICAL APPLICATION
MULTIPARTY ELECTIONS AND COMPETITIVE ELECTIONS

Mexico has had various political parties in its contemporary political history. Multiple parties have participated in presidential, state, and local elections in much of the twentieth century. During the twentieth century, the Institutional Revolutionary Party (*Partido Revolucionario Institucional*, PRI) acted as the hegemonic party, winning every presidential election since 1929 (see Table 6.1) and ruled the country for 71 uninterrupted years. During this period, candidates from opposition parties also competed in presidential elections. However, most observers of democracy did not consider Mexico to be fully democratic until 2000. Many analysts considered that Mexico was in violation of the democratic requirement of competitive elections. However, candidates from multiple opposition parties competed in most of the presidential elections, so why did Mexico not meet the competitive election requirement?

The competitive election requirement in fact does not require that a democratic election be a close race. In many democratic countries, we have instances where candidates won by significant margins over their rivals. Moreover, the Mexican presidential elections of 1988

TABLE 6.1 ■ Mexican Presidential Elections, 1929–2018

Mexican Presidential Elections		
Election year	**Winner**	**Winner's Party**
1929	Pascual Ortiz Rubio	PNR (PRI)
1934	Lázaro Cárdenas	PNR (PRI)
1940	Manuel Ávila Camacho	PRM (PRI)
1946	Miguel Alemán Valdés	PRI
1952	Adolfo Ruiz Cortines	PRI
1958	Adolfo López Mateos	PRI
1964	Gustavo Díaz Ordaz	PRI
1970	Luis Echeverría Álvarez	PRI
1976	José López Portillo	PRI
1982	Miguel de la Madrid	PRI
1988	Carlos Salinas de Gortari	PRI
1994	Ernesto Zedillo	PRI
2000	Vicente Fox	PAN
2006	Felipe Calderón	PAN
2012	Enrique Peña Nieto	PRI
2018	Andrés Manuel López Obrador	MORENA

and 1994 were relatively close elections with, according to the official counts, the ruling PRI candidates receiving only 50.7 percent and 48.6 percent of the total vote, respectively. Therefore, closeness of electoral contests was not the issue.

What many analysts look for is the *ex ante* ("before the event") uncertainty of election outcomes. We may have as many candidates or parties as there may be, but if the system is so rigged that the winner of the election is predetermined, then we cannot regard the election as competitive. Nominally fulfilling the multiparty competition requirement without substance is not sufficient for a country to claim democratic status. In the case of Mexico, there were many accusations of electoral fraud committed by the ruling party, and people knew that the PRI candidates would win the presidential elections before they ever took place. It was not until 2000 that a candidate from an opposition party, the National Action Party (*Partido Acción Nacional*, PAN) won the presidential election and power was peacefully transferred. In that year, Mexico was finally recognized as a democracy.

Liberal democracies must hold elections regularly; that is, they require **periodic elections**. There are autocrats who come to power through democratic elections, but once in power, cancel future elections or hold flawed and noncompetitive elections. In liberal democracies, elections occur at regular intervals. For example, in the United States, presidential elections happen every four years, elections to the House of Representatives every two years, and elections to the Senate are staggered elections occurring every two years for a term of six years. In Japan where a parliamentary system of government is used, general elections to the House of Representatives—the more powerful lower house of the country's national bicameral legislature from which the head of government is chosen—are held at least every four years (elections occur earlier if the lower house is dissolved). On the other hand, elections to the House of Councillors (the upper house) in Japan are held every three years to choose half of its members for fixed six-year terms.

Finally, liberal democracy requires adherence to the principle of the **equal vote**. Often referred to as the standard of "one person, one vote," in liberal democracy, the equal vote requires that the value and weight of the votes of all voters be equal, regardless of race, ethnicity, sex, socioeconomic status, or any other condition.

Civil Liberties

In addition to political rights, liberal democracy also requires the rule of law and the protection of fundamental civil rights, such as the freedom of expression and freedom of association. The **rule of law** is the principle that all people and institutions, including members of government, are subject to and accountable to the law and that there is a fair application and enforcement of the law. In states where the rule of law exists, fundamental rights, including the security of persons and property, are protected from both nongovernmental and governmental actors. In nondemocratic countries, the government is unfortunately often the violator of the rule of law. There can also be societal groups and other non-state actors that violate the rule of law in the form of violent insurgency movements, terrorist acts, drug and human trafficking, and other criminal activities.

According to the Universal Declaration of Human Rights, **freedom of expression** is the right of everyone "to hold opinions without interference and to seek, receive and impart information and ideas through any media and regardless of frontiers" (United Nations, 1948, Article 19). People in nondemocratic countries face restrictions on this right imposed by the government through various measures such as media censorship, regulation, and monopoly of information by state media. Autocratic governments tend not to tolerate criticism. In recent years, the Chinese government has elevated the crackdown and arrests of the activists in Hong Kong critical of Beijing policies. In nondemocratic countries especially, complicity and absence of public criticism does not necessarily mean that the government has the support of citizens. Fearing persecution and repression, many people stay silent or even pretend that they support the autocratic leaders. Because of this, it is difficult to measure the true level of societal support that governments have in nondemocratic countries.

Freedom of association is the right of people to peaceful assembly and association. It guarantees not only the right to form and join organizations; it also guarantees the right to choose not to join organizations. With this right, workers can form and join labor unions, businesses can pursue their interests with a collective voice through their trade associations, and environmentalists can join nongovernmental organizations (e.g., the Sierra Club or Greenpeace) to seek environmental protection. Freedom of association is also crucial in politics because it protects the right to form and join (or not to join) political parties.

In sum, political rights and civil liberties requirements are necessary conditions. That means that all of these elements must be present for a state to be considered a liberal democracy.

PRACTICAL APPLICATION

Pick one country in each of the following categories: low income, middle income, and high income. Do they meet the criteria of liberal democracy? Make sure that you examine each element of political rights and civil liberties.

Nondemocratic Regimes

Regimes that are not democratic go under various labels, such as dictatorship, autocracy, authoritarianism, or some other term. These are general terms that refer to **nondemocratic regimes** and are often synonyms. So far, we have focused on understanding the elements of democracy and classified regimes that do not meet democracy requirements as nondemocracies. However, there are significant variations within nondemocratic regimes regarding the characteristics of the rulers and institutions and how they exercise and maintain power. While there are multiple ways to classify nondemocratic regimes, Barbara Geddes et al. (2014) offer one useful classification scheme using a four-way classification of autocratic regimes: monarchy, dominant party rule, military regime, and personalist rule (see Figure 6.3).

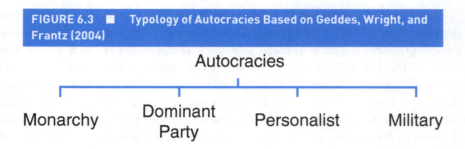

FIGURE 6.3 ■ Typology of Autocracies Based on Geddes, Wright, and Frantz (2004)

Monarchy

Monarchy is a regime where the effective head of government relies on kin and a family network to come to power and stay in power. The royal family typically controls succession. Examples include Qatar and Saudi Arabia. The King of Saudi Arabia, Salman bin Abdulaziz, is the monarchial head of state and head of government of Saudi Arabia and holds absolute power.

Are all monarchies authoritarian? The simple answer is no. There is a major difference between the authoritarian type, often referred to as an **absolute monarchy**, and a democratic **constitutional monarchy**. An absolute monarchy possesses authority not subject to checks by any other individual, group, or institutions, be it legislative, judicial, religious, economic, or electoral. A monarch in a democratic regime is generally a figurehead performing only ceremonial roles. The true lawmaking and law enforcement power in a democratic constitutional monarchy is in the hands of elected officials.

A Closer Look: Absolute Monarchies and Democratic Constitutional Monarchies

For thousands of years, absolute monarchs governed civilizations around the world in one form or another. The unchecked power of the monarchs to make laws and enforce them as they see fit characterized such regimes. In these regimes, monarchs were above the law. This tremendous power still remains in a few parts of the world while others transformed monarchs into figurehead powers.

The legitimacy of such power in the hands of a single person usually comes from a religious doctrine with the top religious leaders giving the approval for a monarch's right to rule. Clerics ordain absolute monarchs as representatives of a deity and therefore possessing the right to rule in its name. The ordination is usually the result of a major military victory by the monarch or one of the monarch's ancestors many generations ago. In religions that worship many deities, monarchs are often viewed as gods and therefore worshiped as such. In the ancient days of Egypt, for example, a pharaoh was given this status. However, few monarchs exist today as "God's Representatives." These cases include states like Oman, Saudi Arabia, and Eswatini.

In many places that have retained their monarchies, they have been transformed into figurehead or ceremonial positions as the states transitioned to democracy. Their authority is symbolic given that they follow the will of the democratic institutions. Sometimes the transition was gradual, as was the case in the United Kingdom. Over time, various governments passed laws that transferred the monarch's absolute power to the democratically elected parliament. In others, a dramatic change in the regime transferred this power to elected institutions while keeping the monarch's position.

Why would people want to keep these monarchs in their weak positions of power and pass on their titles and privileges to their descendants? If they are true democracies, why would these countries have unelected individuals in place with all the tax money needed to maintain their luxurious lifestyles? The answer usually points to the royal families' value as a fundamental part of the societies' cultures. Such societies see their monarchs as apolitical representatives of the country and therefore a critical symbol of unity. As a result, they often possess final signatory power on all laws, even if they usually automatically accept decisions made by democratically elected governments. Sometimes, these monarchs step into the political scene during times of crisis because people see them as legitimate problem-solvers. This was the case when King Juan Carlos I of Spain transitioned his country to democracy after decades of authoritarian rule by General Francisco Franco.

Many European states are democratic constitutional monarchies (e.g., Belgium, Denmark, and Sweden). Outside of Europe, many states still tie themselves to the British monarchy (e.g., Australia, Canada, and New Zealand). Constitutional monarchies—some democratic and some not democratic—also exist in Asia (e.g., Bhutan, Cambodia, Japan, and Malaysia).

Military Regime

A **military regime** is where the military rules as an institution. It is important to note that having a military leader as the head of government or having a politicized military backing the ruler does not necessarily classify the country as a military regime. In a military regime, a group of high-ranking officers hold power, determine who will steer the country, and exercise influence over policy. Consider the case of Brazil between 1964 and 1985. After ousting a civilian president in 1964 in a coup, the military, under the leadership of successive military generals as the country's presidents, ruled the country until 1985. The military generals who acted as presidents followed rules of succession and term limit, and power changed hands peacefully among military generals.

Dominant Party Rule

Dominant party rule is a regime in which a single party dominates political office and policy decisions. In dominant party dictatorships, the ruling party tends to control many aspects of the society, and membership in the party is required to achieve any political ambition. The political elites are typically members of the central organ of the ruling party, which may be called the central committee, politburo, or secretariat. The Communist Party rule in the Soviet Union and the rule by the Institutional Revolutionary Party (PRI) in Mexico until 2000 are examples of dominant party regimes. In the case of the Soviet Union, its constitution stated that only members of the party could hold office. In Mexico, a combination of institutional incentives and electoral manipulation kept the PRI in power (see the Practical Application box at the end of this section).

Personalist Rule

Personalist rule is rule by a dictator unconstrained by other groups or institutions, such as political parties or the military. The ruler, whether military or civilian, controls all policy decisions and the selection of regime personnel. Typically, dictators deliberately weaken parties and the military to prevent challenges to their rule. Personalist regimes tend to have a weak press, employ strong secret police, apply force arbitrarily, and sometimes rely on the cult of personality. Iraq under Saddam Hussein is an example of a personalist regime. Saddam played an important role in the 1968 coup that brought the Iraqi Ba'ath Party to power. While serving as vice president for General Ahmed Hassan al-Bakr, Saddam established security forces through which he repressed opposition and controlled conflicts between the government and the military. By the time he formally became president in 1979, Saddam had consolidated his authority over the state apparatus. Saddam ruled the country with repression, nepotism, and clientelism until 2003 when a coalition led by the United States invaded Iraq to depose him. Other examples of personalist regimes include the regime of Ferdinand Marcos in the Philippines (1966–1986) and the rule by Muammar Gaddafi in Libya (1969–2011).

Autocratic Regimes in the Post–World War II Era

Figure 6.4 presents the number of autocratic regimes in each category since 1946 based on Geddes et al. (2014) *Autocratic Regime Data*. Dominant party regimes predominated the

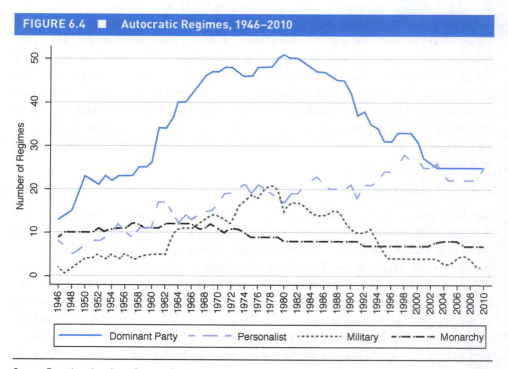

FIGURE 6.4 ■ Autocratic Regimes, 1946–2010

Source: Based on data from Geddes, B., Wright, J., & Frantz, E. (2014). Autocratic breakdown and regime transitions: A new data set. *Perspectives on Politics, 12*(2), 313–331.

autocratic regimes in the post–World War II period, reaching the peak of approximately 50 dominant party regimes in the 1970 and the first half of the 1980s. The dominant party type accounted for more than half of the autocratic regimes in much of the post–World War II era. However, since the late 1980s the autocratic regime type steadily declined. In 2010, there were 25 dominant party regimes, which was 42 percent of all autocratic regimes.

Likewise, the world share of military regimes has declined over time. After reaching 22 military regimes in 1978, this regime type continued to decrease. By 1995, military regimes became the least common type of authoritarian regimes, accounting for less than 7 percent of all the autocracies in the world. In 2010, the share of military regimes further dropped, accounting for only 3 percent (or two military regimes) of the world's autocracies.

In contrast, both the number and share of personalist regimes increased in the post–World War II period. In 1946, there were eight personalist regimes, or one-quarter of all autocratic regimes at that time. By 1998, 39 percent (28 countries) were personalist regimes. By the beginning of the twenty-first century, personalist regimes, along with dominant party regimes, became the most common type of autocracies. Finally, monarchies have demonstrated quite a resilience. The number and share of monarchies have been remarkably stable during the post–World War II period compared to the other types of autocratic regimes. Although the share of monarchies fell in the 20 years following the war, this decline was not due to a decreasing number of monarchies. In fact, the number of monarchies increased from eight in 1946 to 12 by the late 1950s. However, the overall number of autocracies in the world also rose more rapidly, lowering the share of monarchies. Since the 1970s, both the number and share of monarchies fell slightly. Over recent years, there are about seven monarchies, accounting for 12 percent of the world's autocracies.

EXPAND YOUR THOUGHTS

You learned that there are various types of autocratic regimes. Which autocratic regime type do you think would be most stable and durable, and which one or which ones do you think would be most vulnerable to collapse?

PRACTICAL APPLICATION

North Korea has had one of the world's most repressive autocracies. The country has had the dishonor of making Freedom House's "Worst of the Worst" list every year since the organization began publishing it. Conduct research on North Korea. Using Geddes, Wright, and Frantz's classification of autocracies, how would you classify North Korea? What factors were important in making your classification decision? How have the Kim family ruled the country and legitimized their rule?

SUMMARY

You now have a good understanding of states, nations, governments, and regimes. Although frequently used interchangeably, these are distinct concepts. When these terms come up in the remaining parts of the book, it is important to keep in mind the characteristics and functions of each. States are the overall governing structure. Nations are a collection of people that may, or may not, have a state. Governments comprise the leaders and their authority to make and enforce laws. Political regimes are the forms, institutions, and rules of political competition and governance. Furthermore, we examined the characteristics of modern states, which include territory, population, government, diplomatic recognition, and sovereignty. With this knowledge, you are able to understand the complexities found in various states around the world.

It is also important to keep in mind what states do for citizens as well as their abilities to carry out these functions. Modern states are expected to provide political goods and promote economic prosperity. Political goods include security, the rule of law, a functioning legal system, and infrastructure, such as roads, public education, and health care. The ability of states to provide these goods to citizens vary. Failed states are unable to provide the most basic needs for citizens. The dearth of most basic needs and protection and instability in weak and failed states are not simply a domestic problem; they also create challenges for the international community of states because the instability can spill over borders.

Last, you are now able to identify the characteristics of and differences among democratic and nondemocratic regimes. There are different visions of the democratic ideal and various ways to conceptualize democracy. We paid particular attention to the components of liberal democracy, which is the standard understanding of democracy today. The chapter also discussed various types of autocratic regimes and their trends since the end of World War II. We will see in subsequent chapters that not all democracies operate in the same manner. However, they all have the same important characteristics. Similarly, nondemocracies have crucial differences among them that we need to keep in mind as we explore their states' behavior.

KEY TERMS

Absolute monarchy (p. 130)

Civil rights (p. 123)

Competitive election (p. 126)

Consensus democracy (p. 115)

Constitutional monarchy
    (democratic) (p. 130)

Diplomatic recognition (to be a state) (p. 118)

Dominant party rule (p. 131)

Equal vote (p. 128)

Failed state (p. 122)

Fair election (p. 126)

Free election (p. 126)

Freedom of association (p. 129)

Freedom of expression (p. 129)

Government (p. 115)

Heterogeneous state (p. 117)

Homogenous state (p. 113)

Liberal democracy (p. 125)

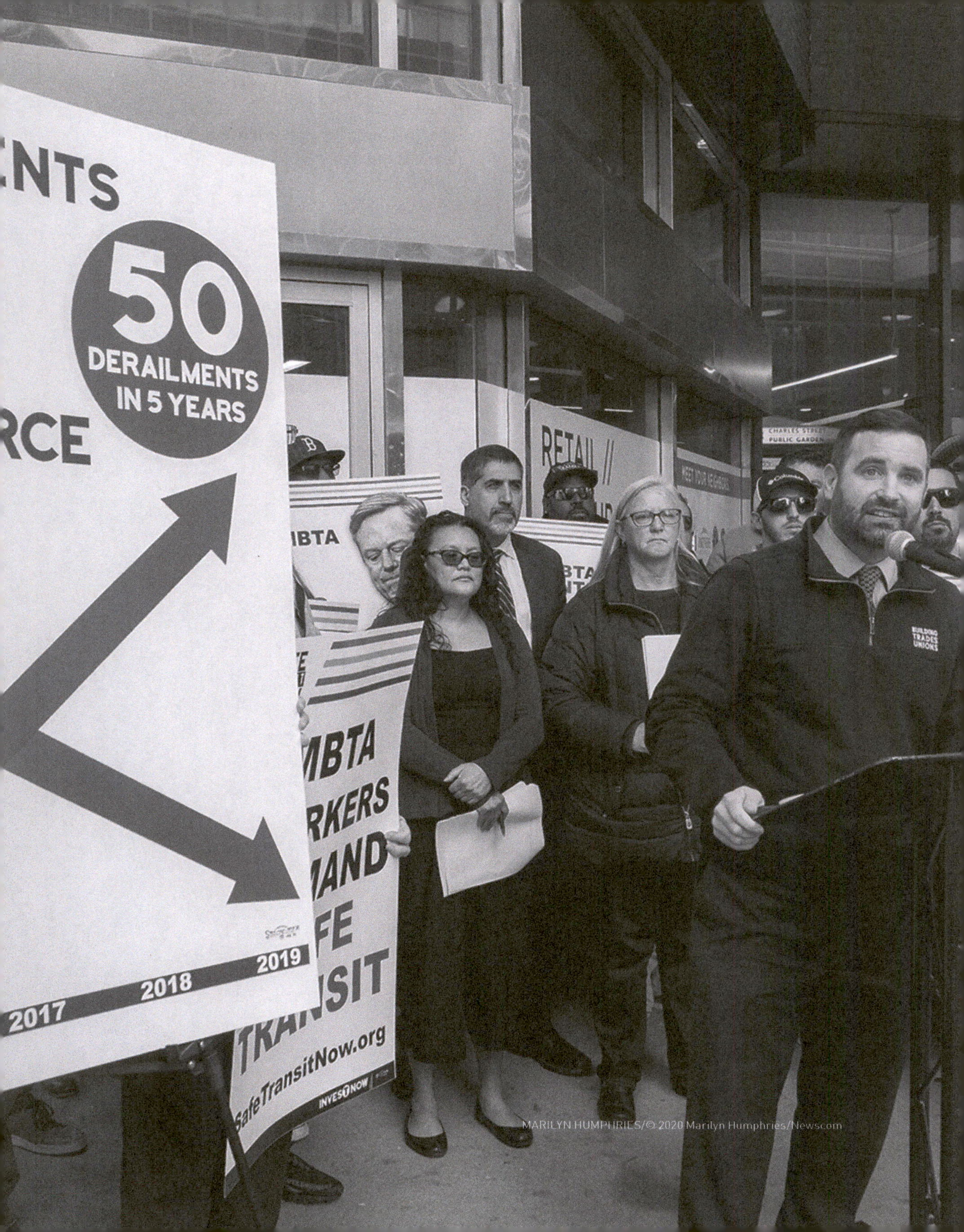

MARILYN HUMPHRIES/© 2020 Marilyn Humphries/Newscom

7 INTERESTS, POLICY, AND PUBLIC GOODS

LEARNING OBJECTIVES

7.1 Discuss the roles and different types of interest groups and various ways by which interest groups can influence the policymaking process.

7.2 Differentiate between national, public, and private interests and models to explain policymakers' motivations for national and public policies.

7.3 Identify examples and characteristics of public goods and common pool resources.

7.4 Conceptualize questions of ecological health and environmental issues as public good and common pool resource questions, and provide examples.

7.5 Describe why individually rational behavior leads to collective action problems that collide with collective welfare and solutions to overcome those problems.

Governments make policies in the name of the public and national interest. They say that they formulate and implement policies that improve the welfare of the citizens and secure and promote the national interests of the country. However, as we are all well aware, most governmental policies are not neutral. In Chapter 1, we discussed that politics is about "who gets what, when, and how." Typically, governmental policies benefit certain groups of people in the society while incurring costs to others, thus creating winners and losers.

Take former U.S. President Donald Trump's "America First" economic policy. To bring back jobs and industry to the United States, President Trump increased tariffs on many imported goods. In 2018, the president imposed a 25 percent tariff on steel from most countries. The big winners of the steel tariff were American steel-producing industries and their workers because the steel tariff made imported steel more expensive for American businesses and consumers to purchase. However, a number of studies also indicated that the steel tariff would not enhance the general welfare of American citizens. On the contrary, analysts argued that the tariff would produce more harm than gains, because the increase in the price of steel resulting from the tariff would hurt the manufacturing companies that use steel as well as U.S. consumers who must pay higher prices for their products.

As the steel tariff example shows, most governmental policies are not neutral; they create losers and winners. We also know that governments do not respond to the concerns and demands of all individuals and groups in the society. Governments, politicians, and policymakers prioritize among many, and often competing, demands and interests. They must decide which ones to accommodate and act on in terms of policy. How do governments determine their priorities? When facing competing demands that cannot simultaneously be satisfied, how do governments choose what policy to implement? For example, since the onset of the COVID-19 pandemic, governments have faced demands for a facemask mandate at the same time as demands for ensuring individual and family choice by banning facemask mandate policies. There are also people who consider that COVID-19 vaccinations should be required while there are others who argue that vaccination should remain an individual choice. How do governments and politicians make policy decisions when there are many alternative choices? Moreover, which governmental institutions facilitate government action and which institutions tend to make governments immobile?

Although we tend to be skeptical about governments' policies—are they really designed to promote general welfare or are they in fact intended to benefit specific peoples and organizations at the expense of general welfare?— there are areas that scholars and policymakers agree benefit the society as a whole. The policies that promote the welfare of all in the community are designed to enhance or protect what is known as public goods and common pool resources.

In this chapter, we will first examine interest groups and how they seek to influence government policy. We then define national and public interests and contrast them with private interests. We will also learn about the properties of "public goods" and "common pool resources" and discuss why we often cannot secure important things that benefit all in the society without government intervention. In particular, we will analyze environmental and ecological issues through the frameworks of the theories of collective goods to understand why there are significant barriers to overcome and effectively address problems of ecological health.

EXPAND YOUR THOUGHTS

Before we begin the exploration of interest group politics, think about policies that the government claims to be beneficial for the general public. Are you really convinced that they promote the welfare of the general public? Who would be winners and losers from those policies?

INTEREST GROUPS

LEARNING OBJECTIVE

7.1 Discuss the roles and different types of interest groups and various ways by which interest groups can influence the policymaking process.

Many political scientists are skeptical about national and popular values. For them, politics is a struggle among competing interest groups to influence public policy. An **interest group** refers to a group of people, businesses, or other entities that are organized on the basis of a particular common interest or concern in their attempt to influence domestic public and foreign policies. Interest groups and political parties share their desire to influence governmental policy. However, they are different in that political parties want to place their members in elective offices, whereas interest groups do not usually pursue elective offices as their goals.

Varieties of Interest Groups

Interest groups are formed in wide ranges of businesses, professions, and issue areas. Some interest groups focus on the economic interests of their members. Agricultural producers' associations may attempt to block importation of competing products from other countries and maintain higher prices for their products through government interventions. Before the North American Free Trade Agreement (NAFTA), now the United States-Mexico-Canada Agreement (USMCA), avocados in the United States were quite expensive. Despite growing popularity of avocado recipes such as guacamole since the 1970s, the United States prohibited the importation of fresh avocados from Mexico until 1993. Throughout the 1980s and 1990s the California Avocado Commission lobbied to prevent imports of fresh and less expensive avocados from Mexico. The California Avocado Commission sought to protect California's avocado growers from competition from Mexico by arguing that allowing Mexican avocados into the United States would spread crop diseases.

In the United States, the energy industry has exerted significant influence over the country's energy and environmental policy. Fossil fuels (oil, gas, and coal) companies, such as Chevron Corp, Exxon Mobil, Koch Industries, and Royal Dutch Shell, spend hundreds of millions of dollars annually in campaign contributions. They lobby policymakers in attempts to promote policies that they consider favorable to their businesses and to block ones that impede their business interests. For example, consider the intense lobbying by the oil industry against the Kyoto Protocol. The Kyoto Protocol is an international treaty adopted in 1997. It mandates that industrialized countries cut their greenhouse gas emissions and asks developing countries to comply to reduce greenhouse gas emissions voluntarily so that they meet target levels. The Kyoto Protocol went into effect in 2005 with 192 parties and without the United States. Many believe that the oil industry lobbying against the Kyoto Protocol led to the failure to ratify the protocol in the United States. The oil and gas industry has been an active interest group in many countries, spending large sums of money on lobbying activities to influence climate change policies.

There are also other types of economic interest groups. For example, labor unions seek to protect workers' rights to organize and bargain collectively. They also seek to protect employment. Some interest groups focus on social concerns. Religious interest groups pursue policies compatible with their values and beliefs, such as opposing legalization of same-sex marriage, abortion, and stem cell research, among others. Other special interest groups, such as the Sierra Club, the National Rifle Association (NRA), and AARP actively try to influence policy related to their specific areas of interest

Organizations such as the NRA, seen here at the annual Conservative Political Action Conference in February 2020, actively try to influence policy related to their specific areas of interest.

Alex Wong/Getty Images

Interest groups can be quite influential. Recent increases in mass shootings in the United States have amplified public concern about guns. Gallup studies have shown an increasing trend in public opinion that favors stricter gun laws in the United States over the past decade, yet Congress has failed to toughen the laws (see Figure 7.1). The NRA, a staunch opponent of stricter gun laws, has wielded significant influence over lawmakers. By spending a lot of money on political campaigns and mobilizing grassroots support, the NRA has been able to deliver effective lobbying over the gun question. Although money is a key factor in the NRA's power as an interest group, politicians also tend to pay greater attention to organized voices and the NRA is well organized and articulate. By contrast, gun control advocates are not as well funded, established, or organized as is the NRA. As such, they have yet to become a powerful voice on Capitol Hill.

How Interest Groups Exert Influence

The **pluralist school** in political science views politics as being played out primarily by nongovernmental groups that use their resources to exert influence over policy. The pluralist school considers that politicians respond to those who can most effectively wield influence. Thus, this perspective focuses on how power and influence are distributed among societal groups in a political process. Interest groups comprise pluralists' important research agenda.

There are many ways interest groups influence the policymaking process. One well-known method is the use of money in political campaigns with the objective of getting politicians elected or pieces of legislation passed or blocked. Simply put, affluence is influence. An interest

FIGURE 7.1   ■   Public Opinions About Gun Law in the United States

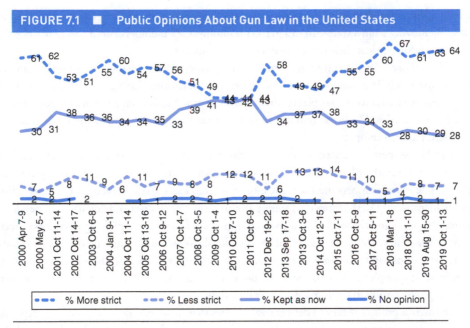

Source: Based on data from Gallup, Inc. (2021, November 23). Guns | Gallup Historical Trends. https://news.gallup.com/poll/1645/guns.aspx

group may see one candidate in an election as more sympathetic to the group's cause than other candidates. In this case, interest groups may use their financial resources to get the sympathetic candidate elected by donating to his or her campaigns. Many people view practices such as this as "buying a politician" because they see the financial contribution as provided in exchange for favorable votes on future legislation. This practice is referred to as *quid pro quo* and may be illegal in many democracies. However, others argue that preventing interest groups from donating to election campaigns is a violation of their right to freedom of speech.

Many countries have addressed this issue by passing legislation to limit the amount of money any one interest group can donate to a campaign to reduce interest groups' influence while not harming free speech. In addition to or instead of donating to individual candidates, interest groups may also donate to political parties where law permits. Interest groups in many countries have made significant financial contributions to parties to influence electoral outcomes.

Interest groups can also use their financial resources to create new policies or transform existing ones. Take as an example the Confederation of Zimbabwe Industries (CZI). The CZI's mission was to expand the level of economic activity for market-oriented businesses that conduct manufacturing and related production. Before the Confederation's interest group activities, the state was the primary actor in Zimbabwe's economy. The CZI's members, however, fell outside the state-run economy and therefore did not benefit from many of its practices. Unless the Zimbabwe economy transformed into an open market, its members would not be able to grow. CZI used their financial resources in the 1990s to employ experts and negotiators to reform Zimbabwe's state-run economy into one that was more market-oriented and open to trade. By moving from a state-run to a market economy, CZI members could compete since the state-run industries lost their government economic support.

A similar use of interest group resources occurred when the national Chamber of Commerce and Industry (CCI) promoted economic reforms in Mauritius during the 1980s. The CCI sought economic reforms that placed their members at a disadvantage when competing with state-run industries. With the removal of government economic support, the CCI members were better able to compete.

Another, somewhat related, method of influence comes from an interest group's membership size and wealth. Membership dues are important sources of funding for many interest groups. The more members there are, the more dues they can collect. Moreover, the more affluent the membership is, the more the interest group can ask for in dues and donations. Therefore, membership size and the level of affluence are important factors in amplifying resources crucial to influence policy. However, the size of the membership can also produce influence, especially if interest groups can mobilize their members to vote for their favored candidates in an election. If an interest group's votes are critical to a politician winning the next election, the politician needs to pay attention to the interest group's demands.

An interest group's ability to deliver sizable votes that influence election outcomes depends partly on electoral systems, the size of electoral districts, and the geographic distribution of the interest group's members. For example, in a plurality (i.e., first-past-the-post) electoral system with a small electoral district, the more geographically concentrated the members of an interest group, the more influence their votes will exert. If the interest group's membership is spread out thinly across a country, its members' votes will comprise a small percentage of the total votes in each electoral district. If instead an election uses a nationwide district with a proportional representation electoral system, then an interest group's votes may account for only a small fraction of the total national votes, but the interest group may still be able to gain a few seats. If they are concentrated in plenty of electoral districts, then they are more likely to get enough of their favored candidates into power and can influence policymaking. We will examine electoral systems and political representation in Chapter 9.

Another method for interest groups to influence the policymaking process is by developing a close association with political parties. The association can be formal or informal. A formal association involves cross-membership between the interest group and the political party. This is the case between the British trade unions and the British Labour Party. In Britain, the major trade unions have a say in many policy positions and the selection of party leaders. Labor unions form a built-in constituency and therefore play an important insider role in the Labour Party. As a comparison, American labor unions have had a very close, yet informal, relationship with the Democratic Party. The labor unions donate to and formally endorse Democratic politicians for office. However, they do not have a formal say in policies that the Democratic Party develops or who the party's leaders will be. Labor unions in the United States have an outsider role in influencing policy. In both the UK and U.S. cases, the influence of the labor unions has steadily declined over the years because of the decline in their membership size.

Finally, interest groups can exercise their influence through the formal role they play in policy formulation. Some political systems structure their policymaking processes to include specific interest groups. One such structure, corporatism, gives labor and business organizations a formal seat at the negotiating table. Corporatism organizes society into various areas of economic and professional sectors, which serve as organs of political representation and exercise control over individuals and activities within their jurisdiction. Government officials broker agreements among various sectors and between labor and business organizations when developing economic policies. The areas of negotiation may involve work safety regulations, health care, retirement pensions, and wages, to name a few. The agreements made are then approved by the legislature and implemented by the government. Scandinavian countries are casebook examples of the corporatist structure.

Corporatism in Mexico was part of the Institutional Revolutionary Party's (PRI's) party structure and an important factor in keeping it in power for so long. The PRI organized Mexican workers into three different organizations: public sector workers, industrial workers, and agricultural workers. One could not belong to a labor union outside these three organizations. Workers could only channel grievances or demands, such as higher wages, through these three organizations. It was then up to the PRI leadership to grant such demands or address grievances. By controlling what workers get, the PRI had the ability to control benefits and therefore had an electoral advantage. After all, would a worker vote against a party that supplied benefits? It is interesting to note that the PRI's secure hold on power ended soon after it dismantled the corporatist structure.

NATIONAL INTEREST, PUBLIC INTEREST, AND PRIVATE INTEREST

LEARNING OBJECTIVE

7.2 Differentiate between national, public, and private interests and models to explain policymakers' motivations for national and public policies.

The discussion in the previous section highlights the importance of interest groups in governmental policymaking. It also suggests that governmental policies are not necessarily created with the welfare of the general public in mind. Rather, they are intended to benefit certain individuals or particular groups.

Nonetheless, when governments adopt a policy—whether a domestic or foreign policy—they justify it on the grounds of "public" or "national" interest. But as previous examples indicate, most policy areas have multitudes of, and often competing, interests and preferences. Occasionally, we speak of a country as if it were a unitary actor with clear and coherent public and national interests. However, manifested state interests tend to reflect the values and interests of those in power. So, when political leaders claim that they are making policies to promote or safeguard public or national interest, many people are naturally and justifiably skeptical.

National Interest

With our skeptical mind (which is a good thing because good scientists are skeptical), let's define what national and public interests are. In general, political leaders seek to protect and promote "national interests" in foreign affairs and "public interests" in domestic affairs. **National interest** is the perceived general, long-term, and continuing goals of a sovereign state in its relation to other states in the international arena. In principle, political leaders formulate foreign policy based on national interest. However, as emphasized earlier, national interest is an elusive and ambiguous concept when put in practice. Foreign policy consensus is rare in many countries. Should the United States work with the Iranian leaders to dismantle the country's nuclear program by providing incentives to do so, or should it pursue a more hard-line strategy that emphasizes economic, political, and possibly military sanctions to pressure Iran into accepting the dismantlement of the program? Would it be more effective to keep China engaged in global economic activities with favorable trade and investment relations in order to improve human rights issues in the country, or would it be more successful if the country faces economic sanctions and diplomatic isolation? Political leaders have also invoked national interest in ways suitable to them and to justify their decisions and the actions of their states. Many political leaders have waged wars and invaded other countries in the name of national interest.

Nonetheless, history is filled with countless actions and decisions that are dubious, or at least controversial, from the standpoint of national interest. For example, many question the motivations of U.S. President George W. Bush's decision to invade Iraq in February 2003. The Bush administration cited threats to world peace posed by Iraq's then leader Saddam Hussein because of his government's alleged development of weapons of mass destruction and its suspected link to the militant Islamist multinational group Al Qaeda, which masterminded the terrorist attacks on the United States on September 11, 2001. President Bush made this decision even though most of the international community, including many U.S. allies, did not support such an operation. The voices disapproving the U.S. invasion intensified after the United States could not find weapons of mass destruction in Iraq and could not establish clear evidence connecting Saddam Hussein to Al Qaeda.

Many professed goals of states in international relations also vary in time and space. For example, global democracy promotion has been one of the foreign objectives of the United States in modern history. However, as U.S. governments' priorities have shifted over time, so have their interest in and emphasis on promoting and safeguarding democracy worldwide. Furthermore, during much of the Cold War, many Soviet leaders vigorously pursued a communist expansionist policy internationally. They wanted to promote changes that would produce one-party dominant regimes like their own. Seeing international communism as their vital national interest, the Soviets helped communist leaders in other countries gain control and remain in power. The government of the Soviet Union also helped crush, with force, threats to communist regimes in Eastern Europe. In response to the Soviet expansionism during the Cold War, the U.S. governments often supported right-wing anti-communist regimes that were highly repressive. The United States was also involved in a number of cases conspiring to subvert governments of other countries, including elected governments, where leaders were suspected to be communist.

The Soviet approach to international communism drastically changed when Mikhail Gorbachev became the General Secretary of the Communist Party of the Soviet Union in 1985. Under his leadership, the Soviet Union began introducing capitalist market reforms to its centralized socialist economy. Unlike his predecessors, Gorbachev also did not quell democracy movements in Eastern European countries in the late 1980s. As the examples of the Soviet Union and the United States demonstrate, professed national interests vary across countries and over time within countries. The Soviet Union wanted to expand the world's socialist regimes, while the United States tried to contain them. Additionally, the Soviet Union had different national interests before and after the Cold War.

Although national interests vary in time and place, scholars of the realist school of international relations maintain that a **state's survival interest**—its very existence—is invariably the ultimate national interest of all states. Survival involves the preservation of the state's territorial integrity, political identity, and autonomy. Defeat in a war or annexation by a more powerful country threatens a state's fundamental identity in the international community. For realists, national security is of paramount concern and lies at the heart of national interest.

In addition to territorial integrity, state autonomy is a key part of national survival. **State autonomy** refers to the ability of a state to act without interference by external forces. This concept is closely related to sovereignty. In Chapter 6, we defined sovereignty as the state's ability to govern autonomously over a given territory. We mentioned as an example that colonies, such as India under Britain and Brazil under Portugal, are not sovereign states because there are higher authorities that control the colonial territories. Sovereignty is a formal legal concept; if an entity is formally subject to control by other entities, it is not sovereign. However, a state can be nominally and legally independent and sovereign while the political leaders of the country may lack the actual power to make decisions for their own country. This is particularly problematic for small and poor countries.

For example, small and poor countries are often told by powerful states and international organizations what to do in exchange for aid and investment. If they are desperate for foreign aid and other types of economic assistance, they may agree to implement policies demanded by those external forces that they would not otherwise adopt voluntarily. An international intergovernmental organization called International Monetary Fund (IMF) has been famous for demanding economic reform as a condition for its loans. Known as **IMF conditionality**, the international financial institution has lent money to countries in economic crises in exchange for the recipient countries' governments undertaking politically and socially unpopular austerity measures, which typically include spending cuts by governments through the elimination of social programs and economic subsidies. Many people are concerned that IMF conditionality limits the loan recipient countries' abilities to make economic policies autonomously.

Public Interest

Public interest refers to state interests when it relates to domestic matters. Public interest involves matters concerning the well-being of the general public. It is an issue in which the entire society has a stake and thus deserves support, advancement, and protection by the government. For example, many societies recognize a healthy workforce as a public interest because it promotes a strong economy. Likewise, many people consider public safety to be of great public interest. Public safety involves safeguarding the public from crimes, calamities, and other potential hazards and threats. A safe environment benefits everyone in the society.

Like national interests, what people recognize as public interest varies depending upon time and place. Equality, freedom, employment, education, private property rights, universal health care, and environmental regulation, for example, may be considered public interests in certain countries at particular times. However, these may not be public interests in other countries or at different times. For example, many consider the protection of private property rights as a paramount public interest in the United States, but socialist countries would consider it to be against public interest.

Do government officials make public policies in the interests of the general public? The **public interest model of government** posits that government officials are motivated to work in the interests of the public, of "the people." This is what U.S. President Abraham Lincoln had in mind in his famous Gettysburg Address when he spoke of "government of the people, by the people, for the people." Once again, many political scientists are skeptical and do not believe that the public interest model of government explains government behavior well. In the previous section, we learned about the influence of interest groups in politics. It is not hard to see that the pluralist school does not buy the public interest model's explanation.

Private Interest

To look into this debate further, it is useful to distinguish between public interest and private interest. **Private interest** is any interest that pertains to individuals or groups whereby the person or the group would gain a particular benefit or advantage that is not available to the general public. Public interest is often contrasted with private interest. Examples of actions due to private interest abound. Workers in the auto industry get up in the morning to go to the assembly plants to earn income to support themselves and their families. Health insurance companies sell insurance policies not thinking about how to improve public health but motivated by profits they generate by selling those policies. Private interests are behind many actions by interest groups. We previously mentioned how farmers' associations seek to keep foreign produce out of their country in order to maintain high prices for their products. Indeed, agricultural lobbies, which keep inexpensive produce from developing countries out of domestic markets, are quite strong in many wealthy industrialized countries. They constitute one of the principal disputes in trade talks between developed and developing countries.

In the public interest model of government, moral motivations, such as helping the poor, protecting the environment, improving education, and promoting economic growth, are believed to generate government policies and actions. In the **private interest model of government**, public officials, including elected politicians, often behave in their own interests rather than those of the public. Their motivations may be power, wealth, or prestige. Or they may be seeking benefits for their families and friends. They evidently do not say that in public, but politicians and bureaucrats could be in pursuit of their private interests when they are making governmental decisions. It is evident in the cases of bureaucratic and political corruption that government officials and politicians are acting in pursuit of their private interests. However, it may be more difficult to discern real motivations in other cases.

For example, one of the common assumptions in political analysis is reelection as a motivation for politicians' behavior. In this theory, politicians attend to their constituents' demands and needs, or promote economic growth and employment, not because they have noble motivations as public servants but because they believe that doing so will help them get reelected. It is difficult to determine, based on their professed goals and behavior, if private interest drives their motivations (i.e., reelection motivation) or if they are genuinely seeking to promote the public interest.

EXPAND YOUR THOUGHTS

As we learned, the public interest model of government posits that government officials are motivated to work in the interests of the general public, and the private interest model of government argues that public officials, including elected politicians, often behave in their own interests rather than those of the public. Which model of government do you think more accurately explains public officials' behavior? Use examples to support your position.

COLLECTIVE GOODS: PUBLIC GOODS AND COMMON POOL RESOURCES

LEARNING OBJECTIVE

7.3 Identify examples and characteristics of public goods and common pool resources.

When we talk about national or public interests, we need to discuss the notion of "public goods." We already know that we must be careful when discussing national or public interests because people often disagree on what is in their interest. Politicians and bureaucrats may also pursue their private interests in the name of public interest. Even when government officials seek to implement policies that they believe to be beneficial for the society, policies still tend to create winners and losers. Are there such things that benefit everyone in the society?

Defining Public Goods

Although a rarity, there are in fact things that are beneficial to everyone in the society without discrimination. They are called public goods. A standard definition of a **public good** is a good that an individual can consume without reducing its availability to another individual and from which no one is excluded. Okay, this is a very technical definition. What does it mean?

A public good has two unique features. First, a public good is **non-rivalrous**. A good is non-rivalrous when its use or consumption by someone does not diminish the availability of the good to another person. It is something that you can use, and by using it, it does not reduce the quantity of the good that you are using. Sounds great, doesn't it? If you think about examples of goods, many of those you come up with probably will not meet the non-rivalry condition. Consider pizza. Is pizza a non-rivalrous good? No, because if you bring pizzas to a party for everyone to enjoy, the slices that you eat will end up in your stomach and will no longer be available to others. Consider parking as another example. A parking spot where you parked your car is no longer available to others at the moment you parked your car. Many goods diminish with use.

EXPAND YOUR THOUGHTS

A public good is non-rivalrous. Can you come up with goods that are non-rivalrous?

Another feature of a public good is that it is **non-excludable**, meaning that we cannot exclude someone from its benefit. Therefore, any good that has restricted access is not a public good. Just like the non-rivalry condition, it is easier to come up with examples that are not non-excludable. For example, college classes you are taking do not meet the non-excludability condition. They are excludable goods because to take these classes, you need to pay tuition and register for them. Even most public services, such as public libraries and public schools, strictly speaking are not public goods. Public libraries typically require their patrons to have a local residency to check out books and use many of their services. If you do not have local residence, the library can deny you certain services or you can use them for a fee. Public schools also tend to require proof of residency to enroll.

EXPAND YOUR THOUGHTS

A public good is non-excludable. Can you come up with goods that are non-excludable?

As you can tell, the conditions of non-rivalry and non-excludability are individually quite demanding. Now think about public goods, which need to satisfy both criteria. Most of the goods we can think of do not meet these two criteria simultaneously. Are there goods that are both non-rivalrous *and* non-excludable?

There are some. One of the examples of a public good is national security. Strong national defense provides peace and security for a state. It is non-rivalrous because you can enjoy the peace and security it offers without diminishing the peace and security available to others. National security is non-excludable because anyone who resides in the country enjoys its benefits. As long as you are in the country, you have protection. Another example of a public good is democracy. Democracy protects fundamental rights of the people. The level of protection that democracy accords does not diminish with more people in the country—that is, democracy is non-rivalrous. Regardless of how many people live in the country, once democracy takes root, they will all have protected rights. Furthermore, if a country is democratic, the state cannot exclude anyone who resides in the country from the benefits of democracy. Thus, democracy also meets the condition of non-excludability so long as the state does not deny a subset of the population their rights. Clean air, lighthouses, and streetlights are also well-known nonpolitical examples of public goods. Can you tell why they are public goods?

EXPAND YOUR THOUGHTS

A public good is both non-excludable and non-rivalrous. Can you come up with examples of public goods not discussed in this chapter? How do they simultaneously meet the conditions of non-rivalry and non-excludability?

Common Pool Resources

A related issue in the discussion of public goods is the notion of shared goods or common pool resources. Think about what the goods in Table 7.1 have in common. They are all non-excludable goods; anyone in the community can use them. You cannot prevent someone from breathing. Public radio is available to anyone in the area; you do not need to pay membership fees to listen to its programs. This makes public radio different from cable or satellite TVs, which usually require a paid subscription to access their programs. Any community members can also go and fish in community fisheries. Are they all public goods? The answer is negative.

Remember that public goods must meet two characteristics: non-excludability and non-rivalry. Although all of the items in Table 7.1 satisfy the non-excludability condition, some of these goods are like regular goods in that if someone uses them, they diminish in quantity. They can even be completely depleted. Therefore, some of those goods do not fulfil the non-rivalry condition; they are rivalrous goods and consequently not public goods. Those goods—non-excludable but rivalrous in consumption—are called **common pool resources** or

TABLE 7.1 ■ Examples of Collective Goods
National security
Public radio
Clean air
Public freeways
Public pasture
Community fisheries

simply commons. Anyone—or any cow—may use public pastures, but the grass consumed by a cow will not be available to another cow, and too many cows on a pasture can end up in overgrazing the grass field. Anyone may be able to fish in the ocean, but overfishing has led to elevated risks of extinction of some species.

EXPAND YOUR THOUGHTS

Common pool resources are goods that are shared (i.e., they are non-excludable) but can diminish and deplete (i.e., they are rivalrous). Which goods in Table 7.1 are common pool resources? Explain. Can you think about other examples of common pool resources?

What is important for public policy is that both common pool resources and public goods, because of their intrinsic features, face unique challenges to their provision and maintenance. Before we examine these challenges, we will look at ecological health as an example of a collective good.

GOOD ECOLOGICAL HEALTH AS A COLLECTIVE GOOD

LEARNING OBJECTIVE

7.4   Conceptualize questions of ecological health and environmental issues as public good and common pool resource questions, and provide examples.

Public goods and common pool resources are non-excludable goods that are shared by everybody. Many scholars and policymakers consider ecological health issues to be questions of public good and common pool resource. Take, for example, ozone depletion—the depletion of the ozone layer in the upper atmosphere of the Earth. It is not only a major environmental problem but also a question of public health. The depletion of the ozone layer enables harmful ultraviolet rays to enter the Earth's atmosphere from the Sun, which causes skin cancer, eye damage, and accelerated aging of skin. Can you tell why the recovery of the ozone layer is a public good? It is because all people living on the Earth will benefit from the reduction of health risk associated with it, and a reduction of health risk to someone will not take away the benefits available to others.

Consider another example: climate change, also known as global warming. Climate change involves the rise in the average temperature of the Earth's atmosphere and oceans. Climate change is responsible for the change in weather patterns, which have become extreme, causing hurricanes with both greater intensity and frequency. It also causes more frequent wildfires, longer periods of drought in some regions, and the rising sea levels that threaten many communities. Some countries, such as Tuvalu, an island country in the South Pacific, face an existential threat due to climate change. Tuvalu faces the risk of completely submerging into the ocean and disappearing from the world map.

PRACTICAL APPLICATION

Climate change is not an abstract concept but is very real for people facing the threat that their countries will submerge in the ocean. Tuvalu, a tiny country in the South Pacific, is under an existential crisis as sea levels rise and weather patterns become increasingly violent as a result of climate change. Many consequences of climate change have not received as much attention from the international community as they deserve, but they have far-reaching effects on communities' vulnerability.

Conduct research on Tuvalu. How has climate change been affecting the people of Tuvalu? What problems have they been facing, and how have they tried to solve these problems? Why do you think it is difficult to obtain international cooperation to solve the problems? How would you handle the issue?

This type of threat from climate change does not occur only in small island countries, although those countries are indeed at a greater risk of being wiped out as a result of climate change. Coastal flooding caused by the rise in sea levels due to climate change threatens many communities in large countries as well. Flooding has become more frequent along the U.S. coastline. According to the U.S. Environmental Protection Agency (2021), coastal flooding has increased the most frequently along the country's East Coast (See Figure 7.2). Rising sea levels impact livelihood in coastal areas in multiple dimensions: by inundating low-lying wetlands and dry land, eroding shorelines, causing more frequent and greater coastal flooding, and raising the flow of saltwater into estuaries and groundwater aquifers in proximity. Many experts predict that multiple U.S. coastal communities will be under water by 2050. Climate change affects some people and countries more than others, but it is certainly affecting everyone. It is an urgent issue for the global community.

Certain environmental issues may be better understood as problems of commons rather than public goods. We can consider various natural resources as commonly owned and depletable. This includes such valuable resources as freshwater, fossil fuels, and natural gas. Conceptualizing resources as commonly owned and depletable can also apply to wildlife. Overhunting and overfishing of wild animals have endangered many species and have led to the extinction of certain species. Consider the bluefin tuna (*Thunnus thynnus*). Catching large bluefin tuna brings a lot of profit for people involved in the fishing industry in many countries. Although providing a livelihood for many people, massive overfishing has threatened the species into extinction.

People agree that protection of the environment and promotion of good ecological health are important and beneficial to everyone on this planet. However, as we noted in Chapter 1, such effort often falls short of expectation even when near consensus exists about its importance and urgency. Because many issues about ecological health are questions of public goods or common pool resources, they encounter distinctive challenges that occur with collective goods. As a result, we are having a hard time promoting and protecting ecological health. We examine those challenges in the next section.

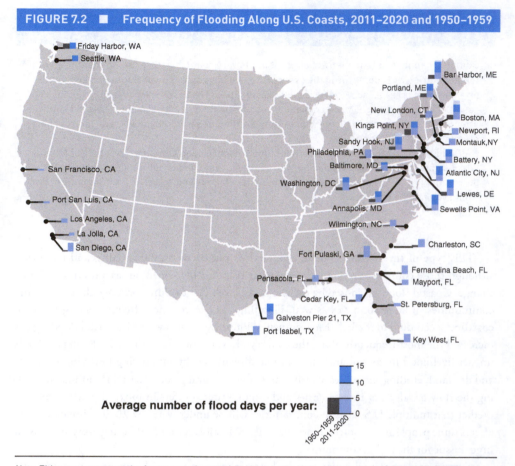

FIGURE 7.2 ■ Frequency of Flooding Along U.S. Coasts, 2011–2020 and 1950–1959

Average number of flood days per year:

Note: This map compares the frequency of coastal flooding in the United States in the 2011–2020 period with the 1950–1959 period. The indicator measures the average number of days per year in which coastal waters rose above a local threshold for flooding at 33 sites along U.S. coasts.

Source: U.S. Environmental Protection Agency. (2021). Climate change indicators: Coastal flooding. Retrieved August 5, 2021, from https://www.epa.gov/climate-indicators/climate-change-indicators-coastal-flooding

FAILURE OF INDIVIDUAL RATIONALITY: COLLECTIVE ACTION PROBLEMS

LEARNING OBJECTIVE

7.5 Describe why individually rational behavior leads to collective action problems that collide with collective welfare and solutions to overcome those problems.

By now, we know that public goods have incredibly fine qualities. They bring benefits, are available to everyone, and remain available even after being consumed. Unlike public goods, common pool resources do shrink and can even disappear with overuse, but they also bring benefits that are accessible to all the members of the community. They could remain available for a long time, if not infinitely, with responsible use. If public goods and common pool resources are so good and beneficial, why are they undersupplied and why is overexploitation of valuable resources such a common, recurrent problem?

Scholars who work with the rational choice (or rational actor) model (see Chapter 5) have provided an apt answer to this puzzle. Recall the expected utility maximizing assumption of the rational choice theory. It assumes that individuals are rational in that they seek to maximize the benefits they can obtain while trying to minimize the costs they may incur. We can measure benefits and costs in monetary and nonmonetary terms. With respect to public goods and common pool resources, rational choice theory predicts that rational actors, in an attempt to maximize their individual utility, behave in a manner that collectively prevents the society from producing desired outcomes. The principal challenge that we face in the provision and maintenance of shared goods is therefore that personally rational choices lead individuals to behave in such a way that collides with the needs and interests of a larger community.

To understand how individually rational decisions may lead to suboptimal social outcomes, we need to understand collective action problems. A **collective action problem** refers to a situation where cooperation among individuals would achieve outcomes that benefit everyone, but this cooperation is prevented by individuals acting in their own self-interest. The consequences are that public goods are undersupplied, and common pool resources are overused.

Collective Action Problem: Incentives for Free Riding

One of the principal collective action problems is a **free rider problem**. A free rider problem is an inherent problem with non-excludable collective goods. It occurs because individuals have an incentive to take advantage of the good available to them without contributing to it and that the good, once provided, is available to everyone regardless of whether they contributed to it. Let's go back to the example of clean air. Clean air is a public good because it is non-excludable and non-rivalrous, and everyone benefits from clean air. You cannot deny people from breathing clean air on the basis of non-contribution. On the other hand, helping to make and keep air clean incurs some, or perhaps substantial, costs. Gasoline is a toxic and highly flammable liquid, and gasoline use contributes to air pollution and climate change. You may need to abandon your gasoline-powered car to buy a more expensive electric car, which produces much lower tailpipe emissions than conventional vehicles do. Or instead of driving your own car, you may need to use a bicycle or public transportation, which is environmentally more friendly but is not necessarily as convenient. Factories may be required to upgrade their operations to introduce clean air technology, which may be expensive. So, trying to help make air clean generates certain costs.

Now, if you are a rational self-interested individual doing a cost-benefit calculation, what would you do, given the non-excludable nature of a public good? You contribute nothing and enjoy the benefit once it is provided. Making air clean requires cooperation by many people and entities. If you contributed and others did not, you would be in a "sucker's" position: You paid the costs, but the benefit (clean air) did not become available. On the other hand, if you do not contribute, you can avoid being a "sucker" if clean air does not happen. If air becomes clean without you contributing, you can still enjoy the benefits of clean air because it is a non-excludable good. Consequently, based on the cost-benefit calculation, free riding seems to be the best choice for you. The dilemma is that if most people think rationally and try to free ride on others' efforts, clean air, which would be in the interest of everyone, would *not* be provided. This is a classic prisoner's dilemma situation we discussed in Chapter 1.

Let's look at another example. Union contracts for public employees resemble public goods. Unions negotiate contracts that benefit public employees regardless of whether or not they are union members. These contracts may include wages, conditions for employment termination, health benefits, leaves, and grievance procedures. Union leaders have argued that mandatory union fees are justified on the ground that everyone benefits from the fruits of collective bargaining. Without mandatory fees, how could they limit free riding by those who do not join unions but still benefit from the outcomes of collective bargaining? In 1977, the U.S. Supreme Court ruled in *Abood v. Detroit Board of Education* that non-union employees in the public sector may be required to fund union activities related to "collective bargaining, contract administration, and grievance adjustment purposes" although unions cannot compel non-union employees to fund political or ideological activities of the union to which they object.

There have been legal challenges by the opponents of mandatory union fees levied from both union members and nonmembers. In 2016, the U.S. Supreme Court heard arguments in the *Friedrichs vs. California Teachers Association* case in which union opponents sought to reverse the 1977 Supreme Court decision that allowed public employee unions to collect "agency fees," also known as "fair share fees." Before the Supreme Court could make the decision, however, Justice Antonin Scalia passed away, and the case was decided by a 4–4 vote, leaving in place the Ninth Circuit decision affirming *Abood*. In 2018, though, in the *Janus v. American Federation of State, County, and Municipal Employees* the Supreme Court ruled that such union fees on public sector employees violate the First Amendment right to free speech, overturning the 1977 decision.

EXPAND YOUR THOUGHTS

As you saw in this chapter, mandatory labor union fees are controversial. Union leaders argue that levying fees from nonmembers as well as from members is justified on the ground that many benefits of collective bargaining, such as paid maternity leave and protection against unjust employment termination, are public goods available to both union members and nonmembers. Opponents of mandatory union fees contend that such fees violate freedom of association and expression. What is your position? Are unions justified to collect fees from members and nonmembers alike for the activities aimed to produce outcomes that benefit all?

Collective Action Problem: The Tragedy of the Commons

One of the major challenges to shared goods and resources is known as the tragedy of the commons. The **tragedy of the commons** explains why individual users of a shared resource system, acting in their self-interest, behave in a manner that is contrary to the common good of all users by depleting or ruining the shared resource.

To understand the tragedy, imagine a fishing village where villagers depend on fishing in a bay for their living. The bay and bay's fish are their shared resources. The bay has a lot of fish, and if each villager captures a hundred fish per week, reproduction of the fish population is possible. However, if they each catch more than one hundred fish a week, then overfishing will destroy the fish population, and eventually there will be no more fish in the bay. With the knowledge of these conditions, what would the villagers do?

Sadly, the theory of the commons predicts that if they are rational and acting independently in their self-interest, they will overfish, leading to the extinction of the shared fish resource in the bay on which everyone depends. Why? If villagers each catch more than a hundred fish per week, their incomes grow by that amount. Hence, they each have an incentive to catch and sell more fish. However, they each also know that if they capture more than one hundred fish per week, they will eventually lose this important resource on which they depend to support their families. Fearing the loss of the valuable shared resource, you would think that each villager would refrain from overfishing. Yet even with this knowledge, the theory of the commons predicts that they will overfish, because even if a villager refrains from overfishing, other villagers may still overfish to make more money. In the end, the villagers who refrained from overfishing may end up in a situation in which they have no extra income and there are no more fish to capture in the bay due to overfishing by others. Consequently, the villagers decide to get extra fish for the extra money in the short run, heavily discounting its long-term implications for their income. If most villagers act in a similar manner (why not?), then soon the worst fear will come true: Overfishing will lead to the extinction of the valuable source of income for all villagers in the community.

This example demonstrates one of the predicaments of common pool resources shared by rational actors making decisions to maximize their individual self-interest. The predicament is that the actors are well aware of the possible adverse consequences of overexploiting a shared resource, but they still act in such a way that collides with not only the collective interest of the community but also their own long-term interest.

Solutions for Collective Action Problems

We saw in the previous sections several examples of collective action problems. Both free rider problems and the tragedy of the commons occur because of the intrinsic nature of public goods and common pool resources. How can we overcome these collective action problems?

Various solutions have been proposed to deal with the problems related to public goods and common pool resources. First is the privatization of the collective goods if privatization is possible. When you privatize a good, you also internalize the costs of its abuse by the users. If you use up all you have, then you—and only you—will not have the resource for future consumption. In other words, the lack of your resource will not affect the welfare of other community members. The fact that you will personally face the consequences of your overuse will likely make you become a more responsible user of your resource. If there is a good way to divide the fish in the bay among the villagers, each villager will become more responsible for how they use their valuable resource. Privatization elevates the value of the long-term interest that individuals have.

A second solution is government intervention. The government can be involved in the provision of public goods and prevention of overexploitation of common pool resources by regulating, monitoring, and sanctioning noncompliant behavior. If the incentive for free riding makes voluntary cooperation by individuals unlikely, the government can create positive incentives for cooperation and negative incentives for undesired behavior. In an effort to reduce air pollution, governments have regulated the amount of pollution that factories can emit into the air, provided tax breaks and other incentives to businesses and citizens who adopt clean air technology, and punished with fines and other methods businesses and individuals who fail to act within the required standards. In the United States, federal, state, and local policies for renewable energy have been a primary driver for the growth of solar, wind, and other renewable energies. Federal tax incentives include the investment tax credit for commercial and residential projects and the production tax credit. The investment tax credit, which is claimed against the business tax liability of the company that develops, installs, and finances the project, has played an instrumental role in the growth of the solar industry.

Is either privatization or national control of resources necessary to protect collective goods? In *Governing the Commons: The Evolution of Institutions for Collective Action*, political scientist and Nobel Laureate in Economics Elinor Ostrom (1990) showed that under certain circumstances user associations can voluntarily form, and do well, in self-regulating their conduct to protect the common good. Ostrom's study indicates that neither privatization nor government intervention is a necessary condition for the management of common pool resources. However, the development of voluntary user associations occurs only under specific conditions, and their enforcement power may be limited. Therefore, many societies have relied on governments to address collective action problems. Unfortunately, neither the state nor the market has been unfailingly successful in solving public goods and common pool resource problems.

The recent report (*Climate Change 2021: The Physical Science Basis*) published in 2021 by the Intergovernmental Panel on Climate Change—the United Nations body for assessing the science related to climate change—predicts that the Earth's temperature rise will continue to significantly worsen in the next 20 years. Greenhouse gas emissions and other human activity are already causing catastrophic impacts on ecosystems and societies around the world. These damages are likely to intensify with potentially disastrous social, political, economic, and environmental consequences. If we do not act immediately with a more sizable undertaking to limit greenhouse gas emissions, the world could become unrecognizable.

Case Study: Climate Change and Government Push for Electric Vehicles

Electric vehicles are part of global efforts to combat climate change. In Europe and China, governments are using regulations and subsidies for automakers to boost electric vehicle production. In July 2021, the European Union made a proposal to prohibit the sale of new gasoline- and diesel-powered cars by 2035. The proposed ban is part of a plan to cut carbon dioxide emissions from vehicles by 55% by 2030 from current levels, and by 100 percent by 2035. The Chinese government is helping Chinese automakers expand into new electric-vehicle markets around the world. The high levels of government involvement in the effort to reduce CO2 emissions via the replacements of fossil-fuel powered vehicles with electric vehicles is not surprising considering that climate change is a public good question. If left with private businesses and citizens to voluntarily take action, we may not achieve the amount of reduction in greenhouse gases needed to effectively curtail and stop global climate change. Electric vehicles are also usually more expensive than gasoline-powered vehicles, and Europe and China have offered cash incentives to consumers to purchase electric cars.

The United States is lagging in the drive for electric vehicles. The electric and plug-in hybrid vehicle share of new car sales in June 2021 was less than 4 percent. The Biden administration has set electric vehicles as an important part of its effort to address climate change. The largest single source of greenhouse gas emissions in the United States is gasoline-powered vehicles, which accounts for more than a quarter of the country's total emissions. In August 2021, President Biden announced an ambitious goal that by 2030, half of all new vehicles sold in the United States should be electric. To achieve this goal, President Biden has called for building a network of 500,000 electric car chargers within the decade, an increase of more than 1,000 percent from the approximately 43,000 charging stations in the United States in 2021. The Biden administration is also moving to toughen auto mileage and pollution standards. President Biden's plan received support from the major U.S. automakers. Executives from the three largest U.S. auto companies, Ford, General Motors, and Chrysler, joined President Biden at the White House, declaring in a joint statement that they target their electric vehicle sales to be 40 to 50 percent of their total new sales by 2030.

As we have seen, ecological and environmental issues often face collective action problems. Hence, governments play a key role in addressing those questions. As President Biden recognized, electric vehicles are the future of the global auto market. As Europe and China shift to electric vehicles with government assistance in regulations and incentives, government inaction in the United States would mean that the country would be behind not only in the global endeavor to tackle climate change but also in the competitiveness of the U.S. auto industry in the rapidly expanding electric vehicle market. The Biden administration recognizes the dual importance of governmental support for electric vehicles and is making crucial steps toward those goals.

SUMMARY

This chapter introduced several types of governmental policies and the forces that can lead to their creation. Various actors influence governmental policy. The pluralist school regards interest groups as exerting significant influence in public policy. We saw that interest groups come in various forms and have different degrees of influence in policy formulation. The important roles that interest groups play in politics in many countries suggest that governmental policies are often not neutral even though governments and political leaders justify their decisions and actions in the name of public or national interest. Rather, interest group politics exemplifies Harold Lasswell's view of politics discussed in Chapter 1: Politics is about "who gets what, when, and how."

Some of the challenges to collective welfare lie in the characteristics of collective goods. We examined two types of collective goods in this chapter: public goods and common pool resources. We can conceptualize many environmental and ecological issues as questions of public goods or common pool resources. The fact that public goods are, by their very nature, non-rivalrous and non-excludable leads to people trying to take advantage of the benefits without participating in the public good's production. We call this a free rider problem. Preservation of shared valuable resources also faces a distinctive challenge known as the tragedy of the commons. In the tragedy of commons, individually rational behavior of maximizing benefits while minimizing costs produces collective action problems. We witness collective action problems in many public policy areas, such as global environmental issues as well as more local common pool resource sharing. Governmental policy, while imperfect, is one way to solve collective action problems. In Chapter 8, we turn our attention to the governmental institutional structures that produce policies, laws, and regulations with which we live.

KEY TERMS

Climate change (p. 150)

Collective action problem (p. 153)

Common pool resources (p. 149)

Corporatism (p. 143)

Free rider problem (p. 153)

IMF conditionality (p. 145)

Interest group (p. 139)

National interest (p. 144)

Non-excludable (p. 148)

Non-rivalrous (p. 147)

Ozone depletion (p. 150)

Pluralist school (p. 140)

Private interest (p. 146)

Private interest model of government (p. 146)

Public good (p. 147)

Public interest (p. 145)

Public interest model of government (p. 146)

State autonomy (p. 145)

State's survival interest (p. 145)

Tragedy of the commons (p. 154)

FURTHER READING

Olson, M. (1997). *The logic of collective action: Public goods and the theory of groups.* Harvard University Press.

8 INSTITUTIONS OF GOVERNMENT

LEARNING OBJECTIVES

8.1 Identify the debates on the role that institutions play in shaping political behavior.

8.2 Describe the characteristics of presidential, parliamentary, and semi-presidential systems, the fundamental differences among them, and their implications for policymaking and political behavior.

8.3 Explain the differences between the types of democratic executives and their primary functions.

8.4 Discuss the principal functions of legislatures and how legislative institutions differ across democracies.

8.5 Describe the key functions of judicial systems and the characteristics of differing judicial systems.

8.6 Analyze the differences between federalism and unitary systems and the reasons for and against the centralization of state power.

8.7 Identify the institutions of nondemocratic regimes and how their functions and goals differ from those in democratic regimes.

In Chapter 6, we learned the differences among states, nations, political regimes, and governments as well as various conceptualizations of democracy and different types of autocratic regimes. In this chapter, we will explore fundamental democratic governmental institutions and structures. We will also examine some examples of institutions in autocratic regimes.

Governmental institutions are the rules, processes, and human behavior that carry out the day-to-day functions of government. Many students reading this chapter are probably thinking, "This is what I thought political science is all about!" Since it took us more than half the textbook to get here, we hope you now know that political science is much more than the study of governmental institutions. Nonetheless, understanding governmental institutions is an important part of analyzing politics because what they do, and how they do it, is interesting and impactful. This chapter will introduce you to basic constitutional structures of government and their varieties employed by different countries in the world.

The formal working structures of government, such as executive offices, legislatures, federalism, and courts, can help explain why political change is difficult or easy to achieve. Some institutions permit swift changes in laws, regulations, and governmental policies. In other institutions, changes are more difficult and much slower to occur. When governmental institutions can quickly address problems, we say they are efficient.

Some people argue that efficiency should not come at the expense of prudence. A quick decision may not necessarily produce the solution that will solve the problems facing society. Constant policy change can also cause uncertainty that may hamper economic, social, and political activities. Therefore, certain countries purposely design their constitutions to slow down decision-making and allow greater deliberation to ensure that solutions are effective. The U.S. Constitution is an example of a constitution that deliberately slows the policymaking process by adding many layers of decision points that each require legislative review and approval. The U.S. political system is designed to make policy change difficult unless there is a solid consensus by different majorities.

While greater deliberation can be a virtue, it is also important to recognize that it does not necessarily lead to effective policies. Nor do we want a government that is immobilized in the face of a social crisis. The design of democratic political institutions must consider the delicate balance between deliberation and participation, on the one hand, and decisiveness on the other.

Some countries design their institutions to preserve the power and ideology of the ruling elite. Although this is more common in nondemocratic countries, politicians in democratic countries have also attempted to change or maintain political institutions, rules, and procedures to maintain their personal benefits.

The high level of interest that politicians and others have in political institutions is testament that political institutions matter. They are not simply different types of government that are inconsequential. To the contrary, political actors care about political institutions because political institutions constrain their choices, encourage certain behaviors, and influence political and policy outcomes.

NEW INSTITUTIONALISM IN POLITICAL SCIENCE

LEARNING OBJECTIVE
8.1 Identify the debates on the role that institutions play in shaping political behavior.

In the old days, political science was mostly a descriptive study of governmental structures. Scholars would focus on the detailed description of governmental institutions, laws, and practices and paid little attention to explaining how these institutions influenced political behavior. Perhaps this is how you learned about politics in your high school government class. In the 1950s, this approach gave way to ones centered on individuals as a dominant paradigm in political science. The new perspectives considered that individuals are key to understanding politics, so they emphasized studying individuals' values and preferences through surveys. They paid scant attention to institutions. Much of what we learned in Chapters 4 and 5 reflects this paradigm shift. One of these new approaches was rational choice theory. An influential rational choice scholar, William Riker, even regarded institutions as nothing but different options in a policy space for political actors. Since institutions simply reflect the preferences of political actors, Riker argued, they might change as political actors' preferences change. Partly as a reaction to this **behavioral revolution** in political science, a new approach to institutions emerged in the 1980s. The **new institutionalism** argues that political institutions are not merely reflections of social forces or individual preferences. Once created, they take on lives of their own and shape the behavior and attitudes of political actors.

Take filibustering in the U.S. Senate. A **filibuster** is a dilatory tactic used to prevent bringing a measure to a vote through a prolonged speech by one or more senators. This tactic takes advantage of the Senate rule that permits senators to speak for as long as they wish, and on any topic they choose, unless cloture votes are approved by three-fifths of the senators. U.S. senators have amply used the filibuster rule to kill or delay bills they oppose.

Institutionalist scholars have also argued that electoral systems shape the behaviors of both candidates and voters. In electoral systems where voters vote for individual candidates, for instance, candidates engage in personalized campaigns that emphasize their own attributes, experiences, and ideology. Conversely, where voters vote for political parties rather than individual candidates, candidates deploy party-based campaigns with much less focus on their own personal characteristics. They focus on what the political party, as a whole, can promise a supporter. In addition, the primary focus in party-centric systems tends to be party leadership, not individual rank-and-file members. Hence, the locus of voter attention and manner of campaigning depend on the type of electoral systems employed. As these examples show, institutions influence political behavior and choices.

Scholars of political institutions today agree that political institutions are consequential. They have implications for how democracy works, for example, with respect to the relationship between the elected and the electorate, the system's ability to make laws, the behavior of elected officials, political conflict among different identity groups, and the stability of democracy, among others. Rather than seeing political institutions as transient and inconsequential, institutionalist scholars regard them as enduring collections of rules, norms, and organized practices. They do not change much in the face of turnover of individuals and are relatively resilient to unique individual preferences or changing external contexts.

EXPAND YOUR THOUGHTS

Do you think institutions influence how people behave in important ways? Or do you think institutions have little influence? Think about an institution that you are involved in. How does the institution influence your behavior? Please come up with specific examples to illustrate your answer.

SEPARATION AND FUSION OF POWERS: PRESIDENTIAL, PARLIAMENTARY, AND SEMI-PRESIDENTIAL SYSTEMS

LEARNING OBJECTIVE
8.2 Describe the characteristics of presidential, parliamentary, and semi-presidential systems, the fundamental differences among them, and their implications for policymaking and political behavior.

Knowledge of political institutions is nevertheless still important. Before we can examine the implications of choosing different types of political institutions, we need to understand the basic differences among them. Many societies have considered reforms of political systems so that they can change some aspect of political behavior. Some societies contemplate or implement extensive political reforms. For example, several countries have considered doing away with a presidential system and adopting a parliamentary or semi-presidential form of government. Certain countries have abolished the second chamber of the national legislature while others have added one. Various countries have undertaken sweeping electoral reforms. Others have had much more limited discussions or small-scale reforms, such as changing the rules of legislative proceedings. Whether we want to undertake sweeping or limited reforms, understanding the characteristics of different institutions, how they work, and what consequences they have for human behavior and society will help us greatly in making good institutional choices.

We begin our exploration by examining democratic institutional arrangements. Political scientists often classify democracies into two basic types based on the system of relation between executive and legislative power: parliamentary and presidential. There is also a third category, semi-presidential, which has features of both presidential and parliamentary systems. Although the number of countries using semi-presidential systems has increased, most of the world's democracies are by far either parliamentary or presidential (with more parliamentary countries than presidential ones). Since parliamentary and presidential systems are the two basic types of government, we will take a close look at these two systems first. We will then examine semi-presidential systems.

Presidential Systems

A **presidential system** is headed by a president who is both head of state and head of government. A popular vote directly elects the president (or in the case of the United States quasi-directly through the Electoral College) for a **fixed term,** a predefined period in office that cannot be shortened. Voters also directly elect members of the legislature in a separate election for fixed terms. The president cannot shorten the terms of the legislators. Neither can legislators legally remove the president from office during the constitutionally defined term under normal circumstances. Presidential **impeachment** procedures allow removal of a sitting president by legislators, but it happens only under extraordinary circumstances and only after meeting rigorous procedural requirements. Since voters select both the president and legislators through direct (or quasi-direct) popular elections, both the president and the legislature are directly responsible to the voters (see Figure 8.1). Presidential systems are **separation of powers** systems because the

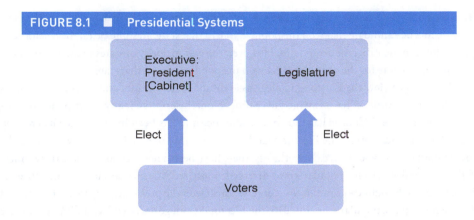

FIGURE 8.1 ■ Presidential Systems

separations of their origins (i.e., elections) and survivals (i.e., fixed terms) make the legislative and executive branches independent of each other.

The United States is the oldest presidential democracy. However, the use of an electoral college (discussed in the following section) to elect the country's president makes it unique from other presidential democracies. Voters elect U.S. presidents for a four-year term, with a possibility of reelection for an additional term. Separate elections select the members of the legislature, the U.S. Congress. Members of the lower house, the House of Representatives, serve two-year terms, and senators serve six-year terms. Those terms are fixed, meaning that the president does not have the authority to dismiss Congress and its members from office during their constitutionally defined terms.

In addition, Congress does not have the power to remove a president unless it demonstrates a president's criminal wrongdoing and follows through the extremely stringent and demanding impeachment procedure. Over more than 230 years under the current constitution, Congress has impeached three U.S. presidents: Andrew Johnson in 1868, Bill Clinton in 1998, and Donald Trump in 2019 and 2021, but they were unable to get enough votes during their trials in the Senate to remove them from office.

Case Study: The Electoral College and Indirect Election of U.S. Presidents

The U.S. presidential democracy uses an indirect method to elect the country's president. All other presidential democracies use a direct popular vote to elect presidents. There have been some countries headed by a "president" who came into power without direct popular elections. However, scholars typically classify these countries as autocracies.

Voters in the United States do not vote directly in presidential elections. Instead, the U.S. presidential elections employ an institution called Electoral College. U.S. voters vote in presidential elections, and these votes, called popular votes, are used to determine each state's electors, who in turn cast their votes in the Electoral College to select the president.

The Electoral College consists of 538 electors. Each state has electors that equal the number of representatives (in the U.S. House of Representatives) plus senators (always two). The District of Columbia currently has three electoral votes. An absolute majority of at least 270 electoral votes is required to win the presidential election. Each state and the District of Columbia determine how the electors will vote. The vast majority of states mandate that each of their electors vote for the candidate that won the popular vote in that state. In some cases, the electors can split ballots among different candidates. However, the vast majority of states mandate that each of their electors vote for the candidate that won the popular vote in that state.

Many people view the Electoral College as an obsolete institution, and several movements to abolish the institution have emerged over time. Nonetheless, like many other political institutions, the Electoral College has shown its endurance and has been in place since its creation in 1787. In practical terms, the Electoral College has mostly produced the same winners as the direct popular vote would have. Nonetheless, there have been a few elections where the winners of the electoral votes and popular votes diverged, most recently in the 2000 and 2016 elections. In 2000, Republican candidate George W. Bush won the presidency against Democrat Al Gore, who won the popular vote. In 2016, the Electoral College declared Republican candidate Donald Trump president against Democrat and popular vote winner Hillary Clinton.

These disparities occur mainly for two reasons. The first reason is the small state bias of the Electoral College. Since all states have two senators regardless of the state's population size, the distribution of electoral votes favors less populous states. Therefore, the Electoral College favors the candidate and the party that command strong support in states with small population sizes. Second, the winner-takes-all method of allocating electors used by all but two states contributes to disproportionality between the electoral and the popular votes. Recall that winner-takes-all means that the candidate with the *most votes*, and not necessarily a majority of the votes, wins.

Outcries for direct popular elections of presidents have tended to increase following controversial elections, like those in 2000 and 2016. Supporters of the Electoral College argue that the current system requires candidates to build a popular base that is geographically broader and more diverse in voter interests than a simple national majority or plurality. Under a direct election, they fear that presidential candidates would focus on appealing only to urban voters in larger states and therefore underemphasize the interests of rural voters in less populated states. Advocates of the direct popular vote argue that the Electoral College is an obsolete institution that contradicts the fundamental democratic principle of one person, one vote. Despite the outcries that occasionally emerge, the Electoral College in the United States is likely to stay for a long time, given the challenges of amending the constitution and because of the partisan and small state interests in maintaining the current institution.

Parliamentary Systems

In contrast to presidential systems, **parliamentary systems** are systems of **fused powers** between the executive and the legislature. Fused powers refer to a condition where the legislative and executive powers are inseparable. This is an important characteristic of a parliamentary system.

In parliamentary systems, a majority of the members of the legislature choose the head of government, who often holds the title of prime minister. The majority could be members of a single political party or a coalition of two or more political parties. The prime minister forms a cabinet, which is commonly referred to as "the government." The cabinet comprises ministers who head the various government departments, called ministries. Ministries are the bureaucracies that oversee the enforcement of laws, rules, and regulations adopted by the legislature and often advise the government on the drafting of legislation.

Voters, on the other hand, directly elect the members of the legislature. The direct popular election of the legislators and parliamentary selection of the prime minister have implications for the chains of responsibility: Governments in parliamentary systems are directly responsible to the majority in the legislature and indirectly responsible to the voters. The members of parliament are directly responsible to the voters (see Figure 8.2).

Due to a government's **legislative responsibility**, a legislative majority in a parliamentary system has the constitutional prerogative to remove a government from office without cause. "Without cause" simply means that a legislative majority can terminate a government without justifying it on criminal misconduct or other formal charges. Perhaps the government is not popular among voters. Maybe the country's economic performance has been subpar and a legislative majority wants another government to form. The prime minister does not need to have violated a law, as would be the case of the presidential impeachment in presidential systems. The procedure of a **vote of no confidence** refers to the method for a legislative majority to remove a government. Governments, on their part, have a power to dissolve the legislature and schedule legislative elections as they see appropriate before their legal legislative terms expire. For example, British Prime Minister Theresa May faced a no confidence vote in her government on January 16, 2019. Many members of her party, as well as the members of the opposition parties, believed that she lost the ability to govern after her proposal on how to leave the European Union (EU) faced defeat. May survived the attempt to oust her from power by 325 to 306 votes. The opposition parties called for the motion of no confidence in an attempt to break a stalemate in the Parliament over how to leave the EU.

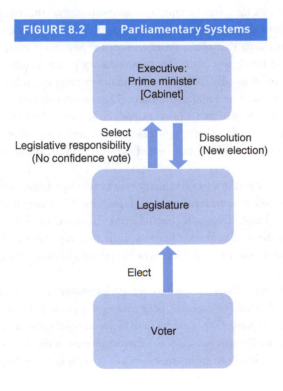

FIGURE 8.2 ■ Parliamentary Systems

Executive:
Prime minister
[Cabinet]

Select
Legislative responsibility
(No confidence vote)

Dissolution
(New election)

Legislature

Elect

Voter

The members of the British Parliament listen to Prime Minister Boris Johnson giving an update on the latest situation in Afghanistan in the House of Commons, September 2021.

Jessica Taylor/UK Parliament via AP

Hence, in traditional parliamentary systems, unlike presidential systems, neither governments nor legislators have fixed terms. The connection that the executive and legislative branches in a parliamentary system have with each other is in both their origins and survivals. These features make parliamentary systems fusions of powers systems.

The United Kingdom is one of the oldest parliamentary democracies. The prime minister leads a government and is usually the leader of the majority party in the British Parliament. The prime minister selects all the remaining ministers. The cabinet members are accountable to the parliament and are members of parliament themselves. In 2011, the British Parliament passed the Fixed-term Parliaments Act,which requires a parliamentary election at least every five years. A passage of a vote of no confidence or a vote of two-thirds of the members can still trigger an early election.

The head of government in a parliamentary system goes by various titles in different countries. The most common is prime minister (UK, Japan), but the person is also called chancellor (Germany), premier (Italy), Taoiseach (Ireland), or even president (South Africa and Spain)! This shows you that the basic difference between parliamentary and presidential systems is not what the head of government is called but how the relation between the government and the legislature is defined.

The unique features differentiating between parliamentary and presidential systems can influence political behavior. For example, political scientists have noticed that political parties tend to be stronger in parliamentary systems than in presidential systems because in the former, the majority party in parliament possesses an inherent interest in the success of the government led by its party leader. This desire unites members of a governing party. In presidential systems, inexperienced politicians can become presidents, and presidents often rely on their own persona and charisma to govern. Unlike parliamentary systems where prime ministers face a possibility of no confidence votes, presidents in presidential systems do not even need party support to stay in office. Some scholars of democracy also argue that because of its flexibility in terms of office and the lesser likelihood of legislative gridlock, parliamentary systems are more conducive to democratic stability than presidential systems.

PRACTICAL APPLICATION

What are the defining characteristics of parliamentary and presidential systems? Select two countries, one that is parliamentary and the other presidential. What differences do you think these two systems generate with respect to candidates' electoral behavior, politicians' legislative behavior, the strengths of parties, and the government's ability to govern?

Semi-Presidential Systems

Not all governing institutions fit neatly into either a presidential or a parliamentary system. Another type of governing system is the semi-presidential system, which is a hybrid of the other two types of systems of government. The French semi-presidential system is one of the best known, but a number of countries, including a few eastern European countries, use this system. Semi-presidential systems have a prime minister and a president who both hold significant authority. Some parliamentary systems have a president that acts as a head of state. Although such presidents in a parliamentary system have important functions, they are primarily ceremonial unless there is a governing crisis requiring their intervention.

In a semi-presidential system, both the prime minister and the president have important legislative powers. Like in parliamentary systems, the majority of members of the parliament selects the prime minister. However, the president must approve the selection. The majority of parliamentary members can also remove the government through a vote of no confidence. A direct popular vote elects a president, as in most presidential systems. The two executives, the prime minister and the president, operate in a manner so that neither is subordinate to the other. In France, the prime minister forms a cabinet and generally legislates over domestic policy. The president is responsible for foreign and security policies. Yet, the president can still veto legislation, although overriding a veto is not difficult.

France has experimented with a semi-presidential system with interesting results. Having a prime minister and president from two different political parties could produce governing tensions, and possibly gridlock, since they would likely have differing ideological points of view. The French refer to the situation of a dual executive from opposing political parties as "cohabitation." In such situations, both executives need to figure out how to live together for the good of the country.

Dual executives from opposing political parties can typically be attributed to incongruent election cycles. In one election cycle to elect the French president, voters may like a political party from the right. In a different election year, while the right-leaning president is still in power, the French voters may elect a left-leaning parliament with the prime minister coming from this party. This was the case with the 1995 French presidential election. Jacques Chirac, the leader of a right-leaning Rally for the Republic party, won over Lionel Jospin, leader of the left-leaning Socialist Party. Two years later, in 1997, the French voters went back to the polls to select members of their parliament. The results produced a left-leaning government with Jospin as the new prime minister. For the next few years, France operated under political executives from opposite ideologies attempting to pass laws.

The solution for continuous gridlock caused by cohabitation occurred in 2000 when the French amended their constitution in order to hold presidential and parliamentary elections at the same time and instituted the concurrent terms of office. Since adopting the constitutional amendment, both the president and prime minister have come from the same political party. The first election since the constitutional amendment, in 2002, saw the reelection of Chirac and a new parliament led by Prime Minister Jean-Pierre Raffarin, the leader of the Union for the Presidential Majority, a right-leaning political party allied with Chirac. Since then, the question of power and leadership between the two have practically been resolved. The president now acts as the leader of the political party in power with the prime minister being the number two person. This has produced a situation where the president generally envisions the legislative agenda and selects the members of the cabinet. The prime minister is the person who gets the ideas through parliament in the form of concrete pieces of legislation.

EXECUTIVE POWER

LEARNING OBJECTIVE

8.3 Explain the differences between the types of democratic executives and their primary functions.

Political executives have existed a lot longer than other governmental institutions, such as legislatures and courts. Political executives also exist in both democracies and nondemocratic states. In the United States, presidents and the cabinet together are called an **administration**. In much of the rest of the world, however, it is referred to as a government. As we defined in Chapter 6, a government is a set of people who have the authority to act on behalf of the state. Presidents are both **head of state** and **head of government** in presidential systems. Head of government is the chief political executive of the country and is responsible for making and carrying out policy decisions. Head of state, on the other hand, is the figurehead of the country and has ceremonial functions, such as greeting and meeting foreign heads of government and representing the country overseas.

In parliamentary systems, a prime minister is head of government, but generally, there is a separate head of state. The head of state may be an elected president. For example, in Italy an electoral college comprising the two chambers of Parliament and representatives of the 20 regions of the country elect their presidents. Since a president in a parliamentary system is only the head of state and not the head of government, the power of the office is not as large as that of a president in a presidential system.

The head of state may also be hereditary. A country's monarch (such as emperor, queen, king, etc.) commonly serves as the head of state where a constitutional monarchy exists. For example, in the UK as of this writing, the prime minister and leader of the Conservative Party is Boris Johnson, who has served as head of government since 2019. Queen Elizabeth II has been the head of state since her coronation in 1952.

In addition to serving as heads of state and heads of government, political executives also commonly oversee national bureaucracies, serve as commander in chief of their country's armed forces, handle diplomatic relations with other countries, act as a chief legislator, and perform the functions of their political party's top leader.

Italian Prime Minister Mario Draghi, German Chancellor Angela Merkel, British Prime Minister Boris Johnson, U.S. President Joe Biden, French President Emmanuel Macron, Canadian Prime Minister Justin Trudeau, and Japanese Prime Minister Yoshihide Suga attend a plenary session during the G-7 summit on June 13, 2021.

PHIL NOBLE/POOL/AFP via Getty Images

PRACTICAL APPLICATION

Find three parliamentary countries and examine how they select their heads of state. How powerful are the heads of state in those countries?

LEGISLATIVE POWER

LEARNING OBJECTIVE
8.4 Discuss the principal functions of legislatures and how legislative institutions differ across democracies.

Today, most countries have national legislatures. All democracies have national legislatures where the sole or at least one of the legislative chambers is a popularly elected body. Such legislatures carry out the roles of representation, lawmaking, and executive oversight. In nondemocratic countries, membership of the national legislature may use criteria other than direct popular elections. In nondemocratic regimes where legislative elections occur, they may not be free, fair, or competitive. In addition, legislatures in nondemocratic states most likely lack real power to make or change laws and regulations. For example, voters do not elect members of the National People's Congress in China by a direct popular election. The provincial assemblies select the members of the National People's Congress. As we detail later in this chapter, researchers consider it a "rubber stamp" legislature that never rejects government-proposed bills.

Representation

In democracies, legislatures have various important roles. First, legislatures provide an arena to represent a wide range of interests in society. **Representation** was the original function of legislatures in Europe where different societal classes could voice their views to the rulers on issues of public concern. For a long time, political representation meant representation of different interests in society by legislators, but the composition of the membership in the legislative body did not reflect the actual ethnic, racial, gender, or socioeconomic diversity in its society. Instead, national legislators have often been homogeneous when considering major demographic characteristics: They have predominantly and typically been male, economically well off and educated, and come from dominant racial or ethnic groups. However, can a practically homogeneous institution effectively represent diverse interests? Many societies still confront this lingering question today.

A more recent trend is **descriptive representation**, which seeks to ensure that the national legislature numerically mirrors the actual societal composition of the population. For example, although women comprise approximately 50 percent of national populations, only 25 percent of national legislators in the world are women. A notable exception is the Nordic countries, where nearly half of the national legislators are women. The United States has not fared well in women's descriptive representation. As of June 2021, women comprise only 27.4 percent of the House of Representatives of the U.S. Congress, which ranks the United States at the 65th place (which it shares with Egypt and El Salvador) in the world, according to the Inter-Parliamentary Union's (2021) *Women in National Parliaments* rankings. As a tool to increase the number of women legislators, a growing number of countries have introduced various types of gender quotas for legislative elections.

Famed Brazilian architect Oscar Niemeyer designed the building of the bicameral National Congress of Brazil, seen here. The smaller Federal Senate chamber features the shape of a shallow parabolic dome. The larger Chamber of Deputies, which represents the people, boasts a symbolic inverted dome in a bowl shape.

CC BY-SA 2.0

The constitution of Mexico is an example of gender quotas for legislative representation. The constitution's Article 41 requires that political parties develop "rules to ensure gender parity in the nomination of candidates in federal and local congressional elections." To enforce Article 41, Mexico's electoral law requires that political parties must guarantee that at least 40 percent of the candidates on their electoral lists are women (or people of the same gender) for both the Chamber of Deputies and the Senate. This means that there could be a minimum of 40 percent or a maximum of 60 percent women. One political party, *Partido Revolucionario Instituional* (Institutional Revolutionary Party, or PRI), voluntarily sets its quota to 50 percent. The National Electoral Institute, the institution responsible for organizing elections in Mexico, can deny a political party's ability to run its candidates should it break this law. Given that the quota requirements refer to candidates and not election outcomes and that the minimum is below the actual percentage of women (currently 51 percent, according to the World Bank Development Indicators), it is possible that women could still be underrepresented in the legislature. In the 2021 elections saw 48 percent of the Chamber of Deputies seats go to women and 49 percent going to women in the Senate. According to the Inter-Parliamentary Union's (2021) *Women in National Parliaments* rankings, this result places Mexico at fifth place in the world.

> ### EXPAND YOUR THOUGHTS
>
> Can a practically homogeneous institution effectively represent diverse interests? To what extent is descriptive representation important for effective political representation? What are the advantages and disadvantages of quota systems to diversify a legislature?

Making Laws

Another primary function of legislatures is **lawmaking**. The process of turning a proposal into a law can be involving. Committees and plenary floors of legislatures examine policy proposals. During deliberation, legislators may receive amendments to modify the original content. Some proposals navigate through legislatures quickly without encountering much resistance, whereas others drag on for a long time with obstructionist tactics employed by legislators and parties. Although legislatures pass or reject legislative proposals, they are not necessarily principal initiators of most enacted legislation. In parliamentary democracies, with tacit or explicit support by a legislative majority, the government is usually the primary agenda-setter and chief initiator of legislation. In many presidential systems, presidents originate many significant laws. However, presidents' ability to pass government bills in the legislature tends to diminish in **divided government**, where different parties control the executive and legislative branches. In presidential systems, presidents also have the power to veto legislation approved by the legislature. Presidential veto authority also varies significantly from country to country. In some countries, presidents have the authority to veto legislation only in its entirety. In other cases, presidents have the ability to veto parts of legislation as well as the entire legislation.

Let's take a look at the U.S. lawmaking process as an example. In the United States, constitutionally, only members of Congress have the prerogative to submit legislative proposals. The only exception is the budgetary bill, which the president introduces. The U.S. president needs to work with members of Congress to submit government initiatives. In addition, the U.S. president retains the power of enactment and veto. Proposals approved by the legislature need a presidential signature of approval before they can become laws. If the president disagrees with the legislation, the president may veto it in its entirety. In the United States, the ability of the president to deny legislation is called the package veto. The U.S. Constitution allows the Congress to override presidential vetoes with a two-thirds vote with both houses voting separately. A proposal becomes a law after the president approves it with their signature or Congress successfully overrides a presidential veto.

In between the initiation of a proposed law and its final vote is the deliberation process. This begins when the speaker of the House of Representatives or the president of the Senate assigns a proposed law to a relevant committee or possibly multiple committees. A legislative committee is a subset of members of the legislature who review proposals that fit their topic of specialization. For example, we can see a committee that reviews proposals associated with education, another for health care, or yet another for military matters. A committee will review the merits of the proposal. If committee members see problems with the proposal, they investigate the issues. This can take the form of gathering data, seeking out expert opinions through testimony, or gathering public input. In the end, the committee can decide on how the proposal will return to the legislature for a full vote. The committee could return it using the original language or introduce amendments. A proposal can also die in a committee. It happens when a committee votes not to allow it to go to the full legislature for a final vote. A committee can also choose not to act on a proposal. The committee chair can prioritize other proposals and end the legislative term without considering it.

If a proposal receives a positive vote from a committee or committees, it will then go to a plenary floor deliberation for further examination. During deliberation, the proposal may receive more amendments to modify the content. There is usually a debate on the final version before the House or Senate conducts a final vote. Each chamber votes on the proposal separately. Often, one chamber will adopt a proposal before it moves to the other where the process begins anew. Some proposals have high importance, leading to similar proposals being processed at the same time. Regardless, if the two chambers vote on the proposals sequentially (one chamber before the other) or at the same time, any differing language between the House and Senate's approved legislation will need to be fixed by a conference committee. This committee includes members from both chambers who adjust the proposals so that they have the same language. After the conference committee revises the proposal, it goes back to each chamber for the final approval.

Some proposals navigate through Congress quickly without encountering much resistance, whereas others drag on for a long time with obstructionist tactics employed by legislators and political parties. There are many occasions when the Congress does not act on proposals during their term. Other cases see it act, but the Congress may run out of time before a final vote. Regardless of the reason, if the proposal does not make the final vote, it will need to start anew in the next legislative term if there is continued interest.

Executive Oversight

A democracy can slide into autocracy if one person, often in the position as an executive, acquires too much power. The need for oversight, therefore, is due to the amount of executive power and the possibility of its abuse. Recall that chief executives serve as the head of government, giving them control of the vast governmental bureaucracy, including the military. The ability to control law enforcement and national security operations can lead to executive abuse without having checks on its powers. To prevent, minimize, and detect executive misconduct and incompetence, legislatures commonly exercise **executive oversight**. The oversight function ensures that the government accounts for its actions and does not abuse its authority.

Legislative oversight of the executive branch is the ability of the legislature to call into question the activities of the executive through investigation and possibly censure or removal of the executive. Such activities include checks pertaining to executive actions. Legislatures have the ability to review, monitor, and supervise governmental agencies, programs, activities, and policy implementation. Oversight can also be broad and ongoing. Such actions can include general areas of congressional activities, such as authorization, appropriations, investigations, and legislative hearings by standing and ad hoc committees.

In some countries, the legislature uses its budgetary power to limit and influence executive actions. For example, the U.S. Congress may deny funding for an activity that the president seeks, such as a military operation. However, in many countries the executive holds more budgetary powers than the legislature.

A direct punishment that a legislature can place on an executive comes in various forms. A **censure** of an executive official or the government is a common method of reproach. A censure is a public reprimand of an official or government that declares that the person or persons acted in a manner that were unacceptable for those who occupy the office. Censure is often an appropriate method to check the powers of an executive when the person did not clearly violate the law. Although censure does not usually accompany additional penalties, such as removal from office, a fine, or prison time, it highlights the misconduct with the objective of shaming the actor into complying with acceptable norms. One could argue that a censure is a very light punishment and may be ineffective in changing an executive's behavior. However, if the person did not violate the law, censure may be the only option open to the legislature.

Another punishment that the legislature can impose on the executive is removal from office. As already discussed, legislatures in presidential systems have the ability to impeach the executive accused of a crime. If found guilty, the president is formally removed from office. We also learned that legislatures in parliamentary systems have the constitutional prerogative to remove the government by a no confidence vote, a procedure that does not require a violation of the law.

Legislative Structures

One last institutional consideration is legislative structures. Do legislators work together as one body, or do they work separately as two independent bodies? This distinction has important implications for political representation and how quickly legislatures can approve the final wording of proposals. If the members sit together as one body, then we refer to the legislature as a **unicameral legislature**, or a legislature with a single chamber. About two-thirds of the world's national legislatures are unicameral. In a unicameral legislature, proposal introduction, deliberation, and votes all take place in the single chamber. In a parliamentary system, the approved proposal becomes law after floor votes. In a presidential system, the legislature-approved bill goes to the president for enactment or veto.

The legislature that comprises two distinct chambers is a **bicameral legislature**. Approximately one-third of the world's legislatures are bicameral. In general, the legislative process in a bicameral legislature requires the approval of a bill in both chambers. This requirement for concurrent approval by two distinct chambers puts an additional hurdle for lawmaking compared to the legislative process in a unicameral legislature.

If the majorities of the two chambers disagree on the content of legislation under examination, many legislatures use some sort of a reconciliation procedure to produce content that is acceptable to the majority in both chambers. The U.S. Congress uses a conference committee, composed of selected members from both houses, to generate a bill that is to be voted up or down in both chambers. In other cases, bills could shuttle between the two chambers until the identical text is approved by both houses. Yet in other cases, one of the chambers, usually the lower house, predominates in the case of bicameral disagreement and adopts the text preferred by the predominant chamber. In most cases, if one of the chambers rejects a bill, then the proposal dies and no further action is taken.

Why would a country decide on having a bicameral system? After all, it makes more sense to have one chamber in the legislature so that the legislative process can operate more efficiently. Although having greater efficiency makes more sense, it may come at the price of reducing the representativeness of the legislature. We often see bicameral systems resulting from historically grounded rationales.

For example, almost all federal countries have bicameral legislatures. Federal countries tend to feature significant internal diversity with unique regional units. In those countries, the lower chamber typically represents the population, and the upper chamber serves to represent the interests of the geographical units, such as states and provinces. Mexico, Nigeria, and the United States are examples. Each country, when they were under colonial rule, experienced different administrative units that eventually became states. After independence, the smaller units wanted to have representation so that the large states would not dominate decisions. Other examples include Germany and Italy. Each is a merger of historically independent kingdoms and principalities. Each previously independent unit wanted a significant say after their respective unifications. It is therefore not surprising that all of our examples have bicameral legislatures: one that represents the subnational units and the other to represent the people as a whole.

Not all bicameral legislatures are the same, however. Bicameral legislatures vary in the relative powers of the two chambers. When one chamber is more powerful than the other, we refer to this arrangement as an **asymmetric bicameral system** (Lijphart, 2012). In general, the chambers hold the labels of "the lower house" and "the upper house." Asymmetric power refers to what a particular legislative body can do and which types of proposals they can debate and approve relative to the other chamber. In many countries, budgetary powers reside in one chamber, and one house can override the decisions of the other house. As we have discussed, controlling the size and allocation of government spending carries a great deal of influence. In addition, the ability of one chamber to disagree with what the other wants and then override its decision clearly makes the first chamber more powerful.

The UK is a good example of an asymmetric bicameral system. The House of Commons is the lower house of the British Parliament and the House of Lords is the upper house. The House of Lords is an unelected chamber whose members the monarch officially appoints, but they require the approval of the House of Commons. Members of the upper house possess noble titles or are leaders in the Church of England. The House of Lords came into being before the House of Commons and for a time it was the only check on the monarchy's power. As democracy evolved, the British established the House of Commons as an elected body representing all the British people. It grew to become more powerful than either the upper house or the monarchy. The House of Lords still regularly reviews and amends bills from the lower house. However, its ability to reject legislation is severely restricted because the lower house can reject amendments by the upper house. Last, while the House of Lords can delay the deliberation of legislation, it cannot do so if legislation involves government spending.

On the other hand, there are also **symmetric bicameral systems**, where the powers of the two chambers are equal and passage of legislation requires approval by a concurrent majority in both houses. For example, the bicameral systems of Brazil, Nigeria, Mexico, and the United States are symmetric bicameral legislatures. The upper houses in these countries (referred to as the Senate in each of these countries) represent geographic units, while the lower houses represent the people. Geographic representation by the upper chamber is common, yet there are other types of representation. For example, the lower house may represent people in narrow geographic districts while the upper chamber may represent the people as a whole with an election where the entire country is a single electoral district.

If the membership characteristics of the two chambers are significantly different, governing becomes more challenging than when there is a great overlap between the two chambers. The incongruence in the membership compositions may be due to different partisan majorities, different electoral or membership selection rules used, or different electoral timings. Studies have shown that legislative gridlock is more likely in bicameral than in unicameral legislatures where the characteristics of the chamber memberships are sufficiently different.

JUDICIAL POWER

LEARNING OBJECTIVE

8.5 Describe the key functions of judicial systems and the characteristics of differing judicial systems.

Judicial systems around the world have some common functions. The most recognizable function is the execution of justice. **Justice** refers to fair treatment under the law. Court rulings need to apply the law equally to all without bias toward someone's characteristics, such as race, ethnicity, gender, or socioeconomic status. Furthermore, courts can rule if the laws themselves are just. They do so by comparing the law and its application to the principles and rights listed in a country's basic law. In most countries, the constitution that establishes their form of government is the basic law. In others, the basic law is a body of law established over time. In yet others, a religious doctrine is the basis of the law. The application of law is often subjective with its roots in the contemporary culture. Many countries once considered slavery as a just institution and it was thus protected by their courts. However, as societal values changed, some courts abolished the institution of slavery because it violated the basic human rights of the enslaved (see the case of *Somerset vs Stewart* in Chapter 5).

A country's judicial system has many layers, each with different functions. A **criminal court**, as the name indicates, tries those accused of committing a crime. Some countries have an **adversarial legal system**, in which the judge is an arbiter, or an impartial referee, between the state (who acts as the prosecutor) and the accused (who acts as the defendant). In such cases, a judge's role is to make sure the proceedings are fair. These circumstances often rely on a jury to be brought together to decide the case. In countries that do not have a jury system, the judge will make the final decision on the case.

Other countries combine the roles of the judge and prosecutor. In an **inquisitorial legal system,** investigating judges discover and examine the evidence against the accused. They also examine the law to determine if the accused is guilty and decide on the punishment. A panel of trial judges then review the evidence and perhaps further question witnesses before giving the final verdict.

Another way to differentiate legal systems is the type of law that they apply. In a **common law system**, governments create laws and leave them to the courts to interpret. Such systems consider each court ruling as a precedent. Once a precedent is set, judges will use it in future cases that are similar in nature. Judges can overturn precedents if they discover a flaw in the prior ruling. Common law works in a hierarchical legal system where courts at higher levels review cases of lower level courts to ensure rulings follow precedent in a just manner.

Under a **civil law system,** a country's legislative system creates laws that do not allow room for interpretation by a judge. The legal codes are precise in detailing the violations, the procedures to follow, and the amount of punishment. It is therefore not surprising that many inquisitorial systems adopt civil law and have an investigating judge prosecute the alleged offense.

Other than criminal courts, countries also have systems in place to rule on the constitutionality of laws and governmental actions. This function of **judicial review** occurs in specialized constitutional courts, which are set up for this purpose. Judicial review is also referred to as constitutional review. In the United States, the Supreme Court performs this function. It can take on cases presented by the federal government, one or more state governments, or individuals. Cases involve the plaintiffs' rights and whether a law violated their rights established in the United States Constitution.

The U.S. Supreme Court, however, only preforms judicial review of laws after their creation and when actors bring a case to the court. In other countries, constitutional courts can review proposed laws if asked. In Germany, Das Bundesverfassungsgericht (Federal Constitutional Court) performs this function if one-third of the German lower legislative chamber petitions the court. Some legal scholars argue that this is a more efficient system since sometimes the constitutionality of a proposed law comes up during debates in the legislature. Instead of guessing if the courts will declare a law unconstitutional, it seems more prudent and efficient to ask the court before passing the proposed law. This would not only save time and expenses but also constitute a proactive way to prevent harming someone's rights. On the other hand, proactive courts have also raised concerns about **judicialization of politics.** The judicialization of politics is the reliance on courts and judicial means to tackle public policy issues, political disputes, and central moral predicaments, and political controversies. This phenomenon has increased dramatically in the late twentieth and early twenty-first centuries in various parts of the world.

The ability to apply the law without outside pressure is also part of the institutional makeup of judicial systems. Consider a controversial case involving the interpretation of a law. Judges could use their judicial expertise to interpret the law, or they could make a decision based on political pressures they receive. One such pressure could be their removal from office if they did not make the "correct" choice. Politicians would then be free to appoint someone that will accept a more politically motivated decision. In many political systems, especially democratic ones, **judicial independence** helps to reduce the chance that political and societal pressures influence judicial decisions.

Many constitutions attempt to have an independent judiciary through appointment and tenure procedures. The appointment of judges by the executive branch, followed by the legislature's approval, raises the chances that expertise will be the primary selection criterion. If voters elect judges, then the process may be more political because judges, just like elected politicians, will have an incentive to make decisions based on how different options raise their chances of winning the next election. However, neither method will guarantee the noninterference of politics in judicial decisions. For example, in the United States, the president appoints federal judges (including members of the Supreme Court), and the Senate must approve them. Research has shown that presidents nominate judges whose ideologies align with theirs and the Senate confirmation process is much easier when those nominations come from the president who holds a majority in the Senate.

Giving judges lifelong tenure is another method to ensure judicial independence. If judges do not need to worry that a decision will lead to their removal, they are less likely to succumb to political pressure.

EXPAND YOUR THOUGHTS

Compare two judicial systems, one that selects judges through appointment with lifelong terms and another in which elections decide which candidates can be judges with fixed terms. In which type of judicial system would you predict judges would have more political pressure? Why do you think this would be the case?

CENTRALIZING OR DECENTRALIZING POWERS OF THE STATE

LEARNING OBJECTIVE

8.6 Analyze the differences between federalism and unitary systems and the reasons for and against the centralization of state power.

The last constitutional feature of governmental structures we examine is the division of power between different levels of government. Many constitutions explicitly limit the concentration of power in one group by dispersing power across many different hands. The separation of powers system was a deliberate institutional choice by the U.S. constitutional framers to divide power across the different branches of government—executive, legislative, and judiciary.

Another method to disperse power is through federalism. **Federalism** is a system that gives considerable autonomy to subnational units while the central government deals with issues of national concerns, such as international commerce, diplomacy, and the like. It is a system that constitutionally guarantees the division of power between the central and regional governments in such a way that each exercises responsibility for a particular set of functions.

Many believe that federalism generates certain benefits. One of the anticipated advantages of federalism is that it protects local autonomy against the possible domination by the center. In addition, countries that adopt federalism tend to be multicultural societies. Therefore, another anticipated advantage of federalism is that local autonomy will enable subnational authority to govern more effectively since they are close to the local population, who may substantially differ from the population outside the area.

Federalism can evolve over time, with the center accumulating more powers or giving more authority to the subnational units. Change usually happens during times of crises or wide debates. When you hear the term *states' rights*, you are likely witnessing a debate regarding federalism. The main questions usually addressed in these debates include how much authority the central government should possess in specific issue areas and how one determines what is best for the local population. Today, certain large countries with diverse regional differences use federalism to keep the country united under one state. In addition to the United States, countries such as Argentina, Brazil, Canada, Germany, Mexico, Nigeria, Russia, Switzerland, and Venezuela employ federal structures.

However, most countries in the world are **unitary governments**. In unitary systems, all major power and policy come from the central government. It is a system in which the central government is supreme while the regional governments are subordinate. Countries with unitary governments tend to have relatively homogeneous populations so there is less need for subnational authority to address local uniqueness. Japan, Costa Rica, and South Korea are a few examples of unitary countries. Because of the concentration of power in the central government, unitary systems tend to allow more efficient policymaking and consistent policies within countries compared to those in federal countries.

Although unitary systems formally concentrate power in the central government, tensions between the center and subnational governments in some countries have led their central governments to delegate some powers to self-governing regional governments. Called **devolution**, the central governments of the United Kingdom and Spain have granted greater autonomy to subnational governments because residents of certain regions in those countries view themselves as distinct from others in the national population. With devolution, the central government retains ultimate authority: It has the legal right under the country's constitution to give and take away authority from the regional governments. In other words, the center allows for the devolution of power to the regions and such transfer of authority is not a permanent constitutional arrangement. This makes devolution different from federal arrangements.

Take the United Kingdom as an example. Britain uses a unitary system of government and it is made up of four distinct regions of people, also referred to as nations. Each region has its own separate history and culture, including its own languages. The following photo shows the four distinct regions of the United Kingdom. At the top is Scotland, below it is England, and on the left side is Wales, with Northern Ireland on the right. . Farthest to the left, we have the

Republic of Ireland, which was part of the UK but has been independent since 1922 (see Chapter 5 for more information). The union of the regions or nations is a complicated history of English conquest of the other three regions. Wales was the first conquered during the medieval era, followed by Ireland in the sixteenth century. After Irish independence, the northern countries remained in the UK. Scotland formally became part of the UK in 1707, although English monarchs ruled it one hundred years earlier due to royal family relationships. Therefore, the peoples of the British islands have had periods of independent kingdoms, with associated cultural and political development, before becoming part of the UK.

The regions comprising the United Kingdom.

iStockPhoto.com/PeterHermesFurian

The call for more regional autonomy in the UK is not new. The Irish case by itself has been a long struggle for autonomy and then independence since conquest. Many Scots fought the English for hundreds of years against becoming part of the UK. They have also continuously called for independence since their incorporation into the UK. There have been votes on seceding from the UK, but none has been successful. Devolution is a method to keep the UK together by giving more power of self-governance to local authority. It established the Scottish Parliament, which includes a prime minister who holds the formal title of the First Minister of Scotland. Northern Ireland and Wales each has its own legislative body, the Northern Ireland Assembly and the *Senedd Cymru* (Welsh Parliament), respectively. England does not have its own regional parliament. Each of these governing bodies was produced by acts of the British (central) Parliament, which also details which policy areas the local authorities can legislate. Since they were not negotiated treaties, the central government has the ability, through the central government's parliamentary legislative process, to suspend or even terminate the regional legislatures. In other words, they exist at the pleasure of the central government. For example, Northern Ireland reverted to direct rule by the center from 2017 to 2020. Regional bodies also do not have the authority to call for an independence vote. The power to call for such a referendum must come from the British (central) Parliament.

EXPAND YOUR THOUGHTS

What are the advantages of unitary systems compared to federal systems? Under what conditions would a unitary approach be more desirable than federal arrangements?

POLITICAL INSTITUTIONS IN NON-DEMOCRATIC REGIMES

LEARNING OBJECTIVE
8.7 Identify the institutions of nondemocratic regimes and how their functions and goals differ from those in democratic regimes.

Institutions of nondemocratic states are different from their democratic counterparts, although they often go by the same names. The incumbent political elites frequently design nondemocratic institutions to preserve and legitimize their power and right to rule. nondemocratic regimes may have laws regulating succession of power, but they tend to regulate the alternation of power among the members of the current elite, such as the rules about hereditary succession in a monarchy and change of the leadership within the ruling political party. In the next two sections, we examine some examples of governing institutions in nondemocratic regimes.

Political Institutions in the People's Republic of China

A dominant party rule is a regime where one party dominates political office and policy decisions (see Chapter 6). It is also called **one-party rule**. Often the legitimacy of one-party rule is in the country's constitution, which may state that only members of a specific political party can hold public office and rule in the name of the people. The rationale for this rule is based on the idea that the specified political party exclusively cares about the needs of the people and it alone knows how to best achieve the country's goals through its ideology. The party leaders have the monopoly on the ability to change the ideology or direction of the country. The constitution may also specify that leadership selection is the current party leaders' prerogative.

China is one of the longest serving among the world's one-party regimes. Since 1949, the Communist Party of China (CPC) has governed the country using its monopoly on power. Although the Chinese constitution does not directly give it the sole right to rule, it does so indirectly by stating that the CPC leads all other political organizations in the country. In addition, the CPC can amend China's constitution during the party's national meetings, called National Congresses.

The CPC controls the state institutions by forming "a state within a state." The CPC's committees form parallel structures with state structures described in their constitution (see Figure 8.3). They are parallel structures because party structures perform the same functions as the state structures and in most cases, the members of the party structures are also members of the state structures. The usual procedure is to make decisions when officials meet in CPC committees and then formally ratify the decisions when they meet in their state capacity. The top of the CPC's hierarchy makes all the critically important decisions and requires all members to follow decisions without obstruction. Therefore, it is not surprising for the state institutions to ratify the party leaders' decisions. In sum, the CPC forms the core of decision-making, which state institutions always approve.

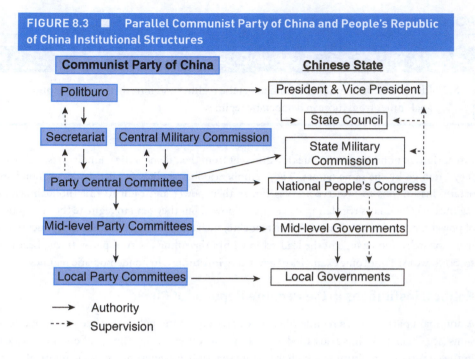

FIGURE 8.3 ■ Parallel Communist Party of China and People's Republic of China Institutional Structures

An examination of Figure 8.3 illustrates how the CPC dominates the state institutions. At the very bottom are the local and mid-level party committees. They oversee the CPC's interests at the town, village, and regional levels. In theory, the respective party members elect the members of the local committees and the mid-level committees every five years. However, the CPC's National Congress elects the powerful Central Committee for a five-year term and oversees the selection of the lower-level committees.

The Central Committee is China's major decision-making body. All decisions that impact the CPC require the Central Committee's approval. This also includes the election of the CPC's most powerful position, the general secretary, who is the party's paramount leader. The Central Committee also selects the members of the most powerful subgroup within the party, the Political Bureau, or **Politburo** for short, as well as the chair of the Central Military Commission. The Politburo comprises the elite of the CPC, including the general secretary. The Central Military Commission controls the operations of People's Liberation Army, which is the formal name of the entire Chinese military.

Each of these CPC institutions has a counterpart in the state. As you can see in Figure 8.3, the members of the local party committees also form the local governments. Since they need to obey the decisions of the CPC's Central Committee, the CPC is effectively in control of these local levels. The national decision-making body is the National People's Congress (NPC), which is China's legislature. The NPC meets for about two weeks and only once a year. As you may imagine, if the CPC institutions had not already made the decisions before the NPC meets, it would be difficult to get much business done within such a short period. Therefore, the CPC's Central Committee, which receives directives from the Politburo, drafts and approves all laws before adoption by the NPC.

The NPC decides who will be China's president and members of the State Council, which is the governing cabinet. However, this is a formality since the NPC elects the CPC general secretary as president and other members of the Politburo often become the vice president and members of the State Council. As you can see, the true authority is within the CPC. The state institutions, which have the formal constitutional powers, simply carry out the orders of the party leadership.

Political Institutions in the Islamic Republic of Iran

The Islamic Republic of Iran is a **theocracy**, which is a regime based on a specific religious doctrine. It is similar to one-party Communist rule in that only a specific doctrine can govern the country. However, the leaders of a state-sanctioned religion substitute the role of the political party. Like the one-party rule, the country's constitution states that a particular religion's doctrines and laws are the only legitimate way to govern. The governing religious leaders justify rule by religious doctrine because a deity or deities handed down the religion to the people as the correct way to live their lives. The religious leaders are well educated in the religion and therefore are the only ones that can interpret its doctrine, making them the guardians of the religion's practice. Under this view, stepping away from the religious rule would mean the country's ruin. The case of Iran illustrates how the institutions of a theocracy put religious rule into everyday practice.

In 1979, a popular revolution removed the U.S.-supported monarch, Shah Mohammad Reza Pahlavi, from power. Multiple political groups participated in the revolution with the single aim of removing the Shah. After the Shah's fall and exile, an Islamic faction led by the Grand Ayatollah Ruhollah Khomeini was able to stabilize the country and form a theocratic regime, which continues to this day. The theocracy's identity is Shia, one of the major sects of Islam. The Shia idea of the Guardianship of the Islamic Jurist legitimizes the regime's right to rule. The Guardianship refers to the authority of the *ulama*, or interpreters of Islam, to serve as custodians or guardians of a society. While many Shia scholars outside of Iran debate the limits to the religious clerics' authority, in Iran an absolute interpretation of the Guardianship doctrine is the basis of the constitution. Religious guardians have total say in the governance of the country. Effectively, this implies that the Iranian state institutions must have clerical membership or at least clerical dominance.

The highest authority is in the hands of the state's executive body, the Supreme Leadership Authority. The current office holder is the Grand Ayatollah Ali Khamenei. He is the second person to hold this position, the first being the founder of the Islamic Republic, Khomeini. In the strict interpretation of the Islamic Jurist Guardianship, the Supreme Leader has the final word on all laws, regulations, and policies. He is also the head of the armed forces, the judiciary, and the state-run media. The position is a lifetime appointment, unless the office holders are unable to carry out their duties.

Technically, the Supreme Leader's appointment comes from another body, the Assembly of Experts. The experts are Islamic jurists and ayatollahs who supervise the Supreme Leader. That being said, court rulings have determined that it is illegal for them to criticize the Supreme

Leader. Membership in the Assembly of Experts also requires the approval of the Supreme Leader. This means that the Supreme Leader, in fact, appoints the body that appoints and dismisses (due to being physically incapacitated) the Supreme Leader. In addition, the Assembly of Experts serve fixed eight-year terms and the Supreme Leader can decline to reappoint them. This puts most, if not all, the power in the hands of the Supreme Leader. Before Khomeini died and left the office vacant, he required the Assembly of Experts to designate Khamenei as his successor. Therefore, the second Supreme Leader was actually handpicked by the first one. The Iranian constitution also states that the Iranian citizens elect the experts. However, another body, the Guardian Council, controls who can run for office and, as mentioned, membership in the Assembly of Experts needs final approval of the Supreme Leader.

The Guardian Council is a 12-member institution that serves as Iran's constitutional court. The Supreme Leader selects six members who are experts in Islamic law. The Iranian legislature selects the remaining six members from a list given to them by the head of the Iranian judiciary, who the Supreme Leader appoints. The Guardian Council has two highly important functions. First, being a constitutional court, it makes the final decision on the constitutionality of all laws. It is important to note that when it makes a ruling on a law's constitutionality, it assesses the constitutionality based on the **Shari'a** or Islamic law found in the Qur'an (Islam's holy book) and not the Iranian constitution. This power allows the Guardian Council to veto any law it deems unfit. Second, the Guardian Council oversees all popular elections. This critical power includes the decision on who can and who cannot run for office. Before the election cycle begins, everyone who wishes to run for office needs to file an application with the Guardian Council. The council then determines if the applicant is devoutly religious enough to seek office. In the case of the Assembly of Experts, the council must also determine if the candidate has sufficiently strong Islamic legal credentials to hold office. The Guardian Council therefore has the ability to maintain the theocratic status quo and block reform.

The Islamic Consultative Assembly or *Majlis* is the Iranian legislature. It is a popularly and directly elected parliament among the candidates approved by the Guardian Council. The ability of the legislature to adopt laws is limited in scope since the Supreme Leader has vast powers to declare edicts. After passing legislation, the new law goes to the Guardian Council for review. If the council agrees, then the law is enforceable. If, on the other hand, the council disagrees with the law's compatibility with the Shari'a, it goes back to the legislature for modification or annulment. Given the limits on who can run for office and legislative power, the Consultative Assembly is designed not to produce reforms unless the Supreme Leader and Guardian Council agree.

The final institution to consider is the office of the Iranian president. The official role of the president is head of government. As mentioned earlier, the powers of the Supreme Leader are vast, which leaves the Iranian president with little influence over political affairs. Although the president is a popularly elected position, all candidates for president require the approval of the Guardian Council, and the final appointment of the president depends on the approval by the Supreme Leader. In addition, the Supreme Leader can remove the president at any time for any cause. For these reasons, the Iranian president is generally not a high-profile or powerful position. In reading the constitution, one could conclude that the president is second to the Supreme Leader. In reality, the president carries very little power, so it is not surprising that the president is not very visible. The exception to this was Mahmoud Ahmadinejad's presidency from 2005 to 2013. A very outspoken and strong believer in the theocracy, he often strongly and publicly criticized Iran's opponents (Israel, Saudi Arabia, and the United States). Ahmadinejad was (and still is) a strong advocate for Iran's nuclear weapons program.

SUMMARY

Governmental institutions shape political decisions because the formal rules and norms influence political actors' behavior. We first examined the major differences between presidential, parliamentary, and semi-presidential systems. Distinct institutional designs concentrate decision-making power in the case of parliamentary systems and disperse it in presidential systems. Semi-presidential systems have a dual executive that would also disperse power in theory. The varied governmental setups translate into differing patterns of legislative efficiencies and outcomes.

We then delved into specialized institutions found in democracies. A head of government leads executive institutions and may serve as a head of state (typically under presidentialism) or we may see another individual acting as head of state (which is common under parliamentary systems). Legislative institutions may be bicameral or unicameral, and in democracies, at least one of the chambers has a formal role of representing the people through direct popular elections. In addition to representation, lawmaking and executive oversights are primary functions of legislatures. We also examined the variation of judicial systems found in democracies. Although each system practices the important principle of the rule of law, they differ in how to carry out this principle.

This chapter also examined how states distribute power across different levels of government. In federal systems, power is constitutionally decentralized. Federal constitutions outline which powers belong to the center and which belong to the subnational authorities. In contrast, unitary arrangements place power in the central government. However, when needed, the central government may devolve power to a subnational authority. The center's ability to decentralize power in unitary systems also implies that it can take back the power when it sees fit.

The last discussion involved the governmental institutions found in some nondemocratic regimes. Through the examples of the institutions of a dominant party regime (China) and theocracy (Iran), we see arrangements that perpetuate power in the hands of a specific group of rulers. In the case of China, only the prevailing ideology of the Communist Party will guide which laws will pass through institutional arrangements. The status quo keeps state power weak relative to the Communist Party's institutions. In the case of Iran, leaders can only use the doctrines of the Shia sect of Islam to create specific laws. Religious leaders keep laws within this doctrine by controlling membership in the decision-making process as well as the process itself.

In the next chapter, we will continue to explore political institutions by examining political parties and electoral laws. We see how the institutional arrangements of elections influence how people vote, how candidates campaign, who wins elections, and even the number of viable parties a democracy will have.

KEY TERMS

Administration (p. 170)

Adversarial legal system (p. 178)

Asymmetric bicameral system (p. 177)

Behavioral revolution (p. 163)

Bicameral legislature (p. 176)

Censure (p. 176)

Civil law system (p. 179)

Common law system (p. 179)

Criminal court (p. 178)

Descriptive representation (p. 172)

Devolution (p. 181)

Divided government (p. 174)

Executive oversight (p. 175)

Federalism (p. 180)

Filibuster (p. 163)

Fixed term (p. 164)

Fused powers (p. 166)

Head of government (p. 170)

Head of state (p. 170)

Impeachment (p. 164)

Inquisitorial legal system (p. 179)

Judicial independence (p. 180)

Judicial review (p. 179)

Judicialization of politics (p. 179)

Justice (p. 178)

Lawmaking (p. 174)

Legislative responsibility (p. 167)

New institutionalism (p. 163)

One-party rule (p. 183)

Parliamentary systems (p. 166)

Politburo (p. 184)

Presidential systems (p. 164)

Representation (p. 172)

Separation of powers (p. 164)

Shari'a (p. 186)

Symmetric bicameral systems (p. 177)

Theocracy (p. 185)

Unicameral legislature (p. 176)

Unitary government (p. 181)

Vote of no confidence (p. 167)

FURTHER READING

Bogdanor, V. (2001). *Devolution in the United Kingdom*. Oxford University Press.

Dreyer, T. (2018, June). *China's political system: Modernization and tradition*. Routledge.

Moe, T. M., & Caldwell, M. (1994). The institutional foundations of democratic government: A comparison of presidential and parliamentary systems. *Journal of Institutional and Theoretical Economics*, *150*(1), 171–195.

O'Connor, V. (2012). *Common law and civil law traditions*. United States Institute of Peace.

The Constitution Forever.
Union and

Bloomberg/Contributor/Getty Images

ELECTIONS AND POLITICAL PARTIES

The institutions of political representation—elections, electoral systems, political parties, and legislatures—play crucial roles in representative democracy. If we are to make representative democracy work, we should understand its basic institutions of leadership selection and interest aggregation as well as institutions of collective decision-making. In Chapter 8, we examined legislatures.

This chapter's focus is elections, electoral systems, and political parties. We start by investigating why people vote—or do not vote. An influential rational choice theory indicates that a rational voter should almost never bother to vote. Yet in reality, more people turn out to vote than predicted by the theory, although there is significant variation in voter turnout across countries. Who votes? Why do people vote? We then consider different electoral rules used in the world. We will take a close look at some of the more popular electoral rules, including plurality voting, majority runoff, alternative vote, and proportional representation. Each type of electoral system uses different methods in converting votes into seats. The differences in electoral systems produce different candidate and voter behavior. They could also generate different electoral outcomes. These differences get us to think about what kind of voter-representative relationship we would like to achieve, how many (or how few) choices we would like to have with respect to the number of political parties and candidates, how representative our democratic institutions should be, and how much we value governmental action over representation of diverse voices and compromise. We will then examine political party systems, inquiring into the factors that influence the number and types of political parties in a society.

Interestingly, elections, legislatures, and political parties, although they are hallmark features of contemporary democracies, are not exclusive to democratic countries. Over the years, nondemocratic countries have increasingly adopted those institutions. No matter how similar they appear, and even though they are also called by the same names, elections and parties in autocratic regimes are completely different from those in democratic countries and serve different purposes. We will look at elections and parties in autocratic regimes at the end of the chapter.

ELECTIONS AND DEMOCRACY

LEARNING OBJECTIVE
9.1   Describe the evolution of democracy and the view and role of elections.

In contemporary democracies, political representation is of paramount importance. When democracy first emerged around the sixth century BC in the city-state of Athens in Ancient Greece, the form it took was quite different from democracy that we know today. In its original form, democracy resembled a town hall meeting in which local people gather to discuss the needs and problems of the community and make collective decisions. The legislative assembly consisted of all adult Athenian citizens (which excluded enslaved people, foreigners, and women). Without intermediaries, Athenian citizens met in the assembly and discussed and voted on the issues that concerned them. This form of democracy is known today as **direct democracy**.

Another interesting feature of Athenian democracy is that the few political and administrative offices that existed were filled randomly by lot, a practice called sortition, to ensure equality of citizens. Athenian democracy did not even use elections to fill principal political and administrative offices. In fact, many at that time considered elections undemocratic because choosing individuals based on their qualifications or attributes meant that people were not treated equally.

Of course, the ancient style of direct democracy is not the democracy that we practice today. We are familiar with democracies where political offices are filled by elections and where legislative bodies consist of elected representatives who make policies on behalf of citizens. This form of democracy where citizens elect their representatives and those representatives gather, speak, deliberate, and make decisions through votes and other means on behalf of those whom they represent is called **representative democracy**.

The prevalence of representative democracies in the contemporary world does not signify that direct democracy no longer exists; direct democracy is still practiced in certain forms and by certain organizations. For example, think about a student organization like a political science honor society in your college where all members meet, discuss, and make decisions for their collective interest and activities. However, political and administrative units have become enormously large. Consider the United States. According to U.S. *Federal Register*, in 2018, 253 million people made up the voting age population in the country. It would be impossible to create a national assembly where all 253 million eligible citizens gather and make decisions for the country. In today's world, political communities are simply too large and direct democracy is plainly impractical as a regular institution of legislative deliberation. Even at the subnational levels (such as state, provincial, and municipal levels), representative democracy with elections is common in most democratic countries.

Our use of representative democracy today elevates the importance of the institutions of political representation. Elections are the primary means to select political leadership in a representative democracy. Electoral systems produce many consequences of our interest, including politicians' behavior, voter-representative relationships, governments' ability to govern, the number and type of political parties, and voter turnout, to name a few.

WHY DO PEOPLE VOTE? THE PARADOX OF VOTING

LEARNING OBJECTIVE

9.2   Explain the logic behind the paradox of voting and the varied patterns of voter turnout in democracies.

One of the fundamental rights in a representative democracy is the right to vote. Although all contemporary democracies guarantee their citizens the right to vote to choose their representatives, **voter turnout**—the percentage of eligible voters who cast a ballot in an election—varies quite significantly across countries. You might think that in many advanced and long-time democracies, voters have ingrained the value of democratic voting and are eager to vote in elections. This is not the case. In many advanced democracies, where voting is not compulsory, voter turnout is rather low. Voter turnout in the United States has been particularly low compared to other countries, hovering around 60 percent of the voting-eligible population during presidential election years, and about 40 percent during mid-term legislative elections (see Figure 9.1). Turnout is even lower for subnational elections. Voter turnout for local elections has historically been lower than turnout for national or state elections in the United States, and is getting even worse. Only about 20 percent of voting age populations on average cast their votes in recent local elections. In some local elections, only about 10 percent of registered voters vote.

Think about the implications for democracy when so few people vote. Suppose that 15 percent of the voting age eligible people voted in an election to elect a representative, and the representative was elected with 50 percent of the vote cast. This would mean that the elected representative had the support of only 7.5 percent of the voting age eligible voters in the district. How representative could a representative democracy be when so few people vote?

However, voter turnout varies considerably not only across the levels of elections but also across countries, and not all countries have problems in getting people to vote. In Australia and Belgium, where voting is required, turnout for national lower house legislative elections has been over 90 percent. In Germany and Sweden, where voting is not compulsory, turnout has been over 80 percent, and in the United Kingdom, Japan, France, and Canada, over 70 percent. Switzerland has been closer to the United States, with only slightly more than 50 percent of the electorate voting in national legislative elections.

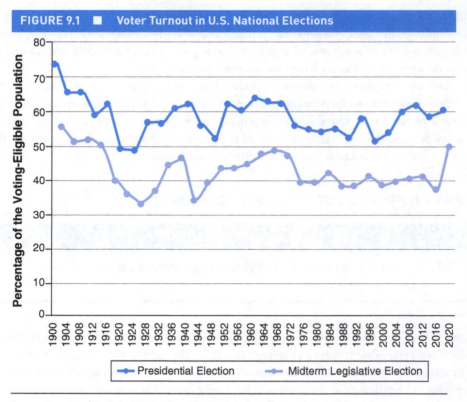

FIGURE 9.1 ■ Voter Turnout in U.S. National Elections

Source: Data from the United States Elections Project. http://www.electproject.org/

Low voter turnout is a problem. It is a problem because an election is a fundamental institution of representative democracy. If many people are not participating in the electoral process, can we still call it a democracy (i.e., government by the people), as the term connotes? Low voter turnout also casts doubt about the legitimacy and representativeness of the government, as mentioned earlier. If, for example, only 40 percent of the electorate vote (which is the recent average turnout for U.S. mid-term national legislative elections) and a representative is elected with, let's say, 50 percent of the vote cast, how representative would the elected official be of his or her constituency? In this example, only 20 percent of the total voters supported the winning representative with ballots.

Hence low voter turnout is problematic. It undermines the fundamental premises of democracy. Why don't more people vote? Most, if not all, of us living in a democratic country would be enraged if our right to vote were taken away. Moreover, if we want to make a difference, if we want to have a say in policy, and if we want our government to listen to us, isn't it essential for us to vote? An election is one crucial mechanism to make governments responsive to the needs and desires of the people and hold them accountable to their actions and outcomes. Our vote empowers us. Our vote is not only the means to select our political leadership but also a key instrument of accountability. We use our votes to reward and punish politicians. Consequently, it is really puzzling that voter turnout is not higher.

Actually, the fundamental puzzle turns out to be: Why do people vote? According to Anthony Downs (1957), a rational voter should almost never bother to vote. Here's why. Voting requires certain efforts and generates costs. To vote wisely, voters need to gather information about candidates, parties, and policy platforms. You would want to know candidates' qualifications, experiences, personalities, beliefs, and more. You would also want to learn about their parties and the candidates' and parties' policy platforms, histories, and general orientations and constituency bases. Gathering information takes time. There are also the physical costs of getting to the polling station, which may require taking time off work, finding transportation, or perhaps forgoing a visit to a dentist. Voters could save the time and resources it takes to vote and use that time and resources for other valuable activities.

Voters should also understand that any one additional vote will hardly make an impact on outcomes. If a voter does not vote, the election results would most likely be the same. As such, even small voting costs make turnout irrational.

So why do people vote? The theoretical prediction based on Down's rational actor model is that voters should almost never vote, yet we observe much higher turnout than one predicted by the theory. The **paradox of voting** refers to the empirical observation that the level of voter turnout is at odds with rational decision-making regarding whether or not to vote based on the cost-benefit calculus and the likelihood that any particular voter's vote would influence the election outcome. We also observe significant variation in voter turnout across different countries and over time. What explains these variations? And given that a lot of people do not vote, who votes?

One explanation for voter turnout may be that voters turn out simply to support democracy and out of a sense of civic duty. Voters might also turn out when the race is very close, which increases the influence of each vote in determining outcomes. Voter turnout may also be related to types of electoral systems used. As we will examine later in the chapter, some electoral systems tend to "waste" many votes while in other electoral systems, almost all votes count in determining the allocation of legislative seats. What other factors might influence voter turnout?

EXPAND YOUR THOUGHTS

Many voters vote and many others do not. Some people vote sometimes but not at other times. What factors influence whether people will vote or not? Are personal attributes, such as level of education, wealth, gender, and ethnicity more important than contextual factors, such as competitiveness of elections, state of the economy, and foreign relations? How important is it for a rational voter to vote knowing that the likelihood that any single vote will affect an election outcome is close to none?

WHO VOTES?

LEARNING OBJECTIVE

9.3 Identify the characteristics of a typical voter.

The less than perfect voter turnout indicates that there are people who vote and people who don't vote. Who votes when voting is not compulsory? Voting populations have certain characteristics. They tend to be better educated and more affluent. They tend to be middle-aged or older, and live in urban and suburban areas. They are also more likely to identify with a political party. Nonvoters display opposite characteristics. They tend to be low-income, young, and less educated, do not identify with a political party, and live in rural areas. Ethnic and racial minorities also tend to vote less often than white people do.

We learned in the previous section that voter turnout is rather low (albeit higher than the theoretical prediction) in many democracies, which puts into question how representative our elected officials and governments are. Low voter turnout might not cause serious harm to the representativeness of our governments if those who vote constitute a microcosm of the electorate as a whole by displaying similar socioeconomic, demographic, and other characteristics. However, this is typically not the case. As mentioned earlier, people who are older and have higher socioeconomic status are more likely to vote. Recent research has indicated that low turnout by minorities and those with lower incomes leads to public policies and spending patterns that are more responsive to the needs and interests of the better-off who, ironically, need less governmental support.

In many societies, women were one of the largest disenfranchised groups for a long time, earning the right to vote much later than men. In 1893, New Zealand became the first country to enfranchise women and formally allow them to vote in national elections. However, women could not stand for election to parliament until 1919. At least a dozen other countries also enfranchised women for national elections before the United States, where women's suffrage was granted only in 1920 with the enactment of the Nineteenth Amendment to the U.S. Constitution. In Switzerland, a country that almost everyone agrees is a mature democracy, women's voting right came really late; women were disenfranchised until 1971.

Traditionally, men were more likely to vote than women in many countries. However, the recent trends show that more women are voting. In the United States, voter turnout rates were higher for men than women until 1980, when a larger percentage of women voted in the presidential election. In terms of the number of people voting, women have been voting in higher numbers than men in every presidential election since 1964 in the United States.

EXPAND YOUR THOUGHTS

Why do racial and ethnic minorities have lower turnout rates in U.S. elections? Why are affluent and educated people more likely to vote than low-income and less educated people? What implications do the lower turnout rates of these demographic groups have in terms of the kind of public policies that elected officials are likely to pursue?

PRACTICAL APPLICATION

Low voter turnout is a problem that many democracies are confronting. What could we do to ensure that people vote? Would you be in favor of introducing compulsory voting to your country? Why or why not?

ELECTORAL SYSTEMS

Variations in electoral systems may at least partially account for the differences in voter turnout across countries. An **electoral system** is a set of laws that regulate electoral competition between candidates or parties, determining the number of seats available in an election, how voters cast their ballots, and how votes are translated into seats. There are three broad categories of electoral systems: majoritarian, proportional, and mixed (see Figure 9.2).

Majoritarian Electoral Systems

Majoritarian electoral systems include electoral systems in which candidates or parties that receive the most votes win. Depending on a particular type of majoritarian electoral system, a candidate may win by plurality or may be required to win a majority of the vote to win the election. Winning by a **plurality** requires the candidate to gain more votes than any other candidates. For example, a candidate could win an election with 38 percent of the vote granted that they won more votes than any other candidates. It does not need to exceed an absolute majority (greater than 50 percent) of the vote cast as long as the candidate's votes exceed those cast for any other candidates. A **majority winner** must receive at least 50 percent + 1 vote to win an election.

FIGURE 9.2 ■ Classification of Electoral Systems Around the World

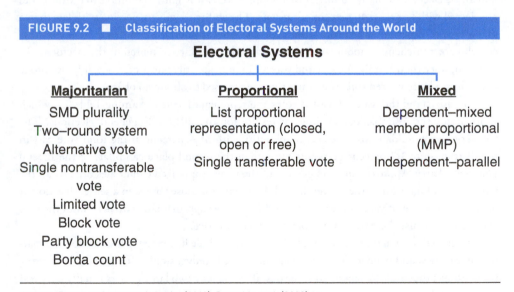

Sources: Based on Bormann & Golder (2013); Reynolds et al. (2008).

Single-Member District Plurality (First-Past-the-Post) Rule

Majoritarian electoral systems include some of the widely used electoral systems such as plurality voting and majority runoff systems. A **single-member district plurality (SMDP) system** is one in which voters cast a single vote for a candidate where candidates compete for a single seat (hence called "single-member district"). The candidate with the most votes wins. It is also known as a "first-past-the-post" and "winner-takes-all" system. Legislative elections in the United States, United Kingdom, India, Canada, and Nigeria use SMDP rules.

SMDP rules have a number of advantages. First, SMDP systems are simple and easy to understand—whoever wins the most votes wins the seat. Second, electoral districts for legislative elections under an SMDP rule tend to be small, and the elected politicians represent well-defined geographic areas. Many consider this to strengthen the voter-representative linkage.

Third, SMDP rules are known to produce and maintain **two-party systems**. (This is called Duverger's law, which we will discuss later in this chapter in relation to political party systems.) SMDP's tendency to limit the number of parties generates various implications and consequences. Because the number of parties is few (in general, just two major parties), SMDP offers clear-cut candidate and party choices to voters. SMDP systems are also associated with single-party majority governments, which facilitates policymaking and governmental action. Single-party governments also make clear who is responsible for policy (compared to minority governments and coalition governments), thus enhancing political accountability. Two-party systems and single-party majority governments that SMDP rules produce also tend to motivate coherent opposition. Extremist parties also do not fare well under SMDP rules.

Although SMDP rules are simple and thus easy to understand and come with many valuable properties, this electoral system also features certain problems. Most notably, SMDP enables a candidate to win without a majority of the vote so a candidate that is not supported by a majority can be elected. In many countries that adopt SMDP, it is not uncommon that candidates are elected with less than 40 percent of the vote. The ability to win an election with less than a majority vote, especially when combined with low voter turnout, is a concern for many observers who are apprehensive about the winning candidate's ability to represent the electorate. In addition, since there is only one seat and voters can indicate only one preference, it is also prone to produce a lot of wasted votes (i.e., votes that are not used to obtain an office).

To understand the issues of wasted votes and representativeness, examine Table 9.1, which summarizes the Wimbledonconstituency results for the 2019 UK general elections. The Conservative candidate won the seat by plurality with 38.4 percent of the total vote cast in the district, only 1.2 percentage points more than the second-place candidate of the Liberal Democrat Party. Approximately 62 percent of the voters supported candidates other than the winning candidate. Since their candidates did not win, for those voters, in a sense, they do not have their representative. In other words, in this example approximately 62 percent of the vote was wasted because these votes were not used to secure office.

Other well-known disadvantages of SMDP rules include its tendency to exclude small parties, minorities, and women due to the fact that there is only a single office available in a district and its propensity to benefit large parties. Because only two large parties usually have real chances of winning the election, SMDP rules also encourage strategic voting; that is, voters may

TABLE 9.1 ■ 2019 Parliamentary Election, UK, Constituency Results (Wimbledon)			
Candidate	**Party**	**Votes**	**Percentage**
Stephen Hammond	Conservative	20,373	38.4
Paul Kohler	Liberal Democrat	19,745	37.2
Jackie Schneider	Labour	12,543	23.7
Graham Hadley	Independent	366	0.7

Source: UK Parliament. https://commonslibrary.parliament.uk/research-briefings/cbp-8749/

cast their votes based on the logic of the lesser of two evils rather than vote for their most preferred candidate in order to avoid their votes being wasted (see Chapter 1 for greater discussion on strategic voting).

Majority Runoff Rule

In a **majority runoff electoral system**, each voter casts a single vote for a single candidate in a single-member district. However, unlike SMDP, it requires that a candidate garner greater than 50 percent of the vote to win the election. If no candidate wins a majority vote, then the two candidates with the most votes move to a second round (often referred to as a "runoff" election) and voters then cast their votes between the two candidates. The candidate with more votes wins the election. Majority runoff electoral systems are the most common type of two-round electoral systems.

Many executive office elections, such as presidential and gubernatorial elections, use majority runoff rules. For example, French and Brazilian voters elect their presidents using majority runoff systems. Table 9.2 shows the results of the 2017 French presidential elections. In the April 23 election (first round), no candidate received more than 50 percent of the votes. Emmanuel Macron and Marine Le Pen, candidates with two highest votes, therefore proceeded to the second round in which Macron won with a decisive 66 percent of the vote.

Majority runoff elections have many advantages. They ensure that the winning candidate is supported by a majority of voters. Hence, majority runoff rules generate fewer wasted votes compared to SMDP rules. They also give voters whose candidates were defeated in the first round an additional opportunity to express their preferences through voting between the remaining candidates in a runoff election. Majority runoff rules also promote diverse interests to coalesce behind the successful candidates after the first-round vote.

Majority runoff rules' disadvantages, compared to those of SMDP rules, mostly result from the administration of the runoff elections, which creates further pressure on the electoral administration in terms of the costs and time. They could also impose additional burden on voters who have to vote twice on separate days. Finally, majority runoff systems are implemented in single-member districts like SMDP rules, which, even though they guarantee that the winning candidate is supported at least by a majority of the voters who voted, still constrain the range of interests that could be represented.

TABLE 9.2 ■ French Presidential Election Results, April 23 & May 7, 2017

Candidate	Party		First round		Second round	
			Votes	%	Votes	%
Emmanuel Macron	En Marche!	EM	8,656,346.00	24	20,743,128.00	66
Marine Le Pen	National Front	FN	7,678,491.00	21	10,638,475.00	34
François Fillon	The Republicans	LR	7,212,995.00	20		
Jean-Luc Mélenchon	La France insoumise	FI	7,059,951.00	20		
Benoît Hamon	Socialist Party	PS	2,291,288.00	6		
Nicolas Dupont-Aignan	Debout la France	DLF	1,695,000.00	5		
Jean Lassalle	Résistons!		435,301.00	1		
Philippe Poutou	New Anticapitalist Party	NPA	394,505.00	1		
François Asselineau	Popular Republican Union	UPR	332,547.00	1		
Nathalie Arthaud	Lutte Ouvrière	LO	232,384.00	1		
Jacques Cheminade	Solidarity and Progress	S&P	65,586.00	0		

Source: Constitutional Council (Conseil Constitutionnel) of France.

The Alternative Vote

SMDP and majority runoff electoral rules are by far the most common majoritarian electoral systems used around the world. In both of these electoral systems, voters can express their preference for only one candidate or party on a ballot. If there is a runoff election, majority runoff systems give voters a second chance to indicate their preferred candidate. You may think that it would be nice if you could express your preferences over all the candidates so that you could indicate which candidate is your most favorite to the one you like the least. **The alternative vote** is a majoritarian electoral system that allows just that. It is a single-member district electoral system where voters rank the candidates running in a district in the order of their preferences. If there is a candidate who receives an absolute majority of first-preference votes, the candidate is elected. If no candidate wins an absolute majority of first-preference votes, then the candidate with the fewest votes is eliminated. The eliminated candidate's votes are then reallocated to the voter's next preferred available candidate until one candidate has an absolute majority of the valid votes remaining.

Let's look at a hypothetical example. Suppose that there are four candidates for mayor in the city of Electopia. Table 9.3 presents the first-preference vote total for each candidate. As you can see, no candidate received a majority vote. Given this, the candidate with the least votes, De Santos, is eliminated, and his votes are reallocated to the remaining candidates based on the voters' next indicated preferences.

Table 9.4 shows how De Santos's 70 votes are reallocated. Forty of his 70 voters indicated Brown as their second preference, 30 voters chose Clinton, and none selected Albertson. Those reallocated votes are added to the remaining candidates' original vote tallies. You discover that no candidate is yet to win a majority vote, requiring another reallocation. This time, with the fewest vote total, Clinton gets eliminated.

In Table 9.5, you see how Clinton's 210 votes are redistributed to the two remaining candidates. Albertson received 30 votes while Brown received 180 votes. By adding those to the

TABLE 9.3 ■ First-Preference Vote Tallies in Electopia's Mayoral Race

Candidate	First-preference votes	Percentage
Albertson	430	43
Brown	320	32
Clinton	180	18
De Santos	70	7
Total	1,000	100

TABLE 9.4 ■ Second Counts of Vote Tallies in Electopia's Mayoral Race

Candidate	First-preference votes	Reallocated votes	Second count total	Percentage
Albertson	430	0	430	43
Brown	320	40	360	36
Clinton	180	30	210	21
Total			1000	100

TABLE 9.5 ■ Third Counts of Vote Tallies in Electopia's Mayoral Race

Candidate	First-preference votes	Second count total	Reallocated votes	Third count total	Percentage
Albertson	430	430	30	460	46
Brown	320	360	180	540	54
Total				1000	100

second count tallies, Albertson now has 460 votes and Brown, 540 votes. Brown wins the election with 54 percent of the vote.

As this example illustrates, voters express their preferences over all the candidates. Even when their most preferred candidate is not a popular candidate, their preferences continue to count until a strong candidate with the ability to win a majority vote emerges. This reduces the incentive for strategic voting and decreases the number of wasted votes.

Another notable feature of this electoral system is that the candidate that is most popular based on voters' first preferences may not necessarily win. In this hypothetical example, the most popular candidate was Albertson, commanding 43 percent of the first-preference votes. If the electoral system used were plurality instead, Albertson would have won the election. However, aside from the 43 percent of voters who voted enthusiastically for Albertson, the candidate was almost everyone else's least favorite. This hurt Albertson's electability under the alternative vote electoral rule. Unless candidates can win an outright majority, they must be liked or at least be found acceptable by the supporters of some other candidates.

The importance of not being disliked also influences candidates' electoral strategies because candidates that are too extreme or too polarizing are unlikely to do well in elections using an alternative vote rule. Due to the value of securing the second preference for the voters of other candidates, the alternative vote also encourages political moderation and bargaining between major and minor parties. Many people also believe that the alternative vote encourages voter turnout by giving voters more options on the ballot for expressing their preferences.

The alternative vote, however, has its weaknesses. First, the system is highly complex and how it works is not easily understood. Voters may not be able, or willing, to acquire sufficient information to rank order the candidates. The requirement to rank order candidates may be particularly demanding when many candidates are in the

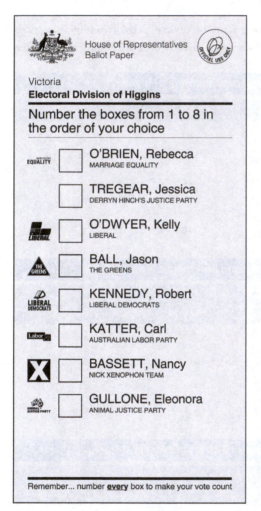

2016 House of Representatives ballot paper used in the Division of Higgins, Australian House of Representatives.

contest. Furthermore, even though the alternative vote considers second and subsequent voter preferences of the candidates until there is a majority winner, just like SMDP and majority runoff rules, it is still an election conducted in a single-member district. As such, the seat allocation can be highly disproportional. Finally, the winner of an election under the alternative vote could be the blandest candidate who is not the first choice of most voters but is not disliked by most because the candidate is simply innocuous and does not stand out.

The alternative vote is also known as instant runoff and **ranked choice voting** (RCV). The best-known example of the alternative vote is the one employed in elections for the lower chamber of the Parliament of Australia. The Fijian legislative elections also use alternative vote. Ireland uses the alternative vote for presidential elections.

Case Study: Ranked Choice Voting in the United States

Although the alternative vote has not been as widely used as plurality voting or proportional representation rules, recent years have seen increasing interest in the alternative vote in the United States. Various municipal elections, including ones in San Francisco, Oakland, Minneapolis, and Las Cruces, have adopted and implemented ranked choice voting. In 2021, New York City began using ranked choice voting for primary and special elections for certain municipal offices, including mayor, public advocate, comptroller, borough president, and city council elections.

Recently, two U.S. states have adopted RCV for federal and state elections. On November 8, 2016, Maine's Question 5, the Ranked Choice Voting Act, passed with 52 percent support. The law requires ranked choice voting for all primary and general elections for Maine's governor, state legislature, and federal congressional offices. On November 6, 2018, Maine became the first U.S. state to use ranked choice voting for the offices of U.S. Senate and House of Representatives.

In the November 2020 general election, Alaskan voters approved a ballot initiative Measure 2 to establish a Nonpartisan Top Four Primary Election system and a Ranked Choice Voting General Election system. These electoral reforms make drastic changes to how Alaska administers elections. Instead of partisan primaries, in which each political party nominates a candidate for the general election in November, the state will hold one nonpartisan open primary, with the top four candidates progressing to the general election conducted with ranked choice voting. However, these changes do not apply to the presidential level, which will retain the traditional system. The proponents of Measure 2 advocated for these sweeping reforms to bring moderation and reduce polarization in politics, as well as to increase opportunities for new faces in politics. Voters in Alaska will vote under the new electoral system in the 2022 general elections.

EXPAND YOUR THOUGHTS

Ranked choice voting has become increasingly popular in the United States. Do you think ranked choice voting would be a good electoral system to replace the single-member district plurality rule currently used in most states to elect U.S. senators and representatives? Why or why not? Would it be a good system to use for presidential elections?

Proportional Electoral Systems

A proportional representation (PR), or simply proportional, electoral system is used in multi-member districts (i.e., there is more than one seat in an electoral district up for competition in an election). Recall that some of the concerns about majoritarian systems are that they waste votes and tend to cause disproportionality, thus distorting political representation. Although majority runoff rules give voters an additional layer of opportunity to express their preferences, they still elect only one candidate per district, and no single candidate can adequately represent diverse interests in the district. **Proportional representation electoral systems** seek to minimize wasted votes and distortion in political representation through proportional allocations of legislative seats based on the shares of votes that political parties receive.

Proportional electoral systems largely fall into two categories: list proportional representation and single transferable vote. Of these two categories, almost all countries that use proportional systems use list proportional representation rules. Under a list PR system, each party presents a list of candidates for a multimember electoral district. Under **closed-list proportional representation** systems, each party presents a ranked list of candidates. Voters vote for the party rather than for individual candidates, and parties receive seats in proportion to their overall share of the vote in that district. For example, let's say District A has 10 legislative seats. If the Social Democratic Party won 20 percent of the district vote, then the party receives two seats (20 percent of the seats) in the district.

Under **open-list proportional representation** systems, each party presents an unranked list of candidates. Voters vote for either a party list or the individual candidate of their choice on a party list. The votes for individual candidates determine post-election ranks of the candidates on their party lists. All votes are pooled at the party level to determine how many seats each party receives. Then seats are allocated to individual candidates in the order of the votes that they gain.

Lower house legislative elections in Argentina, Costa Rica, and South Africa use closed-list PR systems. Brazil and Finland use open-list PR systems. Countries with closed-list PR systems tend to have high levels of party unity, whereas countries with open-list PR systems tend to have relatively low levels of party unity.

PR systems enhance political representation by encouraging the formation of various parties, by giving voters incentives to vote for their preferred party, and by allowing even small parties to win some seats. Small parties are unlikely to gain seats under single-member district majoritarian electoral systems such as plurality rules. Under a PR system, however, small parties can still win legislative seats because seats are distributed to parties proportionally based on the share of votes in the district. For example, if the party you support receives 15 percent of the vote, it obtains approximately 15 percent of the seats allocated to the district. The possibility for even small parties to win seats minimizes incentives for strategic voting, because even votes for small parties count.

If descriptive representation, which seeks to ensure that a legislative body numerically mirrors the societal demographic composition of the population (see Chapter 8), is important for you, closed-list PR systems work well with gender and minority quota systems that many countries have adopted. For example, certain countries have implemented laws that require political parties to secure a certain percentage of seats for women candidates. Parties can comply with this type of gender quota law by alternating men and women candidates on their closed party lists, which cannot be altered by voters. This type of quota to ensure the election of individuals from the traditionally disadvantaged population is hard to implement with majoritarian electoral systems. With open-list PR systems, even if parties reserve a certain percentage of their candidates for women and minorities, voters determine the post-election ranks of the candidates, and there is no guarantee that those candidates will be elected.

At the same time, PR systems tend to create multiparty systems where there are perhaps too many parties for the government to effectively govern. Single-party majority governments are unlikely and legislative negotiations among many different parties can be daunting, leading to policy deadlock. For example, Brazil has over 20 legislative parties and no party has more than 15 percent of the seats in the lower house of its national congress. Can you imagine negotiating a majority to pass legislation in such a context? Because of the lower barriers to the election of small parties, PR systems may lead to the election of extremist parties and candidates.

In many countries with numerous political parties, constructing a multiparty **coalition government** has become a solution to generate a legislative majority. A coalition government comprises two or more political parties that enter a formal agreement to form a government. In parliamentary systems, government forms from within the parliament with the support of a parliamentary majority. Without a parliamentary majority, it would not only be difficult for the government to pass its legislative proposals, but a minority government would also be vulnerable to its removal by a parliamentary majority through a no confidence vote (see Chapter 8 for more details on parliamentary votes of no confidence). Coalition governments are widespread in many European parliamentary democracies, such as Belgium, Germany, Italy, and Netherlands. It is also common to see coalition governments form in some presidential countries with multiparty systems, such as Brazil.

Mixed Electoral Systems

Both majoritarian and proportional systems have advantages and disadvantages. Could we design an electoral system that includes unique features from both systems? In **mixed electoral systems** voters elect representatives using two different systems—one majoritarian and the other proportional. For example, German voters have two votes to elect the members of the lower house of the national parliament called the Bundestag. The first vote is cast for an individual candidate in a single-member district using a plurality rule, and the second vote is to select a party list in a statewide district in the PR tier. Party votes are used to maintain proportionality in the allocation of the Bundestag seats.

There are two types of mixed electoral systems. An independent (or parallel) mixed electoral system is one in which the allocation of the seats in the PR tier does not depend on the outcome produced by the majoritarian tier. For example, Ukraine, which uses an independent mixed electoral system, elects half of its legislators using an SMDP system at the constituency level and the other half using a list PR system in a single national constituency.

In a dependent mixed electoral system (or mixed member proportional system, MMP), the allocation of the seats in the PR tier is dependent on the distribution of seats or votes produced

Ballot of Constituency 252 for the Election of the 16th German Bundestag.

Source: https://commons.wikimedia.org/wiki/ File:Bundestagswahl 2005_stimmzettel_small.jpg. Image in the public domain, CC0.

by the majoritarian formula. Dependent mixed electoral systems use the proportional component of the electoral system to compensate for any disproportionality produced by the majoritarian formula at the constituency level. The German mixed electoral system is of this type.

Mixed electoral systems have become increasingly popular since the 1990s. By adopting a version of a mixed electoral system, politicians and scholars hoped that it would produce positive attributes of both majoritarian and proportional representation systems while minimizing their respective problems. With the PR component, it would enhance diversity in representation and reduce wasted votes. The majoritarian, most commonly single-member district plurality, tier would strengthen the voter-representative linkage by allowing voters to elect a single representative whose mandate is tied to a specific geographic constituency. This would enhance the clarity of responsibility and accountability. The majoritarian tier would also check the proliferation of too many political parties and reduce the challenges of governing that an excessive multiparty system generates. All this sounds great.

However, the assessments of countries that adopted mixed electoral systems have been mixed. For example, popular discontent prompted New Zealand, Italy, and Japan to implement an electoral reform. Those countries adopted a mixed electoral system in the 1990s. The results of these reforms varied significantly, however. The greatest success occurred in New Zealand, where the aim of the reform was to increase party system proportionality, whereas Italy's reform achieved modest success in consolidating party competition around competing blocs. Japan had the least success in achieving its reform objectives as the implementation of a mixed electoral system did little to move away from clientelistic politics and the long-time dominance of the Liberal Democratic Party (Scheiner, 2008).

EXPAND YOUR THOUGHTS

In this chapter, we examined various electoral systems, how they work, and their advantages and disadvantages. We also learned that rational choice theory suggests that rational voters often do not have an incentive to vote and that voter turnout is indeed an issue in many countries. Which electoral system or systems do you think give voters greater incentives to turn out to vote despite the costs associated with voting?

TRENDS IN ELECTORAL SYSTEMS AROUND THE WORLD

Figure 9.3 presents the number of national legislative elections in democratic countries employing majoritarian, proportional, and mixed electoral systems by decade. With the number of democracies growing in the post–World War II period, the use of legislative elections steadily increased by decade (the data for the 2010s include national legislative elections from 2010 through 2016 only). As you can see in Figure 9.3, majoritarian and proportional electoral systems are the predominant types used in legislative elections.

However, the figure also reveals interesting trends. First, the use of majoritarian electoral systems has declined, especially since the last quarter of the twentieth century. This decline is particularly visible when we consider the share of elections conducted using majoritarian

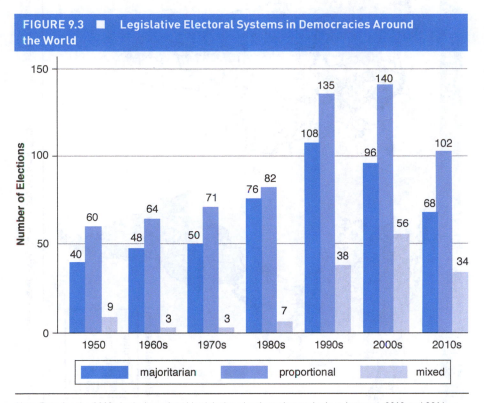

FIGURE 9.3 ■ Legislative Electoral Systems in Democracies Around the World

Note: Data for the 2010s include national legislative elections that took place between 2010 and 2016.

Source: Based on data from the Democratic Electoral Systems, 1946-2016 data set (Version 3.0) (Bormann & Golder, 2013).

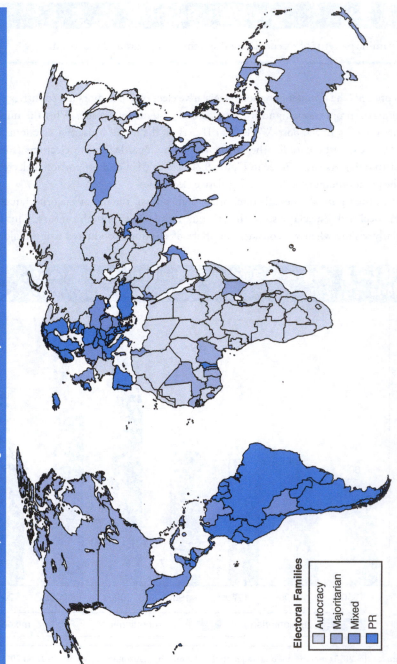

FIGURE 9.4 ■ Map of National Legislative Electoral Systems in Democracies Around the World, 2011–2016

Electoral Families

☐ Autocracy
☐ Majoritarian
☐ Mixed
☐ PR

Source: The map was generated using Bormann and Golder's (2013) Electoral System Family Map App. https://ncb13.shinyapps.io/PartIElections/

TABLE 9.6 ■ Directions of Electoral Reforms			
		New System	
Previous System	**Majoritarian**	**Mixed**	**Proportional**
Majoritarian	Bermuda (BV to SMDP)	Lesotho (SMDP to MMP)	Iraq (TRS to List PR)
	Fiji (SMDP to AV)	Monaco (TRS to Parallel)	Rwanda (FPTP to List PR)
	Montserrat (SMDP to TRS)	New Zealand (SMDP to MMP)	Sierra Leone (SMDP to List PR)
	Papua New Guinea (SMDP to AV)	Philippines (BV to Parallel)	South Africa (SMDP to List PR)
	Mongolia (BV to TRS)	Thailand (BV to Parallel)	Moldova (TRS to List PR)
		Ukraine (TRS to Parallel)	
		Japan (SNTV to Parallel)	
		Russian Federation (TRS to Parallel)	
Mixed		Mexico (Parallel to MMP)	Macedonia (Parallel to List PR)
			Croatia (Parallel to List PR)
Proportional		Bolivia (List PR to MMP)	
		Italy (List PR to MMP)	
		Venezuela (List PR to MMP)	
		Madagascar (List PR to Parallel)	

Key: AV = alternative vote; BV = block vote; list PR = list proportional representation; MMP = mixed member proportional; parallel = mixed member parallel; SNTV = single nontransferable vote; SMDP = single-member district plurality; TRS = two-round system.

Note: Electoral systems for national-level legislatures (for countries with bicameral legislatures, the electoral system is for the lower house) during 1993–2004. Kyrgyzstan changed from a TRS to a parallel system and then back to TRS again within this period and is not included in the table.

Source: Based on information obtained from the International Institute for Democracy and Electoral Assistance (International IDEA), Inter-Parliamentary Union, and Bormann and Golder's Democratic Electoral Systems, 1946–2016 data set.

electoral rules. In the 1970s, 40 percent of legislative elections used majoritarian rules. In the 1990s, legislative elections by majoritarian systems accounted for 38 percent of legislative elections, and in the 2000s, it represented 33 percent. Second, the use of mixed electoral systems increased remarkably since the 1990s. In the 1980s, only 4 percent (or seven) of legislative elections used mixed electoral systems. In the 1990s, the share of legislative elections by mixed electoral systems increased to 14 percent, and by the 2000s, to 19 percent or 56 legislative elections.

The map showing the geographic distribution of electoral systems around the world (Figure 9.4) indicates the lasting influence of colonialism and geographic clustering of electoral systems. For example, former British and French colonies characteristically use majoritarian electoral systems, as their former colonial rulers do. The colonial influence helps explain the prevalence of majoritarian electoral systems in North America, the Caribbean islands, Australia, India, Pakistan, and much of sub-Saharan Africa (Bormann & Golder, 2013). On the other hand, most countries in South America and Europe have historically employed proportional representation systems, although we have witnessed increased adoption of mixed electoral systems in these areas.

An investigation of recent electoral reforms for elections for national legislatures (for lower house elections for countries with a bicameral legislature) confirms the patterns in the recent trend (see Table 9.6). All countries that have changed electoral systems moved in the direction of greater proportionality. Some countries added a PR element to a majoritarian system, thus making it a parallel (or independent) mixed electoral system or MMP (or dependent mixed electoral) system. Others adopted list PR systems, completely abandoning their old majoritarian systems. In contrast, no countries with mixed or proportional electoral systems switched to a majoritarian system. The patterns of electoral system changes reflect the growing interest in many countries in guaranteeing fair political representation for all.

PRACTICAL APPLICATION

If you were to design an electoral system for your country's national legislature, which electoral system would you propose? Explain your choice.

EXPAND YOUR THOUGHTS

In this chapter, we learned of the increasing popularity of proportional and mixed electoral systems and a concomitant decline of majoritarian, particularly single-member district plurality, systems. However, majoritarian electoral systems are often associated with a single-party government, greater clarity of responsibility, enhanced accountability, and decisive governmental action, whereas PR systems tend to generate, in addition to more proportional representation of societal interests, multiparty coalition governments, greater need for political negotiation and bargaining, and slower governmental action and immobility. Both majoritarian and proportional systems can produce democratic virtues of governance and representation, but scholars talk about the trade-offs between the two because an increase in one tends to weaken the other. Given the trade-off, which electoral system would you prefer? By having both majoritarian and PR components, would mixed electoral systems resolve the governance-representation dilemma?

POLITICAL PARTIES

LEARNING OBJECTIVE

9.6   Discuss the functions of political parties, the types of political party systems, and the connection between electoral systems and political party systems.

Political parties play vital roles in democracies. However, there is a considerable variation in the features of political party systems across countries. Given the importance of political parties in democracies, it is important for us to understand what roles they play, the characteristics of political parties and party systems, and what affects the types of political systems that emerge in societies.

The Roles of Political Parties

Political parties perform a number of important functions in a democracy. First, political parties structure the political world. In parliamentary democracies, the majority party or the coalition of parties that constitute a legislative majority forms the government and organizes the legislature. Even in presidential systems, presidents rely on their own political parties and party allies in the legislature to pass legislation.

Political parties also articulate and organize societal interests. **Interest articulation** is a method by which members of a society express their needs and desires to a system of government. Interest articulation can take various forms. For example, members of a society may organize into an interest group to exercise greater influence over policymakers and public opinion by articulating and promoting their interests. Interest articulation may also take the form of personal contact with an elected representative. Political parties commonly represent certain values, goals, ideologies, and policy positions, and serve as important vehicles of interest articulation by organizing various ideas, values, and needs and by simplifying complex reality in a way people can understand and associate with. By doing so, political parties articulate interests in a society.

Another related role of political parties is interest aggregation. **Interest aggregation** refers to the activity that integrates the interests, demands, and needs of individuals into policy programs. Political parties highlight certain issues, set priorities among competing interests, and select issues to be considered for public policy. Both interest articulation and interest aggregation by political parties are essential to producing a responsive government.

Political parties also recruit members and socialize them into the political world. As discussed in Chapter 4, political socialization is the process of acquiring the society's political values and norms. Through political socialization, people develop an understanding of their political identities, opinions, attitudes, and behavior. Political parties recruit and socialize members by teaching them how to speak in public, conduct meetings, take a stance on issues, and negotiate with allies and opponents as needed. Political parties also mobilize people. For example, political parties shore up voter interest and increase voter turnout when campaigning for their candidates.

Political Party Systems in Democracies

Political parties are key actors in democratic countries, but characteristics of political parties vary significantly across countries. One way to classify political party systems in democracies is by the number and size of the parties in a country. In a **dominant party system**, multiple parties exist, but the same party wins every election or almost every election and governs continuously. Elections that dominant parties win are reasonably free, fair, and competitive. It is the voters who keep returning those parties to power of their own will. Japan is an example of a dominant party system in a democracy. Japan's Liberal Democratic Party has won almost every election since World War II and continues to govern the country with only a few brief intermissions. This distinguishes dominant party systems in democracies from dominant party systems in autocracies. Dominant party regimes in autocracies maintain their dominance by banning other political parties altogether or, if elections are held, by setting up a system where only the ruling party can win and take office. Dominant party regimes in autocracies are also called one-party regimes. China, where the Communist Party of China rules unchallenged, is an example of an autocratic variant of dominant party regimes.

In a **two-party system**, there may be more than two political parties, but only two major political parties have a realistic chance of gaining power. The United States and the United Kingdom are examples of two-party systems. In contrast, in a **multiparty system**, more than two parties could potentially win a national election and govern. Mexico since 2000 and Brazil since 1985 have had multiparty systems.

You may wonder why some countries have only one or two major parties while other societies have many parties. Additionally, why do **catch-all parties**—parties that seek to attract people with diverse political viewpoints—play principal roles in some countries, but parties in other systems are ideological or divided along class, religious, linguistic, or regional lines? There are sociological arguments that explain how party systems reflect divisions in the society. There are also institutional explanations that posit that institutions, especially electoral systems, can determine and shape the party system. Societal cleavages, such as religious, class, and urban-rural divides, may provide latent demands for interest representation, but not all cleavages are politicized. Institutional theories argue that political institutions play a significant role in determining how many societal cleavages can become politically salient.

Many studies have demonstrated that electoral institutions affect political party systems. Electoral rules can influence which cleavages become politically activated and how significant these cleavages are. For example, proportional representation systems tend to create many viable parties and may give incentives to politicians to emphasize the differences between their group and other groups. On the other hand, majority runoff and alternative vote electoral rules may motivate politicians to reach out to other groups and moderate politics.

Certain relationships between electoral systems and party systems are considered law-like phenomena. Known as **Duverger's law**, French sociologist Maurice Duverger argued that single-member district plurality rules lead to two-party competition while proportional representation encourages multiparty competition. SMDP rules have a propensity to result in two-party competition due to the mechanical effect of translating votes into seats (which disadvantages small-party candidates) and the psychological effects on candidates and voters. According to Duverger, both candidates and voters understand SMDP's mechanical effect, which deters individuals from competing as small-party candidates (strategic entry) and incentivizes voters to vote for a large-party candidate who may not be their most preferred candidate but has a realistic chance of getting elected (strategic voting). There is an abundance of evidence to corroborate Duverger's law. The United States and United Kingdom, both of which have traditionally used single-member district plurality rules to elect national legislators (except the U.S. states of Maine and Alaska, which have recently replaced SMDP with the alternative vote), have two-party systems. Many countries in Europe and Latin America employ proportional representation electoral systems and have multiparty systems.

PRACTICAL APPLICATION

The U.S. elections have been dominated by two parties: the Republican and the Democratic Parties. It is extremely rare that third-party candidates win elections. Why do you think there is no viable third party in the United States? Certain states have replaced their electoral systems for state- and federal-level elections with ranked choice voting (alternative vote) rules. Would ranked choice voting facilitate viable third-party candidates and lead to a multiparty system in those states?

ELECTIONS AND PARTIES IN NON-DEMOCRATIC REGIMES

LEARNING OBJECTIVE

9.7 Describe the roles that elections and political parties play in nondemocratic regimes.

Although elections and political parties are key institutions of political representation in democracies, political parties exist and elections take place in many nondemocratic countries as well. Even countries that are considered "the worst of the worst" by Freedom House (a nongovernmental organization that conducts research, advocates democracy, and monitors political rights and civil liberties globally) have elections, such as the Democratic People's Republic of

Korea (North Korea). The country's dictator Kim Jong-un was reelected to the national parliament with a unanimous popular vote in 2014! But make no mistake: Parties and elections in autocracies do not perform the same functions or serve the same purposes as those in democracies. Parliamentary elections in North Korea give voters ballots in which only one candidate's name is printed. Kim Jong-un won his reelection by winning 100 percent of the votes cast by his constituency where 100 percent of the eligible voters turned out to vote using the ballot that had only the dictator's name printed. Kim Jong-un did not participate in the country's 2019 elections.

Dictators choose to conduct elections and allow parties and legislatures to exist and operate for the purpose of giving legitimacy to their rule. Democracy became widely accepted as a legitimate form of government during the twentieth century. By the end of the century, elections, legislatures, and parties were taken for granted—rather than being something rare and unique, people now expect these institutions in their societies and around the globe. Take the use of the word *Democratic* in North Korea's official title, Democratic People's Republic of Korea. The rising importance of democracy worldwide and the decline in the legitimacy of nondemocratic governments have led dictators to use a façade of democratic institutions to legitimize their rule, but without empowering those institutions. Elections occur, but they are far from free, fair, or competitive. Parties exist but only with the permission of autocratic governments and as long as they do not pose a real threat to their power. Legislatures operate but they are rubber-stamping bodies approving whatever dictators desire. Even though dictators are not interested in true democracy, they are interested in **democratic legitimacy** under a false pretense.

Authoritarian institutions are also used to acquire information about the level of support that dictators have in society. One of the dilemmas that dictators confront is finding out how much support they have among the people. This is called a **dictator's dilemma**. An actual level of societal support is difficult to assess in autocracies because people are uninclined to reveal their true preferences for fear of retaliation; they are more likely to either stay quiet or say whatever pleases the dictator. By holding elections and allowing parties and legislatures to exist, dictators can obtain some information about the level of support they have and the strength of the opposition to the regime. Dictators sometimes use this information to co-opt potential opposition to their rule by bringing them into the authoritarian institutions and providing benefits to them. **Co-optation** is a political strategy of assimilating opposition and nonmembers into the established group or system in order to manage opposition and preserve political stability. Dictators use both co-optation and repression to quell opposition to their rule.

Another problem that dictators face is that of leadership succession. In democratic countries, the rotation of political offices occurs through elections. But in autocratic countries, elections are generally used to help dictators to stay in power rather than to rotate the political leadership positions. In monarchies, the throne is handed to the familial heir by internal rules. In other autocratic regimes, **authoritarian succession** could be a potentially serious problem threatening the regime's survival. In certain autocracies, such as socialist regimes, political parties not only serve to socialize politicians into appropriate behavior in the authoritarian regime; they also function to raise future leaders and provide a mechanism for leadership selection.

EXPAND YOUR THOUGHTS

Many nondemocratic countries have institutions typically associated with democracies, such as elections and political parties. Why do dictators allow elections to happen and political parties and legislatures to exist?

Case Study: Making "Democratic" Decisions in the Communist Party of China

The use of seemingly democratic principles is found within authoritarian parties as well as the elections they control. The Communist Party of China (CPC) makes decisions using a principle called democratic centralism. Developed by the Soviet Union's first leader, Vladimir Lenin, democratic centralism was a method to maintain party member discipline and was employed by many communist parties during the twentieth century.

Under this principle, the party leaders determined the level at which debate could occur before making a decision. Some issues could be discussed within the CPC's Central Committee, while most important issues are only discussed at the highest level, the CPC's Politburo (see Chapter 8). A majority vote on a proposal follows debates. After the decision has been made, the party leadership does not allow dissent. In other words, even if CPC's members voted against the decision, those members would need to obey the decision as if they were in agreement from the start.

Democratic centralism, therefore, does not meet the full criteria of democratic decision-making. First, CPC leaders decide when and at what level debate is allowed instead of permitting full discussion within the society. Second, by not allowing continued opposition to a decision, it restricts the free speech of individuals.

SUMMARY

Representation is a fundamental principle of modern democracies. Elections, which translate citizen voice to elected representatives, are therefore a critical institution in a democracy. This is why many analysts are concerned about voter turnout in elections. In this chapter, we reviewed recent trends in voter turnout in various countries and found that voter turnout is rather low in many democracies, particularly in the United States. We also examined the paradox of voting, which turns the question of voter turnout upside down and asks why rational voters would turn out to vote.

Some of the explanations for the variations in voter turnout may lie in the various methods used to carry out elections. In exploring the majoritarian, proportional, and mixed electoral systems, it is possible that "wasted" votes and lack of adequate political representation may discourage voting. Although no democratic system can guarantee 100 percent turnout (even in countries with compulsory voting), some electoral systems, such as proportional representation, may have advantages over others in solving the dual problem of low turnout and accurate representation.

However, electoral systems that emphasize representation tend to compromise on governing efficiency given that a single-party majority government becomes less likely. Designs of electoral institutions inherently contain those important trade-offs. Examination of recent electoral reforms for legislative elections around the world reveals a decline in the use of majoritarian systems and an increase in the shares of proportional and particularly mixed electoral systems. In the 1990s and 2000s, many policymakers and scholars were excited about the possibility of mixed electoral systems mitigating the governance-representation trade-off dilemma. The jury is still out on whether mixed electoral systems really produce much anticipated results.

Just like elections, political parties are principal institutions of representation and perform key roles in a democracy. Whereas some countries have only one dominant or two viable political parties, others have many more. Moreover, although some countries have party systems defined by clear ideological, class, or ethnic divisions, catch-all parties are major forces in other countries. Whereas underlying societal cleavages create latent demand for interest representation, types of electoral systems also explain much of the variation in the number and types of political parties in a country.

In the last section, we discussed that not all elections and parties are democratic. Simply having people turn out to vote does not meet minimal qualifications of liberal democracy. Elections must be free, fair, and competitive. Elections in nondemocratic regimes generally do not satisfy these conditions. Instead, they play a role that gives authoritarian regimes the resemblance of legitimacy. Authoritarian leaders also use elections and parties as means of information gathering and institution of political socialization and succession.

KEY TERMS

Alternative vote (p. 200)

Authoritarian succession (p. 214)

Catch-all parties (p. 212)

Closed-list proportional representation (p. 204)

Coalition government (p. 205)

Co-optation (p. 214)

democratic legitimacy (p. 214)

Democratic legitimacy in nondemocratic regimes (p. 213)

Dictator's dilemma (p. 214)

Direct democracy (p. 192)

Dominant party system (in a democracy) (p. 212)

Duverger's law (p. 213)

Electoral system (p. 197)

Interest aggregation (p. 211)

Interest articulation (p. 211)

Majoritarian electoral system (p. 197)

Majority runoff electoral system (p. 199)

Majority winner (p. 197)

Mixed electoral system (p. 205)

Multiparty system (p. 212)

Open-list proportional representation (p. 204)

Paradox of voting (p. 195)

plurality (p. 197)

Plurality winner (p. 212)

Proportional representation electoral system (p. 204)

Ranked choice voting (p. 203)

Representative democracy (p. 192)

Single-member district plurality system (p. 198)

The alternative vote (p. 200)

Two-party system (p. 212)

Voter turnout (p. 193)

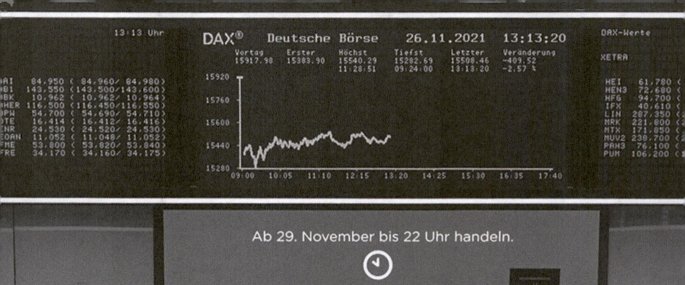

10 ECONOMIC DEVELOPMENT AND POLICY

Why are some countries wealthier than others? What policies have states adopted to promote economic growth and development? What can poor countries do to get out of poverty? Why do we see chronically poor countries, even when they enact policies aimed to solve the problems of poverty and underdevelopment? How do economic factors affect politics and vice versa? These questions fall in the area of study called **political economy**. Political economists, as the name suggests, examine the interaction between politics and economics. The relationship between the two is reciprocal. What would you say is the chance of an incumbent president winning reelection if the economy is doing poorly? Probably not very good. How much influence do large businesses have on international and domestic economic policies? To what extent do state policies and institutions structure economic activities and outcomes within countries? After exploring the concept of economic development, we examine various models of economic development as well as how policies can help or harm economic development and performance. We will also examine how economic conditions influence political change.

Central to this discussion are three basic groups of theories and their related policy recommendations. One advocates government action when the economy is not doing well. Such theorieshold that the state is the only actor with the resources and capacity to solve such large problems. An extreme version argues that government should be leading all aspects of economic growth and development. The last theoretical group claims that governments will do more harm than good if they intervene. In this view, governments' best option is to do nothing. There is much variation in each theoretical group, so we should not consider them monolithic. However, for the purposes of introducing political economy to you, we will examine the fundamental aspects of each theoretical group.

ECONOMIC DEVELOPMENT

LEARNING OBJECTIVE

10.1   Define economic development and explore the classifications of countries based on levels of economic development.

Economic development refers to the process of improving the socioeconomic well-being of people. What we consider high levels, or low levels, of economic development really depends on the reference point based on time and place. For example, what we would consider the height of economic development in 2000 BCE would be dramatically different from the mid-1700s and even more so today. The level of technology strongly influences the level of development. The use of bronze dominated many civilizations in 2000 BCE, while steam engine technology began the industrial revolution in the mid to late 1700s, and today we have witnessed great advancements in many technological fields. Since this chapter focuses on political economy, we will hold advancement in technology as a given. By focusing on the political aspects of economic development, we may be able to explain why level of technology is diffuse globally, yet wealth is not. After all, technological advancements are known throughout most of the world. So why do we not see technological advancement track alongside the level of wealth? Understanding the politics of development helps to provide an answer.

Developed Countries

Commonly, researchers classify countries into two large categories by the level of economic development. **Developed countries** are the wealthiest countries as measured by their per capita income and productivity. Their economies use highly innovative technologies that increase productivity per worker and the production of high-end products. Think about the level of productivity a worker would generate if they assembled items by hand compared to those who have machines assisting them. Workers with machine-aided technologies will be able to produce more items in a given time frame. In addition, production may be more consistent and with output that is of higher quality. Higher levels of production for demanded items will likely produce greater revenues.

Abundant capital in the developed countries enhances their ability to create the next-generation technologies. They have ample money to invest in research and development, in both private and public sectors. Public sector research and development investment are often where financially riskier activities occur. Private investment needs a product to land on the market quick enough to recoup the investment and make profits. Public investment does not require a payoff to a specific set of investors since it is tax funded. Of course, you cannot publicly fund innovation unless you have a sizable tax base, which developed countries do have. Through grants provided to university researchers and research funding given to government agencies, some scientists and engineers produce very innovative technologies. The internet is perhaps the best example of this. The U.S. government funded researchers to develop a communication system based on a network of computers. The goal to develop this alternative method of communication led to the development of the World Wide Web and the daily methods of technology-aided activities we now hold for granted.

Developed countries also have the ability to produce innovative technologies thanks to their high levels of human capital. **Human capital** pertains to the level of skills possessed by the workforce. In simpler terms, a country with high levels of human capital is one with an educated population. Large developed countries are also capable of producing low-tech products and primary commodities. Their economies are therefore very diverse because the skill levels of the workforce are also diverse. However, only highly educated workers can produce the next generation of technologies. Educating a population requires a financial investment, which wealthier countries can do because their population is wealthy enough to afford to educate their children, and their states possess large tax bases that can fund public educational institutions. We will examine the connection between education and the economy more in this chapter.

Developed countries also typically boast advanced financial institutions and other aspects of a large service sector. Financial institutions are the service sector actors that control the distribution of money in an economy. Banks are examples of financial institutions. Banks, however, are not uniform. The banking industry in a country is usually hierarchical with very large lending institutions at the top and smaller ones as you go down the financial pyramid. Also at the top are the national central banks that carry out the financial policies of the state, which will be discussed further in this chapter. Banks are not the only financial institutions. Numerous investment firms are able to use their large wealth to invest in existing or newly created business enterprises. Their purpose is to have their money make more money. Investment firms provide a service for investors who contribute to their funds with the belief that their contributions will grow. Individuals in developed countries often rely on such investments for the fund they plan to use during retirement.

Developed countries today are considered postindustrial societies because the economic share of the service sector is larger than manufacturing. Other types of services are also possible due to their higher skilled workforce. Such services include insurance, health care, information, teaching, and technology maintenance and repair. Unlike manufacturing, a service sector's products are usually not tangible items. Instead, it is an application of knowledge that assists a consumer. Consider, for example, medical doctors. Most of them do not create medicines or even develop the science behind many remedies. They use their acquired knowledge to assist patients to solve their health problems.

Developing Countries

The second category goes by many names: developing countries, lesser developed countries (LDCs), undeveloped countries, underdeveloped countries, the Third World, and the global

South. In this chapter, we will refer to those countries as **developing countries**. This set of countries is very broad: It includes middle-income countries like Mexico and Brazil and poorer ones like Senegal. Developing countries commonly experience persistent high unemployment or underemployment, produce raw goods and low-skill manufactured goods for export, and feature large income inequalities within their societies.

One major problem these countries face is their undeveloped financial markets. Developing countries lack money domestically, so they do not have the ability to invest in innovation in order to grow out of their low development level. Lacking developed local financial markets, developing countries often rely on foreign sources for loans and investments. Without vibrant and prosperous economies, their governments tend to generate low tax revenues, which makes it difficult for governments to finance needed programs, such as education or physical infrastructure. When spending is larger than revenues, governments produce large budget deficits, which they may finance by borrowing or printing money. The practice of raising revenues by printing money is called **seigniorage**. It is an easy way for a government to generate revenues, but it is also prone to cause inflation. When there is more money available, spending increases. If the level of production does not increase to meet the new demand, prices start increasing. Seigniorage is one of the reasons why many developing countries have experienced economic crises. High inflation means that workers' paychecks buy fewer items, causing demands for higher wages. Increasing wages too rapidly, in turn, can increase prices even further.

Many developing countries also have high levels of corruption. **Corruption** is the illegal use of a public office for private gain. While not all developing countries experience high levels of corruption, Transparency International's *Corruption Perceptions Index* indicates that the world's most corrupt countries are poor countries and the countrieswith the least corruption tend to be developed.

Research has shown that corruption undermines economic growth, health of the population, and trust in government institutions. Although corruption occurs both in developed and developing countries, the rule of law is generally weaker in developing countries. This fuels corrupt practices in developing countries. Some public officials are willing to supplement their low salaries by accepting bribes from business people. This type of corruption is an extra "tax" or "government fee" for getting approvals to open up businesses or for construction. These additional costs of doing business resulting from widespread corruption prevent entrepreneurship and are an obstacle to economic development. Corruption also undermines the enforcement of needed regulations. Construction firms, for example, could pay off building inspectors to evade meeting construction requirements. The regulations, however, are in place for citizens' safety. Badly designed infrastructure can undermine development.

Table 10.1 displays certain development indicators discussed in this chapter for select countries. The countries listed represent some of the most and least developed economies. The countries listed first (United States, Germany, Japan, and the United Kiingdom) have high GDPs per capita, which is an indicator of the high levels of their labor forces' productivity. The countries listed at the bottom (Mali, Chad, Liberia, Niger, and Sierra Leone) have some of the world's smallest GDPs per capita. We also see that China's GDP per capita is not very high even though its overall GDP ($14.7 trillion in 2020) makes it the world's second

TABLE 10.1 ■ Development Indicators (2020)					
Country	GDP per capita (Current US$)	Agriculture (% GDP)	Inflation (Annual %)	Postsecondary Educated (Pop %)	Corruption Index
United States	63,543	0.91	1.21	28	67
Germany	45,724	0.66	1.59	28	80
Japan	41,067	1.24	-0.02	35	74
United Kingdom	40,285	0.57	5.57	24	77
China	10,500	7.65	0.67	9	42
Mali	858.92	36.1	1.53	<1	30
Chad	614.47	47.7	11.58	1	21
Liberia	583.27	42.6	1.09	1	28
Niger	565.06	37.1	2.53	<1	32
Sierra Leone	484.52	61.3	4.55	2	33

Sources: World Development Indicators, The World Bank; Transparency International.

largest economy. The level of agricultural production also clearly divides the developed from the developing. The last five economies have a range of approximately 36 to 61 percent of their economies dedicated to agriculture, while the first four have less than 1.5 percent. Inflation is higher among the developing countries than the developed ones. The exception is the United Kingdom, which may be due to economic changes resulting from leaving the European Union, which we discuss in Chapter 12. The higher levels of human capital are evident in the four developed countries, as measured by the percentage of the total population with a postsecondary education. Last, the developing countries have higher levels of corruption. The corruption perception index calculated by Transparency International ranges from 1 (highest level of corruption) to 100 (no corruption). While not completely free of corruption, the developed countries have higher scores than the developing ones.

Now that we know the characteristics of developed and developing countries, we can look into why some countries are wealthier than others are. As stated in the chapter's introduction, arguments regarding how to improve economic performance vary greatly. Some economic policy experts argue that government intervention is critical while others propose a hands-off approach, leaving the process of economic development only in the hands of private markets. We will examine these and other policies and strategies that seek to promote economic development and performance in the next sections.

EXPAND YOUR THOUGHTS

Some argue that corruption is just the way people do business in that country. This refers to the societal norms and, as a result, is not something that will harm economic development. Others argue that corruption does have a negative economic effect and is not necessarily a norm. They cite the number of laws against corrupt activities as evidence that it is not a norm. Which side of this argument would you place yourself? Is corruption a harmless norm, or does it affect economic development?

MARKET-LED DEVELOPMENT

LEARNING OBJECTIVE

10.2 Describe the arguments for and against a market-led development strategy.

Laissez-faire (free market capitalism) delegates development to private forces with limited or no state intervention. The argument rests on the idea that private sector initiatives and competition will generate higher welfare benefits overall. The process begins with the underlying market demand for goods and services that producers (i.e., businesses) seek to satisfy in order to generate profits. In the drive to supply products, multiple businesses seek out customers by outbidding each other through lower prices. Their desire to capture greater market share (and therefore more profits) by lowering prices, drives them to be more efficient to meet the demand of consumers. By being more efficient, firms lower the costs of inputs to achieve the same outputs (products). Reducing the cost of inputs translates into lower production costs and therefore lower prices. Firms that cannot bring goods and services to the market at prices lower than competitors will risk going out of business.

Competition is also a driver for higher quality and innovations. If a firm cannot bring a product to market at a lower price, it can differentiate itself by offering a higher quality and innovative product or service. Offering items that consumers perceive as higher in quality and more innovative allows the firm to continue to be profitable. The most visible example of this is automobiles. The price range for cars is large, with the higher-end manufacturers claiming their prices reflect the higher quality and greater innovations of their products.

In sum, advocates of the free market approach to development claim that everyone benefits. The consumer has access to affordable products because market competition keeps prices low. Businesses that can be more efficient earn profits. People have jobs because market forces need workers to produce products and services. Finally, innovation through new technologies moves the economy forward.

The role of the state is minimal under the market strategy. The state's purpose is to make sure that everyone plays fairly by enforcing contracts made between economic actors. It can also provide the minimum public goods needed for a smooth-running economy. Recall from Chapter 7 that public goods are things from which everyone benefits and are not excludable. Some examples of public goods useful for economic development include transportation infrastructure, energy distribution, and physical security. The strongest advocates of the free market economy will go so far as to say that only contract enforcement and security should be the state's role. They fear that state intervention will distort the equilibrium needed for a producer's ability to supply what consumers demand. State intervention would distort the supply and demand equilibrium and will lead to high prices and reduce the incentives for individuals and private firms to innovate.

Critics argue that the market-led economic development strategy falls short of its promises. The many arguments against a market economy free from state intervention fall into two general categories dealing with labor and environmental issues. If the market is free from state intervention, critics are not convinced that markets will self-regulate in these two areas. The lack of regulation will lead to poor working standards and poor environmental conditions. Instead, critics promote policies that will impose regulations limiting or banning certain business activities or requiring other actions.

These critics are concerned that the market tends to produce highly unequal economic outcomes and harms workers' safety and health. In the struggle to become more competitive and profitable by lowering prices, firms seek to keep wages as low as possible. With low wages, business owners can sell more at lower prices, and selling more goods and services generates higher profits, which critics argue go only to the business owners. Over time, the outcome is income distributions that see wealth concentrated in the hands of a small percentage of people. The need to increase efficiency also leads firms to require each worker to produce more products during the workday. Business owners may also cut costs in areas of workers' health and safety to enhance profitability. The increase in productivity per worker, matched only with lower pay, highly skewed incomes, and hazardous working conditions, creates a class of people referred to as the working poor, people who work full time but do not have the means to meet their basic needs.

To see if the critics have evidence, we need to have an objective measure of income inequality. The Gini index is an index commonly used to measure income inequality. The Gini index ranges from 0 to 100. A zero indicates that incomes are equal for everyone in the country. The level of a country's inequality increases as the value becomes larger. One hundred would mean that one person controls all the income, leaving nothing for the rest of the population. Figure 10.1 illustrates the level of income inequality over time for select countries. As you can see, some of the countries have greater inequality.

If we measure the level of state intervention, we may be able to explain their levels of inequality. To reiterate, classical and neoliberal economists contend that the free market is the best way to promote economic growth and improve the overall welfare of the people. Many politicians, policymakers, and other political pundits also talk about free markets and free trade. How truly free are markets?

The Heritage Foundation publishes the Index of Economic Freedom (IEF). The index assesses the degree of economic freedom in 186 countries. The IEF evaluates 12 areas of freedoms in four different categories: rule of law (property rights, government integrity, and judicial effectiveness); government size (government spending, tax burden, and fiscal health); regulatory efficiency (business freedom, labor freedom, and monetary freedom); and open markets (trade freedom, investment freedom, and financial freedom). The IEF values range from 0 to

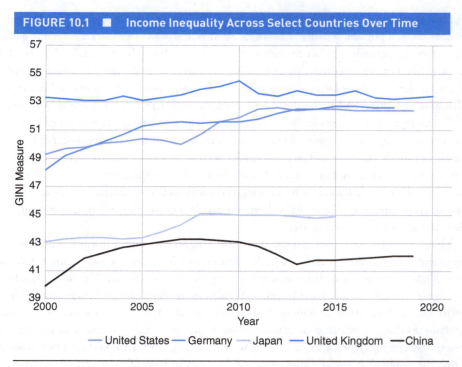

FIGURE 10.1 ■ Income Inequality Across Select Countries Over Time

Source: Based on data from Solt, F. (2020). Measuring income inequality across countries and over time: The Standardized World Income Inequality Database. *Social Science Quarterly, 101*(3), 1183–1199.

100, with higher scores indicating higher levels of economic freedom, or to put it another way, lower levels of market intervention.

Based on this index, the world's freest economies are Singapore and Hong Kong, followed by New Zealand, Australia, Switzerland, Ireland, United Kingdom, Denmark, Canada, and Estonia. The 2020 IEF places the United States the 17th on the ranking of economic freedom. The world's 10 least free economies, in the order of the least free, are North Korea, Venezuela, Cuba, Eritrea, Republic of Congo, Bolivia, Zimbabwe, Sudan, Kiribati, and East Timor. As you can see, all of the unfree economies are nondemocracies, and except for the two freest economies of Singapore and Hong Kong, the world's freest economies are democracies. These patterns may suggest that there is a relationship between markets and political regimes. Indeed, this relationship has been one of the central questions in the study of political economy. Do you think democracies enable freer economies? Or would it be that freer economies require political democracies? Do you think it is a coincidence that the world's first and second freest economies are not democracies?

What are the IEF scores of the three countries at the top of Figure 10.1? Germany went from 65.7 in 2000 to 73.5 in 2020, which corresponds to their increase in inequality. The UK stayed steady, going from 77.6 in 2000 to a small increase, 79.3, in 2020. This corresponds to its high but consistent level of inequality. The United States also stayed steady: 77.3 in 2000 to 76.3 in 2020. The difference, however, is that the U.S. inequality grew during this period. Japan's IEF score from 2000 to 2020 increased from 70.7 to 73.3. China's IEF score was the lowest going from 56.4 in 2000 to 59.5 in 2020.

The critics of the market-led economic development strategy therefore have some evidence for their argument. The developed economies, such as Germany, the United Kingdom, and the United States, all have high Gini Index values and IEF scores. Japan, which is another of the largest developed economies, does not trend as high in inequality, and its IEF score is moderate. The Gini index of China, a country that has been transitioning into a more market-based economy, has also been relatively low, which also corresponds to a low IEF score.

The environment is also a deep concern for critics. To maximize the profitability of business enterprises, owners may not be concerned with how their activities are adding pollutants into the environment. This results in the contamination of air, water, and soil with substances that harm the physical and mental development of children, increase respiratory illnesses, and cause various cancers. There is also the concern regarding how human economic activities negatively influence other species and the global climate. The incentive to limit the release of harmful substances is not present in an economy that requires cost efficiency to lower prices, produce more goods and services, and increase profits.

The problems critics voice should sound familiar if you recall the concept of public goods and the problems of collective action discussed in Chapter 7. Business owners do not have the incentive to give higher wages, provide better working conditions, or limit harmful impacts on the environment because doing so will put them at a disadvantage when competing with other business owners who will not perform these actions. However, if the state can institute regulations, then all business owners would need to comply or face a penalty. The regulation has the effect of leveling the playing field so that competition occurs without a race to lower labor and environmental standards.

EXPAND YOUR THOUGHTS

Sometimes competition can disappear from a market economy. This occurs when one business holds a monopoly in the market. Do monopolies harm or help economic development? Explain your answer using the logic behind market-led economic growth.

CENTRALLY PLANNED (COMMAND) ECONOMIES

LEARNING OBJECTIVE

10.3 Explain the link between centrally planned economies and Marxism, and explain its drawbacks.

The opposing approach to market-led economic development involves total state control of the economic system through its ownership of all resources, land, and enterprises. With total ownership, the state plans out the coordination of all production in order to achieve targeted outcomes. In such systems, the state commands the economy to develop in a certain manner, which gives the strategy its name, the **command (or centrally planned) economy**. The centrally planned economy was the strategy of development employed by communist party dictatorships like the Soviet Union and the People's Republic of China. While many countries have abandoned this strategy, or at least reformed it considerably, North Korea still uses this method for economic development.

The strategy's ideas come from the Marxist critique that capitalism does not benefit everyone and that an egalitarian system can only be achieved when workers own the means of production (see Chapter 3 for a review of the Marxist ideology). The Soviet Union's early days employed differing methods on how to create a socialist economy that would eventually become an egalitarian communist society. The command economy was the method eventually chosen by Joseph Stalin and his followers. In their view, Marxist ideas could only be realized if the state controlled all resources in the name of the workers. The economic development strategy proved to be problematic, as witnessed by countries that suffered through the lack of growth.

Under this strategy, states plan what their economies will look like in some future time interval, usually in five-year increments. The state sets annual, quarterly, and monthly production targets. A central government agency devises plans based on what it believes is achievable. In the former Soviet Union, the State Planning Committee, also known as *Gosplan*, fulfilled this role. Each state-owned enterprise would have a monthly quota to fill so that the economy could achieve its overall targets.

It is important to discuss the level of detail found in the five-year plans so we can understand why they were problematic. The Soviet plans covered *all* production. This included everything from the amount of coal and oil produced, to the number of shoes (including numbers of each size), to volumes of food items, down to the number of paperclips. The state planners based their targets on their estimation of what the economy was capable of producing. To get the correct estimates required a large amount of accurate data funneled to Moscow from all parts of the Soviet Union. This is a massive task for any state bureaucracy, so imagine doing this with pre-computer and pre-internet technology!

The bureaucrats would then design a monumental set of plans that included all farms, mines, factories, and stores in the country. Each unit had its part to play in the plan. Also important to grasp are the supply chain issues. For example, one factory would make tires (output) that would go to an automobile assembly plant as their input. Monthly production quotas needed to match up between those sending and receiving goods. Imagine what would happen if the central plan did not specify enough tires for all the cars made?

The planned targets did not always follow an economic capacity logic. Given that the plan's overall goal was to produce an ideal socialist economy, one that would lead to a Marxist vision of communism, ideological orthodoxy was paramount. Political desires, therefore, often replaced economic reality. The pressures to meet the monthly quotas produced low-quality products, provided little incentive for innovation, and created shortages. At the high point of Stalin's rule, Soviet managers and workers were arrested and imprisoned in forced labor camps if quotas were not met. Fear of imprisonment created incentives to falsify production levels, encouraged corruption among officials who were responsible for reporting on quota fulfillment, and reduced the desire to innovate for fear that it could slow production.

Soviet consumers lining up to get their food rations.

Shepard Sherbell/Contributor/Getty Images

By the 1970s and 1980s, countries that used the central planning strategy faced widespread shortages. The shortages resulted in the rationing of food and other necessities so that everyone would have the minimum amount needed for survival. This often resulted in long lines since the plan did not produce enough stores to distribute goods to consumers. Moreover, many areas only had specialty stores, which meant consumers had to wait in a long line for bread, then go to another store and wait again in line for meat, and so on. People also needed to line up early in the morning because being at the front of the line improved their chances of getting their ration before the store ran out.

This was the life of many people in the Soviet Union, all of Eastern Europe, China, Cuba, North Korea, and parts of Southeast Asia. The few that were exempt from this hard life were members of the countries' communist parties. Party members retained access to special stores that did not suffer shortages. Furthermore, although housing was guaranteed by the state for everyone, party members received the best apartments, leaving the lower quality ones to regular citizens.

These conditions produced an underground market for goods. A state official who was in charge of distribution could take items and then turn around and illegally sell them. Given the shortages, the underground market could set prices very high for those who needed those items. In addition, many officials allowed banned products to enter their countries for a bribe or to sell the products themselves.

EXPAND YOUR THOUGHTS

Failing to meet production quotas was a criminal act in the Soviet Union because the state regarded it as anti-Soviet activity. Yet, falsifying records regarding production outputs was also a crime that carried the same level of punishment. Why would a factory manager choose to lie about production levels and not admit to failing to meet the monthly quota?

Although the last leader of the Soviet Union, Mikhail Gorbachev, attempted to reform the system, states around the world began to abandon their command economies. The command economy strategy's failure to produce continuous economic development ultimately ended communist party dictatorship in the USSR (present-day Russia, parts of Central Asia, and Eastern Europe). Gorbachev tried to liberalize both the economy and the political regime, yet the traditional hard-line communist party leaders did not welcome his ideas. In order to stop the economic and political reforms, the hard-liners attempted a forced takeover, or a coup, against Gorbachev. Since the coup leaders did not have wide support from the military or other party members, they failed in taking over the state. The aftermath, however, was the deep de-legitimization of the system among many leaders who saw the instability within the Communist Party as an opportunity to bring down the Soviet Union. Without the Soviet Union, states under its domain transitioned into market economies and democratic systems.

In contrast, other such states in East Asia and Southeast Asia, including China and Vietnam, were able to transition a significant portion of their economies to market-oriented strategies that produced higher economic development while safeguarding their one-party rule. The leading figure in the Chinese transition was Deng Xiaoping. He first introduced the idea of bringing in market-oriented policies in the 1960s after many years of poor economic performance under Mao Zedong, the Chinese communist regime's founder and paramount leader. However, Deng's ideas ran against Mao's hard-line Marxist views. This led Deng to be removed from the Chinese Communist Party and forced to work in a factory in a rural area for "rehabilitation." It was not until Mao's passing that Deng gradually returned to power and was able to start reforming the economy, which began in 1978. Deng's introduction of market-oriented reforms prompted the dramatic expansion of the Chinese economy, especially in its ability to export manufactured goods. The economic policy changes directly propelled China into becoming the second largest global economy today.

PRACTICAL APPLICATION

Under Mao Zedong, China followed the Soviet model by using central planning with total state control of the country's economic system since the Communist Revolution of 1949. After Mao's passing, Deng Xiaoping selectively began to introduce capitalist reforms into the communist planned economy in 1978. The major negative side effect of rapid economic development due to the reforms was the high levels of pollution. Some would argue that China's lax environmental policies help China to grow quickly. In other words, as soon as they strengthen their environmental policies, they will lose their competitive edge. Do you agree or disagree with this argument? Please explain your answer.

STATE-LED DEVELOPMENT MODELS

LEARNING OBJECTIVE

10.4 Discuss the logic behind each of the various state-led development models, and describe their successes and failures.

There are strategies that aim at the development of a market economy under strong guidance by the state. These strategies, referred to as **state-led development models**, involve active government roles in leading national economic development. Two primary models have been adopted in various countries: import-substituting industrialization and export-oriented industrialization. Each strategy focuses on domestic production, but with different approaches to the global economy. One attempts to limit imports as a means to increase manufacturing. The other sees economic opportunities in expanding trade, especially in its export sector, as a means to grow the domestic manufacturing sector.

Import-Substituting Industrialization

Import-substituting industrialization (ISI) uses trade policy, monetary policy, fiscal policy, and exchange rates to protect and stimulate the creation of new industries for the purpose of domestically producing manufactured goods that a country imports. One way of thinking about ISI is, for example, "Why import televisions when you can make them yourself?" If the state can figure out how to increase the demand for domestically produced industrial goods, the economy will develop.

To achieve this end, the state allocates resources to target industries with preferential credit and protection from competition, particularly from foreign firms, by erecting trade barriers. In many cases, the state owns the business enterprises in areas that require large investments (such as manufacturing of aircraft and oil extraction and refineries) and by establishing development banks that lend considerable credit to key new industries where credit from private institutions may not be available due to risk. ISI was especially popular from around the 1950s through the 1970s in many developing countries. Countries such as Brazil, Mexico, and many other Latin American governments promoted economic development through ISI in the post–World War II era until the sovereign debt crises hit those countries in the 1980s.

The popularity of ISI during this time resulted from the frustrations many countries had over the uneven development between northern developed countries (e.g., the United States, Canada, and Europe) and the southern developing countries (those in Latin America and

Africa). From the late nineteenth century to the end of World War II, the northern countries industrialized and achieved higher economic growth than the southern countries. By the 1950s, the global South was still producing primary goods based on agriculture and mining.

Argentinian economist Raúl Prebisch and others maintained that the lesser developed countries had fallen behind in industrialization and had become dependent on the developed countries' imports for their manufactured goods. Given that the developed economies obtained an industrial "head start," the southern countries would not be able to catch up with their wealthier counterparts in the North unless their states took the lead. In fact, these economists stated that state leadership was necessary to stop the southern countries from sliding further behind.

ISI's basic idea was simple. First, states use their resources to create or support industries that they wish to develop. This could be large and small consumer goods (cars, washing machines, TVs, etc.) or large industrial goods (specialized machinery, transportation vehicles, etc.). To do this, however, required that they solve a very important problem: the lack of money. The advanced banking systems of global North countries enabled those countries to transfer money from their agricultural sectors to their industrial sectors through investment. Profits from the sales of their raw products went into banks, which then lent out the money for industrial investment. For various reasons, this transfer of money did not occur in places like Latin America. The adequate level of funds to invest in industrialization was simply not there. States sought to solve this problem by borrowing money from abroad, mainly from the United States and Europe, to finance their ISI.

Second, in order for the new industries to develop, the state needed to protect target industries from foreign competition. Recall that ISI advocates believed that the "head start" advantages of foreign products would make them more competitive. They believed that foreigners had figured out how to be efficient given their decades of experiences. Potential domestic producers in the global South were still trying to figure out how to be as efficient, if not more so. Since the foreign industrial goods were more efficiently produced, they could be sold at prices that were lower than domestic producers, who were less efficient at producing the same goods.

To give the local industries an advantage, ISI states imposed high tariffs and other restrictions on imports of manufactured goods so that domestic manufactured products would be more attractive to consumers. The high tariffs on foreign imports increased their prices, making the domestic products cheaper for consumers. Keep in mind that the domestic producers did not lower their prices. Goods produced domestically were still expensive, just not as expensive as foreign products due to the additional costs associated with the tariffs applied by the government.

As stated earlier, international commercial banks, mainly from the United States and Europe, were willing to lend large sums of money to many of the ISI countries because of the incorrect idea that sovereign states could not go bankrupt. Moreover, many of the ISI countries were producers and exporters of primary commodities, including oil. The early years of postwar reconstruction and the global South's desire for rapid development produced a large demand for primary commodities and therefore increased their prices. This international commodity boom facilitated reckless lending by the commercial banks even though history had demonstrated that commodity booms were short-lived. The first oil crisis, in 1973, increased oil prices and accelerated lending to ISI countries because the increases in oil profits generated large funds that banks needed to lend. Latin American governments were happy to take these loans and spent the money lavishly.

After being initially successful in many countries, over time, ISI caused massive government debt and inefficient industries. Protectionism made inefficient firms that would manufacture inferior products at high costs. Public financing of state-owned and state-supported enterprises resulted in massive public-sector debt. Manipulation of exchange rates led to price distortions. The availability of cheap credit and large public spending triggered high inflation and then, later, hyperinflation.

The result was that development based on ISI hit a bottleneck. The 1979 oil shock and rising interest rates, significant withdrawals of international credits, hyperinflation, balance of payments crises, and massive foreign debt produced the ultimate crisis: the threat of sovereign debt defaults. This meant that states could no longer pay back the money they owed. Without these payments, the international financial and banking system would collapse.

ISI ended in the 1980s when international institutions, led by the economically more powerful states, forced these countries to look for alternative developmental models. When international credit was no longer available in the early 1980s, ISI governments came close to defaulting on their debts. The International Monetary Fund, the U.S. and European governments, and private international creditors (such as Citibank) devised economic adjustment and reform programs that these borrower countries had to accept as a condition for securing further loans and restructuring their old ones. These programs, based on neoliberal principles, required the slashing of government spending, privatization of public enterprises, deregulation of the domestic market, and removal or lessening of barriers to international trade.

The experiences of the Latin American countries and others give us important lessons and puzzles. Why didn't the governments of these countries abandon ISI policies when they began causing widespread economic problems? Are all ISI policies prone to economic problems and crises? What would you do differently if you believe that economic development would not happen in currently underdeveloped countries without state intervention?

One alternative development strategy was neoliberalism. Partly as a response to the failures of ISI policies, neoliberal economics began to dominate development debates in the 1980s. **Neoliberalism** is based on laissez-faire economics and advocates development and economic policies based on free market, free trade, and minimal government intervention. It is a market-led development strategy that also focuses on international openness. In other words, neoliberalism advocates for classic liberal economic policies (see Chapter 3 for a refresher) in both domestic and international areas. Advocates wanted not only reforms to remove state leadership of, and intervention in, the domestic economy; they also wanted these economies to be open to international trade and foreign investment. The economic crises in Latin America, Africa, and some Asian countries were viewed as a result of the excessive government interventions in the economy and trade protectionism, which distorted prices, led to inefficient industries (due to trade protectionism and lack of competition), and removed incentives to innovate.

Export-Oriented Industrialization

Export-oriented industrialization (EOI) is another alternative approach to economic development where the state takes a leading role. EOI is also known as the developmental state model and the Asian development model due to the experiences of several Asian countries (and quasi-countries), such as Japan, South Korea, Taiwan, Thailand, China, among others. The governments in EOI countries guided development by selectively assisting target industries producing goods and services for export. The East Asian states introduced the EOI strategy when many other developing countries implemented ISI strategies. The EOI strategy was somewhat the opposite of ISI. With ISI, states sought to close themselves off from international trade. With EOI, they wanted trade to fuel their economic development.

The EOI strategy usually started with a focus on light manufacturing, such as textiles. States helped those industries compete internationally. The next stage was to facilitate the growth of industries that manufactured consumer durables and high-tech products such as automobiles, televisions, refrigerators, and computers (some of these items were "high-tech" during the early years of EOI). EOI was considered successful in achieving economic growth with equity and human capital development in East Asian countries. Advocates of EOI pointed out that competition in overseas markets was one cause of these firms' success. In addition, the money coming in from export sales helped to bolster their countries' financial markets, which fueled more investments at home and abroad. The high contrast of EOI successes and ISI failures led to the conclusion among many policy proponents that EOI was the future for economic development.

The EOI model of development was highly regarded until the 1997–1998 Asian financial crisis. Some critics argue that the developmental state was not an important factor in East Asian development and that developmental states have adopted as many failed policies as successful ones. Others point out that the combination of close ties between the government, banks, and firms and lack of transparency in developmental states tend to create moral hazards that nurture corruption. During the Asian financial crisis, critics argued, particularly pointing to the practices in South Korea, developmental states fostered "crony capitalism," which led to the financial crises in many Asian countries. Although economic crises hit many Asian developmental states, in contrast to Latin America where the debt crises in the 1980s generated prolonged and widespread economic recessions (the 1980s in Latin America is known as the "lost decade"), many of those Asian economies rebounded relatively quickly.

PRACTICAL APPLICATION

Conduct an internet search to locate the World Bank's *World Development Indicators*' data bank. Once you are there, choose one country classified either as a "lower middle income" or as "low income" country. Which developmental strategy would you suggest for the country? Why?

EDUCATION AND INFRASTRUCTURE POLICIES

LEARNING OBJECTIVE

10.5 Describe how human capital and infrastructure development help economies develop.

Within various strategies, there are a few sets of policies, called **structural policies**, that are critical in assisting economic development. The first set of policies are those that improve the likelihood of individuals' attaining higher levels of education, or the development of human capital. Human capital is a crucial component of economic development because a dynamic economy needs an educated workforce and diverse skills. People that possess high skills and knowledge are more likely to create the innovations that advance an economy.

Elementary and secondary education is compulsory in most countries, and public education at these levels is offered free of charge using tax money. However, the quality of public education and enrollment varies significantly across countries. In many countries, the quality of public education is abysmal and people with financial means choose private schools. Educational inequality is one of the structural causes of wealth inequality, as children of wealthy families receive better education and enjoy many more career opportunities after schooling. Children of guardians with less financial means tend to go to poorly funded public schools and face

An example of a public works project: The Tehri Dam, India.
Hans Georg Roth/Getty Images

significant barriers to personal and professional development. It is worth noting that education—particularly good public education—played an important role in successful East Asian countries and economies that have achieved remarkable economic achievements with relative equity in income distribution.

Sophisticated and complex economies require a highly skilled workforce. College and postgraduate education have become increasingly common and necessary in job markets of such economies. If the total cost of educating college graduates and other members of a technically skilled workforce is in the hands of individuals, then the likelihood of producing such a workforce is low if the starting point has many people in poverty. People who had modest beginnings, and who received a publicly financed education to fulfill their potential, have created many innovations. The state can fund education to produce generational economic benefits and unleash human aspirations.

The development of infrastructure is also a factor that produces long-term effects. There are many public works, which are state-financed infrastructure projects, that lower the costs of economic production. A simple example is an adequate road system. Roads that are in good condition and connect important markets reduce transportation costs, which then lowers the price of goods. For example, if a firm making ceramic floor tiles transports its products on poorly constructed or maintained roads, the firm will incur an additional cost because it will need to package its products more securely to prevent damage. The ceramic tile firm could build its own road, but doing so will dramatically increase the transportation costs and therefore its prices. However, the firm can pay taxes, along with other road users, and the state can build the infrastructure for their collective use.

Often developing countries do not possess enough resources to build adequate infrastructure needed for economic development. To finance such projects, the state may need to take out loans. If there is not enough money domestically, the loans will need to come from international lenders. The World Bank and many international regional development banks offer loans and grants to developing countries for infrastructural development projects. The states may also borrow from private lenders. The financing of public works through borrowing is not a financial burden if the projects accelerate economic development. With greater economic growth, the state can take in more tax revenue that can go toward paying off the debt incurred by such public works. However, if the projects do not produce growth, or some other factor negatively affects the economy, the state will have difficulty paying back lenders.

Public works projects can also fall short of their intended purposes due to politicians' efforts to maintain power. Politicians, especially in a democracy, want to deliver policies and projects that produce employment and a vibrant economy. Public works projects provide short-term employment for construction and related areas in the region where the project is located. The project can also generate long-term benefits for the economy. Frequently, the allocation of such public works projects follows a political logic of constituency service by reelection-seeking politicians and power maintenance rather than the logic of economic efficiency and necessity. Sometimes these **pork barrel projects**—public works projects sought by politicians, with political objectives, through the appropriation of government budgets for their electoral districts—do not see their completion and do not deliver long-term benefits.

Corruption also plays a role in public works not producing, or reducing, promised benefits. When there is corruption, projects end up costing more than necessary because individuals wish to pocket gains. Perhaps the project itself was promised to specific contracting firms because they paid off state officials and politicians. Project quality could be compromised if builders bribe state inspectors to approve faulty construction. The higher project costs resulting from corruption lower the benefits of the project. Consider, for example, the construction of a dam that will produce hydroelectricity. The final kilowatts-per-hour price of the electricity the dam produces will be greater if corruption increases the cost of the dam. This higher price will negatively affect homes and businesses and thereby reduce the benefits from the project.

GOVERNMENT INTERVENTION IN MARKET ECONOMIES

LEARNING OBJECTIVE

10.6 Identify the main components of fiscal and monetary policies, and explain how each type of policy impacts demand for goods and services.

Depression era Chicago soup kitchen.

U.S. National Archives

In times of economic downturn, many states intervene in the economy to restore and promote economic growth, employment, and stability. Take, for example, one of the deepest and longest lasting global economic crises, the Great Depression (1929–1939). The desire to address the interrelated problems of high unemployment, low economic growth, bank failures, and housing and farm foreclosures was in the minds of many during these years. U.S. President Herbert Hoover (1929–1933) held fast to the belief that state invention in solving the economic crisis would harm, and not help, since he and many others believed that market forces, by themselves, would bring back economic growth in the long run.

The president that succeeded him, Franklin D. Roosevelt (1933–1945), believed that without a quick and effective response, the survival of capitalism, and even democracy, was in danger. He pointed to the rise of fascism and communism in Europe, as well as the start of antidemocratic movements in the United States, as reasons to implement economic policies that would help in the short term. The antidemocratic movements used the extreme economic downturn as evidence that the market-led economic development strategy was a failure and needed to be abandoned for a strong state that could control economic forces. With the threat of growing antidemocratic movements, Roosevelt sought a quicker solution to deal with the Depression than simply waiting for the market to resolve the crisis.

What are some of the tools Roosevelt and future leaders used to get their economies out of trouble? We will examine the fiscal and monetary policies that states frequently use to manage economic performance. Governments use fiscal and monetary policies to incentivize consumers and firms to either spend during economic downturns or reduce spending when economies expand too rapidly.

Fiscal Policy

Taxing and spending by states are at the heart of **fiscal policy**. All states tax their residents for the money needed to fulfill obligations. By spending money and taxing less, states circulate more money in the economy and as a result incentivize consumers and businesses to spend more of their money. Increases in government expenditures stimulate an economy by, for example, purchasing items produced in the private sector and building public works projects. In both cases, employment increases. More people working means more people who are able to spend on items that they need and want. Advocates of increased government spending claim that such actions have multiplier effects. That is, every dollar the government spends produces more than one dollar in economic growth.

The other side of fiscal policy is the reduction of taxes. By taxing less, people and firms have more money to spend. Keynesian economics—named after British economist John Maynard Keynes (1883–1946)—advocate that tax cuts should target people in the middle- to lower-income brackets because this is where the restrained demand lies. This means that they are more likely to have a great impact on aggregate spending than tax cuts on the wealthy.

Taxing less and spending more may cause a budget deficit. A budget deficit occurs when revenues (money coming into the government) are smaller than expenditures (money leaving the government). This may not be a problem if it is a short-term condition. As the economy grows, tax revenues could increase and government spending can be rolled back. Cutting back on spending and increasing taxes would be a way to pay back the debt acquired during the budget deficit years. However, politicians often find it politically more popular to spend more and tax less than spend less and tax more. After all, what is the likelihood of citizens voting for a politician who promises to raise their taxes and cut social spending? Without certain institutional limits, therefore, budget deficits are common among governments in many countries.

Monetary Policy

Monetary policy is the management of the money supply (the total value of money available in an economy at a given time) and interest rates. The common objectives of monetary policy are to control inflation and improve employment. When interest rates are high, people are less likely to purchase items with large price tags, such as houses and cars. They are reluctant because they understand that the monthly loan payments will be large. In addition, they are concerned that the overall cost is not equal to the worth of the item. For example, under high interest rates, the new car you purchased could require half your monthly take-home pay. The high interest rate could also mean that the car you purchased for $20,000 would end up costing you $40,000 (principal plus interest) when your loan has been paid off. Would you still buy it? By lowering the interest rates, consumer demand should increase, as does the overall economic growth because producers supply more goods to meet the greater demand. Politicians have incentives to lower interest rates and keep them low given the positive outcomes for consumers.

The problem is that lowering interest rates, and keeping them low too long, creates inflationary pressures. Recall that when money is more readily available, people spend. After all, that is the goal. However, what happens when consumer spending outpaces the ability of firms to produce goods? Increased demand relative to supply causes prices to rise. Producers may not increase supplies of goods fast enough for various reasons. It could be due to the length of time needed for building new production facilities such as manufacturing plants. Another reason could be that producers do not have the money to increase production. In addition, some producers may not want to expand production because they fear that demand for their goods would eventually shrink and leave them with too many goods. To make sure monetary policy is used for economic benefits instead of political gains, some political economists advocate for an institutional method that keeps decisions on interest rates in the hands of individuals with expertise and experience in knowing when to decrease and then eventually increase interest rates to limit inflation.

In many countries, monetary policy is generally in the hands of central bank officials who make decisions on interest rates based on how well the economy is performing. To do this, central banks monitor inflation rates to ensure price stability. When inflation is higher than an acceptable rate, or when central bankers evaluate that the economy is "overheating" and thus anticipate high inflation, monetary authorities may raise interest rates and restrict credit to combat inflationary pressures. When central bankers are free from political pressures, we say that the country has **central bank independence**. Central bank independence is critical in keeping inflation rates low. However, politicians may wish to use monetary policy instruments to boost consumption to counteract economic downturns for political gain. Politicians may want to take advantage of monetary policy as they would use fiscal policy to benefit their political objectives.

In extreme cases, high inflation can cause political instability. When prices dramatically increase, average consumers will be able to buy less with the same income. Just imagine working hard knowing that your paycheck will buy you less and less over time. Frustration may manifest in street demonstrations and erupt into violent actions against the state. This was the situation Germany faced under the Weimar Republic (the regime in power before the Nazis) between 1921 and 1923, when inflation was at approximately one trillion percent over these years (yes, you read that correctly). At the highest point of hyperinflation, workers received their pay multiple times a day so that they could purchase goods before they became unaffordable. Demonstrations and street violence between communists and Nazis ended with the Nazi seizure of power. Major economic interest groups like banks and industry supported the regime change because the Nazi leaders promised political and social stability and believed that the Nazis would safeguard their property rights.

High inflation can be a continuing concern for all countries, especially developing countries. One contemporary example is Venezuela, which experienced inflation rates above a million percent in 2018. The economic hardships led to a political crisis with massive street demonstrations demanding that President Nicolás Maduro resign, which he refused. The instability also caused waves of economic refugees wanting to leave Venezuela for neighboring Colombia. The political crisis continued into 2019 when the Venezuelan National Assembly invalidated the results of the 2018 election citing illegal voter manipulation by Maduro. They installed Assembly Speaker Juan Guaidó as acting president, who was promptly arrested by Maduro.

EXPAND YOUR THOUGHTS

Governments could use monetary policy to boost employment by lowering interest rates. Critics of expansionary monetary policies argue that monetary policy should not be a tool for increasing employment if high interest rates lead to inflation. What is your opinion about using monetary policy to boost employment?

Counter-Cyclical Economic Policies

In general, interventionist policies to combat economic downturns follow the Keynesian economic principle of government action to either increase or decrease aggregate demand. Advocates believe that all capitalist economies go through business cycles marked by high points of growth followed by declining performance. Although it is possible for markets to self-correct the economic declines, as free market proponents maintain, it would take time and risk that political and social forces would attempt to overturn the market system because of the economic downturn's adverse effect on living conditions. To smooth out the highs and lows of economic performance, governments can adopt **counter-cyclical economic policies** to jump-start the economy at low points and prevent demand from outpacing supply of products and services at high points.

Intervention can take place in the form of state fiscal expenditures (i.e., government budgets) and interest rate adjustments as previously discussed. **Expansionary fiscal policy** aims to increase the money supply in the economy by using budgetary tools to increase spending and/or cut taxes. **Expansionary monetary policy** seeks to boost demand for goods and services by lowering interest rates. Expansionary fiscal and monetary policies put more money in the hands of consumers and businesses and thereby increase demand for products and services. In contrast, **contractionary fiscal policy** and **contractionary monetary policy** are intended to reduce the money supply and demand by decreasing government spending and by raising taxes and interest rates. The goal of expansionary fiscal and monetary policies during economic slumps and recessions is to increase aggregate demand by putting money in the hands of consumers. Conversely, governments use contractionary fiscal and monetary policies to cool down an overheated economy and counteract inflationary pressures.

EXPAND YOUR THOUGHTS

According to Keynesian fiscal policy recommendations, governments should increase spending and cut taxes during economic downturns in order to stimulate the economy. The resulting debt would be paid for when the economy improves by decreasing spending and increasing taxes. Do you think that a voter would support an election candidate that promises to increase taxes and cut government programs during economic good times in order to pay off the debt incurred during the bad economic times? Does your answer create a dilemma for the advocates of deficit spending as a method to recover from economic downturns?

SUMMARY

Countries around the world differ not only in their political culture and institutions but also in their levels of economic development. Economic development refers to the level of economic well-being and prosperity and can be explained by many factors. In this chapter, we focused on diverse development strategies adopted by various states over time to explain the effects that politics has on economics and economics has on politics. Each strategy can be classified by the amount of state intervention. In the market-led model, the state plays a minimal role when compared to other models of economic development. The model with the highest amount of state control is the centrally planned (command) economy. States that use this model own and control all aspects of economic production. To a lesser extent, state-led models introduce heavy government policy guidance and control in an attempt to develop economies.

Each model has its advantages and disadvantages. The analysis of their advantages and disadvantages, as well as country experiences, helps us assess why some countries are more successful than others in producing economic gains. Those strategies that failed ended with economic policy reforms, regime change, or, in the worst case scenario, state failure. The cases of the centrally planned economies and import-substituting industrialization are among the strategies that have been replaced due to the poor economic performances that countries experienced. The fall of the Soviet Union and the similar regimes in Eastern Europe are our evidence of how economics can dramatically influence politics.

We also saw that governments intervene during economic downturns in many types of economies. To promote growth and preserve economic and political stability, governments use the tools of fiscal and monetary policies to manage the level of demand. By using counter-cyclical economic policies, governments can stimulate demand when it is too low and reduce it when it is too high. The aim of counter-cyclical economic policies is to smooth out the highs and lows of the country's economic cycles and promote stability. The successful use of counter-cyclical policies may sometimes require making unpopular decisions. Decision-makers who are independent of the political process can make choices they feel are necessary even when they are unpopular.

KEY TERMS

Central bank independence (p. 239)

Command (or centrally planned) economy (p. 228)

Contractionary fiscal policy (p. 241)

Contractionary monetary policy (p. 241)

Corruption (p. 222)

Counter-cyclical economic policies (p. 240)

Developed countries (p. 220)

Developing countries (p. 222)

Economic development (p. 220)

Expansionary fiscal policy (p. 240)

Expansionary monetary policy (p. 241)

Export-oriented industrialization (p. 234)

Fiscal policy (p. 238)

Human capital (p. 221)

Import-substituting industrialization (p. 231)

Laissez-faire (free market capitalism) (p. 224)

Monetary policy (p. 239)

Neoliberalism (p. 233)

Political economy (p. 219)

Pork barrel project (p. 236)

Seigniorage (p. 222)

State-led development models (p. 231)

Structural policies (p. 235)

11 DEMOCRATIZATION

LEARNING OBJECTIVES

11.1 Describe the historical waves of democratization, the evolution of the meaning of democracy, and the current state of democracy around the world.

11.2 Explain the concept of democratic consolidation, the characteristics of consolidated democracies, and the challenges to democratic consolidation.

11.3 Discuss modernization theory and why the middle class is an important factor for democratization.

11.4 Examine the cultural characteristics that scholars believe are important for democratization, and the debates and controversies associated with cultural explanations.

11.5 Discuss how international environments affect domestic political regime change and how democratization in one country may spark democratization in other countries.

11.6 Identify various explanations for the breakdown of democratic regimes.

As the twentieth century came to a close, Nobel Economic Sciences Laureate Amartya Sen was asked what he thought was the most significant event of the twentieth century. This was not an easy question to answer. The twentieth century was full of notable developments, such as the two world wars; the rise and fall of Nazism, fascism, and communism; the Holocaust; the development of nuclear weapons and the Cold War; decolonization; explorations to the moon; the emergence and spread of the Internet; and the Great Depression. After pondering a while, Sen chose, without difficulty, the rise of democracy as the most important development that happened during the twentieth century.

Today, we look around and see a world where democracy is taken for granted. Democracies are found in almost all corners of the world. In many countries, disputes are resolved in peaceful manners through democratic elections, legislative deliberations, and court rulings. Democratic elections create winners and losers. In many countries, lost parties accept their defeat, and peaceful alternations of power take place on a regular basis. People are free to organize for a cause, and their right to free speech is guaranteed. The media reporting includes criticisms of government policies and actions. Opposition to incumbent governments is not only tolerated but is taken for granted and embraced as a sign of a healthy democratic regime. Democracy is no longer an exclusive feature of the Western countries; we've witnessed democracies in Asia, the Americas, and Africa as well.

Of course, nondemocratic regimes still exist, but they are on the defensive. Dictators around the world today have to explain why they do not have a democratic regime. As we saw in Chapters 8 and 9, some dictators even try to mask their autocratic governments in a cloak of nominally democratic institutions by holding elections, although those elections are not free, fair, or competitive. They allow legislative bodies and political parties as long as those institutions do not truly challenge the rulers. Even the world's worst dictators seem to want to present their countries as democracies, even though their use of the term *democracy* differs. Political leaders in some autocratic countries have named or renamed their countries using adjectives and words like *democratic* or *people* (as in Democratic People's Republic of Korea, People's Republic of China, and Democratic Republic of the Congo) as if calling themselves and their countries democratic would give them democratic legitimacy.

Despite the wide acceptance of democracy as the legitimate form of government today, democracy on a global scale is in fact a relatively recent phenomenon. Furthermore, experiences of democracy and autocratic regimes have diverged among countries. The varied experiences of countries generate many questions. What factors influence whether countries will democratize? What explains why some democracies survive while others backslide to authoritarianism? Can a democracy survive and thrive in any country, or does it require a certain type of society, culture, or economy?

Democratic transition and stability have been one of the enduring questions in political science and among policymakers. In this chapter, we will examine histories of democratic transitions and the current state of democracies in the world. We will then review major theories of democratization that emphasize economic, cultural, and international factors in explaining countries' democratic transitions and stability. The last section of the chapter discusses breakdowns of democracies.

HISTORICAL WAVES OF DEMOCRATIZATION

LEARNING OBJECTIVE

11.1 Describe the historical waves of democratization, the evolution of the meaning of democracy, and the current state of democracy around the world.

For those of us living in democracies, it may come as a surprise that the fervor for democracy is a relatively new phenomenon. For much of the twentieth century, most countries were not democratic. A large majority of the countries around the world were authoritarian as late as the mid-1970s. A turning point came in the late twentieth century when a number of countries began to abandon their authoritarian regimes and adopt democratic institutions. Unlike previous cases of democratic transitions, the late twentieth century democratization was really a worldwide phenomenon. Nonetheless, the democratic movement was not always successful. While many countries that adopted democratic institutions have fully democratized and stayed democratic, many others did not complete transitions to full democracies. In yet others, democratic institutions collapsed and were replaced by authoritarian regimes.

Democratization is a political phenomenon by which a nondemocratic country moves to adopt democratic institutions and practices. Democratization is a complex, multistep phenomenon. It involves the removal of an authoritarian regime, conducting a founding election of a new democratic regime, and adhering to the norms and institutions of political rights and civil liberties of liberal democracy. A founding election is the first relatively free, fair, and competitive national-level election held upon or after a country's transition to a new democratic regime. The departure of a dictator does not guarantee that the country will transition to a democracy. In fact, many autocratic regimes have been replaced by other autocratic regimes. Nonetheless, we can identify certain historical periods in which a number of countries democratized.

Democratization Waves and Reverse Waves

Although modern democracy is largely a twentieth-century phenomenon, its beginning goes as far back as the start of the nineteenth century. However, its spread worldwide was not continuously upward. Looking over two hundred years of history of modern democracy, we can spot periods of global democratic expansion and contraction. One well-known work on the historical patterns of democracy is Samuel Huntington's 1991 book, *The Third Wave*.

Huntington recognized three democratization waves and two counter-waves in human history. Each wave featured modal patterns of regime change during a specific period. If significantly more countries were becoming democratic than becoming or staying autocratic, then a democratization wave was happening. If, by contrast, significantly more countries were becoming autocratic than democratic, then a reverse wave was occurring. Huntington noticed that a counter-wave followed each democratization wave. Table 11.1 summarizes democratization and reverse waves that Huntington identified in his now classic 1991 book.

According to Huntington, the first democratization wave began in 1828 and was influenced by the American and French Revolutions. During the nearly one hundred year period, democracies slowly and gradually spread to certain countries. "Democracy" during the first wave, however, would not meet the requirements of liberal democracy today. What was especially lacking in the beginning was universal enfranchisement. Huntington counted as a democracy if a country met the minimum democratic requirements he established for this period: (1) The head of government is either directly or indirectly elected through a popular election; and (2) at least 50 percent of the male adult citizens (of the dominant racial group) had the right to vote. According to Huntington, countries such as the United States, United Kingdom, France, Switzerland, Italy, and Argentina met the minimum democratic requirements of the time.

The first democratization wave ended and a reverse wave emerged in the 1920s. The reverse wave occurred during the interwar period, and the world witnessed the rise of totalitarian and authoritarian regimes. Adolf Hitler seized power in 1933 and founded the Nazi regime in

TABLE 11.1 ■ Waves of Democratization Recognized by Huntington		
Wave	**Period**	**Examples**
First Democratization Wave	1828–1926	United States, United Kingdom, France, Switzerland, Italy, Argentina
Reverse Wave	1922–1942	Italy, Germany, Portugal, Spain, Argentina, Brazil, Japan
Second Democratization Wave	1943–1962	West Germany, Italy, Austria, Japan, Uruguay, Brazil, Costa Rica, Argentina, Peru
Reverse Wave	1958–1975	Argentina, Brazil, Bolivia, Ecuador, Chile, Uruguay, Korea, Indonesia, Africa
Third Democratization Wave	1974–???	USSR/Russia, Eastern Europe, East Asia, Latin America, and more

Source: Huntington (1991).

Germany. Military coups took over governments in many European and Latin American countries. Political systems in countries such as Italy, Germany, Portugal, Spain, Argentina, Brazil, and Japan, where nominally democratic institutions existed, gave way to blatantly authoritarian or totalitarian regimes.

With the end of World War II, a new impetus for democratization began in the 1940s, starting the second democratization wave. During this period, Japan, Italy, and West Germany reemerged from the ruins of the war to become democracies. Many Latin American countries also experimented with democratic institutions. During the second democratization wave, democratic institutions emerged or reemerged in places like West Germany, Italy, Austria, Japan, Uruguay, Brazil, Costa Rica, Argentina, and Peru.

As the Cold War intensified in the postwar period, however, the democratization wave once again gave way to another reverse wave. Communist Party dictatorships took over most of the countries in Eastern Europe and spread to other parts of the world. Many colonies in Africa achieved independence, yet decolonization of Africa led to the multiplication of nondemocratic regimes in the region. The most dramatic reversals took place in Latin America, where military coups brought down democratic governments in Peru, Brazil, Bolivia, Argentina, and Ecuador in the 1960s. Military coups of the 1970s in Chile and Uruguay also ended the relatively successful democracies in Latin America. Most Central American countries suffered brutal dictatorships, civil wars, and communist insurgencies and counter-communist violence in the 1960s and 1970s. In Pakistan, Indonesia, and South Korea, the military also took over governments in the 1950s and 1960s.

In April 1974, the Portuguese military overthrew the authoritarian Estado Novo (New State) regime in a coup, ending nearly a half century of autocratic rule and paving the way for the country's democratization. Huntington marked 1974 as the beginning of a new global

FIGURE 11.1 ■ Freedom in the World Map

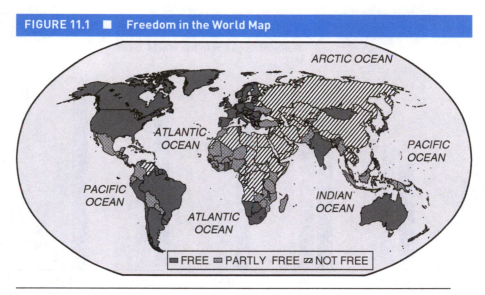

Note: Freedom House is a nongovernmental organization that monitors democratic status of countries in the world. On the map, solid countries are rated as "free" (liberal democracy), those with dots "partly free," and those with stripes "not free" (autocracy).

Source: Sarah Repucci and Amy Slipowitz (2022) The Global Expansion of Authoritarian Rule. FREEDOM IN THE WORLD 2022, Freedomhouse.org.

democratization wave. This new democratization wave signified a truly worldwide movement toward democracy. Communist party dictatorships in Eastern Europe and the Soviet Union collapsed, being replaced by democratic institutions. Many military regimes, personal dictatorships, and other types of authoritarian regimes in Latin America, Asia, and Africa were also supplanted by democratic regimes. In 1974, according to one estimate, democracies accounted for only one-quarter of the countries in the world. Today, about half of the countries are fully democratic, and many more have adopted some democratic institutions (see Figure 11.1). Huntington called this worldwide regime change to democracy **third wave democratization.**

When the third democratization wave ended and whether we are currently in a reverse wave have been a matter of scholarly debate. If a wave represents a significant movement in one direction of regime status change involving many countries, then the third democratization wave appears to have ended by the early 2000s. As Figure 11.2 presents, from 1974 to 2004, the percentage of democracies constantly increased, and concomitantly, the percentage of autocracies continuously declined. From 2004 to 2014, however, the proportions of democracies and autocracies stayed the same. Furthermore, if we examine fluctuations in the levels of democracy and autocracy, many countries have become less free or more repressive even though these movements may not have changed those countries' regime classifications. More recently, Freedom House registered a slight increase in the share of autocratic regimes. These latest developments have raised concern among democracy advocates about prospects of democracy in the world.

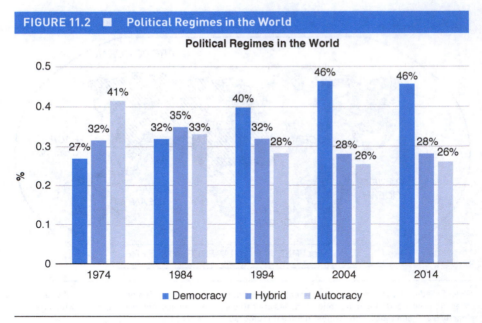

FIGURE 11.2 ■ **Political Regimes in the World**

Political Regimes in the World

■ Democracy ■ Hybrid ■ Autocracy

Source: Based on data from Freedom House. https://freedomhouse.org/

Evolution of the Meaning of Democracy in Practice

In Chapter 6, we examined various classificatory schemes of political regimes. When we think about democracy today, universal adult suffrage is an essential and indispensable tool. A universal voting right is what makes "government by the people" possible. Consequently, universal adult suffrage is a core definitional element of the concept and measurement of democracy, no matter whether one conceptualizes democracy in terms of liberal democracy, Robert Dahl's (1971) polyarchy, or Freedom House's free society.

Indeed, today we take for granted universal adult suffrage as a fundamental component of democracy. Just imagine that a government declares its country to be democratic without universal adult suffrage. We bet hardly anyone will be willing to accept the country as a democracy. Even most dictatorships with elections these days have universal adult suffrage! However, this was not always the case. In the past, many countries had some restrictions on voting rights. Women, people of color, those without an education, those who were poor, and people without property commonly did not have the right to vote in various parts of the world, even in places that were considered democratic with the standard of that era. Other dimensions of political and civil rights have also evolved over time.

Given that the standard of democracy has changed over time, what criteria would a researcher use to identify and count the number of democracies during the first democratization wave? Samuel Huntington counted some 30 countries as "minimally democratic" during the period 1828 to 1926. As discussed in the previous section, the scholar used two criteria. First, suffrage must be given to at least 50 percent of the adult male population. Huntington accepted multiethnic and multiracial societies as democracies if at least 50 percent of the adult white male population were enfranchised. This method permitted him to count countries like the United States as democratic despite the fact that a large majority of the total adult population did not have the right to vote in the nineteenth century. The second requirement was that the head of government must be elected periodically. As you can tell, these criteria are much less stringent than the criteria for democracy today. In fact, they would not be considered democracies at all if today's understanding were applied! Nonetheless, a focus on political competition rather than participation enabled the scholar to identify democratic countries historically based on the view of democracy at that time.

Many longitudinal data of political regimes typically do not include the question of suffrage as a criterion to determine whether or not a country is democratic. For example, the Center for Systemic Peace's Polity Project provides political regime characteristics and regime transitions from 1800. The Polity Project's coding of democracy considers "competitiveness of political participation," "competitiveness and openness of executive recruitment," and "constraints on the chief executive" but does not examine the extent of suffrage or civil liberties.

EXPAND YOUR THOUGHTS

Our understanding of democracy has changed over time. As we learned, for a long time, *universal* adult suffrage was not a component of modern democracy although most agreed that a sufficient percentage of citizens must have the right to vote. Instead, many political scientists focus on political competition—the election of the head of government and the legislature in multiparty competition and peaceful alternation of office in accordance with electoral results—when they analyze democracy historically. What are the pros and cons of focusing on political competition in conceptualizing and analyzing democracy? Do you consider it a valid approach, or would you say universal adult suffrage should not be omitted as a part of the definition of democracy? Why?

Case Study: Democratic Transition in Brazil

Democratic transitions can be fast, happening quickly in a short period of time, such as the ones that happened in many Eastern European countries in 1989. It can also be a gradual, prolonged transition. Democratization tends to go through a measured protracted process, particularly when the political transition is initiated by the outgoing authoritarian leaders. Such was the case in Brazil's most recent democratic transition.

The Brazilian military came into power in the 1964 coup and ruled the country until 1985. During the 21 years of the military regime, successive military generals served as the country's president. In 1974, moderate General Ernesto Geisel became president and began a process of political liberalization called *abertura* (opening in English). Geisel devised a plan for a gradual opening of the authoritarian regime and an eventual return to democracy. The only opposition party at that time, Brazilian Democratic Movement (MDB), was allowed to run election campaigns almost freely, exiled citizens were allowed to return home, and the extraordinary powers of the military government were repealed. In 1979, Geisel's handpicked successor and another moderate, General João Figueiredo, became president.

President Figueiredo continued the path laid by Geisel and guided the country back to democracy by overcoming the strong opposition from military hard-liners. To quell the opposition inside the military regime, Figueiredo signed an amnesty law pardoning those convicted of "political or related" crimes between 1961 and 1978 so that those responsible for repression and other crimes during the authoritarian period would not be prosecuted after civilians took control of government. An **amnesty law** retroactively pardons or discharges a select group of people, usually members of security and armed forces, government officials, politicians, opposition leaders, and others, from criminal liability for the unlawful acts that they perpetrated. The amnesty law in Brazil also pardoned political and related crimes committed by both armed and nonviolent opposition groups to the military rule. President Figueiredo also did away with the two-party system that the military government imposed in 1966 (which operated with a single official progovernment party, ARENA, and a single official opposition party, MDB), allowing new parties to be formed. The president also instituted direct elections of state governors.

The election of a new civilian president by the national congress serving as an electoral college was scheduled for 1985. In 1984, Brazilians mobilized the *Diretas Já* (Direct Election Now!) movement and demanded a direct popular election of the president. Despite the growing popular movement and the media attention, the proposal failed to pass the congress. An internal dispute about candidate selection caused a split within the pro-military party and defection by certain influential politicians, including José Sarney, weakening the military's grip of the

The indirect election of the president in Brazil, 1985. The Brazilian National Congress served as an electoral college for this crucial election, paving the way for the country's transition to civilian rule after 21 years of military rule. President-elect Tancredo Neves (in the middle) was hospitalized on the eve of his inauguration and died without ever taking the oath of office.

Célio Azevedo/Senado The Commons/Flickr

electoral process. Those defectors formed a new party and worked with opposition parties to elect Tancredo Neves of the PMDB (Party of the Brazilian Democratic Movement—former MDB) as president with Sarney as his vice president. In January 1985, Tancredo Neves was elected, defeating the candidate supported by the military.

Unexpectedly, the president-elect fell severely ill on the eve of his inauguration and his running mate, José Sarney, a long-time supporter of the military regime, was inaugurated as vice president and served in Neves's place as acting president. Neves passed in April without ever taking the oath of office, and Sarney formally became president.

Democracy From Above: Political Liberalization and Democratic Transition Game

When thinking about democratic transitions, you may be seeing an image of a popular revolution where the masses, demanding freedom, drag the dictator out of a palace and take control of the government in transforming the country into a democracy. This form of democratic transition is rather rare. In many cases, democratic transitions are negotiated processes that involve many different individuals and groups, both from the autocratic regime and from civil society. Moreover, some democratic transitions are initiated by the authoritarian leaders of the autocratic regime. The Brazilian democratic transition we just examined is such a case. Why would authoritarian leaders initiate democratization and voluntarily give up power?

There are various reasons why authoritarian leaders voluntarily relinquish power and accept democratization. One such explanation was provided by Adam Przeworski (1991), who developed a model of democratic transition based on the strategic interactions among authoritarian elites and mobilized civil society actors. In Przeworski's model, there are two key actors: liberalizers within the authoritarian government and mobilized civil society actors who are assumed to be seeking democracy. The process begins with liberalizers who will decide whether they will open up the political space to the civil society or not. This is called **political liberalization**, which is the process of loosening government control over people and the society. Liberalizers consider political liberalization not because they intend to democratize the country but because of their internal power struggle with the authoritarian regime's hard-liners. Through political liberalization, liberalizers hope that civil society actors will serve as their allies against regime hard-liners. In other words, liberalizers intend to mobilize popular support to consolidate their power against the regime's hard-liners. What liberalizers seek to achieve is thus not a democracy but a broadened dictatorship where mobilized civil society actors are co-opted. Therefore, liberalizers are not democrats.

Once political liberalization begins, civil society actors need to decide whether they will accept being co-opted to enjoy greater but incomplete freedom, or if they will organize further to demand full democratization. If they believe that the authoritarian regime would successfully repress the organized civil society demanding full democracy, then they would enter into agreement with the liberalizers, and the outcome would be a broadened dictatorship. If, on the other hand, they believe that the regime is not strong enough to repress the organized civil society, they would mobilize further and demand full democratization. The difficulty for liberalizers at this point is that neither repression nor democratization is an attractive outcome to them. They definitely are not interested in full democratization. Yet, using force to repress the organized civil society would strengthen the position of the hard-liners vis-à-vis the liberalizers within the regime. Liberalizers, by assumption, would prefer to democratize using repression if the civil society continues to organize. However, the liberalizers' most preferred outcome is a broadened dictatorship in which they rule without being challenged by either the hard-liners or the civil society opposition. So, what would liberalizers do?

All actors are assumed to be rational and engaged in strategic behavior. Given this assumption, the liberalizers would choose political liberalization over the status quo, the existing state of affairs, if and only if they believe that civil society actors will agree to enter into the broadened dictatorship. If they believe that civil society actors will continue to mobilize, no political opening would be initiated. This logic makes sense. Nevertheless, we occasionally see political liberalization ending up in full transition to democracy. How would we explain this?

Przeworski explains that political actors often make choices without having all of the information, which may cause errors when evaluating alternative strategies. In this political liberalization game, full democratization occasionally ensues because the liberalizers miscalculate the strengths of the organized civil society. The underestimation of the organized civil society's strength causes liberalizers to incorrectly believe that civil society actors prefer political liberalization and a broadened dictatorship to the other two alternatives: maintaining the status quo or insisting on full democratization (which entails a significant risk of repression). Hence, political liberalization takes place, leading to a stronger than expected civil society continuing to organize against the authoritarian regime and the liberalizers accepting full democratization against their initial intent.

In sum, according to Przworski's model, top-down democratization does not require true democrats who are genuinely committed to a democracy. In fact, in the scholar's model, democratization from above occurs as a result of authoritarian leaders' miscalculations.

CONSOLIDATION OF DEMOCRATIC REGIMES

LEARNING OBJECTIVE

11.2 Explain the concept of democratic consolidation, the characteristics of consolidated democracies, and the challenges to democratic consolidation.

Implementing a founding election is a significant accomplishment for formerly authoritarian countries and represents a key milestone in democratic transitions. To get to that point, authoritarian leaders must either be ousted or agree to hold an election that will replace them. Those elections must be organized and conducted in a reasonably free, fair, and competitive manner—uncharted territory for many who have lived in authoritarian systems. Political parties need to form, recruit, and support their candidates. Parties also need to create identities and policy platforms that distinguish themselves from other parties. Citizen education about how elections are conducted is necessary. Proper training of electoral administration staff is also indispensable.

For many new democracies, consolidating democracy is equally challenging. **Democratic consolidation** occurs when there is the broad acceptance of democracy as the permanent and the only legitimate form of political activity in the society. It happens when democracy has become "the only game in town" and all significant actors adhere to democratic rules of the game and expect others to do so as well.

But how do we know in practice if a democracy is consolidated? Huntington (1991) proposed a "two-turnover test." Before we can consider a country a consolidated democracy, according to the two-turnover test, one party must win the founding election and then a different party must win a later election and peacefully replace the first party in government. Unfortunately, passing this two-turnover test is not proof that the democracy has consolidated. There are many democracies where power has changed hands, but not all significant actors have accepted democracy as the only game in town.

For example, Colombia has been an electoral and unconsolidated democracy for several decades. The country's presidency has changed hands between rival political parties. Nonetheless, long-standing widespread violence and serious human rights abuses by the left-wing revolutionary guerrillas, drug traffickers, paramilitary groups, and government security forces have challenged its democracy. Although the government and the country's main revolutionary group, Revolutionary Armed Forces of Colombia, signed a peace accord in 2016, its implementation has been delayed. Resistance to the accord has developed, raising concerns about the country's democracy.

Peru is another example. The most recent period of military rule (1968–1980) ended when Peruvian voters elected Fernando Belaúnde Terry as president in the May 1980 elections. In 1985, Alan García of the main opposition party, American Popular Revolutionary Alliance, won the presidential election and took office, fulfilling the two-turnover test requirements. However, democracy was far from the only game in the country. In the 1980s, Peru suffered from violent insurgent movements from revolutionary and terrorist groups, including the Shining Path (Sendero Luminoso) and the Túpac Amaru Revolutionary Movement. Those groups threatened and disrupted elections, particularly in rural areas; killed numerous civilians, including politicians and candidates; and detonated bombs and destroyed properties in Lima and other urban areas.

The presidential election of 1990 was highly competitive with multiple candidates and no clear favorite. It also occurred in the context of fear and citizen dissatisfaction with how democracy was performing. Terrorist attacks were intensifying, the economy was faltering, corruption was rampant, and voter confidence in politicians and traditional political parties was waning. The Peruvian voters elected Alberto Fujimori, a relatively unknown mathematician, in the second round of the majority run-off elections to the presidency. Once in office, President Fujimori undertook drastic measures to combat the country's economic crisis and tried to subdue terrorist activities. In April 1992, frustration with the opposition-controlled Congress was mounting, and the president dissolved Congress and seized total control of the government. President Fujimori subsequently adopted a new constitution, held congressional elections, carried out austerity measures and market-oriented economic reforms, and implemented heavy-handed antiterrorist measures. These measures were successful in stabilizing the Peruvian economy and crushing the insurgent groups, which made President Fujimori highly popular among citizens in the 1990s. However, the Peruvian citizens obtained better economic performance and public security by sacrificing their democracy.

These Colombian and Peruvian cases and the experiences of many other countries indicate that Huntington's two-turnover test is not a solid test of democratic consolidation. We are skeptical about whether there could ever be a definitive test of democratic consolidation. So far, we do not have one.

Many researchers have analyzed citizens' attitudes toward democracy as an alternative way to evaluate the degree of democratic consolidation. In essence, researchers use survey questions to find out the degree of citizen commitment to democracy. If survey respondents express that they support other (nondemocratic) forms of government, it is clear that they are not committed to democracy. However, even when respondents indicate their support for democracy, their support may be conditional, contingent on democracy producing desired outcomes such as economic growth and public security. Consequently, many researchers are interested in finding out the proportion of the population who have an unfettered commitment to democracy.

Other researchers have also examined the passage of time as a proxy for democratic consolidation with the understanding that the longer a democracy endures, the more consolidated it becomes. In the absence of a definitive test of democratic consolidation, only time will tell whether a democracy is entrenched enough in the society to last for a long time.

PRACTICAL APPLICATION

What is the difference between a democratic transition and democratic consolidation? Find a country where democracy has recently been adopted but not consolidated. What factors support your evaluation that the country's democracy has not consolidated?

EXPAND YOUR THOUGHTS

Democratic consolidation is hard to know in practice. Some scholars say democratic consolidation is not a useful analytic concept because it is hard to conceptualize and measure. If you were to assess whether a country's democracy has been consolidated or not, what indicators would you look for? Is democratic consolidation a useful and measurable concept? Why or why not?

EXPLAINING DEMOCRATIZATION: ECONOMIC DEVELOPMENT

LEARNING OBJECTIVE

11.3 Discuss modernization theory and why the middle class is an important factor for democratization.

Under what conditions do countries democratize and stay democratic? This question has occupied the minds of many political scientists and policymakers for decades. Various explanations have been proposed to help us understand why some countries democratize sometimes but not other times and why certain democracies are durable, but others are precarious or even collapse.

Among the economic explanations, **modernization theory of democracy** has been the most influential explanation. It is widely believed that economic development is closely related to democratic development. Classic modernization theory, such as the one developed by Seymour Martin Lipset (1959), argues that economic development makes democracy more likely to emerge and more likely to survive once it has been adopted. According to the theory, economic development leads to the development of a large middle class with certain characteristics: educated, tolerant of diverse views, secular, realistic, and capable of effectively participating in the political process. Thanks to their education and wealth, middle-class people are not susceptible to demagogic, extremist, or utopian ideas. These people also believe in their political efficacy and so demand their empowerment and participation, resulting in a transition to democracy. Once democratized, the values and attitudes of the middle class make democracy strong and less vulnerable to breakdown.

In contrast, poor countries' societies are characterized by a mass of impoverished and uneducated people at the bottom and a handful of rich people at the top with a small middle class underneath them. The interests of these different societal groups are not compatible with each other, and the intensity of **distributional conflict** over who gets what and how much is likely to be high in these countries. In such societies, politics is viewed as a zero-sum game (in which someone's gain is your loss; see Chapter 1) and political moderation and compromise—two well-known ingredients of a functioning democracy—are unlikely. The elite in this type of society have an inherent interest in repressing the poor and keeping them disenfranchised. These factors make democracy less likely in poor countries.

For his book *Social Origins of Dictatorship and Democracy: Lord and Peasant in the Making of the Modern World,* Barrington Moore (1966) conducted a comparative analysis of modernization in Britain, France, the United States, China, Japan, Russia, Germany, and India. Moore argued that class structures and interclass alliances at particular points in time can explain the types of social revolutions that occurred and political regimes that followed. Moore emphasized the importance of industrialization and the rise of a middle class for a democracy to emerge. According to Moore, "We may simply register strong agreement with the Marxist thesis that a vigorous and independent class of town dwellers has been an indispensable element in the growth of parliamentary democracy. "*No bourgeois, no democracy*" (1966, p. 418 [emphasis added]).

As you can see, modernization scholars conceive economic development much more broadly than economic growth, which can simply be defined as an increase in the production of economic goods and services. This is commonly measured by an expansion in the gross domestic product (GDP). Although economic growth is important, economic development involves not only increases in financial wealth but also industrial expansion and societal changes. In modernization theory, wealth, education, industrialization, and a large middle-class population are considered crucial to the development of a stable democratic society.

Does modernization theory have empirical validity? In other words, are higher levels of economic development correlated with (a) higher levels of democratic development, (b) a higher probability of transition to democracy, and (c) a lower probability of democratic breakdown? One way to examine the first hypothesis is to see whether democracies are on average more economically developed than autocracies.

Figure 11.3 presents the box plots of GDP per capita in purchasing power parity (PPP) for democracies and autocracies. GDP per capita in PPP considers and adjusts to price differences among countries when comparing the wealth of countries. Although economic development implies much more than GDP per capita, many researchers use GDP per capita as a simple proxy for economic development. The box plots show for each regime category the median value of GDP per capita (the middle line inside the box) as well as the values for the 25th percentile (the bottom of the box), 75th percentile (the top of the box), minimum, and maximum, excluding outliers. It is clear that democracies are on average wealthier than autocracies. The median GDP per capita of democracies is $15,639, whereas the median GDP per capita of autocracies is $6,458. That means that democracies are on average more than twice as wealthy as autocracies. The dispersion of values indicates that democracies are more varied than autocracies in terms of the levels of wealth, but much of the variations are in the upper (i.e., wealthier) direction. The

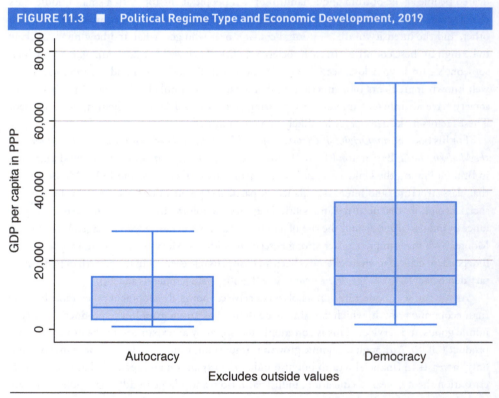

FIGURE 11.3 ■ Political Regime Type and Economic Development, 2019

Note: Democracies include countries with Freedom House's political rights ratings of 4 or lower. Autocracies include countries with political rights ratings of 5 or higher. GDP per capita is the 2019 purchasing power parity values based on the constant 2017 international dollar.

Sources: Based on data from Freedom House and *World Development Indicators*.

analysis of the data lends support for modernization theory. Nonetheless, this is just one test. We encourage you to test the second and third hypotheses as well.

EXPAND YOUR THOUGHTS

Think about wealthy oil-exporting countries, such as Saudi Arabia. Many of these countries are not democratic. In what ways are they *not* a negation of modernization theory?

PRACTICAL APPLICATION

China's economic development in the past few decades has been astonishing. The country has been developing at an average rate of approximately 10 percent annually for the past four decades. Do you think China will democratize in the near future, say within the next 10 years? Why or why not?

PRACTICAL APPLICATION

Modernization theory suggests that higher levels of economic development are correlated with (a) higher levels of democratic development, (b) a higher probability of transition to democracy, and (c) a lower probability of democratic breakdown. How would you test these hypotheses?

EXPLAINING DEMOCRATIZATION: CULTURE, ATTITUDES, AND BELIEFS

LEARNING OBJECTIVE

11.4 Examine the cultural characteristics that scholars believe are important for democratization, and the debates and controversies associated with cultural explanations.

Many studies examine the roles of culture, values, attitudes, and beliefs in democratic transitions and development. There are two principal perspectives in the political culture approach. The first, **cultural primordialism**, focuses on factors, such as geographic location, religion, and ethnicity, that are relatively stable over time. Cultural primordialists argue that cultural characteristics are hard to change, and certain cultures are more compatible or incompatible with democratic institutions and practices. Many cultural primordialists have long believed and maintained that only "Western" and "Christian" culture provides a suitable base for the development of democracy. To sustain their claim, cultural primordialists emphasize that modern democracy originated in the "West," where the Enlightenment's emphasis on individualism, natural rights, and liberty developed as cultural values.

Cultural primordialists have considered that various cultures are not conducive to democratic development. For example, many thought that democracy would be difficult to take root in societies with Catholic culture. They viewed the Catholic Church to be authoritarian and thought the hierarchical Catholic culture would be more suited for authoritarian systems of government. The authoritarian experiences of Spain, Portugal, Italy, and much of Latin America during the first three-quarters of the twentieth century gave credence to this perspective. However, many of these countries democratized during the third democratization wave in the last quarter of the twentieth century. As a result, a revisionist view emerged, which attributes democratization of predominantly Catholic societies to changes in the Catholic Church. Over time, the Catholic Church came to embrace the liberal principle, the autonomy of the state from the church, and the freedom of religion, resulting in the reconciliation between the Catholic Church and liberal democracy.

Students read books during a gathering to mark World Mental Health Day at an Islamic junior high school in Banda Aceh on October 14, 2021. Indonesia, the world's most populous majority Muslim country, has made remarkable strides from authoritarian to democratic rule since the collapse of the Suharto regime in 1998.

CHAIDEER MAHYUDDIN/Contributor/Getty Images

Today, many cultural primordialists, including Samuel Huntington (1996), warn that Islam and Confucianism are especially incompatible to democratic values. Some features of Muslim societies that are considered particularly problematic for democratization include their alleged inability to separate religion from politics, intolerance toward other religions, and treatment of women. In

Confucian societies, some values allegedly hinder democratic development, such as hierarchy over equality, deference for authority over liberty, and emphasis on collectivism over individualism.

However, other scholars have criticized the cultural primordial perspective as **ethnocentrism**. They argue that cultural primordialists are evaluating other cultures according to their own preconceptions, which originate from the standards and customs of their own history and culture. Critics have also pointed out that many cultural primordial views are too simplistic and ignore the wide diversities that exist within groups of countries labeled Muslim or Confucian societies, among others. For instance, China, South Korea, Singapore, and Japan may all be considered Confucian societies, but they all have unique histories, dissimilar political systems, and different cultures. Moreover, in any culture and religion, one can find values and practices that are compatible with democracy as well as those that are not compatible with it. Keep in mind that Protestant countries have had practices that would be considered undemocratic today.

Over the past several decades, many political scientists specializing in political culture have sought to scientifically measure predominant national cultures rather than use cultural stereotypes. These scholars employ modern survey techniques to gauge mass beliefs and analyze national culture. **Civic culture** is a cluster of shared values and attitudes held by the people in a society, which is measured by responses to survey questions. Beginning with Almond and Verba (1963), the civic culture school has identified fundamental mass beliefs, such as interpersonal trust and political tolerance, that should exist for the development of a vibrant civil society and a stable democratic regime. Although primordial views have persisted, the civic culture approach has become an important area in the scientific study of democracy and democratization.

EXPAND YOUR THOUGHTS

Consider cultural primordialists' explanation about the impact of culture. To what extent are cultural primordial arguments valid? What cultural attributes do you think are crucial for the development of democracy in a country? Explain your answer.

EXPLAINING DEMOCRATIZATION: INTERNATIONAL FACTORS

LEARNING OBJECTIVE

11.5 Discuss how international environments affect domestic political regime change and how democratization in one country may spark democratization in other countries.

International environments also influence political regimes and regime transitions within countries. Following World War II, many countries democratized as a result of the insistence of the Allied Powers. Among those that democratized following the Second World War included former totalitarian countries of Japan, (West) Germany, and Italy, which were defeated in the war. Democracy also emerged in Latin America. Some newly independent states in Asia also introduced democratic institutions. However, this democratic wave did not last long. The superpower conflict between the United States and the Soviet Union intensified in the 1960s, which contributed to the rise of autocratic regimes. On one hand, Soviet expansionism led to the proliferation of communist party dictatorships. The anticommunist policies of the United States, on the other hand, led to the breakdown of democracies and quasi-democracies in various places. They were replaced by repressive right-wing authoritarian regimes. During the height of the Cold War, the world share of democracies declined substantially.

The international political climate then changed again. With the tension between the United States and the Soviet Union subsiding in the 1980s, there were also shifts in U.S. and Soviet foreign policies. Most notably, the Soviet Union under Mikhail Gorbachev's leadership did not intervene militarily when communist party rule was threatened in Eastern Europe. The United States also became increasingly unwilling to support repressive dictatorships with terrible human rights records even if they were anticommunist. Around the same time, norms of liberal democracy spread widely and became embraced by many countries, peoples, and organizations. These changes at the international level created a hospitable environment for democracy and valuable support for those promoting democracy.

Many people believe that international environments, especially international regional environments, have transmissible effects. Democracy can be viral. If a country democratizes, that may trigger its neighboring countries to democratize as well. This phenomenon is called **demonstration effects**, also referred to as snowballing effects and contagion effects. In essence, this perspective argues that successful democratization in one country leads to democratization in another country in its proximity. Successful democratization in a country demonstrates to peoples in other nondemocratic countries that an overthrow of a dictatorship is possible—that the dictator is not invincible—and that democracy can be attained. There are also learning effects: Other countries can learn from earlier democratizers' experiences in terms of successful and failed strategies. They can study what strategies worked and what did not.

The expansion in global communications and transportation technology has produced an environment where demonstration effects take place more frequently and with greater ease. Today, it is difficult to control information. Ideas, peoples, and news move across national borders much faster than they used to. Political phenomena transmit easily, resulting in a map like Figure 11.1 where democracies are clustered with other democracies, and nondemocracies are also found with other nondemocracies.

The fall of the communist party dictatorships in Eastern Europe is the epitome of a demonstration effect. The socialist regimes in Europe fell one after another in 1989 and were replaced by democratic regimes. The ongoing economic crisis in Poland led the Communist leaders to initiate a series of negotiations with regime opposition Solidarity leaders. The result was the partly open parliamentary elections in June 1989 in which one-third of the Sejm (lower house) seats were freely contested. The Communists were defeated at the polls, which created a political crisis. The Communists' failure to form a government led to more rounds of negotiations with Solidarity. On September 12, the Sejm voted to approve Prime Minister Mazowiecki and his cabinet. For the first time in almost half a century, a non-Communist government took office.

Since Poland's democratization, other Eastern European countries—Hungary, East Germany, Czechoslovakia, Bulgaria, and Romania—one after another eliminated the one-party dictatorships in 1989 and sought democratization. In 1991, the Soviet Union, once a feared force, collapsed as well.

PRACTICAL APPLICATION

Find an example of demonstration effects with respect to democratization. How did democracy spread? What triggered the first democratization?

DEMOCRATIC BREAKDOWN

LEARNING OBJECTIVE

11.6 Identify various explanations for the breakdown of democratic regimes.

Thus far, we have examined the conditions in which countries become democratic. However, regime change is not a teleological unidirectional phenomenon. Many countries have experienced democratization as well as democratic collapse. Some countries experience multiple episodes of democratic breakdowns. Authoritarian-to-authoritarian transitions are also common. **Democratic breakdown** occurs when institutions of democracy are subverted and not immediately restored. In this section, we will look at some of the factors of democratic breakdowns. But before we consider why democracies collapse, let's first examine how democracies fail.

How Democracies Die

The ways in which democratic regimes end are not uniform. Democracy can die rapidly in a matter of a few weeks, a few days, or even a few hours. When a democratic regime fails so quickly, it is called a **rapid death of democracy**. Democracies experience a rapid death when they are subverted in a successful coup d'etat. A coup is typically led by a small group of armed forces conspiring to oust an incumbent political leader. It is not uncommon that those soldiers and officers work with other societal or political groups (such as private businesses and opposition politicians) to remove the incumbent political leaders.

Chile saw its democracy die rapidly in 1973. On September 11, Army General August Pinochet led the attack on the presidential palace, demanding the resignation of democratically elected Socialist President Salvador Allende. Allende refused to surrender. When Allende realized that there was no way for him to leave the palace as president, he took his life. In a matter of several hours Chilean democracy was toppled by a military coup. Within a month of the coup,

Coup of September 11, 1973, in Chile. Bombing of La Moneda (presidential palace).

Biblioteca del Congreso Nacional de Chile

the military government killed thousands of leftists, both real and perceived, and forced their disappearances. Disappearances, imprisonments, and tortures of political opposition continued. The Chilean democracy was not restored until 1990.

Another pattern of a democracy's rapid death is perpetrated by incumbent political leaders. Often referred to as *autogolpe* or self-coup, various political leaders, who were democratically elected to lead their country, closed the national congress and the court and suspected or eliminated the national constitution. As we saw earlier in this chapter, when Peruvian President Alberto Fujimori sent tanks to the national congress, purged the court, and abolished the national constitution in an act dubbed as *fujigolpe* on April 5, 1992, the short-lived Peruvian democracy (which began in 1980) died.

Democracy can also die a slow death. A **slow death of democracy** refers to the process in which a country's democratic institutions gradually deteriorate, eventually to the point that democracy no longer exists. It can take many years for a democracy to die a slow death. From the 1980s to the end of 2015, Venezuela experienced a slow death of its democracy, with gradual deterioration of the country's democratic institutions and the rule of law.

Case Study: Slow Death of Democracy in Venezuela

Venezuela democracy's slow and gradual collapse and the country's downfall into complete political and economic chaos is perhaps one of the most tragic political developments of the last quarter century. After the fall of dictator Marcos Pérez Jiménez in 1958, Venezuela maintained its democracy at a time when most Latin American countries saw their democracies subverted in the 1960s and 1970s. Because of the relative stability of democracy in Venezuela on a continent where democratic institutions kept collapsing, its democracy had been considered successful, although with various shortcomings.

Venezuela's democracy from the 1950s to the 1990s rested on the Punto Fijo Pact agreed on by the major political parties. The signing parties would respect the election results, rotate the presidency, and share oil revenues. The two-party system it created (originally three, but the third party lost significance over time) worked relatively well in providing political stability, but by the 1990s the system was discredited due to corruption, poverty, and economic crises that Venezuelans were experiencing. In this context of political and economic declines, then Lieutenant Colonel Hugo Chávez led one of the military coups against the government in 1992. The coup failed, and Chávez was arrested and imprisoned. In 1993, President Carlos Andrés Pérez of the Democratic Action was impeached for corruption. Public confidence in the traditional parties continued to deteriorate. In 1998, out of prison, Chávez won the presidential election and became president of the country in 1999.

Chávez launched what he called the "Bolivarian Revolution" and implemented "twenty-first century socialism." A Constituent Assembly filled with Chávez's allies drafted a new constitution in 1999 and reformed the national congress and the judicial system. Chávez would rule the country by decree, which prompted political opposition groups to complain about the lack of fair opportunities for participation. In addition, international human rights activists, such as the Human Rights Watch, were expelled from the country. Private businesses were alarmed by Chávez's rule and sought to overthrow him, albeit unsuccessfully, in a coup in April 2002. As Venezuela's democratic institutions and civil liberties weakened, Chávez fell ill with cancer in 2011 and died in office in 2013.

Chávez was the central figure in Venezuelan politics for 14 years. His death left a void that was filled by Nicolás Maduro, his vice president. Not equipped with Chávez's charisma or visions, Maduro relied on being his charismatic patron's heir, continuing *chavismo* (which refers to Chávez's ideology, programs, and governing style), and suppressing the political opposition. As political and economic crises deepened, Maduro became more and more dependent on repression and autocratic rule. Venezuela at the end of the twentieth century was a relatively wealthy country with a large middle class and a long-time democracy. Today, Venezuela is a failed state, facing an acute humanitarian crisis in which millions of Venezuelans struggle to meet basic needs. The dire hardships in Venezuela have caused massive migration and a refugee crisis, with millions of Venezuelans having fled their home country.

Why Do Democratic Regimes Collapse?

Many explanations have been proposed to account for the breakdown of democratic regimes. Theories that focus on economic development, culture, and institutions find culprits within these countries that experience democratic breakdowns. Others focus on international conditions that foster or hinder democratic governance.

As discussed earlier in this chapter, classic modernization theory posits that economic development is related to transitions to, and the stability of, democracy. Modernization scholars argue that democracy is unlikely in poor and highly unequal societies. Even if a democratic regime is adopted in this type of society, it would not be stable. Hence, democracies that appeared in many Latin American countries during the early and mid-twentieth century were fragile and vulnerable to populist appeals, such as Juan Perón in Argentina and Getúlio Vargas in Brazil. These countries were also vulnerable to military coups supported by business interests, which instituted bureaucratic authoritarian regimes in the 1960s and 1970s.

Although Lipset (1959) claimed that economic development was necessary for both becoming and remaining a democracy, Przeworski et al. (2000) contend that economic development does not affect the probability of democratic transitions but does strongly influence the chance of democratic survival. Their study found that no democracy has collapsed in a very wealthy country.

Others argue that types of economic assets are more important than the level of wealth per se. They contend that democracy will not thrive in places that rely on **fixed assets** (i.e., economic activities related to land and are not mobile or easily redeployable), such as natural resource extraction and agriculture. Democracies are more likely to emerge and sustain in countries where major economic activities are based on **flexible assets** (properties and resources that can be redeployed relatively easily), such as manufacturing and banking.

Culture is another social feature that many believe to influence not only the emergence but also the stability of democratic regimes. As mentioned, Western Protestant culture has long been held as an important prerequisite for a successful democracy. According to this perspective, Protestant culture explains why the United States and the United Kingdom, two of the world's longest living democracies, have been able to maintain democracy for so long. In contrast, many Latin American countries have experienced repeated breakdowns of their democratic regimes. Proponents of this perspective believe that the installation of democracy in places that are culturally different from the West will lead to an unstable democracy at best, or its collapse at worst.

Many political scientists also consider political institutions as key factors to explain democratic instability and breakdown. Referring to "**perils of presidentialism**," Linz and Valenzuela (1994) contend that presidential systems are particularly susceptible to democratic breakdowns. They argue that presidential systems have an inherent tendency to generate executive-legislative conflict without a constitutional mechanism to resolve it. Presidential systems, where the president and members of the legislature are elected separately, tend to produce legislative gridlock. Because of the fixed terms of office and mutual independence of the branches of government, unlike parliamentary systems, the system does not allow the removal of a sitting president or a dissolution of the legislature before their terms end. Since there is no constitutional means to resolve this crisis, the military intervenes as *poder moderator* (moderating power) in the form of a military coup.

In contrast, according to the perils of the presidentialism perspective, executive-legislative conflict is less likely in parliamentary systems because the prime minister and the cabinet are selected by the legislature in this regime type. In the event of such conflict, parliamentary systems have built-in conflict resolution mechanisms: for the legislature, a vote of no confidence to remove the government that lost support of the legislature; and for the government, dissolution of the legislature and early parliamentary elections.

Critics of presidential systems also contend that the majoritarian tendencies of presidential systems tend to generate tension and polarization as there is only one office for which all forces vie for with the highest premium. This elevates political stakes in winning presidential elections. Furthermore, an election of an antisystem candidate, such as President Hugo Chávez of Venezuela, who was a leader of a failed 1992 coup, is more likely in presidential systems. In a nutshell, critics maintain that presidential systems are not conducive to democratic stability. According to those critics, the United States is an exception rather than the rule.

However, some scholars argue that it is not the institution of presidentialism that is perilous to democracy but the combination of presidentialism and multiparty systems. This argument implies that the United States, with a two-party system, is not an exception for being a stable democracy. Others argue that the higher rate of democratic breakdowns in presidential countries is rooted not in flawed institutions but rather in the tendency of societies with unfavorable conditions for democracy to choose a presidential, rather than parliamentary, system. Yet others have shown that after experiencing a democratic breakdown, parliamentary systems have poorer subsequent records in maintaining democracy than presidential systems. In short, recent research has increasingly found that the relationship between systems of government and democratic survival is more nuanced than previously argued.

The international environment also creates conditions that are hospitable, or conversely adverse, to democracy. During the Cold War, Soviet expansionism and U.S. anticommunist policies led to a series of coups and insurgency movements in many parts of the world, including the U.S.-supported coups against the elected governments of Guatemalan President Jacobo Arbenz Guzman in 1954 and Chilean President Salvador Allende in 1973. Scholars also argue that regional levels of democracy critically affect the stability of the democratic regimes of the countries within the region. This means that democracy is less likely to emerge, and less likely to survive, if installed in a region filled with autocracies.

As a way to promote democratic development and prevent its reversal, some regional organizations have adopted democratic conditionality for their membership. **Democracy conditionality** is the requirement that certain international organizations have adopted in a treaty or protocol statement that member states must adhere to democratic principles to become and remain a member of the organization. For example, the European Union (EU) and the Common Market of the South (MERCOSUR) require their member states to maintain their democratic status.

PRACTICAL APPLICATION

Pick one country where democracy collapsed in the past decade. Which theory of democratic breakdown best accounts for the demise of democracy in the country you chose?

Regional Integration and Democratic Conditionality

One of the notable international developments since the late twentieth century is the formation of regional integration blocs in various parts of the world. **Regional integration** refers to the process in which countries merge their economies and political decision-making. The European

Union (EU) is one of the oldest and most developed regional integration blocs. There are some 40 regional integration projects in total (Genna & Hiroi, 2015) with varying degrees of integration. Most of the regional integration blocs have remained primarily economic integration projects. Instituting a common external trade policy among member states is usually the first step. There are various reasons for countries to form and join regional integration organizations. Economic prosperity and political stability are the most predominant goals for most states.

Many of these regional integration organizations have something called a democracy clause. A democracy clause is a treaty or protocol statement that requires member states to adhere to democratic principles. A democracy clause formalizes a regional organization's democratic conditionality discussed in the previous section. Currently, 12, or approximately 31 percent, of the 40 regional integration organizations have a democracy clause (see Table 11.2). Why do largely economic regional integration blocs require democracy as a condition for their membership?

There are two main reasons. First, politics and economics are closely intertwined. Economic prosperity requires an environment that promotes investment and other economic transactions. Such an environment is not possible without political stability. Moreover, since regional integration member states are integrated with one another, political instability in one country has negative spillovers to other member states. So successful regional integration requires region-wide political stability. Democracy is an important way to ensure political stability in the region by

TABLE 11.2 ■ Regional Integration Organizations With Democracy Clauses	
Regional Integration Organization	**Year of Implementation**
European Union	1988
Andean Common Market	1989
Central American Integration System	1991
Southern African Development Community	1994
Common Market for Eastern and Southern Africa	1995
Georgia-Ukraine-Azerbaijan-Moldova	1997
Common Market of the South	1998
African Union	2000
Pacific Islands Forum	2000
East African Community	2001
Economic Community of West African States	2001
Economic Community of the Great Lakes Countries	2006

Source: Genna & Hiroi (2015).

helping to avert abrupt and violent government changes through coups or insurgencies. Many regional integration blocs have instituted democratic conditionality through a democracy clause to ensure collective political stability.

Second, some political leaders find an intrinsic value in democracy and recognize the existence of domestic antidemocratic forces that threaten democratic institutions in their countries. Those pro-democracy leaders may externally commit their countries to maintaining democracy by signing a democracy clause of a regional integration organization of which their country is a member. They do so in the hope that democracy would be harder to reverse if their country is officially committed to it by an international treaty. For example, political leaders of the MERCOSUR (Common Market of the South) original member states (Argentina, Brazil, Paraguay, and Uruguay) introduced a democracy clause to their regional integration bloc as an insurance against possible future attempts to subvert their fledgling democratic institutions. The MERCOSUR members suspended Venezuela's membership in the organization because it has failed to adhere to democratic principles.

SUMMARY

Over time, countries have increasingly adopted democratic regimes. Although there have been ebbs and flows in the global democracy movements, the overall trend is in an upward direction. By the end of the twentieth century, democratic regimes counted nearly half of the countries in the world. Once instituted, democracies face various challenges to consolidation, and democratic breakdown is not uncommon among nascent democracies.

The chapter reviewed various explanations for democratization. Political phenomena tend to be multicausal, as we saw in Chapter 2. Many factors influence countries' transitions to democracy and democratic stability. We first examined an economic cause of democratization with a particular emphasis on the role of economic development and the middle class. Modernization theory posits that economic development leads to the development of a stable democratic society. Another set of explanations we explored focus on a society's political culture. There is much debate and controversy regarding what cultural attributes are important for democratization. We explored two cultural perspectives: cultural primordialism and civic culture. The last set of explanations we examined stressed how the international environment promotes or hinders democratization. One major international influence is a country's neighbors. Known as demonstration effects, the likelihood of a country democratizing increases when its regional neighbors are democracies or are democratizing.

Finally, we delved into the question as to why democratic regimes break down. We revisited the economic, cultural, and international explanations, and we examined institutional explanations to evaluate what factors threaten democratic stability. In the 1990s, the institutional approach emphasizing the perils of presidentialism gained wide currency due to the contrasting experiences of countries adopting presidential and parliamentary regimes in the earlier period. However, more recent scholarly work casts doubt on this perspective. As is the case with democratization, a mix of factors may be important to explain democratic breakdown.

KEY TERMS

Amnesty law (p. 252)

Civic culture (p. 261)

Cultural primordialism (p. 259)

Democratic breakdown (p. 263)

Democracy conditionality (p. 267)

Democratic consolidation (p. 255)

Democratization (p. 247)

Demonstration effect (p. 262)

Distributional conflict (p. 257)

Ethnocentrism (p. 261)

Fixed assets (p. 266)

Flexible assets (p. 266)

Founding election (p. 247)

Modernization theory of democracy (p. 257)

No bourgeois, no democracy (p. 257)

Perils of presidentialism (p. 266)

Political liberalization (p. 253)

Rapid death of democracy (p. 263)

Regional integration (p. 267)

Slow death of democracy (p. 264)

Third wave democratization (p. 249)

FURTHER READING

Cheibub, J. A. (2022). Presidentialism and democratic performance. In A. Reynolds (Ed.), *The architecture of democracy: Constitutional design, conflict management, and democracy*. Oxford University Press.

Hiroi, T., & Omori, S. (2002). Perils of parliamentarism? Political systems and the stability of democracy revisited. *Democratization, 16*(3), 485–507.

Mainwaring, S. (1993). Presidentialism, multipartism, and democracy: The difficult combination. *Comparative Political Studies, 26*(2), 198–228.

12 INTERNATIONAL PEACE AND CONFLICT

Let's start this chapter with a question that may challenge your view of the world. On any given day over the past few years, were most countries in a peaceful relationship, or were they mostly in conflict with each other? If you follow the news, you might think that countries are more likely to be in conflict than in peace. States do get themselves into disputes, but the number of interstate conflicts is smaller than you might think. In addition, the number of armed conflicts, including wars, among countries has greatly declined since the end of the Cold War. Although conflicts such as wars are actually rare, their consequences in human and economic terms are very large. This is what motivates political scientists to understand and explain why they arise.

In this chapter, we will examine various types of conflicts and peace maintenance throughout the world. We ask why interstate wars and other armed conflicts sometimes occur and why peace tends to prevail most of the time. We will also look into why wars and other armed conflicts have declined over the past few decades so that we can see if the trend will hold into the future.

CONFLICT AND COOPERATION AMONG NATIONS

War is a large-scale organized conflict between politically defined groups. We define **peace** simply as the absence of war or militarized conflict. It is does not necessary mean that states have friendly relations with each other. **Interstate wars** occur between states and is what we normally think about when we talk about war.

An **international dispute** is a disagreement between two or more states. Disputes can include states accusing each other that they are performing unfair trade practices, have infringed on their territory, or broken a treaty obligation, to name three examples. As we will learn, states often settle disputes, so they rarely escalate into wars. States usually settle problems among themselves or use one of many international organizations to produce a peaceful resolution. When international dispute does not find a way for a peaceful settlement, it may motivate conflicting states to solve the dispute through force. This occasionally leads to a war.

Most armed conflicts these days are found within countries and are referred to as **civil wars**. Civil wars have two or more political groups fighting each other to determine who will ultimately control the state. These wars may include conflicts between ethnic, religious, regional, or economic groups. Although domestic in nature, political groups fighting a civil war often receive support from a foreign state, especially if such states have an important stake in who will win the war.

In contrast, cooperation among states has increased since the late twentieth century. The increase in international cooperation has led to greater **interdependence** among states where citizens, businesses, and other organizations of two or more states rely on each other to achieve their goals and foster their welfare. Greater international cooperation and interdependence do not mean that disputes, conflicts, and wars among states are now almost extinct. Conflicts still occur, disputes still arise, and wars still break out.

The study of international relations focuses on simple, broad questions: Why do countries sometimes fight wars to settle their differences, what explains periods of peace, and why do some states find it easier than others to collaborate with other states? The attempt to answer these questions is as old as human civilization itself. One of the earliest attempts to explain war can be found in *The History of the Peloponnesian War* by Thucydides (5th century BC/1940). Thucydides served as an Athenian general during the long war (431–404 BC) between Greek city-state leagues led by Athens, on one side, and Sparta, on the other. His thoughts became the foundation of **realist theory**, an approach that dominated international relations for thousands of years.

As the scientific method became more utilized in political science since around the mid-twentieth century, many began to question if realism was a useful theory. Those scholars developed new theories of international relations. These new theories revisited the basic questions of international relations and developed new answers. We will explore some of the leading theories of war and conflict later in this chapter. However, we first need to define the types of relations among states.

Interstate relationships fit into a range of options from which leaders can choose. We know from history and current events that any given pair of states have multiple issues that need attention. These can include basic problems such as where is the dividing line that separates their countries? Should a state be allowed to influence the internal politics of the other state? What kind of trade relationship should states have with each other? Is one state trying to help the other state's enemies? The list is long, and dominant issues have changed over time. One new area of concern is **cybersecurity**, which involves the ability of actors to protect themselves from attacks on their computer systems and networks. These attacks seek to steal data, disable systems, and/ or spread false information. At the heart of many of these questions are perceptions. Does a state view the other state as a friend or an enemy, or perhaps a little of both?

Figure 12.1 places different relations between states into three broad categories: conflict, neutrality, and cooperation. Before detailing what these three concepts mean, it is important to know that states can have parallel and linked foreign policies. The concept of **parallel foreign policies** describes the condition where a state can have a dispute over one issue while cooperating in other areas. Under this condition, we would need to mark multiple points on the conflict-cooperation spectrum to see where a pair of countries fit. For example, the United States and European countries have had many trade disputes that brought them into the conflictual side of the spectrum. Yet, at the same time, they are very cooperative regarding security under the North Atlantic Treaty Organization (NATO) military alliance.

Linked foreign policies do not differentiate between issues. If two countries are in conflict over one issue, the conflict will spill over into other issues. For example, many state leaders expressed dissatisfaction about Iran's desire to develop and maintain nuclear weapons. Their conflict with Iran on the nuclear weapons proliferation issue spilled into their economic relations when they decided to cut off trade and investment. Iran, of course, did not like these economic sanctions, which has deepened the conflict that the country has had with several countries, including the United States.

Neutrality is in the center of the conflict-cooperation spectrum, where state leaders can choose to acknowledge the existence of other states, including problems they may have with these states. However, they prefer to limit interactions or not take sides on an issue. The classic example of neutrality is Switzerland, a country that has no formal military alliances and only joined the United Nations in 2002. The country is engaged in international economic exchanges and treaties, but in limited ways. Neutral states have very restrained interactions with other states and attempt to be friendly with all states.

On the left side of the spectrum are all the possible degrees of conflict that countries can have with each other. **Conflict** includes a wide array of disputes that occur among states due to diverging interests those states hold. Conflict can come in many forms. States may have relatively small disagreements that can be settled fairly quickly among themselves or through mediation by a third actor. Perhaps a state believes that another state is not upholding promises made in a trade treaty or that it is not treating its citizens well.

FIGURE 12.1 ■ The Spectrum of International Relations

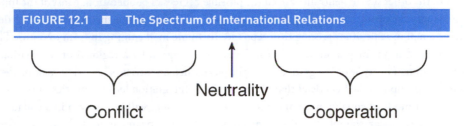

However, some conflicts are acute and can escalate into a war. Before the outbreak of World War II, Adolf Hitler annexed several territories; this action caused conflict between Germany and other European powers. Efforts to stop the German military and territorial expansion were unsuccessful and resulted in war between the opposing sides after Germany invaded and occupied Poland.

War is the extreme point of conflict. Wars use force and cause destruction of properties and human lives. Sometimes, a party in a war can achieve a total victory with the other side surrendering unconditionally. An unconditional end to a war requires that the losing side obey all of the winner's terms without negotiation. The winner may achieve more than simply resolving the original issue that sparked the war.

Compare, for example, two wars that the United States fought in the twentieth century. The war with Japan, which was a part of World War II, involved the attack on Pearl Harbor. The war's end resulted in much more than restitution for the attack. When Japan unconditionally surrendered to the United States, the United States removed the leadership that conducted the war, had many of the leaders tried for war crimes and crimes against humanity, executed the guilty, created a new governing regime for the country, and made sure that the United States would have a long-term military presence in Japan. In other words, the United States remade Japan's politics and maintained a strong presence.

Another war that the United States fought in Asia was with Vietnam. U.S. involvement started in 1955 and escalated until its end in 1975. The issues surrounding the U.S. involvement began soon after the countries of French Indochina won their independence. Vietnam entered into the Cold War rivalry and was divided between the North (Democratic Republic of Vietnam) and the South (Republic of Vietnam). The communist North, which was supported by the Soviet Union, sought the unification of the country. Both sides could not come up with a peaceful resolution, leading the North to begin a war for unification. The United States allied with the South by providing arms, military forces, and other assistance. The financial cost of the Vietnam War, along with the growing popularity of the antiwar movement, created an unsustainable position for the United States. The war ended with the United States and the Vietnamese sides signing the Paris Peace Accords in 1973. Soon after the U.S. forces left the South, it was taken over by the North and a new united country, the Socialist Republic of Vietnam, was declared. The peace that followed between the former enemies recognized Vietnam's sovereignty as the main part of the conditional surrender. Given the conditions of the surrender, the United States would not pay restitution for the damage and deaths caused by the war.

On the other side of neutrality are all the possible degrees of **cooperation**. Most of the interactions among countries on any given day occur on this side of the spectrum. Cooperation can be small in scale, like agreeing to accept and distribute mail coming in from overseas. The extreme end is an integration of political decision-making under a regional or international organization. This type of integration may take place when countries believe that making decisions as a group is more beneficial than doing so alone. Integration locks countries into a more permanent mode of collaboration, meaning that specific issues will be resolved in a collaborative manner. A clear example of regional integration is the European Union (EU), an entity that joins member states together to make decisions regarding a large array of economic, political, and social issues. We will examine, in more detail, the EU and other aspects of international cooperation in Chapter 13.

PRACTICAL APPLICATION

What are some current examples of conflict, neutrality, and cooperation among countries? Please be sure to define each term and that your examples match the definitions.

INTERNATIONAL ACTORS

LEARNING OBJECTIVE

12.2 Identify the major actors involved in international relations, their interests, and how they make decisions.

Answering the fundamental questions of why we observe international cooperation or conflict requires us to identify the actors involved and how and why they make their decisions. Some scholars argue that states of the international system are the most important actors in international relations. Some would go so far as to say that they are the only actors that matter in analyzing international relations. As defined in Chapter 6, a state is an administrative apparatus that makes and implements public and foreign policies and uses coercive power to rule in a given territory. Identifying the state as a principal actor also assumes that the state is unitary. This means that any changes in the power of domestic political groups or who leads the state will not change a state's behavior. Therefore, scholars with this approach doubt the relevance of domestic politics in international relations.

On the other hand, there are scholars who believe that individual state leaders are important and comprise another set of international actors that we should consider in any analysis. National leaders interact with each other at the domestic level to decide on foreign policy and at the international level with other leaders. These actors are the heads of state and government (presidents, prime ministers, etc.) and those who are entrusted to assist them in foreign or defense policy. **Foreign policy** pertains to the positions and approaches that a state has with other states. **Defense policy** refers to the positions and approaches that a state uses to protect itself from foreign enemies. Each state usually has someone who holds the title of minister of foreign affairs or minister of defense. In other states, like the United States, the title of the office is secretary of state or secretary of defense.

When scholars examine the role of individuals, they often focus on how relevant state institutions shape individuals' decisions and actions. Known as the institutional approach, these scholars argue that a person's decisions are modified or limited by formal and informal rules and norms of institutions. This is where bureaucratic considerations come into play. Bureaucracies have set procedures for information gathering and distribution that may impact an individual's decision. Bureaucracies are also where policy decisions are carried out. An experienced leader may consider the critical role bureaucracies play when crafting a decision, since some bureaucracies do not like change and may not go along with new policies. Therefore, the state's bureaucracy is an important actor to consider when analyzing international relations because it may influence the decisions of other actors.

Another approach to understanding individual actors' decisions and behaviors is psychological. Psychological analysis focuses on the emotional characteristics of leaders. Researchers analyze the personality traits displayed in prior decisions and attempt to match how a leader's personality leads to particular decisions. To better ground how personality impacts decisions, some scholars examine leaders' biographies to see how events in their early development may impact decisions. Others investigate if there are patterns of decision-making among similar personality traits across many leaders instead of exclusively examining a single leader.

Interest groups within countries can also be important actors since they may influence national leaders' foreign and defense policy decisions. An interest group is an organized association that seeks to either maintain policies or change them (see Chapter 7). We saw earlier in this book that interest groups play a role in the formulation of various policies. As in the domestic policy areas, interest groups have various motivations to influence foreign and defense policy. Some interest groups have an economic stake in these policies. If your business is in the arms industry, then you would like to see your government spend more on defense. To be more effective, you would join with other defense industry firms to persuade your government to spend more or at least not cut defense spending.

However, economic incentives are not the only motivations that drive interest groups. For example, certain interest groups try to influence the relations their state has with another state. In the United States, the American Israel Public Affairs Committee promotes strong alliances between the United States and Israel. Yet other interest groups attempt to influence a specific issue regarding defense policy. The antinuclear weapons groups in Europe and the United States are this type of interest group. Although not as visible as during the Cold War, these interest groups seek to pressure states into reducing the number of such weapons on their territories.

At the international level, there are **transnational actors**, or organizations that transcend nation-state identity. **International nongovernmental organizations** (INGOs) are entities that advocate specific policy positions in global affairs. The word *nongovernmental* in the term indicates that they do not formally represent any states' interests. INGOs are independent organizations that try to influence or maintain policies at the national or international level. Greenpeace is a global environmentalist organization that uses direct action and lobbying to address global issues like climate change and commercial whaling. They publicly address issues they view as important and offer policy recommendations for states and international governmental organizations to follow.

Another set of transnational actors are **multinational corporations** (MNCs). Similar to INGOs, MNCs do not represent specific states. They are business enterprises that have headquarters and operations in two or more countries. Among the largest well-known MNCs include Microsoft, Nestlé, Coca-Cola, Toyota, and Exxon. MNCs vary greatly in the scope of services and products they provide. Large MNCs have a global reach in that their operations, services, and products are found in numerous countries. They influence international politics by advocating for policies and regulations that allow them to continue or expand profitable operations. Some developing countries try to attract MNCs with lax labor and environmental regulations. MNCs also tend to favor policies that facilitate capital mobility (e.g., policies that allow MNCs to easily invest in and take money out of a country). MNCs may also seek to lower their tax obligations by leveraging their ability to introduce investments and jobs in exchange for favorable business conditions.

MNCs are also strong advocates for open trade policies. Their global scope of operations means that their supply chains could be disrupted if trade is restricted. A supply chain is the network of suppliers and producers that contribute to getting parts made and transported for the manufacturing of a final product or delivery of a service. An examination of your smartphone will tell you that the various parts come from different corners of the globe. Sometimes the smartphone parts pass across borders multiple times before they are sent to yet another country that hosts the final assembly plant. Then, smartphones need to be distributed around the world. To reduce the cost of the devices to consumers, MNCs want countries to limit or eliminate the tariffs (taxes) and other barriers to trade.

POWER OF INTERNATIONAL ACTORS

LEARNING OBJECTIVE

12.3 Explain how international actors' power will impact their behavior.

The actors discussed in the previous section vary in their power to influence international politics. We say that actors hold power if they are able to change the behavior of another actor in a desired way. We observe the use of power when one state employs overwhelming military force on another to change the latter's behavior. We can also witness power in more subtle ways. For example, governments of countries that receive foreign aid may believe that the donor countries will cut off aid to them if they do not allow elections. Their desire for aid may prompt them to hold elections even if they wish otherwise. In this instance, states that give foreign aid have power over states that receive aid.

It would be inaccurate to assume that one type of actor is automatically more powerful than another type. For instance, there are some large MNCs that are more powerful than some small states. However, we cannot say that all large MNCs are as powerful as all states. Instead, we can argue that particular actors are more or less powerful than other actors. For instance, China is overall a much more powerful state in world affairs than the small South Pacific state of Fiji.

Power, although very important in theory, is a challenge to measure in a systematic way. How do we know if an actor is powerful? It is very easy to say that a state, for example, was powerful because it won a war or got what it wanted in an international negotiation. Yet, inferring power by observing outcomes is not very useful if we want to predict an outcome. We need a measure of power that is independent of a particular outcome.

Scholars of international relations have tried to systematically measure the power of states. One of the common ways to measure a state's power is to examine the economic size, natural resources, and demographics of a country to determine how these elements compare to those of other states. Economic size is usually measured by the country's gross domestic product (GDP), which is the value of all products and services produced by a country's economy. GDP is a suitable measure of state power because wealthy countries can often change the behavior of other countries. Wealth improves the ability to increase military-related production, invest financially in other countries' economies, and provide foreign loans and aid, which enhance the state's leverage over other states that lack these abilities. Natural resources can be considered a separate category from GDP, although they can be related. If a country is rich in natural resources and has the ability to economically exploit them, then economic wealth (GDP) and natural resources are related.

Demographics can also be an indicator of power. Simply put, the larger a country's population is, the greater is the potential for the size of the state's military and economy. One important demographic characteristic pertinent to a state's power is the percentage of adults who are able to serve in the armed forces. In most countries, conscription is restricted to young men, although there has been a trend in having young women also serve in combat roles. The distribution of age groups also matters because it indicates the share of the national population that can contribute to military or military support during wartime. Even in peacetime, the age distribution, particularly the size of the working age population, is germane to state power as it determines the share of the national population that can contribute to a state's economic might.

Table 12.1 lists the countries with the 10 largest economies as measured by total GDP in 2020. The United States has the largest total GDP. Combining this wealth with 3.74 percent of GDP military expenditure makes it the most powerful even though its population size ranks behind China and India. China has the second largest economy in the world but spends less on its military. However, the larger population size means that it has considerable demographic power. The remaining eight states are less powerful but have a major status when considering their alliances. The United States, Germany, UK, France, Italy, and Canada are all members of NATO. Therefore, their combined strength easily makes it the largest force on the planet. Also, the United States has a strategic alliance with both Japan and South Korea.

Being powerful does not necessarily imply that the actor always seeks to influence other actors' behavior. Three factors affect whether an actor will choose to exercise its power. The first is **issue saliency**, or how much an actor cares about the particular issue in question. As you can imagine, the more an actor cares about an issue, the more likely it will want to exert its power to resolve the issue in its favor. An actor's favored outcome on an issue is called their **preference**. Among two or more actors, preferences can overlap (meaning that there is little difference in their preferred outcomes), or there could be large differences. The third factor is the power of the other actor vis-à-vis an actor's own power. An actor is more likely to exercise its power and

TABLE 12.1 ■ The Power of Major States (2020)

State	GDP (Billions US$)	Military Spending (Percentage of GDP)	Population (Millions)
United States	20,937	3.74	329.5
China	14,723	1.75	1,402.1
Japan	5,065	1.00	125.8
Germany	3,806	1.40	83.2
United Kingdom	2,708	2.25	67.2
India	2,623	2.88	1,380.0
France	2,603	2.07	67.4
Italy	1,886	1.57	59.6
Canada	1,643	1.42	38.0
South Korea	1,631	2.85	51.8

Source: World Development Indicators, The World Bank.

coerce or induce other actors to accept its preferred resolution when the other actor is less powerful. However, exercise of power is much less meaningful when dealing with more powerful actors.

Let's look at Nigeria and the role it plays in maintaining political stability in West Africa. In 2002, Nigeria intervened militarily in the Ivory Coast's domestic politics. The Ivory Coast government was fighting against rebels who sought to topple it. Why would Nigeria send in its military to deal with the domestic problem of a neighboring state? Nigeria is clearly the region's most powerful country when we look at the size of its economy, population, or military. Knowing about its regional power only provides a partial answer to the question, that is, Nigeria's capability. Issue saliency and preferences explain the country's motivation behind this action.

West Africa has a history of political instability. The region has suffered a number of armed rebellions and coups against governments. Political instability in one country affects neighboring countries by causing disruption in economic activities, spillover violence, and refugees seeking assistance. Therefore, a strong desire for political stability exists. This desire to have regular and peaceful change of power is enshrined in the democracy clause (see Chapter 11) of the Economic Community of West African States (ECOWAS), of which both Nigeria and the Ivory Coast are members. Consequently, Nigeria cares greatly about this particular issue. What is Nigeria's preference regarding the rebellion in the Ivory Coast? Its preference is for the Ivory Coast to settle domestic problems peacefully, perhaps through the democratic process in order to maintain stability in the region. It would also prefer that states enforce the ECOWAS treaty.

Therefore, we would expect Nigeria to intervene in the Ivory Coast's domestic affairs not only because it can (power) but also because it has high issue saliency and a strong preference regarding its neighbor's instability.

PRACTICAL APPLICATION

List some examples of the most powerful states, INGOs, and MNCs. In what ways can the examples on your list impact international affairs in their favor? In other words, what makes them so powerful?

INTERNATIONAL ISSUES

LEARNING OBJECTIVE

12.4   Discuss current major international issues.

This section provides an overview of some issues in international relations that have been prominent over the past few decades. We will examine traditional theories of war and peace in the next section to give us insights as to how states seek to solve these issues.

Civil War

Civil war involves armed conflict between two or more opposing groups in a country with the aim of controlling the existing state or creating a new one. Although this may sound like a domestic problem, it generates international implications and may require international action. Take, for example, **refugee crises**. People attempting to escape the violence produced by civil war will seek refuge in another country. Depending on the number of refugees and the economic conditions of the receiving country, the influx of people can produce political challenges.

In recent years, Europe has experienced large waves of mass migrations from people attempting to escape armed conflict in Libya, Syria, Iraq, and as far as Afghanistan. The introduction of so many migrants has caused disputes among the European countries regarding how to handle them. Questions arose as to who would be responsible for giving them refugee status, how they would be able to migrate across the continent, and how to distribute refugees among the European countries.

The financial and social responsibilities of the receiving countries have made the question regarding how many refugees each country should accept acute. The financial aspect involves how to pay for housing, health care, education, and other living expenses. Should the money come from a common pool, or should each country pay the expenses on its own? Socially, many Europeans are concerned about how the refugees will integrate into their societies. The problems in the refugees' home countries are likely to continue for the foreseeable future, so there is a strong likelihood that many, if not most, will not return once they establish themselves in the receiving country. This often pits groups that welcome refugees against groups opposed to their relocation in the receiving country.

Another humanitarian issue that arises from civil wars is the international community's intervention in stopping the killings and destruction. Civil wars in the distant past were viewed as exclusively domestic problems and the world community refrained from intervening. Since the end of World War II and the creation of the United Nations, the new, more interventionist norm has become dominant. That is, the international community assumes the responsibility of bringing the disputing parties in a civil war to the negotiating table and ending the fighting as soon as possible. During and after developing a peace settlement, international forces often come in to keep the peace by enforcing cease fires, separating combatants, and monitoring activities on the ground.

In many civil wars, combatants unfortunately participate in war crimes and crimes against humanity. The prohibition of such crimes is governed by international agreements such as the Geneva Conventions. The **Geneva Conventions** set the standards of international law for ethical treatment in war, including the basic rights of wartime prisoners, protection for wounded and sick military and noncombatant civilians, protection for the civilians in a war zone, and protection for the medical personnel and facilities. War crimes and crimes against humanity can result from orders given by top political and military officials or committed by people further down the command structure. Regardless, treaties give the international community the authority to punish these criminals. The past procedure had been to establish special tribunals to try accused individuals for specific conflicts. Early modern era examples include the Nuremberg

Za'atari camp in Jordan for Syrian refugees, July 18, 2013.
U.S. Department of State

Trials (which convicted Nazi leaders) and the International Military Tribunal for the Far East (also known as the Tokyo Trials, which convicted Japanese government leaders). More recently, special tribunals passed judgment on war crimes that occurred during the Balkan (Yugoslavia) and Rwandan civil wars (see Chapter 5). The expense and time necessary to create special tribunals for each specific instance gave way to establishing a permanent international court. Since 2003, the International Criminal Court, located in The Hague, Netherlands, has served as a permanent tribunal to try accused individuals for the international crimes of genocide, crimes against humanity, war crimes, and the crimes of aggression.

Domestic and International Terrorism

Terrorism is the use of violence and threats to intimidate the people through fear to achieve political objectives. Terrorism, like civil wars, has taken on an international dimension. Terrorist groups comprise individuals that use terrorism to achieve their objectives. Because these groups are generally small when compared to their state adversaries, they apply a strategy that frightens people, like blowing up densely populated areas to inflict mass damage and deaths. The unpredictability of their violence puts the general public on edge. Terrorists project a perception of great strength with the intent to scare societies into submitting to their demands.

In domestic terrorism, terrorists use their tactics to achieve domestic aims. Examples include the Irish Republican Army (IRA; Britain), Euskadi Ta Askatasuna (ETA; Spain), and the Ku Klux Klan (KKK; United States). Their tactics are generally unsuccessful since they have yet to achieve their goals. The IRA can trace their work as a terrorist organization since Ireland gained independence from Britain, with the exception of the northeast corner (known as Northern Ireland). Although the IRA has been active for about one hundred years, there are no prospects for achieving their stated goal of Northern Ireland leaving Britain and joining the Republic of Ireland. Similarly, the ETA aims to separate the Basque region from Spain, which they have been attempting since the late 1950s without success. The KKK has sought to advance white supremacy in the United States through the subjugation of Blacks and other racial and ethnic minorities. Its terror tactics attempted to enforce racist norms that included voter suppression and other violations of constitutionally mandated civil rights. Although strong during its early years, the KKK has since been waning. Although many terrorist groups have not met their aims, they have not been deterred from carrying out their acts. The strategies in capturing terrorist members usually rest on domestic law enforcement, although states often rely on international cooperation when domestic terrorists work outside their country.

International terrorism is different in that international terrorist groups do not solely target their domestic government or society. They believe that foreign governments use their home governments and therefore target the former as the true culprits behind their grievances. The basic strategy is to frighten the foreign government and people into not interfering in the domestic activities of their country. They believe that once the foreign influence is removed, they are more likely to achieve their domestic aims.

One of the best-known international terrorist organizations is al-Qaeda, which masterminded the terrorist attacks in the United States on September 11, 2001. Its leadership promotes an ideology that there is an international conspiracy to destroy Islam. At the heart of that effort, its leaders argue, is the use of Muslim governments, like Saudi Arabia, as tools for United States, Israel, and other Western powers' goals. The strong Western influence in predominantly Muslim countries is used as evidence. Al-Qaeda leaders claim that as Islam is undermined in these countries, it will lose followers and therefore end as one of the world's more popular religions. To end this perceived trend, al-Qaeda's leadership strongly encourages their followers to plan and carry out attacks in the United States and Europe in order to force these states to change their foreign policies. If foreigners, particularly the United States, remove their support, then it will be easier for al-Qaeda to destabilize the Middle East and remove current governments from power. Its ultimate goal is to create a global Islamic theocracy that adheres to their fundamentalist interpretation of Islam.

Given al-Qaeda's international scope of operations and decentralized methods of planning, combating the organization requires international cooperation. The members of the **North Atlantic Treaty Organization** (NATO), which is a military alliance made up of European states, the United States, Canada, and Turkey, attempted to capture the al-Qaeda leaders responsible for the September 11 attacks when they invaded Afghanistan, which was home to the al-Qaeda base of operations. The group's principal leader, Osama bin Laden, was eventually killed by U.S. forces in Pakistan 10 years later. While many experts agree that al-Qaeda still has some degree of centralized leadership, it has become more of a movement since the war in Afghanistan began. With splinter groups and other like-minded individuals in the world, their operations are still ongoing.

EXPAND YOUR THOUGHTS

Some believe that the global efforts currently in place to address the issues of civil wars and domestic and international terrorism are effective. Others see such efforts as ineffective and a waste of resources. Take a position on this debate by picking one issue area and one international agreement to see if global collaboration has worked in lowering the likelihood that a civil war or terrorism will occur.

THEORIES OF CONFLICT AND COOPERATION

LEARNING OBJECTIVE

12.5 Describe the various theories of international conflict and cooperation.

Why do some states cooperate to solve issues in international relations? Why do some countries find themselves in disputes? Why do some of these disputes end in an armed conflict? War has been a recurring and enduring pattern of behavior among peoples since the beginning of recorded history. Many political scientists have studied the causes of international wars and conditions for peace. International relations theories can help us answer many of these questions. Each theory makes important assumptions about world affairs to simplify complex reality. As you read the theories, you may agree or disagree if the assumptions are correct. The question that needs to be answered is: Do any of these theories explain relations among states well?

Power Transition Theory

Many international relations theories focus on the power of states in explaining cooperation or conflict. Such theories are called state-centered theories. One such theory, **power transition theory**, holds that the international system is hierarchically ordered based on the level of state power. At the top of the hierarchy is the most powerful state, referred to as the **preponderant power**, which informally governs the international system with the aid of other powerful states. We say "informally governs" because no world government or global constitution exists. Today, the United States arguably holds the position of the preponderant power and countries like Britain and other major European powers help the United States to informally govern the international system. Together they establish the conditions of the international system that is mutually beneficial to the preponderant power and its allies. These conditions are called the **international status quo**, which is a general term that captures the acceptable norms and processes of the international order. Examples include the recognized borders of countries, which states are allowed to have nuclear weapons (and which ones are prohibited), what is considered a legitimate territorial takeover, and the legitimacy of the various international institutions, to name a few. We can also think about the status quo as a set of private goods established by the preponderant power and enjoyed by states that ally with it. The preponderant power and the allied great powers are, by definition, satisfied with the status quo they create.

The remaining states in the international hierarchy can be broken down into two groups: smaller satisfied states that benefit from the status quo and great, middle, and smaller sized states that are dissatisfied by the status quo. The dissatisfied group can choose to fight against the preponderant power and its allies or accept the status quo. An example of a state that dislikes the status quo is Iran. Iranian leaders believe that they have the need for nuclear weapons to protect their country against the larger states and perhaps to influence the Persian Gulf region. Since Iran is a dissatisfied state, the United States and its allies have placed economic sanctions on the country in an effort to prevent it from acquiring nuclear weapons. These sanctions prevent Iran from enjoying international benefits, such as the international trading and financial systems established by the United States and its allies.

In addition to hierarchies at the global level, power transition theory states that hierarchies also exist at the regional level. The regional hierarchy has a local preponderant power at the top with a set of allies supporting the regional status quo. In Latin America, for example, Brazil holds the preponderant position. Nigeria holds this position in West Africa. Power transition theorists consider India the preponderant power in South Asia. Each of these local preponderant powers have the largest economies and populations in their respective regions.

Central to power transition theory is what happens when there is a serious challenge to the international (or regional) status quo by a state, which we will refer to as the challenger. As Figure 12.2 shows, over time, a preponderant state's power begins to plateau. It does continue to grow but not as rapidly as it did in the past. The challenging state, however, has achieved the ability to grow at a faster pace due to major domestic policy changes and its large population size. In the years leading up to the point when the preponderant power and the challenger are at parity, the challenger could not attempt to change the status quo. Since such a challenge would likely result in a war, the challenger would likely lose because of its weaker position. Therefore, the challenger would not initiate a war. After all, why start a fight it will not win? Instead, the challenger would need to wait until it could win this major war, one that would change the international status quo. This would likely occur when the challenger has just exceeded the parity condition with the preponderant power (i.e., the transition point).

If the challenger is successful in changing the international status quo by winning a war against the previous preponderant power, it would become the new preponderant power. Therefore, the theory argues that when two countries achieve approximately equal power, with one being dissatisfied, a major war will occur. This was the case when Germany attempted to become the preponderant power in World War I and again in World War II.

The power transition point can be peaceful if the new preponderant power is satisfied with the status quo established by the old one because they agree on the core structure of the world order. This explains why the United States and Britain did not engage in war during the U.S. rise in power. The United States was satisfied with the international order that Britain established (a relatively free capitalist international economy and liberal democracy), and Britain was satisfied with the changes that the United States wished to make. For example, Britain favored the U.S. leadership in creating the post–World War II international institutions like the International Monetary Fund, the World Bank, and the United Nations. These institutions would become the foundation of the new postwar global order.

In sum, according to power transition theory, power distribution among states do not alone explain relationships among states. Knowing how satisfied a state is with the international or regional conditions is also important.

FIGURE 12.2 ■ States' Power Over Time and Development of a Power Transition

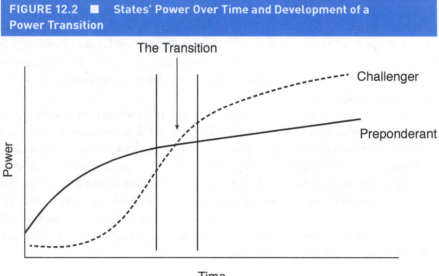

Balance of Power

Another and much older, state-centered theory is **balance of power theory**. Its explanation for why some countries go to war or cooperate is also based on relative power. However, the logic and conclusions are different from those of power transition theory. Balance of power theory assumes that the international system is **anarchy** since it lacks a set of self-enforcing global institutions. Instead, states rely on themselves if they wish to be secure in an international system of unequal powers.

The theory argues that as countries grow in power, they will become more aggressive. To deter an aggressive posture and develop international stability and peace, countries balance against the strongest state. In a situation where there are two powerful countries, their near equal strength deters aggression by one or the other. By matching each other's strength, one side is unlikely to attack the other because the prospect of winning a war becomes more uncertain. If there is no second country that is equally powerful, then countries can form limited and temporary alliances to balance against a larger power. Small countries are unlikely to ally with a large power because, according to the theory, the large one will take advantage of the smaller one. The larger power may also seek out alliance members in case the alliance formed against it becomes too large. In sum, the international system maintains peace if states balance each other's power through alliances.

The critical component is the limited and temporary nature of the alliances. If states cannot easily switch alliances to continue the balancing strategy, then one side will become larger than the other. Since being more powerful leads to aggression according to the theory, the likelihood of war increases as the alliances within the international system become more unbalanced. The theory therefore predicts that no state will be in a permanent alliance with another since such an alliance will produce instability in the international system.

Deterrence assumes that states start wars thinking that they will win and that they can best prevent being attacked by having a powerful military. The idea is to increase the costs of being attacked to the point where the costs outweigh the benefits of a potential victory, or increase the odds of the attacker losing the war. In sum, if both sides of a conflict are equally matched in power, then the probability is very low that either side will start a war because they are uncertain about whether they can win. The **nuclear deterrence** strategy was one of the important uses of the balance of power logic, which intended to produce stability among competitive states that possessed nuclear weapons.

The deterrence strategy took a bold step forward with the invention of nuclear weapons. As you know, nuclear weapons have a tremendous killing and destruction capacity, more so than any conventional (nonnuclear) weapon. The one atomic bomb that the United States dropped on the Japanese city of Hiroshima on August 6, 1945, killed approximately 140,000 people out of a population of approximately 350,000 people. Most died within a matter of seconds, and others died over the course of several months due to injuries or radiation poisoning. The Hiroshima bomb is considered weak by today's standard since it only used approximately 2 percent of its nuclear material. Modern nuclear weapons have much higher explosive yields and can kill and destroy cities with millions of people.

Combining nuclear weapons technology with deterrence produced the new strategy of **mutually assured destruction** (MAD). The idea is that if two or more opponents could guarantee the total destruction of all states, then they will not attack each other. Mutual annihilation means that no victor will come out of the nuclear weapons exchange since all states involved would be destroyed. Since neither side could win such a nuclear exchange, neither side would start an attack. MAD was the weapons strategy used by the United States and the Soviet Union during the Cold War. In fact, the Cold War's central theme was MAD.

Both sides manufactured enough weapons to destroy each other many times over. Yet, the logic behind nuclear deterrence was that you needed this amount of destructive power so that you would not need to use them (since aggression against a nuclear power would be deterred). Advocates of nuclear deterrence credit the strategy for the absence of a direct war between the United States and the Soviet Union, even though they had many incidents that could have escalated into a war.

Critics of nuclear deterrence see three problems. The first is the occurrence of an **arms race**. Since deterrence means that states will not start a war because of the potential attackers' inability to win, the logical action for states would be to create more weapons. The more military power you have, the larger your chances are of winning a war. Now, if your opponents see you arming yourself, they will want to create more weapons. When you see that they are more heavily armed, you want to arm yourself even more. The outcome is to have a race to see who can have the most weapons. Critics argue that arms races can exert potentially destabilizing effects. Moreover, the cost of building and maintaining massive amounts of nuclear weapons and their systems means sacrificing other spending priorities, such as health care, education, and economic development.

The second problem, which also generates a potentially destabilizing effect, is **nuclear proliferation**. Nuclear proliferation is the spread of nuclear weapons across the globe. Those who wish to stop proliferation argue that nuclear proliferation would increase the likelihood of using these weapons. A relevant question that could be asked is, if nuclear deterrence works in preventing wars, then why not let every state have a full nuclear arsenal? Why would the international system's major powers stop countries like Iran or Saudi Arabia from having the weapons? The active prevention of these and other states from developing nuclear weapons technology and system may tell us that nuclear deterrence may not be as stabilizing as advocates claim.

In the end, nuclear deterrence rests on human rationality. In Chapter 5, we learned about the limitations of human rationality. The assumption of human rationality is the third problem that critics of nuclear deterrence point out. How confident can you be that political leaders are perfectly rational and can effectively engage the calculus assumed by nuclear deterrence theory? What would be the consequences if political leaders of nuclear states miscalculate or are misinformed? What if an event makes an unexpected turn and conflict escalates? So long as there is a chance that political leaders may not behave in the way predicted by the theory, risk for nuclear wars exists. Such a risk may result in catastrophic outcomes.

Democratic Peace

Sometimes scholars observe an interesting relationship that lacks an explanation. **Democratic peace theory** came out of such an observation. The observation was simple: In all the wars between countries, none have been between democratic states. While the observation is solid, there is debate as to why this is the case. It is important to note that most scholars do believe that democracies have some tendency to be warlike. The evidence demonstrates that democratic states are as likely to fight a war as an autocratic state. They just are likely to avoid fighting another democracy.

One explanation for the democratic peace notes that democracies share the same norms of dispute settlement. Within democracies, disputes are usually settled through arbiters, like court judgments. Abiding by the decisions of an independent ruling body fits the principle of the rule of law. If the rules and international institutions are legitimately created by democratically accountable leaders, then the institutions can effectively settle disputes, thereby reducing the likelihood of fighting a war to resolve the disagreements.

As democracies grew in number, they fostered the development of international institutions that would settle disputes in ways similar to those found in their domestic politics. One current example is the **International Court of Justice** (ICJ), which is sometimes referred to as the World Court. The ICJ is an institution that the United Nations created with the purpose of using international law to settle disputes among states. The ICJ's rulings are advisory since it lacks enforcement power. Enforcement power would come in the form of an international police force or other similar agency. If such a law enforcement agency existed, states might see the need to obey the ICJ rulings even when they disagree. Since the states of the international system have yet to create an enforcement agency, they voluntarily follow the ICJ rulings. The idea of accepting the rule of law as a norm is what democratic peace scholars believe separates democracies from autocracies.

Another explanation centers on **democratic accountability**. Democratically selected leaders are unlikely to enter into unpopular wars since doing so may lead to their removal from power through elections. Since they are accountable to the electorate and the theory assumes that they wish to remain in power, politicians will consider the level of support among the voters before starting or continuing wars. Autocratic leaders are generally not accountable to public opinion, at least not in a direct way. They tend to survive in office through the support of powerful societal groups and so only need to consider the views of a smaller, select group of people. Furthermore, autocratic leaders are more likely to control information, which allows them to manipulate the information regarding the war and influence the public to accept it.

Opinion formation regarding war assumes that the average citizen will accept the need for war if the benefits outweigh the costs. The average citizen bears a large amount of the costs of war due to death and destruction, reduced security, and economic rationing. They will therefore need to believe that the war is worth the sacrifices. Leaders need to think carefully before engaging in war, and once initiated, may need to quickly end it. If both countries are democracies, these thoughts are given double attention and are known to both sides. Accordingly, the likelihood of settling a dispute through a peaceful process increases since support for war is difficult to obtain for either of the two democratic states.

Commercial Liberal Peace

According to the **commercial liberal peace theory**, the world's high level of economic interdependence produces important factors that help us explain why some countries engage in war and others do not. **Economic interdependence** refers to the degree to which a country's domestic economy relies on one or more foreign economies. Greater interdependence increases the economic costs of war. You are unlikely to want to have an armed dispute with a close trading and investment partner because loss of trade and investment would harm your economy and reduce the state's capabilities.

For example, suppose that you rely on a trading partner for manufacturing inputs, such as oil and steel. Fighting a war with a trading partner would reduce or perhaps end your supply of oil and steel. Those resources are critical for manufacturing and running instruments of war such as tanks, submarines, and airplanes. Or perhaps a trading partner supplies a rare earth element not found in your country that is important for producing batteries. Given the need for batteries in many products (including instruments of war), it would not be a good idea to fight a war against a supplier.

In addition, economic interdependence increases the effectiveness of economic sanctions to stop countries from engaging in undesirable actions. Economic sanctions involve limiting or ending economic transactions such as trade and investment to change a target country's behavior. The use of an economic sanction is only effective if the target country has economic relationships with the sanctioning countries. If the targeted country is isolated from the global economy, sanctions would have little to no meaning.

Another reason why likelihood of war would decrease with greater economic interdependence lies with the development of effective global economic institutions. Wars sometimes occur as a result of economic disputes. If one state takes actions that may harm the economies of other states, the states harmed will likely seek a remedy for the problem. Without joint institutions, the disputing parties may not be able to peacefully resolve the problem because no independent and capable agency is in place to assist. Consider the inability to pay back a foreign debt. In the past, when one country could not pay back its debt to another, and the debt was large enough to harm the banking system of the lending country, the lending country would militarily invade and occupy the borrowing country in order to receive payments.

This occurred in 1861 when France removed the Mexican government of President Benito Juárez and installed a monarchy under Emperor Maximilian. At issue was Mexico's inability to repay its debts. Both the British and Spanish governments supported the French invasion and occupation because Mexico also owed them money and France agreed to collect their debts in return for their support. It took an armed revolt by the Mexican people to remove the French from the country. The invasion and occupation, which ended in the French withdrawal, was not the most efficient method to solve the issue. However, given the lack of another remedy, it was the one the French used.

If we fast-forward to the early 1980s, we see a different approach and outcome to a similar dispute. Mexico, again, was not able to pay back its foreign debt. The Mexican government defaulted on its debt in 1982 and created conditions that could have triggered an international financial crisis, one that would have affected both wealthy and poor countries. Consequently, it was in everyone's interest to develop a plan to maintain stability in the financial markets. Instead of a costly invasion and occupation to recover the loans, countries worked with international economic organizations, such as the International Monetary Fund, to negotiate how Mexico could restructure its finances and be able to meet its debt payment obligations. The result was a set of plans of restructured payments so that Mexico could pay its debts to both private banks and international intergovernmental lending institutions.

Constructivism

Constructivism, another explanation for conflict and cooperation, examines how countries view themselves, other countries, and the international system. Before we take a closer look at the theory, let's conduct a thought experiment. Imagine a room full of people interacting with each other. You can decide if the interaction is social or work related. They are discussing things, making plans, or, in some cases, trying to ignore each other. They know each other, or at least they think they know everything important about the people they are interacting with. They formed these views from previous interactions or what they heard from others. There are no rules about how everyone can behave; there are only norms of behavior. As you imagine this situation, think about all the possible interactions that are happening. Sometimes there are fights as well as firm agreements. There could be some activities that enhance collaboration, while some are plotting to harm others. The interactions also enhance the reputations of some. However, some interactions cause people to start reevaluating reputations of others. Moreover, every once in a while, a new person enters the scene requiring some new views and reassessments. Now, if you were to substitute people with states, you have the basic understanding of constructivism.

Constructivists anthropomorphize states by placing human qualities on these nonhuman entities. Of course, states are governed by people. Constructivists argue that state leaders reflect the characteristics of the state. Leaders get to their positions because they embody the ideals of the societies they represent. Since the focus is on the social attributes of states, these theorists question the central role of material power in explaining international relations. The wealth, military size, and natural resources that the state commands are not as important as what the state does and how it behaves in the international system. Constructivists argue that ideas, identity, and social interactions provide better explanations. The theory's name comes out of the assumption that all interactions are socially constructed and based on historical patterns of behavior. Like in the thought experiment, states develop a perceived identity of each other. Therefore, as countries interact, they develop ideas regarding each other and the system as a whole. Some states identify certain states as ones that will seek peaceful resolutions to challenges, involve international institutions in resolving disputes, and wish to develop friendships. Certain other states are identified as more aggressive toward some states due to historical interactions, while passive with other states. In sum, if you understand the past social interactions of states, you will then understand how they will treat each other today and into the future.

The constructivist theory's focus on the perceptions of states' identities generates important implications for international relations. If the international community identifies a particular state as an actor that cannot be trusted, then the community may view the state's actions as belligerent. Take for example, the contrast in the international community's approaches toward nuclear proliferation by India and Iran. India did not receive condemnation from the international community after it began developing and then fully developed its nuclear weapons technology. The community trusted India when it stated that its weapons are exclusively for defensive purposes. The community, on the other hand, has aggressively tried to limit, if not end, Iran's development of nuclear weapons. The view of Iran's ambitions in its region creates distrust within the international community. They do not accept the possibility that Iran will use such weapons exclusively for defensive reasons. The lack of trust promoted the international community to actively stop Iran through diplomatic actions and economic sanctions.

PRACTICAL APPLICATION

What explains specific cases of cooperation or conflict? Using one theory discussed in the chapter, how does it help you explain why the states collaborated in trying to solve the problem?

EXPAND YOUR THOUGHTS

There has been a long dispute between China and Taiwan. Both claim to be the legitimate state of China. In fact, Taiwan's official name is "The Republic of China." China wishes to officially annex the island so that together they can become one unified country. Taiwan enjoys protection from the United States, which many argue prevents China from invading and taking Taiwan. Do you think that war between China and the United States is likely to occur as a result this dispute? Use one international relations theory discussed in this chapter to support your answer.

SUMMARY

There are many ways to describe the types of relations between states. Some are conflictual, while others are more cooperative. This chapter reviewed the possible interactions among states and how best to explain their behavior. We first defined the range of possible relations between states so as to conceptualize our dependent variable. We then identified the actors involved. While many scholars have traditionally aimed their attention exclusively to states, others note that entities such as multinational corporations (MNCs) and global interest groups may also play important roles. By knowing major international actors' interests, we are more likely to know their policy preferences. From this starting point, we can begin to explain their behaviors.

In addition to identifying international actors' interests, it is important to identify the sources of theirpower. Powerful actors use their power to leverage weaker actors if they believe such action will produce a desired outcome. However, having power does not always imply using it. The salience of an issue to an actor is also a critical factor.

We also reviewed current major international issues facing states and non-state actors. Civil wars and domestic and international terrorism are issues that have captured the attention of actors over the past few decades. These issues are fundamentally different than the traditional international relations issues because they deal with domestic instability due to weak or failed states and non-state actors.

The last section provided overviews of various theoretical explanations for conflict and cooperation. Some of the theories emphasize the distribution of power in the international system to understand state interactions, with some contradictory conclusions. Power transition theory predicts war when two major states are approximately equal in power and if the challenger is dissatisfied with international order that the preponderant state created. On the other hand, balance of power theory states that equally matched states are less likely to engage in war. Democratic peace theory emphasizes the regime type of states, with democracies being less likely to fight wars with each other. Commercial liberal peace theory claims that what is important is how economically interdependent states are: The more interdependent they are, the less likely states will fight wars. The last theory, constructivism, focuses on the identities and social relations of states as good indicators for explaining their behavior.

This chapter focused primarily on the conflictual side of international relations. As mentioned in the chapter's introduction, we study these types of relations not because they occur frequently but because of their destructive reality or potential. In the next chapter, we will focus on cooperation among states, which happens frequently and brings many mutual benefits.

KEY TERMS

Anarchy (in relation to the international system) (p. 288)

Arms race (p. 289)

Balance of power theory (p. 288)

Civil war (p. 274)

Commercial liberal peace theory (p. 291)

Conflict (p. 275)

Constructivism (p. 292)

Cooperation (p. 276)

Cybersecurity (p. 275)

Defense policy (p. 277)

Democratic accountability (p. 290)

Democratic peace theory (p. 290)

Deterrence (p. 288)

Domestic terrorism (p. 284)

Economic interdependence (p. 291)

Foreign policy (p. 277)

Geneva Conventions (p. 283)

Interdependence (p. 274)

International Court of Justice (p. 290)

International Criminal Court (p. 284)

International dispute (p. 274)

International nongovernmental organizations (p. 278)

International status quo (p. 286)

International terrorism (p. 284)

Interstate war (p. 274)

Issue saliency (p. 280)

Linked foreign policy (p. 274)

Multinational corporations (p. 278)

Mutually assured destruction (p. 289)

Neutrality (p. 275)

North Atlantic Treaty Organization (p. 285)

Nuclear deterrence (p. 288)

Nuclear proliferation (p. 289)

Parallel foreign policy (p. 275)

Peace (p. 274)

Power transition theory (p. 286)

Preference (p. 280)

Preponderant power (p. 286)

Realist theory (p. 274)

Refugee crisis (p. 282)

Terrorism (p. 284)

Transnational actors (p. 278)

War (p. 274)

Doug Armand/Getty Images

13 OUR GLOBALIZING WORLD

LEARNING OBJECTIVES

13.1 Identify the characteristics and forms of globalization and regionalization.

13.2 Examine the types and functions of international institutions.

13.3 Describe the missions and functions of major global institutions.

13.4 Identify the European Union's main institutions and the challenges that the EU has faced in recent times.

13.5 Discuss the differences and similarities of various regional integration organizations.

13.6 Identify the principal critiques of globalization.

Technological advancements allow us to interconnect with parts of the world in seconds. A generation or so ago, it would have taken weeks or months for the average person to correspond with someone a continent away using regular mail. Telephone long-distance calls were available, but many could not afford the charges. Now, many people have the ability to chat in real time. While advancements in technology provide us with the means to interact across large distances, political agreements among countries and favorable domestic politics give us the capacity to take advantage of these technological advancements. This chapter introduces globalization and its companion concept, regionalization. We will see what needs to happen politically, behind the scenes, before someone can open a smartphone app and start interacting with anyone, or anything, across the world. We will examine what drives globalization, regionalization, and interdependence and why states create international institutions. Although globalization has brought about many benefits to people across the globe, it has also created new problems and challenges. We will explore some of these challenges and the costs of globalization after examining the basic concepts, actors, institutions, and examples of globalization and regionalization.

GLOBALIZATION AND REGIONALIZATION

13.1   Identify the characteristics and forms of globalization and regionalization.

Globalization is one of those concepts that people often use or hear, but many cannot define it. It is the process of producing ever greater interdependence among peoples across political borders. Many also say that globalization is making national borders less and less relevant. As we saw in Chapter 12, interdependence pertains to mutual dependence between and among citizens, businesses, and other organizations of two or more states to achieve their goals and foster their welfare. This growing interdependence brings together international and domestic inputs and outcomes (see Figure 13.1).

What happens in one country can affect other countries and produce international political outcomes on many issues. For example, in the late 1990s, the Thai government's decision to devalue the country's currency caused a financial crisis that hit many countries, including Malaysia, Indonesia, South Korea, and eventually Russia, Brazil, and Argentina. The problem spread across countries and continents because of the global financial networks that did not have effective international regulations to prevent such a crisis. Various agreements between states allowed the open exchange of financial instruments. However, none of them regulated such transactions. The lack of this regulation led to the market failure.

International outcomes can also shape domestic politics as we become more interdependent. While we may believe that international influence on domestic politics is more likely in small countries, large and powerful countries are not immune. For example, in 2002 the United

FIGURE 13.1   ■   Global Interdependence

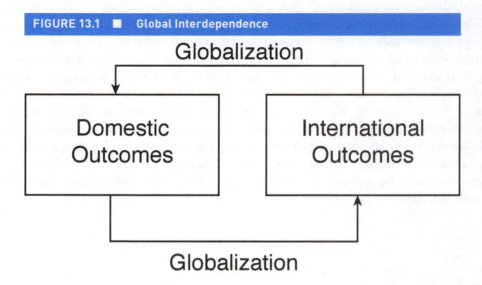

States imposed trade restrictions on steel imports due to its domestic politics. However, after the World Trade Organization (WTO) ruled that the United States violated its trade commitments, the George W. Bush administration removed the restrictions in the following year. Establishing a global trading arrangement like that of the WTO comes with rules that all member states need to follow; otherwise, states will start to take advantage of each other, often because of domestic pressures. The Bush administration imposed the trade restrictions on steel in response to the requests by the U.S. steel industry. President Bush saw the political advantage of going along with the request. Yet, continuing with the steel tariff after the WTO ruling would result in long-term problems if the international trade arrangement fell apart.

We can observe globalization in three different dimensions: economic, political, and social. The economic dimension is the most obvious, and some scholars argue that it drives the other two. Look at every object within a few feet around you right now. Most, if not all, of these items have a label stating, "Made in ...." The fact that you can purchase a product in your local store that was made halfway across the world is a result of many years of negotiations among states. Trade agreements allow goods to come into your country (also known as imports) with a lower level of taxes, referred to as **tariffs**, or perhaps free of tariffs.

In addition, foreign products need to meet certain standards, which are negotiated among states, before they can enter the domestic markets of trading partners. Take, for example, paint or products that have paint on them. Decades ago, many countries banned the use of lead in paint because of the harmful effects on human health and childhood development. What if some countries do not have such a ban and want their firms to trade lead-based paint and painted products globally? Open trade on paint would require all states to agree to either ban lead or not ban lead. If they decide to agree on a ban on the trade of lead-based paint and painted products, even those states that did not ban lead before the agreement would have to ban such paint products. Otherwise, their paint would be prohibited from entering a country that has a lead ban.

States also negotiate treaties that govern the treatment of foreign investment. Such treaties often protect foreign investment as well as limit the amount of money allowed to leave the country. Firms take risks in investing in a foreign country. Aside from the usual business risks, such as believing that people will buy their products, they might run the risk that the host state will take their property. Since the firm is a foreign entity, it may not enjoy all the rights given to citizens of that country. In addition, a change in leadership or policy may result in the confiscation of the firms' properties. Agreements among states would safeguard firms and therefore reduce this risk. From the other perspective, states also take a risk in allowing a foreign firm to enter their country. Often firms invest millions of dollars in a country due to a special arrangement between the firm and the host state. The agreement could include low or no taxes for the firm. Other incentives could also be given to bring the firm into the country. States do this because large investments by MNCs would boost the host country's economy. However, if the firm decides to leave and take all that investment with it, then it could produce economic hardship. To prevent a large flight of money, states may require foreign firms to sign an agreement that stipulates how much, and under what terms, they can take their capital out or simply create laws that would do the same.

Finally, there must be a way to settle disputes among states if one accuses the other of not honoring their treaty obligations. In some cases, states establish international institutions for the sole purpose of settling disputes. In Chapter 12, we introduced one such institution, the International Court of Justice, which we will discuss in detail later in this chapter. However, many international institutions have in their charters methods to solve disputes. They usually set up a panel of impartial experts who listen to the different arguments and then come up with a decision that all actors need to accept. In fact, charters establishing international institutions often declare that members have to use the charter's dispute settlement procedure and accept the final decision produced by the procedure.

A closer look at the 2002 steel dispute gives us a good example. When the Bush administration increased tariffs, members of the WTO who believed they were harmed by the tariffs filed a dispute. The filing triggered the establishment of a panel of experts who would review all the evidence and decide if the United States was in violation of the WTO rules. Officials draw these experts from an established pool of individuals whose training and experience match dispute. Since our example involves the steel industry, individuals such as lawyers, economists, and business people with related knowledge would join the panel. In addition, all parties would have a say in the panel membership. The procedure required settlement of the dispute based only on the rules and merits of the case. After the panel ruled that the United States was in violation of WTO rules, it gave the members harmed by the U.S. steel tariffs the right to increase their tariffs on any goods if the United States did not lower its steel tariff. In this particular example, the members did not need to raise tariffs because the United States agreed to lower its steel tariffs.

The political dimension of globalization refers to joint decision-making among states. As countries become more economically interdependent, it becomes necessary to move away from unilateral decisions and more toward multilateral decisions. Consider international trade once again. Countries adopt many regulations associated with product safety, such as the example previously mentioned regarding prohibiting lead in paint. This is to ensure that consumers do not purchase items that could harm their health. When countries trade, one side may send a product that cannot be sold in the receiving country because the item does not meet specific standards. Therefore, although there is free trade among the countries, trade can stop if product standards are not the same. To produce a common standard, countries make joint decisions. As more and more countries make joint decisions, we witness convergences of policies and regulations. States need to create joint decision-making bodies in order to make multilateral decisions. We will discuss such international institutions in the next section.

The social dimension of globalization is something we experience in our daily lives when we personally connect with people and events across the world. Social media and real-time reporting of events bring the world closer to us. Prior to our technological advances, the news people read, listened to, or saw, came from public or private outlets that determined what was newsworthy and how information would be filtered. Today, almost anyone can be an on-the-spot reporter by capturing images and videos on smartphones and posting them on any number of social media feeds. One of the key political examples of social media's role in disseminating information was the Arab Spring uprisings in the early 2010s, which attempted to bring down authoritarian regimes across North Africa, Bahrain, Syria, and Yemen. The spread of news via social media that depicted people in open rebellion in Tunisia sparked similar actions across the region.

Technology has also helped people connect in less dramatic ways. Before the creation of the internet and social media, the way you could meet a person from another country was to either visit the other country and make friends or for someone to visit your country and form a friendship. Today, you can meet anyone around the world that shares your interests through specialized forums and pages on social media. This opportunity is widely available since social media accounts are usually free and the only cost is the device and access to the internet. Being able to communicate with people in foreign countries opens up opportunities to identify with a diversity of individuals.

Similar to globalization, but on a smaller scale, is regionalization. **Regionalization**, or regional integration, is the process of integrating the economies, politics, and societies of countries in a specific part of the world. Regionalization is an attempt by states and non-state actors to become integrated either because global efforts are not progressing fast enough or due to the special needs of a geographic region. The most advanced case of regional integration is the European Union (EU), which we will discuss later in this chapter. However, the EU is not the sole case of states seeking regional integration. We will introduce other cases found in Africa, Asia, and South America.

PRACTICAL APPLICATION

How has globalization affected your life? How different would your life be if we lived in a world without globalization? Examine some technological advancements that occurred early in your life. How have the advancements you identified intersected with globalization? Provide at least three specific examples.

TYPES OF INTERNATIONAL INSTITUTIONS

LEARNING OBJECTIVE

13.2 Examine the types and functions of international institutions.

International institutions facilitate the process of globalization. States create these institutions through treaties that define their purposes and operations. Although international institutions have at their core the desire for greater cooperation among states, they vary in their ability to control the behavior of members. The effectiveness of international institutions strongly depends on how much states are willing to contribute to their success since enforcement of agreements and decisions rely on states themselves and not an external force.

The first type of international institutions is an **intergovernmental organization** (IGO). IGOs are made up of states that cooperate when making decisions based on rules and norms they create. States establish IGOs to govern agreements on a wide scope of issues. They can cover areas such as investment, the environment, and human rights, to name a few. Among IGOs' limitations is their inability to do anything unless member states make decisions. In other words, IGOs lack independent decision-making authority. Their task is to provide the structure for states to meet and make joint decisions.

IGOs differ in that some are global in scope while others are regional. The International Monetary Fund (IMF) is an IGO with members from every part of the world. Its membership covers 190 countries, working to foster global monetary cooperation and secure international financial stability. The Cooperation Council for the Arab States of the Gulf, also known as the Gulf Cooperation Council (GCC), limits its membership regionally. Its membership consists of all Arab states of the Persian Gulf (Bahrain, Kuwait, Oman, Qatar, Saudi Arabia, and the United Arab Emirates) except Iraq. Another difference among IGOs is what they do. Some limit their activities to specific issues. The IMF, as stated earlier, though having a global membership, focuses on a narrow set of functions since their goal is to help resolve issues involving a state's financial stability. The GCC, albeit regional, deals with multiple areas of cooperation: economic, security, and social, to name a few. One IGO that enjoys global membership and handles a broad scope of issues is the United Nations. We will look at the United Nations in detail later in this chapter.

The latter part of the twentieth century began the development of another type of international institution: supranational organizations. **Supranational organizations** hold sovereignty over member states; that is, they make decisions that member states must follow. The member states decide who will lead such organizations, but the leadership then decides on how to staff the organization. Since a supranational organization needs to be independent and unbiased, the leadership and staff are not loyal to any one country. Although they are still citizens of their home country, their decisions focus on the needs of all members and must follow the treaty obligations agreed to by the member states. One global example of a supranational organization is the International Criminal Court (ICC). The ICC judges rule based on the entire body of international law regarding human rights and conventions of war. If their rulings were biased, then the ICC would lose credibility. Therefore, it is in the best interest of a supranational organization to be fair to all actors when making decisions.

EXPAND YOUR THOUGHTS

Some people believe that their country's membership in a global IGO is a mistake, whereas others believe it is highly important to belong to global IGOs. What do you think are the advantages and disadvantages of states joining supranational institutions? Do IGOs have more advantages than supranational institutions? Provide specific examples to support your position.

THE RISE OF GLOBAL INSTITUTIONS

LEARNING OBJECTIVE
13.3 Describe the missions and functions of major global institutions.

Many current major global institutions emerged as outcomes of agreements made shortly after World War II (WWII). National leaders at the time believed that WWII occurred at least partly because of the lack of international coordination and cooperation. The League of Nations, created after World War I, was ineffective in many ways and was an example of how not to operate a global institution. Not wanting to make the same mistakes again, proponents of effective global institutions sought ways to improve how states would commit to international peace. This section briefly outlines the purposes and functions of some of the most important global institutions.

The United Nations

The **United Nations** (UN) is an international intergovernmental organization with the mission to promote and maintain international peace, security, and prosperity. The UN helps states increase international security through multiple organs within it. There are six UN organs in all.

The **UN Security Council** manages conflict resolution among members. Of the 15 members, 5 are permanent and 10 are temporary members that rotate based on two-year terms. The permanent members include Britain, China, France, Russia, and the United States. They became permanent members because they were the main victors of WWII and, as a result, formed the foundation of the UN. The nonpermanent members are states that are part of five regional groupings: Africa, Asia-Pacific, Eastern Europe, Latin America and the Caribbean, and Western Europe and other states. Security Council resolutions often deal with actions to prevent or stop aggression. The members of the Security Council make decisions using a basic rule: For a resolution to pass, at least 9 of the 15 members need to vote in favor of it, with no negative vote from any of the 5 permanent members. This decision rule gives the permanent members veto power to block any action. The uneven powers among Security Council members have been the cause of multiple calls for reform. Suggested reforms would either expand the number of permanent members or revoke the veto power altogether. Unlike decisions made by other UN organs, Security Council resolutions are binding on all UN members, meaning that all members must follow Security Council decisions or face penalties. However, in reality penalties are difficult to formulate and apply, which leads some states to go against Security Council resolutions.

The **UN General Assembly** is the largest UN organ comprising every member state. Decisions follow the "one country, one vote" principle. Important decisions need a two-thirds majority, while others need a simple majority. Important decisions include issues associated with peace and security, the UN budget, admission of new members, removal of existing members, and appointments of the Security Council's nonpermanent members and the choice of the UN Secretary-General. Decisions that do not include the operating budget, membership, and appointments are nonbinding. The members do not need to follow nonbinding decisions. It is therefore not a surprise for a member state to vote in favor of a General Assembly resolution and then not follow it in practice. Some scholars believe that members vote in favor of certain resolutions to improve their reputation on the international stage, especially if the voting in favor of a resolution carries little cost.

The **UN Secretariat** is the UN's bureaucratic organ. The staff of the Secretariat are employees of the UN and therefore must not bias their functions in favor of any member state. The staff conduct much of the background work that facilitates UN activities by performing tasks such as translations, data gathering, report writing, and management of UN operations. At its head is the **UN Secretary-General**, who is often the key UN spokesperson. The Secretary-General's formal duties include the appointment and supervision of approximately 44,000 international civil servants, bringing up important matters to the General Assembly and Security Council, and the annual reporting to the membership. Given the position's high profile, the current and past Secretaries-General have come from smaller countries to ensure neutrality.

The International Court of Justice (ICJ), which we introduced in Chapter 12, settles legal disputes between member states. The ICJ should not be confused with the International Criminal Court (ICC). The ICC is the permanent tribunal that tries individuals accused of crimes against humanity and war crimes. The ICJ, instead, is a legal remedy for issues among states that, in the past, may have been settled using war. The General Assembly appoints 15 judges for nine-year terms. No two judges can come from the same country and there is an informal understanding that judges need to represent not only geographic diversity but also the world's legal diversity. The ICJ rulings are binding since, before proceeding, all parties must agree to abide by the court's decisions.

The **UN Economic and Social Council** (ECOSOC), as the name indicates, focuses on the economic and social issues facing members, especially those problems that may threaten international or domestic security. Its functions are to primarily identify, discuss, seek out information through scientific reporting, and offer recommendations. In the past, they have created goals for development, especially for economies that face major barriers to improve their welfare. The ECOSOC addresses environmental issues given how such issues also influence economic development. Therefore, its recommendations often emphasize the need for sustainable development. The General Assembly selects 54 UN member states to become members of ECOSOC for staggered three-year terms.

The **UN Trusteeship Council** is the UN organ that helps former colonial territories transition into self-governing, independent states. In 1945, when the UN began, the Trusteeship Council played an essential role given the number of territories seeking independence. By 1994, all the territories under its jurisdiction became independent. This left the organ without a real mandate. Today, it requires a majority in the General Assembly or the Security Council for the Trusteeship Council to resume operations.

Global Economic Institutions

Post-WWII leaders also considered that the states' inability to coordinate national economic policies precipitated the onset of the war. They believed that creating effective global economic institutions would remedy the problems that limited coordination among states. We spotlight three of the most influential global intergovernmental economic institutions: the International Monetary Fund (IMF), the World Bank, and the World Trade Organization (WTO).

The International Monetary Fund

The **International Monetary Fund** (IMF) is charged with maintaining international monetary stability. It assists countries when they are facing problems with the value of their currency, foreign exchange reserves, and banking institutions. The original plan to stabilize the values of member states' currencies was to establish a fixed exchange rate system. A fixed exchange rate keeps the value of a country's currency mostly constant with regard to another currency. For example, if a country fixes the value of its currency to the U.S. dollar, then the value will not change vis-à-vis the U.S. dollar unless the governments make an adjustment. This is different from a floating (or flexible) exchange rate, which allows the market to decide how much currencies are worth. Under the old IMF system, called the **Bretton Woods system**, all the member states' currencies were fixed to each other's through the U.S. dollar. The U.S. dollar was then fixed to a specific value of gold (referred to as the gold standard). The idea was that the system would allow all of the currency values to be stable and would thereby produce greater certainty for global economic exchange like trade. In the early 1970s, the United States, due to its own economic problems, could no longer support the system and abandoned the gold standard. The result was the collapse of the fixed rate Bretton Woods system. The end of the Bretton Woods system led to the adoption of a floating system, which we have today.

The IMF continues its mission to maintain a stable global financial system by intervening when a troubled economy seeks assistance. Intervention comes in the form of loans with conditions. Commonly referred to as IMF conditionality, the government of a country requesting financial aid from the IMF must agree to adjust its macroeconomic and structural policies to overcome the problems that led it to seek financial assistance. The reforms follow an economic point of view known as the **Washington Consensus**, named so because of the IMF's location in Washington, D.C. Under this economic viewpoint, which is in line with neoliberalism, financial stabilization occurs when government budgets are dramatically cut in an attempt to reduce overall government debt. The large cuts in government budgets, referred to as **austerity programs**, usually hit the poorest citizens hardest because of heavy cuts to government-funded social welfare programs. So long as the country holds IMF loans, it must maintain low government spending.

The World Bank

The **World Bank** is another global intergovernmental economic institution. It is actually not a single institution but five: International Bank for Reconstruction and Development (IBRD), International Development Association (IDA), International Finance Corporation (IFC), Multilateral Investment Guarantee Agency (MIGA), and International Centre for Settlement of Investment Disputes (ICSID). The first two (IBRD and IDA) are the institutions that are the best known and contribute the most to the World Bank's mission of improving economic prosperity, especially among poor countries. They provide loans for national projects that demonstrate the potential to boost economic performance. The amount of interest charged on the loans is anywhere from current market rate to zero interest, depending on the wealth of the borrowing country. Projects develop physical and social infrastructure without which it would be difficult for the national economy to develop. Physical infrastructure projects may include dams for hydroelectricity production or development of information connectivity. Social infrastructure includes projects that would improve educational opportunities and health. The World Bank also provides grants, which is money that has no interest and is not paid back, for special urgent projects, such as disaster relief.

EXPAND YOUR THOUGHTS

Many people are critical of the Washington Consensus. They argue that the austerity programs that result from the conditions set by the IMF and the World Bank do not really help the countries receiving loans. What are the benefits of receiving loans with such conditions? Do the benefits outweigh the costs?

The World Trade Organization

The **World Trade Organization** (WTO) is the intergovernmental organization that governs global trade by overseeing the **General Agreement on Tariffs and Trade** (GATT). The WTO also fosters trade negotiations and settles trade disputes. The GATT is the global treaty that spells out all the costs, regulations, products, and services that are traded among member states. Once a state joins the WTO, it receives the lowest tariff terms that a member state gives to all other WTO members. The GATT is an evolving agreement first established in 1947 and then revised seven times after subsequent negotiation rounds. Each round lowered barriers to international trade and added more member states. The latest round of negotiations, referred to as the Doha Round, began in 2001. As of 2022, it has not been concluded.

Another important function of the WTO is its role in dispute settlements. As mentioned earlier in this chapter, when one or more members accuse others of violating the GATT, they can ask a panel of WTO-assembled experts for a ruling. If the dispute panel sides against the violating member(s), it allows the injured members to retaliate by increasing tariffs on the violator until it is once again in compliance with the trade rules.

Let's take a detailed look at a recent case of a dispute and how it was resolved. In September 2020, the World Trade Organization's dispute settlement panel ruled that the United States, under the Trump administration, violated international trade rules by imposing extra tariffs applicable only to China on $200 billion worth of Chinese goods. With the ruling, China, in theory, would be able to levy retaliatory tariffs on billions' worth of U.S. goods. However, the U.S. government appealed the decision to the WTO's appeals court, which was not functioning because the Trump administration refused to approve new members for it. With the final verdict not in sight, this ruling had a symbolic, rather than practical, significance.

What happened between the filing of a dispute and the WTO decision? As mentioned, one of the roles the WTO has in administering the GATT is its ability to settle disputes among member states. This is similar to how domestic law is carried out. All parties to the GATT need to follow the rules listed, such as any agreement or contract between individuals. When one or more members believe that another member or members are in violation of the GATT, the accusing side can file a dispute. The dispute lists how the accused side violated the agreement. At first, all sides meet to see if they can reach a settlement.

If the members cannot reach a settlement, then the accusing side can request that a panel of experts be assembled to hear both sides of the dispute and make conclusions and recommendations. China's complaint rested on the United States' unilateral increase of tariffs in 2018 and 2019 on only Chinese products with the accusation of unfair Chinese trade practices. China's complaint against the United States had two parts. First, China argued that if it was in violation of GATT rules; the United States should have filed a dispute instead of increasing tariff rates on its own. Second, China complained that the motivation for tariff increases was not due to GATT violations on China's part but rather an attempt to limit Chinese imports to the United States for economic reasons.

What was the United States' claim against China? The U.S. government believed that China had violated Article XX(a)'s concept of "public morals." It accused China of theft, extortion, cybercrimes, economic espionage, theft of trade secrets, and anticompetitive behavior. Under the dispute settlement rules, the United States would need to provide evidence that such activities took place.

The dispute panel concluded on September 15, 2020, that the United States did not demonstrate the burden of proof that China had harmed U.S. public morals or that it organized efforts to do so. As a result, the panel recommended that the United States reduce its tariffs to the level in line with the GATT. At the end of October 2020, the United States filed an appeal against the ruling. As mentioned, the Trump administration blocked the appointments on the Appellate Body in 2018 and made it unable to function. Until the appeals process can move forward, the trade dispute between China and the United States will be in limbo.

THE EUROPEAN UNION

LEARNING OBJECTIVE

13.4 Identify the European Union's main institutions and the challenges that the EU has faced in recent times.

The efforts to integrate Europe began shortly after the end of World War II as a means to create a stable and peaceful region. The **European Union** (EU) has been successful in this broad mission as demonstrated by the fact that there have been no wars between European states since the EU's formation. This is quite a feat given that Europe has had interstate wars each generation since the fall of the Roman Empire, which happened approximately 1,550 years ago.

FIGURE 13.2 ■ Map of the European Union

The foundation of what we now know as the EU began when the original six member states (Belgium, France, Germany, Italy, Luxemburg, and the Netherlands) negotiated the Treaty of Rome (1957). Since its founding, the EU expanded to 28 member states and is now 27 after the United Kingdom left the EU in 2020. In addition, there are a half dozen states that are seeking admission into the EU. During the years of its development, the EU unified the members economically by establishing a single market where products, services, capital, and people could move freely across borders. Nineteen member states have also replaced their national currencies with a single currency called the euro.

Another interesting fact is the EU's adoption of a set of symbols that are similar to those used by countries. For example, it has an anthem, a motto, and a flag. The EU flag is flown or displayed alongside national flags, in front of government buildings, and during important ceremonies and meetings; it also sits behind national leaders in their official portraits. The anthem, Beethoven's "Ode to Joy," is performed at official EU functions. The EU motto, "United in Diversity," speaks to the notion that diversity can be preserved while the states and people unite under a common cause of peace and prosperity.

The member states are joined politically through various complex institutions, many of which have growing supranational powers. It has a legislative institution called the European Parliament that votes on laws that govern the region. The Parliament shares legislative powers with the European Council and its associated institution, the Council of the European Union. European citizens, in a continent-wide election using a proportional representation system, directly elect the members of the European Parliament. The members of the European Parliament form political party groups that are ideologically tied together and are not grouped along national lines. This means that members from leftist, centrist, or rightist parties group themselves together regardless of which country they come from.

The European Council and its associated institution, the Council of the European Union, are similar to an upper chamber of a bicameral legislature. The member states' heads of government (or in some cases the heads of state) make up the European Council. The Council of the EU include the ministers of all the member states. This body has the strongest say in the creation of EU law and regulations. The European Council generally manages the evolution of the EU since major advances in integration start and end with them. The advances come in the form of new treaties, which are ratified by national legislatures.

The European Commission is the main bureaucracy of the EU. This institution introduces new laws and regulations for the European Parliament and Council of the European Union to consider. In addition, the institution oversees the enforcement of EU laws and regulations and manages the EU's budget. The commission is broken down into 27 separate commissions that oversee specific economic, social, or cultural matters.

The EU does not have an individual in the role of "leader" of the organization. Instead, it has a decentralized form of leadership. The president of the European Council heads the meetings of that institution and serves as the chief mediator for disputes among member states' governments. There is also the president of the European Commission, who heads the EU bureaucracy. The EU's High Representative of the Union for Foreign Affairs and Security Policy heads European External Action Service, which is the EU's diplomatic service and foreign and defense ministry. Last, the Council of the European Union has its own president. Its presidency rotates every six months among the member states' heads of government. Therefore, there are four individuals at any time who can speak for the EU.

The European Court of Justice (ECJ) is the "supreme court" of the EU since it has the final say on the interpretation and equal application of the law. It rules on the constitutionality of existing EU laws and addresses member states' noncompliance cases. The European Council appoints the ECJ's 27 judges, one for each member state. However, all 27 judges do not usually sit as one body. Instead, they hear cases in panels made up of 3 to 15 judges. The ECJ is an effective court even though it has no direct way to enforce its decisions. The court, instead, relies on each member state's judicial system to carry out its verdicts.

EXPAND YOUR THOUGHTS

Is the EU a supranational organization? One way to think about an answer is to examine the institutions that make up the EU. Which of the EU institutions we learned about in this chapter are supranational, and which are intergovernmental? After this assessment, what can you say about the supranational character of the EU? Is it more supranational or more intergovernmental? Be sure to explain your answer.

The EU has faced several challenges over the past couple of decades that have tested its ability to continue existing. The 2008 international financial crisis that hit most developed countries challenged the EU's ability to coordinate member states' actions in the areas of government spending and bank regulations. One potential threat was the ability to continue with the single currency. Anti-euro advocates called for their country to leave the common currency because it limited their governments' flexibility to handle the crisis. The call for leaving the common currency was strongest in Greece, although this desire was also voiced in many EU member states. The crisis drew to a close when member states developed stricter banking regulations by moving more financial oversight to the EU level. In other words, leaders believed that more, not less, economic integration was the solution.

The international refugee crisis challenged member state collaboration and unity when in 2015, over a million refugees attempted to enter Europe from countries like Syria, Iraq, Libya, and Afghanistan. In fleeing war, political persecution, and poverty, they risked their lives crossing the Mediterranean Sea in dangerous vessels or treacherous journeys over land. Many refugees used their limited funds to pay human smugglers, who often put migrants in danger. The refugees' arrival in Italy and Greece overwhelmed these governments' ability to help them. Those who were able to get into Italy or Greece continued their migration further north. Many EU member states, however, started closing or restricting border crossings in violation of EU law. Recall that freedom of movement is a basic EU principle as well as EU law. Therefore, closing borders jeopardized the foundation of the EU. The crisis was partially resolved with EU member states agreeing to a quota system, where each member state would accept a specific number of officially admitted migrants and greater EU border surveillance.

The latest crisis, Brexit, began in 2016 and was not resolved until the very end of 2020. Brexit is the abbreviation for the British (United Kingdom) exit from the EU. In June 2016, the British citizens voted, in a national referendum, to leave the EU . Reasons for leaving rested on dissatisfaction with how much decision-making power the United Kingdom had to share with its fellow EU states. Advocates for leaving the EU believed that the UK was no longer a sovereign state because it needed to follow EU laws and regulations. One central complaint for those who argued to leave was the ability for EU citizens to freely work and live in the UK. This anti-immigrant argument, many scholars note, had a strong xenophobic element.

Overall, those who wished to leave the EU did not like the continuing efforts to integrate Europe into what they saw as a "United States of Europe." Their arguments were summed up in the common slogan of "taking back control." Advocates wanting to remain in the EU stressed all the benefits of membership. These included the economic benefits from trade and investment as well as the ability to work, live, and study in the EU. The pro-EU campaign also cited the important role that the British voice exerted in European politics and how it was more powerful in global affairs as a member of the EU than being on its own.

EU treaty law allows member states to leave. It sets up a two-year negotiating phase after a member state officially declares its desire to leave. However, it took nearly twice that amount of time, and three UK prime ministers, to negotiate a full exit. Much of this delay was due to the complexity involved in leaving while maintaining some degree of economic relationship between the EU and UK. The exit became complete when a new economic relationship began on January 1, 2021. Some argue that the full implications of Brexit are yet to be realized. Aside from the economic uncertainty is the future of Britain itself. Although the overall national vote was clear (52 percent voted to leave), parts of the UK, like Scotland and Northern Ireland, had a majority that voted to remain. Given that some Scots have had a long desire to break away from the UK, Brexit may give them the big push to do so.

OTHER CASES OF REGIONAL INTEGRATION

LEARNING OBJECTIVE

13.5 Discuss the differences and similarities of various regional integration organizations.

Regional integration is not exclusive to Europe, and we can find cases in every region around the world. However, other cases are not as integrated as the EU. Most cases are simple free trade areas. This means that the states agreed to either dramatically lower or eliminate tariffs on most or all goods and services. The following are some examples of regional cooperation that have integrated beyond free trade areas.

The Southern Common Market

The Southern Common Market, or MERCOSUR using the Spanish language acronym (MERCOSUL is the Portuguese acronym), is a South American regional integration bloc. It includes Argentina, Brazil, Paraguay, and Uruguay as full original members and seven other countries as associate members. Venezuela was once a full member; however, its membership is under suspension due to its lack of democratic practices. The original four members of MERCOSUR founded the organization in their earlier days of re-democratization.

To safeguard democracy, they agreed that MERCOSUR can only include functioning democracies and to sanction or suspend members that fall short of following democratic principles (see Chapter 11 on democracy clauses).

MERCOSUR has institutions that are very similar to those of the EU. In fact, many of the founding leaders saw the EU as a model for regional integration in South America. The institutions include a council, commission, and parliament. The major difference between these institutions and their similarly named EU counterparts is in the authority they possess. The latter are far less powerful than the EU institutions and are considered more intergovernmental than supranational.

All MERCOSUR members, full and associate, enjoy free trade among themselves. However, during past economic downturns, members have violated the free trade agreement and unilaterally increased tariffs. The full members have a common tariff for all goods coming into them from outside the trading bloc. This means that any one member cannot change their national tariffs unless the other three do as well. The commitment to a common tariff also requires the four member states to negotiate free trade agreements with others as a single group. The member states are therefore prohibited from signing independent free trade agreements. Having a common tariff has frustrated some of the member states due to the slow pace in reaching free trade agreements with others. For example, the negotiation for a free trade agreement between MERCOSUR and EU has taken approximately 22 years, and while it is entering into its concluding stages, it has yet to be a fully ratified treaty. The slow pace has prompted some members, such as Brazil and Uruguay, to seek out free trade partners on their own.

Economic Community of West African States

Africa is home to multiple examples of regional integration, including the African Union, which seeks to economically and politically integrate the entire continent. One of the more prominent cases is the **Economic Community of West African States** (ECOWAS). It includes 15 West African members. Some of the members have free trade among themselves, others joined under a common external tariff, and yet others have a common currency.

ECOWAS institutions also parallel those found in the EU and MERCOSUR. The ECOWAS Commission is the bureaucracy that oversees the operation of the group. The Community Parliament is the organization's legislature, whose members are selected by the member states. The Community Court of Justice does not operate as a supreme court. Instead, the body settles disputes among the member states. The heads of government together are members of the ECOWAS Authority, which is the principle decision-making body. The Bank for Investment and Development (EBID) financially aids ECOWAS efforts to integrate. The EBID does this by providing loans and grants to both private entities and public agencies for infrastructure projects and economic programs.

ECOWAS is unique in two ways. First, the level of integration is split between the states that are former colonies of France and Britain. The French-speaking member states are already joined together under a common currency. The English-speaking member states are tied together economically and are planning to create a common currency, the eco. The longer-term plan is for the entire organization to have a single common currency. However, the French-English rivalry has scholars questioning their ability to do so. Second, ECOWAS has a strong security component, the ECOWAS Monitoring Group (ECOMOG), which is made up of the militaries of the member states. The ECOWAS Authority established ECOMOG as a way to maintain stability in a region where civil wars and coups are rather frequent. When given permission by the region's leaders, ECOMOG will intervene in countries facing militarized domestic conflict.

Association of Southeast Asian Nations

The **Association of Southeast Asian Nations** (ASEAN) includes 10 members that seek to integrate their economies and develop higher levels of collaboration. The ASEAN members' desire not to interfere in each other's domestic affairs makes this organization unique compared to other regional integration organizations. The member states attempt to balance their desire for greater cooperation while maintaining high levels of sovereignty and independence. The desire for this balance implies that they have a small number of institutions, which are purely intergovernmental. This includes the ASEAN Secretariat, which is a relatively small bureaucracy, and a council, which is made up of the national leaders. They are also challenged in achieving higher levels of integration because they trade more with the outside world than with each other. They have used their level of cooperation, however, to sign free trade agreements as a bloc with their main economic partners, such as Australia, China, and Japan, instead of competing with each other for separate free trade agreements.

The member states believe that greater integration can be best achieved by focusing on three dimensions, which they refer to as communities. The Political Security Community seeks to ensure peace and stability in the region through the creation of rule-based structures. The Economic Community attempts to create a single market that will have the free flow of goods, services, investment, and capital. The Socio Cultural Community works toward developing a region that promotes high levels of quality of life, equitable access to opportunities, and human rights.

COSTS OF GLOBALIZATION

LEARNING OBJECTIVE
13.6 Identify the principal critiques of globalization.

One may conclude that globalization has benefited the world because it brings states, economies, and people together like never before. After all, who can argue with the global and regional institutions' lofty goals of ensuring a more secure and prosperous world? While the goals may not be up for argument, there are many who have serious concerns regarding *how* institutions, states, firms, and individuals try to realize these goals and if these goals are being achieved.

One critique is the large influence wealthy countries have over less wealthy ones. The IMF and World Bank voting method demonstrates how little say the less wealthy states have. These global economic institutions do not follow a "one member, one vote" method in making institutional decisions. Instead, the number of votes that member states possess depends on how much money they contribute to the international institutions. The larger their GDP is, the more they contribute. In turn, votes are weighted based on the contribution size. This gives the wealthier members a larger vote share. As Figure 13.3 shows, the world's wealthiest countries, also known as the **Group of Seven (G-7)** (Britain, Canada, France, Germany, Italy, Japan, and the United States), together hold 41.3 percent of all IMF votes. The United States alone controls 16.5 percent of the vote. To create a majority vote, the G-7 only needs a few more states, like those listed in the figure. In the end, the remaining 176 member states would need to follow the decisions of a small group of states.

Another concern involves what some call the **democratic deficit**. Critics believe that more and more important decisions are taken out of the hands of democratically elected leaders and given to individuals that are not accountable to the citizens they affect. In a democracy, voters can vote incumbent politicians out of office if they do not like the policies they implement. However, voters cannot remove IMF or World Bank officials even when they require their governments, which receive loans, to make dramatic policy changes with which the voters disagree. Moreover, even if voters were to remove their country's elected leaders who accepted such loan conditions, the international lending institutions would require the same set of policies from the next government. This creates a situation where unelected officials of international institutions are making public policies for a country, and voters in that country cannot hold those who are responsible for the policies accountable.

This was the Greek case in 2015. Both the EU and the IMF required austerity cuts in exchange for providing the Greek government with loans to stabilize their banking system. The Greek voters, however, voted against the austerity program in a national referendum and

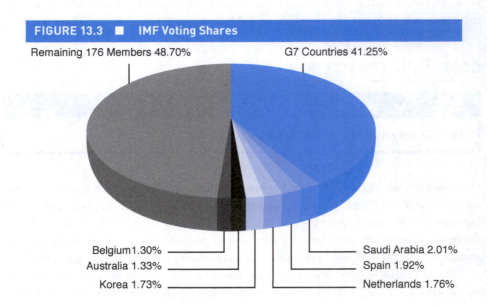

FIGURE 13.3 ■ IMF Voting Shares

Remaining 176 Members 48.70%

G7 Countries 41.25%

Belgium 1.30%
Australia 1.33%
Korea 1.73%

Saudi Arabia 2.01%
Spain 1.92%
Netherlands 1.76%

then later voted out politicians who attempted to implement austerity. Each new government campaigned to get tough with the international lenders, only to acquiesce to the EU and IMF in the end.

The last critique involves **social dumping**. According to the critics, the poorer regions carry a disproportionate share of the negative aspects of globalization. Open trade and the ease of foreign direct investment allow multinational corporations to move production from high-cost areas to low-cost ones, and then sell to consumers anywhere in the world their lower priced products. By lowering the cost, prices can also drop and sales increase, as do profits. While this sounds like good news for the consumers and producers, it may sustain negative impacts. The lower costs of doing business is, in large part, made possible by low wages and lax labor and/or environmental regulations in less wealthy countries. Individuals work for little pay and under conditions that are not acceptable in a wealthy country. The poor working conditions are a result of the absence of government regulations (or their enforcement) that would give workers safe and healthy workplaces. In addition, under conditions of high unemployment, workers can be easily dismissed from their place of work if they complain. Another issue is the nonexistence or low levels of environmental regulations that give producers the opportunities to increase the pollution of the local environment by manufacturing processes that contaminate the air, water, and soil. The promise of increasing economic development through trade and foreign investment falls short when considering the degradation of daily life.

The shifting of production to less regulated parts of the world and the subsequent increase in the levels of pollution also have had an effect on global climate, which began with the advent of large-scale industrialization. The link between human activity and the average rise in global temperatures is a hotly contested issue in the United States but less so around the world. The large body of evidence accumulated over decades of research by the international body of scientists points to a rise in both greenhouse gas levels and temperature. While the Earth has experienced periods of climate change, our current period coincides with our industrial activities and not with natural trends. The buildup of greenhouse gases, such as carbon dioxide (CO_2), methane (CH_4), nitrous oxide (N_2O), and ozone (O_3), from burning fossil fuels (oil, gasoline, natural gas, and coal) produces an atmospheric shield that prevents thermal radiation from escaping into the atmosphere. The trapped heat increases both air and ocean temperatures, which in turn produces harmful consequences for many species of life, including humans. The melting of glaciers increases sea levels, harming coastal cities and islands. Shifting weather patterns increase catastrophic floods and droughts. In addition, as humidity and precipitation patterns change, infectious diseases can spread into new areas.

Although globalization has contributed to the problem of global climate change, the high levels of established cooperation through international institutions may be helpful in producing solutions. The reduction of greenhouse gases needs a global commitment, especially among the largest emitters, since the actions of a small group of countries are unlikely to produce significant changes. The problems preventing a global commitment are in the short-term economic concerns that make some countries reluctant to cooperate.

Reducing greenhouse gases requires efforts and investments in, for example, shifting from fossil fuels to renewable forms of energy and increasing fossil fuel efficiency to lower the levels of greenhouse gas emissions. The solution, unfortunately, incurs costs. The switch to renewable energy requires investment in infrastructure and technologies. Increasing fuel efficiency and reducing greenhouse gas emissions can lead to higher prices for products like automobiles and trucks. Some countries that have large acreages of rainforests, like Brazil, are asked not to cut them down because plants and trees absorb CO_2. Many in Brazil, however, argue that not exploiting the rainforest for timber, grazing, and farming will reduce the country's ability to grow economically. They point out that wealthy countries in Europe and the United States exploited their forests in the past, which helped their economic development. The reduction of greenhouse gases challenges us with collective action problems (see Chapter 7) and poses a prisoner's dilemma (see Chapter 1). Solutions require a balance between costs and benefits to induce global cooperation.

States have started to develop global efforts to reduce greenhouse gases. The latest effort was in 2015, when members of the UN negotiated, signed, and enacted the Paris Agreement. The member states agreed to keep the current level of average temperature change below 2°C. It also set a goal to lower this change to 1.5°C. The Paris Agreement is an advancement from previous accords because it set limits on carbon emissions, obliges the periodic assessment of achieving goals, and requires that less wealthy countries obtain financial support. Each state that signed on to the agreement must individually adhere to its commitments. The major question left unanswered is if the states, especially the major contributors of greenhouse gases (China, United States, and EU members) will do their part to reduce their emissions.

PRACTICAL APPLICATION

How globalized are we? Is globalization as extensive as people say? Are we as globalized as we think we are? Think about how you would measure globalization. What are some important indicators that you need to see have increased over the past 50 years that would convince you that the world is globalizing? Explain your answer.

SUMMARY

Globalization and regionalization are phenomena that embody the ongoing changes around us. In an interconnected world, what happens at the international level affects domestic politics, and the domestic politics of a country can have global implications. Whether we are analyzing greater interdependence at the global or regional level, the international institutions created by states facilitate the process. Such institutions bring together states to build greater collaboration and cooperation, as well as settle disputes among them.

International institutions vary in how much authority they possess and the functions they perform. Intergovernmental organizations bring together states to discuss and agree on issues, but many do not have the ability to make binding decisions. Instead, IGOs are venues for mutually acceptable outcomes to which states agree to adhere. In contrast, states give supranational institutions the ability to make independent decisions that they themselves must accept. Functions of international organizations can span from the specific to the general. The World Trade Organization, for example, has the specific role of managing global trade. The United Nations, on the other hand, has many organs that cover a great many issues.

We took a close look at regional organizations in this chapter. The European Union is an effort to bring states together in deeper integration than what we see at the global level. The EU has a mix of intergovernmental and supranational institutions that join the economies, politics, and societies of the continent. For over six decades, it has gradually built a system uniting the European states under a single market, currency, and set of laws while successfully handling multiple crises. We also examined other regional organizations (MERCOSUR, ECOWAS, and ASEAN). These cases show that deeper economic and political collaboration among states can be found on every continent. They also demonstrate that there is no one set path for integration.

We also reviewed a few critiques of globalization. We saw the uneven power that wealthier states have in making important decisions affecting the politics and economies of developing countries. Another is the lack of democratic accountability in global decision-making. Finally, we examined the issue of social dumping. Critics emphasize that the removal of the barriers to global economic exchange is harming labor and environmental conditions. They voice the need for greater international action in these areas. If international institutions can help states cooperate, then global crises, like climate change, can be effectively addressed.

KEY TERMS

Association of Southeast Asian Nations (p. 313)

Austerity program (p. 305)

Bretton Woods system (p. 305)

Democratic deficit (p. 314)

Economic Community of West African States (p. 312)

European Union (p. 307)

General Agreement on Tariffs and Trade (p. 306)

Globalization (p. 298)

Group of Seven (G-7) (p. 314)

Intergovernmental organization (p. 302)

International Monetary Fund (p. 305)

Regionalization (p. 301)

Social dumping (p. 315)

Southern Common Market (p. 311)

Supranational organization (p. 302)

Tariff (p. 299)

UN Economic and Social Council (p. 304)

UN General Assembly (p. 303)

UN Secretariat (p. 304)

UN Secretary-General (p. 304)

UN Security Council (p. 303)

UN Trusteeship Council (p. 304)

United Nations (p. 303)

Washington Consensus (p. 305)

World Bank (p. 305)

World Trade Organization (p. 306)

GLOSSARY

Absolute monarchy An absolute monarchy possesses authority not subject to checks by any other individual, group, or institutions, be it judicial, legislative, religious, economic, or electoral.

Administration An administration, a term most often used in the United States, is a deliberative body made up of the president and members of the cabinet.

Adversarial legal system Adversarial legal systems determine the outcome of trials with a judge as an impartial referee, the state (who acts as the prosecutor), and the accused (who acts as the defendant). Juries usually determine the outcome of the trial. In countries that do not have a jury system, the judge will make the final decision on the case.

Alternative vote The alternative vote is a single-member district majoritarian electoral system where voters rank the candidates running in a district in the order of their preferences. If there is a candidate who receives an absolute majority of first-preference votes, the candidate is elected. If no candidate wins an absolute majority of first-preference votes, then the candidate with the fewest votes is eliminated and those votes are reallocated to the voter's next preferred candidate that is available until one candidate has an absolute majority of the valid votes remaining. The alternative vote is also known as ranked choice voting and instant runoff.

Amnesty law An amnesty law is a law that retroactively pardons or discharges a select group of people, usually members of security and armed forces, government officials, politicians, opposition leaders, and others, from criminal liability for the unlawful acts that they perpetrated.

Analytic thinking Analytic thinking is a process of solving problems by breaking down their complexity into components and seeing how the parts fit together. The aim of analysts is to put the puzzle pieces together so that they can solve the problem at hand.

Anarchy (in relation to the international system) An anarchic international system is one with no central authority. In an anarchic international system, states must rely on themselves (and no other) for survival.

Arab Spring The Arab Spring is a wave of antigovernment protests, uprisings, and armed rebellions by citizens demanding democratic reforms that took place in various countries in North Africa and the Middle East in 2011.

Arms race An arms race is a situation when two or more actors feel so threatened by the other actors' level of armaments that they will increase their levels of armaments as well. The reactive increase in arms sparks another round of increases by the other actors.

Association of Southeast Asian Nations The Association of Southeast Asian Nations (ASEAN) is a regional organization composed of 10 member states that seek to integrate their economies as well as develop higher levels of collaboration.

Asymmetric bicameral system An asymmetric bicameral system is one where a legislative chamber (usually the lower house) has more power than the other chamber (usually the upper house).

Austerity program An austerity program is a way to solve a country's economic problems through large cuts in government budgets, such as eliminating business subsidies and cuts in education and social programs. Critics argue that austerity policies hit the poorest citizens hardest because the heavy government spending cuts include substantial reduction in social welfare programs.

Authoritarian succession In many autocratic regimes, leadership succession poses a challenge because the rules of leadership succession are not clear unlike in democracies where political offices rotate by elections.

Authority Authority is the power or right to give orders, make decisions, and enforce compliance. Hierarchies are a traditional method of allocating authority so that members of an organization know the power positions of actors.

Balance of power theory Balance of power theory is a theory of international relations that explains that peace can be achieved when states are equally powerful and a war is likely to break out when there is a very powerful state whose power is unmatched by other states or alliances of states.

Behavioral revolution The behavioral revolution in political science is an approach that centers on individuals as the key to understanding politics through emphasizing the study of values and preferences obtained through surveys.

Belief system A belief system is the collection of views a person has regarding how the world operates and how the world ought to be. The views can incorporate an ideology or include a mix of differing ideological components.

Bicameral legislature A bicameral legislature has two houses, a lower house and an upper house, which make independent decisions regarding the creation of new laws.

Bounded rationality Bounded rationality is the idea that we make decisions that are rational but within the limits of the information available to us and our cognitive capabilities.

Bourgeoisie In Marxist terminology, the bourgeoisie is the owners of the means of production in the capitalist system.

Bretton Woods system The Bretton Woods system was an international monetary arrangement where all the member states' currencies were fixed to each other's through the U.S. dollar. It ended in the early 1970s.

Capitalism In Marxism, capitalism is a stage in the historical progression of economic systems that followed feudalism. The industrialized economic system is one in which the owners of the means of production, called the bourgeoisie or capitalists, exploit the industrial workers to generate economic surplus.

Catch-all party A catch-all party is a type of a political party that seeks to attract people with diverse political viewpoints

Censure A censure is a public reprimand of an official. It concludes that the person or persons acted in a manner that is unacceptable for those who occupy the office.

Central bank independence Central bank independence is a condition where central bankers are free from political pressures in making monetary policy decisions.

Civic culture Civic culture is a cluster of shared values and attitudes held by the people in a society. These values and attitudes are measured by responses to survey questions.

Civic engagement Civic engagement is any set of voluntary actions by individuals, often within groups. People participating in civic engagement identify and try to solve problems in their local community, country, or even around the world.

Civil law system A civil law system is one where a country's legislative system creates laws that do not allow room for interpretation by a judge. The legal codes are precise in detailing the violations, the procedures to follow, and the amount of punishment.

Civil rights Civil rights refer to individual freedom and fair treatment. This includes the rule of law, freedom of expression, freedom of association, etc.

Civil war Civil wars are armed conflicts within a country between two or more political groups who seek to take control of the state.

Classical liberalism Classical liberalism emphasizes individual liberty, individual rights, and private property, and calls for minimum intervention by the government in the affairs of private agents.

Climate change Climate change, also known as global warming, involves the rise in the average temperature of the Earth's atmosphere and oceans. Climate change is responsible for the change in weather patterns.

Closed-list proportional representation A closed-list proportional representation system is a type of list proportional electoral system where the order of candidates elected is determined by the party itself, and voters are not able to express a preference for a particular candidate.

Coalition government A coalition government comprises two or more parties that enter a formal agreement to form a government.

Cognitive dissonance Cognitive dissonance is the perception of contradictory information that produces stress and discomfort. People avoid cognitive dissonance by dismissing information that contradicts their beliefs.

Collective action problem A collective action problem refers to a situation in which individuals acting in their self-interest would prevent cooperation among them to achieve outcomes in which everyone would be better off.

Collectivist attitudes A collectivist attitude is an attitude that professes the importance of cooperation and group efforts in producing successful outcomes. The attitude also emphasizes the impact of group outcomes over individual ones.

Command (or centrally planned) economy Command or centrally planned economy is a development strategy where states plan what their economies will look like in some future time interval, usually in five-year increments. A central government agency devises these plans and sets annual, quarterly, and monthly production targets.

Commercial liberal peace theory Commercial liberal peace theory of international relations claims that wars are unlikely among economically interdependent states.

Common law system A common law system is one where governments create laws, but courts have the ability to interpret them by creating precedent rulings.

Common pool resources Common pool resources are goods that are non-excludable but rivalrous in consumption. Common pool resources are sometimes referred to simply as commons.

Communal society Communal society is one where people participated in hunting and gathering activities.

Communism Communism is a political ideology that seeks equal, classless society whose principles Karl Marx and Friedrich Engels firmly established. In Marxism, communism is the final stage of human development. At this stage, workers' ownership and management of production would lead the state, considered the instrument of the ruling class, to become obsolete and disappear.

Competitive election A competitive election ensures that voters have meaningful choices. At minimum, there must be two candidates from at least two different political parties.

Conflict Conflict includes a wide array of disputes that occur among states due to diverging interests those states hold.

Consensual societies Consensual societies are societies with high levels of interpersonal trust and individuals willing to associate with community groups. Cooperation is easy in these societies as is reaching mutually acceptable decisions.

Consensus democracy A consensus democracy prioritizes representation and inclusiveness. It promotes the idea that democracy should represent as many citizens as possible, that a simple majority should not govern unfettered, and that power should be shared by different groups.

Conservatism Conservatism seeks preservation of the current political and socioeconomic system or seeks to return to a political and social system more in line with traditional values. Conservatives believe that humans are morally and intellectually imperfect, and human nature, if not controlled, can lead to social breakdown.

Constitutional monarchy (democratic) A democratic variant of constitutional monarchy has a monarch who is generally a figurehead with only ceremonial roles. The true lawmaking and enforcement power is in the hands of elected officials.

Constructivism Constructivism is a theory of international relations that claims that states' behaviors can be explained by their identities and reputations.

Contentious societies Contentious societies are societies with low levels of interpersonal trust and deep divisions among individuals and groups. Members of such societies have difficulty in cooperating or reaching mutually acceptable decisions.

Contractionary fiscal policy Contractionary fiscal policy is when the state decreases spending and increases taxes because the economy is doing well and debt needs to be paid.

Contractionary monetary policy Contractionary monetary policy is when the state increases interest rates due to high (anticipated) levels of inflation.

Cooperation Cooperation is the condition among states where they seek to work together for mutually beneficial outcomes.

Co-optation Co-optation is a political strategy of assimilating opposition and nonmembers into the established group or system in order to manage opposition and preserve political stability.

Corporatism Corporatism is a functional organization of a society into various areas of economic and professional sectors serving as organs of political representation and exercising control over individuals and activities within their jurisdiction.

Corruption Corruption is the illegal use of a public office for private gain.

Counter-cyclical economic policies Counter-cyclical economic policies attempt to jump-start the economy at low points and prevent demand from outpacing supply of products and services at high points.

Criminal court A criminal court tries those accused of committing a crime.

Critical theory A critical theory describes the problems in society and the reasons behind the need for change.

Cultural primordialism Cultural primordialism focuses on factors, such as geographic location, religion, ethnicity, etc., that are relatively stable over time. Cultural primordialists argue that cultural characteristics are hard to change, and certain cultures are more compatible to democratic institutions and practices and certain other cultures are incompatible with them.

Cybersecurity Cybersecurity involves the ability of actors to protect themselves from attacks on their computer systems and networks. These attacks seek to steal data, disable systems, and/or spread false information.

Defense policy Defense policy refers to the positions and approaches a state uses to protect itself from foreign enemies.

Democratic accountability Democratic accountability is the means citizens have to hold elected officials responsible for their decisions. Citizens can reward officials by supporting them in elections when citizens like the results of officials' decisions or not vote for them in cases when decisions do not produce desirable outcomes.

Democratic breakdown Democratic breakdown occurs when institutions of democracy are subverted and not immediately restored.

Democratic conditionality Democracy conditionality is the requirement that certain international organizations have adopted in a treaty or protocol statement that member states must adhere to democratic principles to become and remain members of the organization.

Democratic consolidation Democratic consolidation occurs when there is the broad acceptance of democracy as the permanent form of political activity in the society. It happens when democracy has become "the only game in town."

Democratic deficit The democratic deficit is a criticism of globalization. It states that more and more important decisions are taken out of the hands of democratically elected leaders and given to individuals who are not accountable to the citizens they affect.

Democratic legitimacy in nondemocratic regimes Many autocratic regimes use institutions associated with democracy, such as elections, legislatures, and political parties, to boost the legitimacy for their rule without giving real power to those institutions.

Democratic peace theory Democratic peace theory is a theory of international relations that explains why democracies do not fight wars with each other.

Democratic socialism Democratic socialism advocates for change through elections and other democratic means. Through elections, democratic socialists seek to create laws and policies that would gradually reform their economies with the aim to create a more equitable society.

Democratization Democratization is a political phenomenon by which a nondemocratic country moves to adopt democratic institutions and practices.

Demonstration effect Demonstration effects refer to the phenomena that political events and regimes could be contagious, having influence beyond where they originated. The democratic theory of demonstration effects argues that successful democratization in one country leads to democratization in another country in its proximity.

Dependent variable A dependent variable is the outcome or effect requiring explanation and caused by one or more independent variables.

Descriptive representation Descriptive representation seeks to ensure that the national legislature numerically mirrors the societal demographic composition of the population.

Deterrence Deterrence assumes that states start wars thinking that they will win and envisions that the best way to prevent an attack is by having a powerful military.

Developed countries Developed countries are the wealthiest countries as measured by their per capita income and productivity. Their economies use highly innovative technologies that increase productivity per worker and the production of high-end products.

Developing countries Developing countries commonly have persistent high unemployment or under-employment, produce primary commodities for export as well as low skill manufactured goods, and have large income inequalities within their societies.

Devolution Devolution is a process where a central government delegates some powers of self-governance to subnational governments. The delegation of power may not be permeant and is up to the discretion of the central government.

Dictator's dilemma In autocratic regimes, an actual level of societal support is difficult to assess for dictators because people are uninclined to reveal their true preferences for fear of retaliation.

Diplomatic recognition (to be a state) A state needs diplomatic recognition by the international community of states, especially by the more powerful ones, that it is a sovereign state. It happens when it is legally recognized by the community of states as the sole legitimate governing authority within its territory and as the legal equal of other states.

Direct democracy Direct democracy occurs when the people, without intermediaries (such as representatives) discuss and make collective decisions (through voting and other decision-making methods) regarding the issues that are important to them.

Distributional conflict Distributional conflict is a conflict or competition over the division of resources; that is, it is about who gets what and how much.

Divided government Divided government occurs when different political parties control the executive and legislative branches.

Divine right Divine right is the claim that political leaders may make that they rule on behalf of a deity or multiple deities.

Domestic terrorism Domestic terrorism refers to the actors and their terrorist activities within a country.

Dominant party rule Dominant party rule is a regime in which a single party dominates political office and policy decisions.

Dominant party system (in a democracy) In a dominant party system, multiple parties exist, but the same party wins every election or almost every election and governs continuously.

Duverger's law Duverger's law states that single-member district plurality rules lead to two-party competition while proportional representation encourages multiparty competition.

Economic Community of West African States The Economic Community of West African States (ECOWAS) is a regional organization of 15 members states with a mix of members having free trade among themselves and others joining together under a common external tariff and single currency.

Economic development Economic development refers to the process of improving the socioeconomic well-being of people.

Economic interdependence Economic interdependence refers to the degree to which a country's domestic economy relies on one or more foreign economies.

Electoral system An electoral system is a set of laws that regulate electoral competition between candidates or parties, determining the number of seats available in an election, how voters cast their ballots, and how votes are translated into seats.

Environmentalism Environmentalism centers on concerns of ecological well-being, specifically the improvement and preservation of the natural environment by advocating for cleaner air, water, and soil.

Equal vote The equal vote principle of liberal democracy requires that the value and weight of the votes of all voters be equal, regardless of race, ethnicity, sex, socioeconomic status, or any other conditions. It is often referred to as the standard of "one person, one vote."

Ethnocentrism Ethnocentrism refers to the practice of evaluating other cultures according to the preconceptions originating from the standards and customs of one's own history and culture.

European Union The European Union (EU) is a regional organization with currently 27 member states whose aim is to unite their economics and politics.

Executive oversight Executive oversight is the ability for a legislature to evaluate and possibly limit the power of the executive.

Expansionary fiscal policy Expansionary fiscal policy aims to increase the money supply in the economy by using budgetary tools to increase spending and/or cut taxes.

Expansionary monetary policy Expansionary monetary policy seeks to increase demand for goods and services by lowering interest rates.

Export-oriented industrialization Export-oriented industrialization is a strategy where states guide development by selectively assisting target industries producing goods and services for export. It is also referred to as the developmental state model.

Failed state Failed states effectively have no national government that can enforce policy. The state is so weak that it virtually loses control over part or all of its territory.

Fair election A fair election guarantees all candidates and parties the right to compete on a level-playing field.

Fascism Fascism is a radical right-wing ideology that promotes extreme nationalism, seeks to blame outsiders for a country's problems, and emphasizes the supremacy of the state.

Federalism Federalism is a system that gives considerable autonomy to subnational units while the central government deals with issues of national concern. Such a system constitutionally guarantees the division of power between the central and subnational governments.

Feminism Feminism is an ideology centered on recognizing and eliminating discrimination and inequality of women in all aspects of society.

Feudalism In feudalism, the nobility emerged as the dominant class and serfs and peasants as the exploited class. The nobility owned the lands while peasants were required to work the lands and send their surplus output to the nobility.

Filibuster A filibuster is a dilatory tactic used to prevent bringing a measure to a final vote.

Final solution The final solution was the specific plan to remove all Jews from their homes, steal their property, and then systematically murder them in gas chambers or through forced labor.

Fiscal policy Fiscal policy refers to how the state taxes its residents and how it spends the collected taxes.

Fixed assets Fixed asset economic activities are economic activities related to land and are not mobile or easily re-deployable, such as natural resource extraction and agriculture.

Fixed term Fixed term refers to a predefined period in office that cannot be shortened.

Flexible assets Flexible assets are properties and resources that can be re-deployed relatively easily, such as manufacturing and banking.

Foreign policy Foreign policy pertains to the positions and approaches a state has with other states.

Founding election A founding election is the first relatively free, fair, and competitive national-level election held upon or after a country's transition to a new democratic regime.

Free election Free election refers to the right of voters to cast their votes for the candidates or the parties of their choice, free of constraints or coercion.

Free rider problem A free rider problem occurs because individuals have an incentive to take advantage of the good available to them without contributing to it when the good, once provided, is available to everyone regardless of whether they contributed to it. A free rider problem is an inherent problem with non-excludable collective goods.

Free trade agreement A free trade agreement is a treaty between two or more countries that reduces barriers to imports and exports among them. Such agreements allow goods and services to move more freely among countries.

Freedom of association Freedom of association is the right of people to peacefully assemble and associate.

Freedom of expression Freedom of expression is the right of everyone to hold opinions without interference and to seek, receive, and impart information and ideas through any media and regardless of frontiers.

Fused powers Fused powers refer to a condition where the legislative and executive powers are inseparable. This is an important characteristic of a parliamentary system.

Game of attrition A game of attrition involves interactions where actors attempt to "wait out" each other in the hope that the other side will give up eventually.

Game of chicken The game of chicken refers to a situation where players benefit if the other side yields and where the worst outcome for both sides is when neither side backs down, resulting in an outright collision.

General Agreement on Tariffs and Trade The General Agreement on Tariffs and Trade (GATT) is the global treaty that spells out all the costs, regulations, products, and services that are traded among member states.

Geneva Conventions The Geneva Conventions are international agreements that set the standards in international law for the ethical treatment of people in war, including the basic rights of wartime prisoners, protection for wounded and sick military and noncombatant civilians, protection for the civilians in a war zone, and protection for the medical personnel and facilities.

Genocide Genocide refers to the targeted mass murder of a specific group of people, especially those of a particular ethnic group or nation. Examples include occurrences during the Holocaust, the Ottoman Empire's genocide of Armenians, Rwanda, and Bosnia-Herzegovina.

Globalization Globalization is the process of producing ever greater interdependence among peoples across political borders.

Government A government is a set of people who have the authority to act on behalf of the state. In other words, a government is the means through which state power is exercised and state policy is established and enforced.

Greenhouse gases Greenhouse gases are carbon dioxide, methane, nitrous oxide, and other substances human activities release into the atmosphere and function like a blanket, trapping the Sun's heat, causing the planet to warm.

Group of Seven (G-7) The Group of Seven (G-7) is a group formed by the world's wealthiest countries. They include Britain, Canada, France, Germany, Italy, Japan, and the United States.

Head of government Head of government is the chief political executive of the country and is responsible for making and carrying out policy decisions.

Head of state Head of state is the figurehead of the country and has ceremonial functions, such as greeting and meeting foreign heads of government and representing the country overseas.

Heterogeneous state A heterogeneous state is one in which many ethnic, religious, or other identity groups exist within its borders. A heterogeneous state may be multinational or multicultural.

Historical materialism Historical materialism is a theory of human development that emphasizes the internal contradictions in the system of material production and economic relations as the engine for societal development

Holocaust The Holocaust is the systematic murder of the European Jews by the Nazis.

Homogenous state A homogenous state is a country in which a significant majority of its population shares the same national identity.

Human capital Human capital pertains to the level of skills possessed by the workforce. In simpler terms, a country with high levels of human capital is one with an educated population.

Hypothesis A hypothesis is a simple, clear, and testable statement regarding the relationship between a dependent and independent variable. Researchers derive hypotheses from theories and test them as part of the scientific method of analysis.

Ideology An ideology is a comprehensive system of beliefs about political, social, and economic institutions; processes; and goals. It is a system of beliefs that explain, evaluate, and provide remedies for social problems. A political ideology offers a critique of a country's politics and then proposes a vision of the way in which the world ought to be.

IMF conditionality IMF conditionality is the condition of emergency financial loans that the International Monetary Fund makes to countries in economic crises in exchange for the recipient countries' governments undertaking politically and socially unpopular austerity measures, which typically include spending cuts by governments through the elimination of social programs and economic subsidies.

Impeachment Impeachment refers to the procedures that allow the removal of a sitting president by legislators. It can happen only under extraordinary circumstances, such as the accusation of breaking the law, and only after meeting rigorous procedural requirements.

Import-substituting industrialization Import-substituting industrialization is a development strategy that uses trade policy, monetary policy, fiscal policy, and exchange rates to protect and stimulate the creation of new industries for the purpose of domestically producing manufactured goods that a country usually imports.

In-group favoritism In-group favoritism is the desire to distribute resources to members of the in-group and keep resources away from members of the out-group (people who are not members of the in-group).

Independent variable An independent variable is the factor that will explain the changes in the dependent variable.

Individualistic attitude An individualistic attitude is an attitude that favors the importance of individual efforts in developing their futures and taking exclusive responsibility for outcomes. Individualists do not view the role of others or the state as a method to make their lives better.

Inquisitorial legal system Inquisitorial legal systems have investigating judges that discover and examine the evidence against the accused. They also examine the law to determine if the accused is guilty and what the punishment will be. A panel of trial judges then review the evidence and perhaps further question witnesses before giving the final verdict.

Institutional racism Institutional racism is a condition where societal, economic, and political institutions have embedded racist norms. Although individuals acting in these institutions may not believe themselves to be racists, the rules and policies produce uneven advantages and disadvantages based on the person's race. An example would be harsher prison sentences for crimes committed by Blacks compared to those committed by whites in the United States.

Interdependence Interdependence is a condition where citizens and businesses from different countries rely on each other to achieve their goals and foster their welfare.

Interest aggregation Interest aggregation refers to the activity that integrates interests, demands, and needs of individuals into policy programs.

Interest articulation Interest articulation is a method by which members of a society express their needs and desires to a system of government.

Interest group An interest group refers to a group of people, businesses, or other entities that are organized on the basis of a particular common interest or concern in their attempt to influence domestic public and foreign policies.

Intergovernmental organization Intergovernmental organizations (IGOs) are made up of states that cooperate to make decisions based on rules and norms that the states create.

International Court of Justice The International Court of Justice is an institution of the United Nations created with the purpose of using international law to settle disputes among states.

International Criminal Court The International Criminal Court serves as a permanent tribunal to try accused individuals for the international crimes of genocide, crimes against humanity, war crimes, and the crimes of aggression.

International dispute An international dispute is a disagreement between two or more states.

International Monetary Fund The International Monetary Fund (IMF) is an intergovernmental institution charged with maintaining international monetary stability. It assists countries when they are facing problems with the value of their currency, foreign exchange reserves, and banking institutions.

International nongovernmental organizations International nongovernmental organizations are non-state actors that advocate specific policy positions and try to influence or maintain policies at the national and international levels.

International status quo The international status quo is a general term that captures the acceptable norms and processes of the international order.

International terrorism International terrorism is the act of terrorism carried out by transnational actors.

Interstate war Interstate wars are wars between states and is what we normally think about when we talk about war.

Issue saliency Issue saliency refers to how much an actor cares about a particular issue in question.

Judicial independence Judicial independence is a condition that helps to reduce the chance that political and societal pressures influence judicial decisions. The judicial system is free from political pressures from other branches of government.

Judicial review Judicial review is the power some courts have that allows them to rule on the constitutionality of laws and governmental actions.

Judicialization of politics The judicialization of politics is the reliance on courts and judicial means to tackle public policy issues, political disputes, central moral predicaments, and political controversies.

Justice Justice refers to fair treatment under the law.

Laissez-faire (free market capitalism) Llaissez-faire, or free market, capitalism delegates economic development to private forces with limited or no state intervention.

Lawmaking Lawmaking is the process of turning a proposal into a law.

Legislative responsibility Legislative responsibility refers to the constitutional prerogative of a majority in a parliamentary system to remove a government from office without cause.

Liberal democracy Liberal democracy is based on a procedural view of democracy and emphasizes institutions, rules, and procedures that govern political competition and participation as well as protection of civil liberties.

Liberal feminism Liberal feminism is a branch of feminism that advocates legal reforms to advance women's rights so that women can fully enjoy the political and economic rights advocated by the classical liberal ideology.

Liberalism Liberalism commonly refers to classical liberalism although there is another variant of liberalism, modern U.S. liberalism. Classical liberalism holds individual liberty in high regard and advocates civil liberties under the rule of law.

Linked foreign policy Linked foreign policies are foreign policies that spill over into other foreign policies.

Majoritarian democracy A majoritarian democracy emphasizes majority rule and is based on a concentration of power. In an ideal-type majoritarian democracy, an elected (single-party) majority is given an unfettered mandate to govern within its term to implement its policy decisively. A majoritarian democracy promotes government decisiveness, clarity of responsibility for policy and government performance (policy and performance responsibility is clear because who the majority is is clear), and accountability.

Majoritarian electoral system Majoritarian electoral systems include electoral systems in which candidates or parties that receive the most votes win. Single-member district plurality (first-past-the-post), majority runoff, and alternative vote are examples of majoritarian electoral systems.

Majority runoff electoral system In a majority runoff electoral system, each voter casts a single vote for a single candidate in a single member district. If a candidate garners greater than 50 percent of the vote, the candidate wins the election. If no candidate wins a majority vote, then the two candidates with the most votes move to a second round (often referred to as a "runoff" election) and voters cast their votes between the two candidates. The candidate with more votes wins the election.

Majority winner A majority winner must receive at least 50 percent + 1 vote to win an election.

Marxist feminism Marxist feminism is a branch of feminism that argues that gender inequality is part of the larger set of inequalities found in the capitalist system. Marxist feminism advocates the demise of the capitalist system so that women can enjoy full political and economic rights.

Mass media Mass media are any method of communication that attempts to reach a wide audience.

Materialist values Materialist values are political values that place an emphasis on physical and economic security as opposed to self-expression and quality of life. Materialist values are on one end of a spectrum of values associated with postmaterialist theory. Postmaterialist values are on the other end of the spectrum.

Media echo chambers Media echo chambers refer to programing where the audience tunes in because they are likely to agree with host's views. They echo each other's views.

Military regime A military regime is where the military rules as an institution. In a military regime, a group of high-ranking officers holds power, determines who will steer the country, and exercises influence over policy.

Mixed electoral system In mixed electoral systems voters elect representatives using two different systems—one majoritarian and the other proportional.

Modern U.S. liberalism Modern U.S. liberalism combines ideas of civil liberty and equality with support for social justice and equalization of opportunity through government intervention.

Modernization theory of democracy Modernization theory of democracy posits that economic development makes democracy more likely to emerge and more likely to survive once it is adopted. According to the theory, economic development promotes the development of a stable democratic society through the expansion of the middle class.

Monarchy Monarchy is a regime where the effective head of government relies on kin and a family network to come to power and stay in power.

Monetary policy Monetary policy is the management of the money supply (the total value of money available in an economy at a given time) and interest rates.

Multinational corporations Multinational corporations are business enterprises that have headquarters and operations in two or more countries.

Multiparty system In a multiparty system, more than two parties could potentially win a national election and govern.

Mutually assured destruction Mutually assured destruction is a nuclear deterrence strategy that attempts to raise the costs of a nuclear war so high that no rational state would use its nuclear weapons.

Nation A nation refers to a group of people who perceive themselves as sharing a sense of belonging and who often have a common language, religion, culture, and/or historical experience.

National interest National interest is the perceived general, long-term, and continuing ends of a sovereign state in its relation to other states in the international arena.

Nationalism Nationalism is an elevated sense of national consciousness that emphasizes a unity of a nation and promotion of its interests and culture to the detriment of the interests of other nations.

Negative-sum game A negative-sum game is a situation in which the sum of gains and losses is smaller than zero.

Neoliberalism Neoliberalism is based on laisse-faire economics and advocates development and economic policies based on free market, free trade, and minimal government intervention.

Neutrality Neutrality is a condition where state leaders can choose to acknowledge the existence of other states, including problems they may have with them, but prefer to limit interactions or not take sides on an issue.

New institutionalism New institutionalism is an approach in political science that views political institutions as not merely reflections of social forces or individual preferences. Once created, they take on lives of their own and shape the behavior and attitudes of political actors.

New social movement New social movements are similar to traditional movements but differ in that they attempt to influence not only the changing of laws and policies but also societal norms and values.

No bourgeois, no democracy "No bourgeois, no democracy" is a phrase found in the study by Barrington Moore about the social origins of dictatorship and democracy. Moore emphasized the importance of industrialization and the rise of a middle class for a democracy to emerge.

Nondemocratic regime Nondemocratic regimes are ones that do not meet the criteris for (liberal) democracy. Nondemocratic regimes go under various labels, such as dictatorship, autocracy, and authoritarianism.

Non-excludable A good is non-excludable when no one can be excluded from its benefit.

Non-rivalrous A good is non-rivalrous when its use or consumption by someone does not diminish the availability of the good to another person.

Non-zero-sum game A non-zero-sum game produces an outcome that is either more or less than zero. This means that one's gain does not necessarily come from another's loss. It is possible that all players win; it is also possible that all players lose.

Normative theory Normative theory concerns evaluative judgements about what is right or wrong, just or unjust, or desirable or undesirable in a society. It does not seek to explain politics in the scientific sense but attempts to explain why things are undesirable based on specific value judgments.

Norms Norms are behaviors and practices that a society views as acceptable and expected. In politics, acceptable behaviors can help advance a political agenda, whereas unacceptable ones can harm the ability to advance a political agenda.

North Atlantic Treaty Organization The North Atlantic Treaty Organization (NATO) is a military alliance made up of European states, the United States, Canada, and Turkey.

Nuclear deterrence Nuclear deterrence is a strategy that uses the balance of power logic. Under such a strategy, nuclear weapons are a means to produce stability among competitive states.

Nuclear proliferation Nuclear proliferation is the spread of nuclear weapons across the globe.

One-party rule One-party rule is an authoritarian system where only one political party is allowed to govern a country.

Open-list proportional representation An open-list proportional representation system is a type of list proportional electoral system where voters can indicate not just their preferred party but also their favored candidate within that party.

Ozone depletion Ozone depletion is the depletion of the ozone layer in the upper atmosphere of the Earth. It is a major environmental problem.

Paradox of voting The paradox of voting refers to the empirical observation that the level of voter turnout is at odds with rational decision-making regarding whether or not to vote based on the cost-benefit calculus and the likelihood that any particular voter's vote would influence the election outcome.

Parallel foreign policy Parallel foreign policies refer to the condition where a state can have a dispute with another state over one issue while cooperating with that same state in other areas.

Paris Agreement on Climate Change The Paris Agreement on Climate Change is an international environmental treaty signed by 196 states. This agreement established the intentions of those states to reduce their greenhouse gas emissions.

Parliamentary systems Parliamentary systems are democratic regimes where the legislature and executive are inseparable and the executive has the main responsibility for legislation.

Parsimonious theory A parsimonious theory is a theory that can explain a phenomenon with few factors.

Patriarchy Patriarchy is a social system in which men hold power and privilege and predominate in government, moral authority, economic roles, and social functions.

Patriotism Patriotism is the devotion to one's country.

Peace Peace is the absence of war or militarized conflict. It is does not imply that states have friendly relations with other states.

Perils of presidentialism "Perils of presidentialism" is a proposition advanced by Juan Linz and others that due to their inherent features, presidential systems are particularly susceptible to democratic breakdowns.

Periodic election A periodic election is one of the requirements of liberal democracy where elections must be held with regular intervals.

Personalist rule Personalist rule is rule by a dictator unconstrained by other groups or institutions, such as political parties or the military. The ruler, whether military or civilian, controls all policy decisions and selection of regime personnel.

Pluralist school The pluralist school views politics as being played out primarily by nongovernmental groups that use their resources to exert influence over policy. The pluralist school considers that politicians respond to who can most effectively wield influence.

Plurality winner Winning an election by a plurality requires the candidate to gain more votes than any other candidates. There is no requirement to garner an absolute majority (greater than 50 percent) of the vote cast.

Politburo Politburo, or Political Bureau, is the top decision-making body of the Communist Party of China (CPC). It is small and comprises only the top leadership of the CPC.

Political attitude A political attitude is an established way of thinking or feeling about something or someone that a person expresses in their political behavior. A person's political values help explain the types of attitudes expressed. Examples can include attitudes toward authority, society, and individualism.

Political behavior Political behavior pertains to any form of individual or group engagement in the political process or any activity that has political or policy consequences.

Political culture Political culture refers to a society's shared norms and values that are relevant to the analysis of politics. Whereas culture includes many different norms and values, not all aspects of culture is important to the study of politics.

Political economy Political economy is the examination of the interaction between politics and economics and their reciprocal relationship.

Political goods Political goods include security, the rule of law, a functioning legal system, and infrastructure, such as roads, public education, and health care.

Political liberalization Political liberalization is the process of loosening government control over people and the society.

Political psychology Political psychology examines how people process information involved in political decision-making with attention to conscious and unconscious processes involving emotions.

Political realism Political realism is a political philosophy that attempts to explain and prescribe political activities and relations. It views politics as the struggle for power. Political realists thus believe that only the powerful can rule.

Political regime A political regime is a set of formal and informal rules, norms, and institutions that determine how the government is organized and how governmental decisions are made.

Political rights Political rights are the rights of citizens to political participation and include such fundamental rights as the right to vote and the right to compete for elected office.

Political science Political science is the examination of politics using the scientific method.

Political socialization Political socialization is the process of acquiring the society's political values and norms. Individuals learn their values and norms from primary and secondary agents, either directly or indirectly.

Political trust Political trust is the trust citizens have for political institutions and politicians.

Political values Political values are the values that exert an impact on political behavior. Values are ones that an individual or society holds in high regard.

Politics Politics is defined as "who gets what, when, and how." In other words, politics is about how people distribute and obtain resources and power within a society and across countries.

Polyarchy Polyarchy is a definition of political democracy developed by Robert Dahl. It focuses on two fundamental dimensions of democracy—contestation for office and broad participation of citizens—and defines political democracy as the set of institutional arrangements that permits public opposition and establishes the right to participate in politics.

Pork barrel project A pork barrel project is a public works projects sought by politicians through the appropriation of government budgets for their electoral districts with political objectives.

Pork barrel project A pork barrel project is a public works project sought by politicians, with political objectives, through the appropriation of government budgets for their electoral districts.

Positive-sum game A positive-sum game is a situation in which the sum of gains and losses is greater than zero.

Postmaterialist values Postmaterialist values are political values that place an emphasis on self-expression and quality of life as opposed to economic and physical security. These values are on one end of a spectrum of values associated with postmaterialist theory. Materialist values are on the other end of the spectrum.

Power transition theory Power transition theory is a theory of international relations that explains states' behaviors by examining their relative powers and satisfaction with the international status quo.

Preference Preferences are an actor's favored outcomes in any given situation.

Preponderant power The preponderant power is the state in the international system or region that has the greatest power, as measured by the economy, military, or population.

Prescriptive constitutional government Prescriptive constitutional government, supported by Edmund Burke, is a government based on a constitution that is the "historical choice of successive generations, the successful inheritance of those who have gone before, and the embodiment of the wisdom of the species over time."

Presidential systems Presidential systems are democratic regimes where there is a separation of power between the legislature and the executive. Each holds different roles in the legislative process, and voters elect members using different electoral systems.

Primary agents of political socialization Primary agents of political socialization are individuals, groups, and institutions that are the most important actors in the process of political socialization. For the average person, primary agents include family and educational institutions.

Prisoner's dilemma A prisoner's dilemma is a situation where people do not or cannot work together even when it is beneficial to do so, resulting in a socially worst outcome.

Private interest Private interest is any interest that pertains to individuals or groups whereby the person or the group would gain a particular benefit or advantage that is not available to the general public.

Private interest model of government In the private interest model of government, public officials, including elected politicians, often behave in their own interests rather than those of the public.

Procedural view of democracy The procedural view emphasizes institutions, rules, and procedures that govern political competition and citizens' rights.

Proletariat The proletariat is the exploited working class in a capitalist system who could only sell their labor since they owned no property.

Proportional representation electoral system A proportional representation (PR), or simply proportional, electoral system is used in multimember districts. Proportional representation electoral systems seek to minimize wasted votes and distortion in political representation through proportional allocations of legislative seats based on the shares of votes that political parties receive.

Public good A public good is a good that an individual can consume without reducing its availability to another individual and from which no one is excluded. Examples include clean air, strong national security, and democracy.

Public interest Public interest involves matters that concern the well-being of the general public. It is an issue in which the entire society has a stake and thus deserves support, advancement, and protection by the government.

Public interest model of government The public interest model of government posits that government officials are motivated to work in the interests of the public, of "the people."

Radical feminism Radical feminism argues that the patriarchy is the fundamental organization of society and that the social system is characterized by the intentional domination and oppression of women by men through societal norms and traditions.

Ranked choice voting Ranked choice voting refers to the alternative vote electoral rule. It is a single-member district preferential majoritarian electoral system where voters rank-order candidates. If there is a candidate who receives an absolute majority of first-preference votes, the candidate is elected. If no candidate wins an absolute majority of first-preference votes, then the candidate with the fewest votes is eliminated and her/his votes are reallocated to the voter's next preferred candidate that is available until one candidate has an absolute majority of the valid votes remaining.

Rapid death of democracy Rapid death of democracy refers to a fast process in which a democratic regime fails and does not immediately return to democracy. Democracies can die rapidly in a matter of a few weeks, a few days, or even a few hours.

Rational actor model The rational actor model is based on rational choice theory, which seeks to explain human behavior in terms of expected utility maximization—the quest for maximizing anticipated benefits and minimizing anticipated costs—by individuals or groups.

Realist theory Realist theory is the oldest theory of international relations. It argues that states are the only important actors and that a balance of power among them will preserve a lasting peace.

Realpolitik Realpolitik is politics or diplomacy based on practical rather than ideological or moral considerations

Refugee crisis A refugee crisis is a situation when people attempt to escape the violence at home produced by conditions such as a civil war and will seek safety in another country. It becomes a crisis when the receiving country cannot handle the number of refugees.

Regional integration Regional integration refers to the process in which countries merge their economies and political decision-making. The European Union (EU) is one of the oldest and most developed regional integration blocs.

Regionalization Regionalization is the process of integrating the economies, polities, and societies of countries in a specific region of the world.

Religious fundamentalism Religious fundamentalism refers to the unwavering belief that an individual or a group of individuals has in the infallible and absolute authority of a sacred religious text or teachings of a particular religious leader or deity.

Representation Representation is the act of expressing the preferences of a constituency.

Representative democracy Representative democracy is a form of democracy where the people elect their representatives and those representatives gather, deliberate, and make decisions (through votes and other means) for the society on behalf of those whom they represent.

Resource curse Natural resource curse is an idea that being endowed with significant amounts of natural resources, such as oil and diamonds, is not a blessing but rather a curse for economic development, democracy, and political stability.

Revolution A revolution is a complete change of a country's political system often, but not always, through a violent overthrow of the previous political regime.

Right to compete for elective office In a liberal democracy, the right to compete for elective office needs to be guaranteed for practically all adult citizens without discrimination.

Rule of law The rule of law is the principle that all people and institutions, including members of government, are subject to and accountable to the law and that the law is fairly applied and enforced.

Satisficers Satisficers are individuals that choose the option that will satisfy their needs and desires without putting too much effort into making sure they are considering every single possible choice.

Scapegoating Scapegoating is blaming "outsiders" for one's problems and is one of the key features of fascist belief.

Scientific method The scientific method is a systematic way to test hypotheses and answer questions using observable data.

Scientific theory A scientific theory is a theory that is well tested using the scientific method and offers a broad explanation of natural or social phenomena.

Secondary agents of political socialization Secondary agents of political socialization are individuals, groups, and institutions that are the second most important actors in the process of political socialization. For the average person, secondary agents include peers, friends, media, and social organizations.

Seigniorage Seigniorage is a government's practice of raising revenues by printing money.

Separation of powers Separation of powers is a defining characteristic of a presidential system. It refers to the checks the legislature and the executive branches of government have on each other.

Shari'a Shari'a refers to the law found in the Qur'an, Islam's holy book.

Single-member district plurality system A single-member district plurality (SMDP) system is one in which voters cast a single vote for a candidate where candidates compete for a single seat (hence called "single-member district"). The candidate with the most votes wins. It is also known as a "first-past-the-post" and "winner-take-all" system.

Slave society A slave society is one where forced labor is institutionalized in the form of slavery.

Slow death of democracy A slow death of democracy refers to the process in which a country's democratic institutions gradually deteriorate, eventually to the point that democracy no longer exists. It could take many years for a democracy to die a slow death.

Social contract theory A social contract theory explains why and whether members of society need to comply with the fundamental social rules, laws, and institutions of the society.

Social dumping Social dumping is a criticism of globalization. It states that the opening of trade and capital mobility allows multinational corporations to transfer environmentally and socially undesirable practices to countries with little to no labor and environmental regulations.

Social equity Social equity refers to developing conditions of equal opportunity and fairness to all members of a society. Environmentalists point out that the economically disadvantaged often live in the more polluted areas of a country due to the community's lack of political ability to fight against businesses that produce environmental problems.

Social identity group A social identity group is one with membership restricted to people who believe they hold the same identity. Social identity is socially constructed and therefore can vary from society to society.

Social identity theory Social identity theory explains how improved self-esteem develops through group formation and helps to explain intergroup behavior, which is behavior between groups.

Social movement A social movement is a complex, decentralized, and sometimes coordinated grouping of people who wish to produce political, economic, or social change by creating new laws and policies or by repealing laws and policies with which they disagree.

Social rights Social rights are the rights of citizens to socioeconomic well-being. These rights may include, for example, public education, pensions, employment, decent wages, national health care, and so forth.

Social science Social science is the study of human interactions and societies.

Social trust Social trust is the type of trust people have for one another and for social institutions.

Socialism Socialism is an ideology that seeks to change political systems that support a market-based economy to one where opportunities and resources are more evenly distributed. In the Marxist stage theory of development, socialism is the stage in which the level of exploitation is reduced by the elimination of private property and the collective ownership of production is established.

Southern Common Market The Southern Common Market (MERCOSUR) is a South American regional organization that seeks to integrate the economies of member states. Its current full members are Argentina, Brazil, Paraguay, and Uruguay.

Sovereignty Sovereignty refers to states' authority to govern autonomously over a given territory.

State A state is an administrative apparatus that makes and implements public policies and uses coercive power to rule within a given territory. Modern states have all of the following elements: territory, population, government, diplomatic recognition, and sovereignty.

State autonomy State autonomy refers to the ability of a state to act without interference by external forces.

State of nature State of nature is a concept used in social contract theories and refers to a hypothetical condition of human life before government or society.

State-led development models State-led development models are strategies that promote the development of a market economy under strong guidance by the state.

State's survival interest A state's survival interest involves the preservation of the state's territorial integrity, political identity, and autonomy. According to the international realist school, survival is the ultimate and common goal of all states.

Strategic interaction Strategic interaction refers to a calculative interaction between players in which a player's ability to obtain the desired outcome is dependent on the move of at least one other player and in which all players know this and make calculated moves in order to attain the best possible outcome.

Strategic voting Strategic voting occurs when voters, instead of voting for their most preferred candidate, vote for another candidate in order to prevent a candidate that they really dislike from winning.

Strong state A strong state is a state that is generally capable of providing adequate political goods and economic well-being to its citizens.

Structural policies Structural policies focus on developing the critical assistance needed for economic development. Examples include educational policies and infrastructure policies.

Substantive view of democracy The substantive view of democracy classifies political regimes in terms of the outcomes that they engender. This view essentially argues that democracy should secure social rights of the people and that countries should be judged based on the extent to which they guarantee and deliver those outcomes.

Supranational organization Supranational organizations are created by states and hold sovereignty over member states; that is, they make decisions that require member states to follow.

Surplus value *Surplus value* is a term used in Marxism. It denotes profits that the owners of the means of production generate through their ownership of land, factories, or other resources.

Sustainable development Sustainable development is the principle that advocates economic development without compromising the environmental conditions for future generations. Sustainable development, therefore, requires a balance between economic and environmental progress.

Symmetric bicameral systems A symmetric bicameral system is one with both legislative chambers being equal in power.

Tariff A tariff is a government tax on an imported good.

Territory A territory is a geographic area with clearly defined borders separating itself from other states.

Terrorism Terrorism is the use of violence and threats to intimidate people through the creation of fear due to desired political objectives.

Theocracy A theocracy is a governing regime based on a specific religious doctrine.

Theory A theory is an explanation or estimation of how the world works. Theories include a set of interrelated concepts and propositions that explain or predict events, behaviors, and other types of phenomena in a systematic way.

Third wave democratization Third wave democratization pertains to the worldwide regime change to democracy since the mid-1970s.

Tragedy of the commons The tragedy of the commons explains why individual users of a shared resource system, acting in their self-interest, behave in a manner that is contrary to the common good of all users by depleting or ruining the shared resource.

Transaction costs Transaction costs are the time, effort, and any other resources required to make and enforce individual and collective decisions.

Transnational actors Transnational actors are individuals or groups that do not identify with a specific state and operate in two or more countries.

Trust Trust is the feeling people have when they believe others will act in a way that may benefit them, or at least not harm them, without the need to review their actions for possible harm.

Two-party system In a two-party system, there may be more than two political parties, but only two major political parties have a realistic chance of gaining power.

UN Economic and Social Council The UN Economic and Social Council focuses on the economic and social issues facing UN members, especially those problems that may threaten international or domestic security.

UN General Assembly The General Assembly is the largest UN organ comprising every member state that has an equal vote on nonbinding resolutions.

UN Secretariat The Secretariat is the UN's bureaucratic organ whose staff are employees of the UN and therefore must not bias their functions in favor of any member state. The staff do much of the background work that facilitates UN activities by performing such tasks as translations, data gathering, report writing, and management of UN operations.

UN Secretary-General The Secretary-General is the head of the UN Secretariat and is the chief spokesperson of the UN.

UN Security Council The Security Council is the organ of the UN that manages conflict resolution among members. It has 15 member states, of whom 5 (Britain, China, France, Russia, and the United States) are permanent members with veto power.

UN Trusteeship Council The UN Trusteeship Council is the organ that helped former colonial territories transition into self-governing, independent states. It is currently inactive.

Unicameral legislature A unicameral legislature has one house that deliberates on lawmaking.

Unitary government Unitary government refers to a governing system where all major power and policy come from the central government. The central government is supreme over the subnational governments.

United Nations The United Nations (UN) is an international intergovernmental organization with the mission to promote and maintain international peace, security, and prosperity.

Universal adult suffrage Universal adult suffrage gives the right to vote to all adults in a society.

Variable A variable is a measurable property or trait of people or things that can take on different values and changes across time and space.

Vote of no confidence A vote of no confidence is the procedure in a parliamentary system where the legislature can remove a prime minister from power.

Voter turnout Voter turnout is the percentage of eligible voters who cast a ballot in an election.

War War is a large-scale organized conflict between politically defined groups.

Washington Consensus The Washington Consensus is a neoliberal economic viewpoint that professes that financial stabilization occurs when government budgets are dramatically cut in an attempt to reduce overall government debt.

Weak state A weak state is a state that insufficiently provides political goods or economic well-being to its citizens.

World Bank The World Bank is a group of five lending institutions that provide loans and grants for national projects that demonstrate the potential to boost domestic economic development.

World Trade Organization The World Trade Organization (WTO) is the intergovernmental organization that governs global trade by overseeing the General Agreement on Tariffs and Trade, fostering trade negotiations, and settling trade disputes.

Zero-sum game A zero-sum game is a situation in which one player's win is another player's loss. If the total gains and losses of the players are added up, the sum equals zero.

REFERENCES

CHAPTER 1

Box-Steffensmeier, J. M. (1996). A dynamic analysis of the role of war chests in campaign strategy. *American Journal of Political Science*, *40*(2), 352–371.

Lasswell, H. D. (1936). *Politics: Who gets what, when, how*. Whittlesey House.

Norton, M. I., & Sommers, S. R. (2011). Whites see racism as a zero-sum game that they are now losing. *Perspectives on Psychological Science*, *6*(3), 215–218.

CHAPTER 2

Friedman, M. (1953). The methodology of positive economics. In *Essays in positive economics* (pp. 3–43). University of Chicago Press.

Ross, M. (2006). Is democracy good for the poor? *American Journal of Political Science*, *50*(4), 860–874.

CHAPTER 3

Burke, E. (1790). *Reflections on the revolution in France*. Macmillan.

Carson, R. (2002). *Silent spring*. Houghton Mifflin Harcourt.

Hobbes, T. (1968). *Leviathan*. Penguin Books. (Original work published 1588–1679)

Locke, J. (1952). *The second treatise of government*. Bobbs-Merrill.

Machiavelli, N. (1908). *The prince* (W. K. Marriott Trans.). Dutton & Co. (Original work published 1532)

Marx, K., & Friedrich, E. (2002). *The communist manifesto*. Penguin. (Original work published 1848)

Mill, J. S. (1859). *On liberty*. John W. Parker & Son.

U.S. Census Bureau. (2020). *Income and poverty in the United States: 2019*. https://www.census.gov/library/publications/2020/demo/p60-270.html.

Wollstonecraft, M. (2014). *A vindication of the rights of woman*. Yale University Press. (Original work published 1792)

CHAPTER 4

Edgerly, S., Thorson, K., & Wells, C. (2018). Young citizens, social media, and the dynamics of political learning in the U.S. presidential primary election. *American Behavioral Scientist*, *62*(8), 1042–1060.

Inglehart, R. (1977). *The silent revolution: Changing values and political styles among western publics.* Princeton University Press.

Maslow, A. H. (1943). A theory of human motivation. *Psychological Review, 50*(4), 370.

CHAPTER 5

Mamdani, M. (2001). *When victims become killers: Colonialism, nativism, and the genocide in Rwanda.* Princeton University Press.

Putnam, R. D. (1993). *Making democracy work: Civic traditions in modern Italy.* Princeton University Press.

Tajfel, H., & Turner, J. C. (1979). An integrative theory of intergroup conflict. In M. J. Hatch & M. Schultz (Eds.), *Organizational identity: A reader.* Oxford University Press.

Tajfel, H. (1982). Social psychology of intergroup relations. *Annual Review of Psychology, 33*(1), 1–39.

CHAPTER 6

Alvarez, M., Cheibub, J. A., Limongi, F., & Przeworski, A. (1996). Classifying political regimes. *Studies in Comparative International Development, 31,* 3–36.

Bush, G. W. (2002, September 17). [White House statement]. https://georgewbush-whitehouse.archives.gov/nsc/nssall.html

Dahl, R. A. (1971). *Polyarchy: Participation and opposition.* Yale University Press.

Geddes, B., Wright, J., & Frantz, E. (2014). Autocratic breakdown and regime transitions: A new data set. *Perspectives on Politics, 12*(2), 313–331.

Lijphart, A. (2012). *Patterns of democracy: Government forms and performance in thirty-six countries* (*2nd* ed.). Yale University Press.

North, D. (1981). *Structure and change in economic history.* Norton.

Paddock, C. (2009). *Obama: Creator of history.* Epitome Books.

Rotberg, R. I (Ed.). (2004). *When states fail: Causes and consequences.* Princeton University Press.

Tilly, C. (1985). War making and state making as organized crime. In P. Evans, D. Rueschemeyer, & T. Skocpol (Eds.), *Bringing the state back in* (pp. 169–186). Cambridge University Press.

United Nations. (1948). *Universal declaration of human rights.* https://www.un.org/en/about-us/universal-declaration-of-human-rights

Weber, M. (1946). Politics as a vocation. In *From Max Weber: Essays in sociology* (H. H. Gerth & C. W. Mills, Trans.). Oxford University Press. (Original work published 1918)

CHAPTER 7

Intergovernmental Panel on Climate Change. (2021). *AR6 climate change 2021: The physical science basis.* https://www.ipcc.ch/report/ar6/wg1/

Ostrom, E. (1990). *Governing the commons: The evolution of institutions for collective action.* Cambridge University Press.

U.S. Environmental Protection Agency. (2021). *Climate change indicators: Coastal flooding.* https://www.epa.gov/climate-indicators/climate-change-indicators-coastal-flooding

CHAPTER 8

The Inter-Parliamentary Union. (2021). *Women in national parliaments.* http://archive.ipu.org/wmn-e/classif.htm

Lijphart, A. (2012). *Patterns of democracy: Government forms and performance in thirty-six countries.* Yale University Press.

CHAPTER 9

Bormann, N.-C., & Golder, M. (2013). Democratic electoral systems around the world, 1946-2011. *Electoral Studies, 32,* 360–369.

Downs, A. (1957). *An economic theory of democracy.* Harper.

Reynolds, A., Reilly, B., & Ellis, A. (Eds.). (2008). *Electoral system design: The new international IDEA handbook.* International Institute for Democracy and Electoral Assistance (IDEA). https://www.idea.int/sites/default/files/publications/electoral-system-design-the-new-international-idea-handbook.pdf

Scheiner, E. (2008). Does electoral system reform work? Electoral system lessons from reforms of the 1990s. *Annual Review of Political Science, 11,* 161–181.

CHAPTER 10

Heng, L., & Judith, S. (1983). *Son of the revolution.* Vintage Books.

Keynes, J. M. (2018). *The general theory of employment, interest, and money.* Springer. (Original work published 1936)

Overy, R. J. (1996). *The Nazi economic recovery 1932–1938.* Cambridge University Press.

Prebisch, R. (1950). *The economic development of Latin America and its principal problems.* United Nations.

Sakwa, R. (2005). *The rise and fall of the Soviet Union.* Routledge.

Solt, F. (2020). Measuring income inequality across countries and over time: The Standardized World Income Inequality Database. *Social Science Quarterly, 101*(3), 1183–1199.

Smith, A. (1776). *An inquiry into the nature and causes of the wealth of nations.* Methuen.

Smith, H. (1976). *The Russians.* Ballantine Books.

Xiaoping, D. (1996). *Selected works of Deng Xiaoping: 1975-1982.* Foreign Languages Press.

CHAPTER 11

Almond, G. A., & Verba, S. (1963). *The civic culture: Political attitudes and democracy in five nations*. Princeton University Press.

Dahl, R. A. (1971). *Polyarchy: Participation and opposition*. Yale University Press.

Genna, G. M., & Hiroi, T. (2015). *Regional integration and democratic conditionality: How democracy clauses help democratic consolidation and deepening*. Routledge.

Huntington, S. P. (1991). *The third wave: Democratization in the late 20th century*. University of Oklahoma Press.

Huntington, S. P. (1996). *The clash of civilizations and the remaking of world order*. Simon & Schuster.

Linz, J. J., & Valenzuela, A. (1994). *The failure of presidential democracy*. Johns Hopkins University Press.

Lipset, S. M. (1959). Some social requisites of democracy. *American Political Science Review, 53*(1), 69–105.

Moore, B. (1966). *Social origins of dictatorship and democracy: Lord and peasant in the making of the modern world*. Beacon Press.

Przeworski, A. (1991). *Democracy and the market: Political and economic reforms in eastern Europe and Latin America*. Cambridge University Press.

Przeworski, A., Alvarez, M., Cheibub, J. A., & Limongi, F. (1996). What makes democracies endure? *Journal of Democracy, 7*(1), 39–55.

Przeworski, A., Alvarez, M. E., Cheibub, J. A., & Limongi, F. (2000). *Democracy and development: Political institutions and well-being in the world, 1950-1990*. Cambridge University Press.

CHAPTER 12

Burchill, S., Linklater, A., Devetak, R., Donnelly, J., Nardin, T., Paterson, M., Reus-Smit, C., & True, J. (2013). *Theories of international relations*, Macmillan International Higher Education.

Hobson, C. (2017). Democratic peace: Progress and crisis. *Perspectives on Politics, 15*(3), 697–710.

Lemke, D. (2002). *Regions of war and peace* (Vol. 80). Cambridge University Press.

Organski, A. F., & Kugler, J. (1981). *The war ledger*. University of Chicago Press.

Powell, R. (1990). *Nuclear deterrence theory: The search for credibility*. Cambridge University Press.

Thucydides, A. T. (1840). *The history of the Peloponnesian War: Illustrated by maps, taken entirely from actual surveys; with notes chiefly historical and geographical* (R. P. G. Tiddeman, Trans./Ed.). T. Combe. (Original work published 5th century BC)

Waltz, K. N. (2001). *Man, the state, and war: A theoretical analysis*. Columbia University Press.

Wendt, A. (1999). *Social theory of international politics* (Vol. 67). Cambridge University Press.

CHAPTER 13

Bayart, J. F. (2007). *Global subjects: A political critique of globalization*. Polity Books.

Beck, U. (2018). *What is globalization*? John Wiley & Sons.

Karns, M. A., Mingst, K. A., & Stiles, K. W. (2015). *International organizations: The politics and processes*. Lynne Rienner.

McCormick, J. (2017). *Understanding the European Union: A concise introduction*. Palgrave.

Steger, M. B. (2017). *Globalization: A very short introduction*. Oxford University Press.

INDEX